Brother Enemy

BROTHER ENEMY

The War after the War

NAYAN CHANDA

HARCOURT BRACE JOVANOVICH, PUBLISHERS

San Diego   New York   London

Copyright © 1986 by Nayan Chanda

Library of Congress Cataloging-in-Publication Data

Chanda, Nayan.
  Brother enemy.

  Includes index.
  1. Indochina—History—1945–   I. Title.
DS550.C48   1986   959'.053   85-24745
ISBN 0-15-114420-6

Designed by Michael Farmer
Printed in the United States of America
First edition
A B C D E

To my father, who inspired it all,
and to Geetanjali, who made it happen.

Contents

Contents

Maps appear on pages xii, 50, 55 and 337.
Photographs appear on pages 161–168 and 305–312.

Acknowledgments

E. H. CARR described the commonsense definition of history as a body of ascertained facts. According to this view "the facts are available to the historian in documents, inscriptions and so on, like fish on the fishmonger's slab. The historian collects them, takes them home, and cooks and serves them in whatever style appeals to him." Carr rightly challenged this definition by raising the fundamental question, What is a historical fact? What passes as a fact of history is in fact made into such by a historian's conscious decision. However, for a historian attempting to write a history of the Third Indochina War the problem is more basic than that of exercising subjective judgment in choosing facts from a plethora of events. There simply may not be enough relevant information to choose from. Other than relating self-serving selections of confidential documents, the Communist governments of China, Vietnam and Cambodia are unlikely to open their archives to independent historians.

I undertook to write this very preliminary, and of necessity, incomplete account with a full awareness of my limitations. But while I am too close to the events to attempt a historian's objectivity in seeking facts I enjoy a certain advantage over future historians. In the fifteen years I have followed developments in Indochina, I have had the opportunity not only to witness some of the dramatic events but also to talk to all the protagonists and many of the foreign observers who have followed the events on a daily basis. I have been particularly fortunate to have access to sources on all sides and have a glimpse of the secret calculations and behind-the-scene maneuvers leading up to the conflict. In fact, one redeeming feature in this bitter and seemingly uncompromising struggle between former comrades has been the occasional self-doubt and self-critical attitudes I have found in private conversations with Vietnamese, Chinese, and Cambodian officials. This book owes a great deal to those nameless officials on all sides who shared with me information that did not necessarily show their governments in a favourable light.

I owe a special debt of gratitude to Prince Norodom Sihanouk for spending dozens of hours in telling me his extraordinary life story. Many of the personalities figuring in this book have given me a lot of their time and helped me in different ways in researching the story. I am grateful for their cooperation.

Seth Lipsky and William Shawcross bear the responsibility of pushing me to write this book, and the editor of my magazine, Derek Davies, carried his encouragement to the extent of giving me six months off to begin the research. I am indebted to the Research School of Pacific Studies, Australian National University, and especially to David Marr for offering me a visiting fellowship that enabled me to do the historical research.

Many friends, colleagues, scholars, and diplomats have read parts of the manuscript and have offered valuable comments and suggestions. Since I am almost certain that none would perhaps agree with this book in its entirety, I shall spare them the embarrassment of naming them specifically.

I am grateful to Graham Aliband, Desaix Anderson, Alain and Michele Archambault, Jan Austin, Dorothy Avery, Jacques Beaumont, Elizabeth Becker, Stanley Bedlington, Madhu Bhaduri, Chanthou Boua, Mohammed Bouabid, Lyall Breckon, Terry Breese, Richard Breeze, Fred Brown, Raymond Burghardt, James Burnet, Timothy Carney, David Chandler, Parris Chang, Helen Chauncey, Michael Chinoy, Kraisak Choonhavan, Evelyn Colbert, Shyamala

Cowsik, Maryse Daviet, Patrice and Brigitte de Beer, Philippe Devillers, Neelam Dhamija, Nguyen Huu Dong, Michael Eiland, David Elliott, Donald Emmerson, Harold Evans, Philippe Franchini, John Girling, Banning Garrett, Jim Gerrand, Tushar and Rajeshwari Ghose, William Gleysteen, Donald Gregg, Wang Gungwu, Sandor Gyori, Harry Harding, Lilian Harris, Barbara Harvey, David Hawk, Bob Hawkins, Hollis Hebbel, Stephen Heder, Bill and Peggy Herod, Murray and Linda Hiebert, Richard Horne, Mario Iseppi, Raphael Iungerich, Stephen Johnson, Paul and Sophie Quinn-Judge, Jerome Kanapa, Stanley Karnow, Kasem Kasemiri, Henry Kenny, Donald Keyser, Ben Kiernan, Allen Kitchens, Tommy Koh, Gabriel Kolko, Charles Lahiguera, Dennison Lane, James Lilley, Michael Lombardo, Michel Lummoux, Steve Lyne, John MacAuliff, Jamie Mackie, A. Madhavan, Kishore Mahbubani, Abdul Majid, Robert Manning, Glenn May, John Mcbeth, George McQuillen, Charles Meyer, Atsuo Miyake, John Mohanco, Don Oberdorfer, Jean-Christoph Oberg, Bill O'Malley, Roland-Pierre Paringaux, Arun Phanupong, Douglas Pike, Jonathan Pollack, Gareth Porter, Mark Pratt, Kailash Puri, Ken Quinn, Dragoslav Rancic, Sean Randolph, K. Ranganathan, David Reese, Philippe Richer, Robert Ross, Daniel Roussel, Malcolm Salmon, Kernial Sandhu, Renji Sathiah, Turid Sato, Jean Sauvageot, Tonia Shand, Robert Shaplen, Frank Sieverts, Amarjit and Bhagwant Singh, Pami Singh, Richard Solomon, Daniel Southerland, Simon and Elise Spivak, Michel Strulovici, Roger Sullivan, Robert Sutter, Frank Tatu, Carlyle Thayer, Jerry Tinker, William Turley, Lorenzo and Adriana de Vignal, Sarasin Viraphol, Jusuf Wanandi, Steve Wasserman, William Wilmott, Joseph Winder, William Wise, Leonard Woodcock, Maria Zammit.

I profoundly feel the loss of Denzil Peiris, Pravesh Kumar, and S. Sivaramakrishnan, who helped me so much and are not here to see the fruit of their encouragement.

I am deeply indebted to Lynn Nesbit for her effort to see this book published and my editor, Marie Arana-Ward, for being so patient in guiding me through the difficult process of completing the manuscript. This book, of course, would not have been written without Amit and Ateesh, who had to do without their father for a long period.

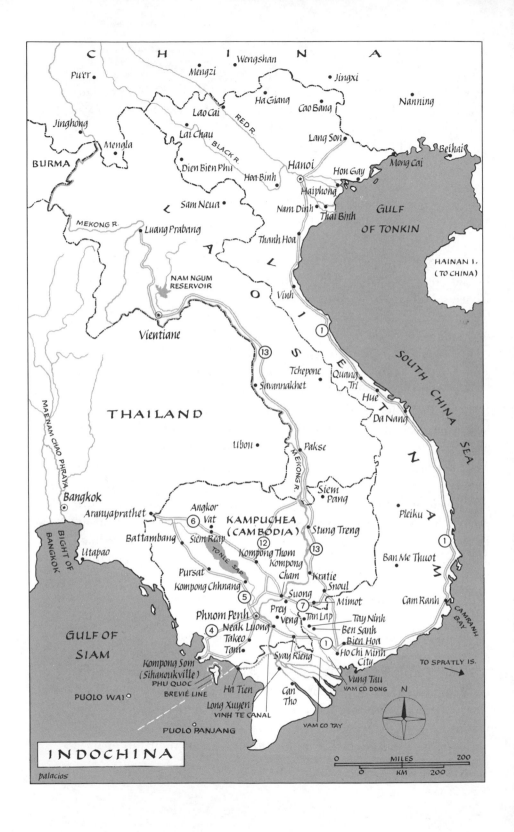

INDOCHINA

C H I N A

Pu'er

Mengzi

Wengshan

Jingxi

Nanning

Ha Giang

Cao Bang

Jinghong

Lao Cai

RED R.

Lai Chau

BLACK R.

Lang Son

Beihai

Mengla

Dien Bien Phu

Hoa Binh

Hanoi

Hon Gay

Mong Cai

BURMA

Haiphong

Sam Neua

Nam Dinh

Thai Binh

GULF
OF TONKIN

MEKONG R.

Luang Prabang

Thanh Hoa

HAINAN I.
(TO CHINA)

NAM NGUM
RESERVOIR

Vinh

L

A

Vientiane

O

13

Tchepone

Quang
Tri

S

SOUTH
CHINA
SEA

Savannakhet

Hue

THAILAND

Da Nang

Ubon

Pakse

MEKONG R.

T

Siem
Pang

Bangkok

Pleiku

Aranyaprathet

Angkor

6 Vat

KAMPUCHEA
(CAMBODIA)

Stung Treng

E

Battambang

Siem Reap

12

Kompong Thom

13

Ban Me Thuot

MAENAM CHAO PHRAYA

Utapao

TONLE SAP

Kompong
Cham

Kratie

N

Pursat

Snoul

BIGHT OF
BANGKOK

Kompong Chhnang

5

Suong

7

Mimot

Cam Ranh

A

Phnom Penh

Prey
Veng

Tan Lap

Tay Ninh

CAMRANH BAY

GULF OF
SIAM

4

Neak Luong

Ben Sanh

M

Takeo
Tani

Bien Hoa

1

Kompong Som
(Sihanoukville)

Svay
Rieng

Ho Chi Minh
City

TO SPRATLY IS.

PHU QUOC

Ha Tien

Vung Tau

PUOLO WAI

BREVIÉ LINE

VAM CO DONG

N

Long Xuyen

Can
Tho

VINH TE CANAL

VAM CO TAY

PUOLO PANJANG

MILES   200

KM   200

palacios

Cast of Characters

Zbigniew Brzezinski	National Security adviser to Jimmy Carter
Deng Xiaoping	Vice-Chairman of the Chinese Communist Party
Han Nianlong	Vice–Foreign Minister of China
Heng Samrin	President of People's Republic of Kampuchea
Hoang Tung	Editor of Vietnamese Party daily *Nhan Dan*
Richard Holbrooke	U.S. Assistant Secretary of State for East Asia and the Pacific
Hua Guofeng	Chairman of the Chinese Communist Party
Huang Hua	Foreign Minister of China
Ieng Sary	Vice-Premier and Foreign Minister of Democratic Kampuchea

Cast of Characters

Khieu Samphan	Prime Minister of Democratic Kampuchea
Kriangsak Chomanan	Prime Minister of Thailand
Li Xiannian	Vice-Premier of China
Le Duan	Secretary-General of the Communist Party of Vietnam
Le Duc Tho	Politburo member of Communist Party of Vietnam
Le Thanh Nghi	Chairman of Vietnamese Planning Commission
Nguyen Co Thach	Foreign Minister of Vietnam
Phan Hien	Vice–Foreign Minister of Vietnam
Pham Van Dong	Prime Minister of Vietnam
Pol Pot	Secretary of the Communist Party of Kampuchea
Norodom Sihanouk	Former Head of State of Cambodia
So Phim	Chairman of Democratic Kampuchea's Eastern Zone
Souphanouvong	President of Lao People's Democratic Republic
Cyrus Vance	U.S. Secretary of State
Vo Nguyen Giap	Defense Minister of Vietnam
Leonard Woodcock	U.S. Ambassador to China

Brother Enemy

Introduction:
The Exit

DARKNESS FELL like fate on Saigon on April 29, 1975. By 6:30 P.M. a power cut had blacked out the city, but in a way this was almost a blessing, because it cloaked the shame of defeat. I stood on the terrace of the Hotel Caravelle under a fine drizzle, watching Saigon's last night. Giant American helicopters, red lights pulsating and projector lamps flashing occasional shafts of piercing white light, hovered, clattering, before swooping down on rooftops to pluck remaining Americans and some of their Vietnamese associates to the safety of the United States Seventh Fleet lying offshore in the South China Sea. Moments later they zoomed up, their engines groaning deafeningly, to melt into the monsoon-shrouded sky. Against the backdrop of a sky crisscrossed by incandescent tracer bullets, the helicopters looked like giant fiery dragonflies engaged in some macabre dance over a dying city.

Below, a darkened and silent metropolis, known as both the Jewel of the Orient and the Whore City, awaited its conquerors. Its tall buildings were silhouetted against the flashes of rockets exploding over the horizon and the dull, orange glow of burning ammunition dumps at the Tan Son Nhut air base. Boulevard Le Loi and Tu Do Street, slicked by drizzle and almost deserted, glistened momentarily in the headlights of passing cars that rushed families of army officers and other rich Vietnamese to barges waiting on the Saigon River. Once in a while, bursts of gunfire erupted from the dock area as soldiers fired to scare away desperados attempting to board the boats. These were the last tremors of the frenzy that had gripped South Vietnam since the fall of Hue and Danang in March. The rush to flee the advancing Communist juggernaut was petering out. Earlier in the evening, I had watched as hundreds of Vietnamese pressed against the iron gates of the American embassy, waving bits of paper—identity cards, affidavits, even wads of dollar bills—in a bid to be allowed up to the embassy helipad. But they were clearly weary and dejected after a day of clawing and battering at the locked gates, which were manned by marines with rifles. Hundreds still jammed the stairwell of the buildings designated for the evacuation by helicopter, but as night wore on, hope was extinguished like a candle.

There are times when history brusquely accelerates, and this was one; the end had come with breathtaking speed. When the North Vietnamese army, led by portly General Van Tien Dung, struck at the Central Highlands town of Ban Me Thuot on March 10, it sent shudders all the way through the Nguyen Van Thieu regime. This was yet another audacious move by the Communists, following their seizure of Phuoc Binh Province in January. But few had seen it for what it had turned out to be—the beginning of the end. Faced with the new challenge, Thieu reversed his former policy of fighting for every inch of territory. His orders for a tactical withdrawal from Pleiku and Kontum in the Central Highlands, for the transfer of an elite unit from Hue, produced a swift strategic debacle. As the demoralized Thieu troops fled in complete disorder, Hue, Danang, and Nha Trang—and the rest of the South—fell like skittles to the North Vietnamese in just three weeks.

By early April the Communists were tightening their noose around Saigon. The Americans stepped up both the airlift of arms and the evacuation of their Vietnamese employees and friends. The war finally came to Saigon the day after Thieu had himself slipped out of the country aboard a U.S. Air Force C-118. In the early morning of April 27, I was rudely awakened by an explosion— the first Communist rocket to hit Saigon had struck the Hotel Majestic, a block away from my apartment. A Communist agent in the South Vietnamese air force, the same man who had bombed Thieu's palace earlier, returned on the twenty-eighth with his plane to attack the Tan Son Nhut air base. This devastating blow and an increasing rain of rockets and shells finally ended the fixed-wing airlift organized by the Americans.

Operation Frequent Wind, launched by the U.S. Navy on the afternoon of April 29 to evacuate Americans and Vietnamese by helicopter, halted by the morning of the thirtieth. From the roof of the Hotel Caravelle, North Vietnamese tanks seemed to crawl like a line of ants on Route 1 leading from Bien Hoa. From this battlefield grandstand I watched a lone helicopter drop out of the gray sky and settle on the helipad of the concrete, matchbox-like American embassy. Within a few minutes it was airborne again, with the last of the marine guards aboard. Pink smoke bellowed up from the canisters dropped to keep away any Vietnamese who hoped to scramble aboard. Banking sharply to avoid the transmission tower of the General Post Office, the helicopter climbed steeply across the Saigon River to disappear over the eastern horizon. It was 7:35 A.M. Twenty-one years after the Central Intelligence Agency's Colonel Edward Lansdale had arrived in Saigon to supervise the training of an anti-Communist Army of the Republic of Vietnam, the curtain finally fell on the American adventure in Indochina.

Four hours later, as I sat alone in the office of the British news agency, Reuters, opposite the presidential palace, pounding out a dispatch about Communist flags' being flown over the Saigon suburbs, I heard the roar of diesel engines and armored treads. Through the open door I saw a camouflaged tank flying a blue, red, and gold Vietcong flag rumbling toward the palace. I grabbed my camera and ran out of the office. As I crossed the park that lay between the Reuters office and the presidential palace, the tank fired a salvo in the air and broke through the cast-iron gate into the grounds of the palace. Soldiers in pith helmets and baggy green uniforms, and some with their tank helmets still on, jumped out of the tank and leapt up the stairs to plant the Vietcong flag. They had reached the end of the Ho Chi Minh Trail; the war was over.

I was dazed by the onrush of events, finding it hard to believe that the Vietnam War, a war that I had almost grown up with, had ended. A year before, when I had taken up residence in Saigon as the Indochina correspondent of the *Far Eastern Economic Review*, I knew that the Paris Peace Agreement worked out by Henry Kissinger and Vietnamese Politburo member Le Duc Tho was virtually dead. The cease-fire violations had lapsed into localized military campaigns. But nobody, not even the Communist planners in Hanoi, had expected the debacle. By mid-April, however, it had become evident that a decisive moment was near. At the insistence of my editors in Hongkong I had convinced my wife to leave Saigon, but I resisted their suggestion to leave. "No story is worth your life," my editor said in a message. "Get out if there is any danger." In a letter pigeoned out to Hongkong on April 25 I answered that I could not leave "without witnessing the final act of the drama." Only five days after that letter got off, the curtain dropped. I watched with a heavy heart as many of my Vietnamese friends left, as families were separated, as the wrenching exodus took place. I saw the misery of thousands who had fled from the rolling Communist tide on the central coast to the haven of Saigon, only to be trapped again in Saigon. Yet there was relief that the end came without the bloodbath that many had feared. The long separation between the South and the North was ending in a curious way, with the Saigonese milling around North Vietnamese T-54 tanks to chat with shy boys in green from the North. There was anxiety about what the future held, but there was the feeling that Vietnam at last was at peace, that over time all else would sort itself out.

Little such assurance was to be found in neighboring Cambodia, where the curtain had come down thirteen days earlier. During my last trip to Phnom Penh in January 1975, I had seen the Khmer Rouge noose tighten around the capital. The city's population, bloated by nearly two million refugees who had moved to Phnom Penh to flee from the war, was terrorized by rocket attacks. The Khmer Rouge cut all the roads, and soon the sole lifeline to the world outside was the Mekong River. Desperate American attempts to organize a Berlin-style airlift of food and fuel had to be abandoned as the Pochentong Airport came under attack. A weeping president Lon Nol left the country, followed soon by the American personnel. On April 17 the Khmer Rouge had marched into the capital to drive out the citizens at gunpoint. Two weeks later the foreigners who had taken refuge in the French embassy were bundled out to Thailand on trucks, and Cambodia—a shrinking bleep on the horizon—suddenly vanished.

As the Second Indochina War was ending, a new war between comrades and brothers was in the making. Hardly had the imperialist enemy left the scene, when age-old rivalry and suspicion surfaced. The comrades of yesterday started asserting their national interests against one another. But, cloaked in secrecy and camouflaged behind rhetoric of revolutionary solidarity, it was largely an invisible feud. Little did I know that I would spend the best part of the following decade covering a conflict that was unfolding just when peace seemed to have broken out in Indochina. For me it was like watching an image on a photographic plate growing sharper over the years as I traveled in Indochina and China—from the killing fields of Cambodia to the battle-scarred hills of the China-Vietnam border—and talked with countless people on both sides of the fence. Trying to piece together the missing parts of the jigsaw puzzle of the new conflict, I have since done hundreds of interviews with policymakers and officials of all the major powers and neighbors of Indochina involved in the drama. This book is the result of the inquiry I began twelve years earlier.

The fall of Saigon and Phnom Penh was followed by bloody clashes between the victorious Vietnamese and Cambodian Communists over the control of islands in the Gulf of Thailand. Khmer Rouge leader Pol Pot soon launched a program of forced march to socialism in order to grow strong quickly and face the hereditary enemy, Vietnam. Soon the bloody purges against opponents suspected of sympathy for Vietnam spilled into direct attacks on Vietnamese villages and massacres of civilians. To the Khmer Rouge, it was a preventive war of survival against a historic enemy predestined to "swallow" Cambodia. To the Vietnamese, Cambodian hostility with backing from China was a replay of history. Vietnam's millenary enemy, China, was seen as attempting to subjugate Vietnam by a pincer move from the north and the southwest. As it had many times in its thousand-year struggle against the Middle Kingdom, Vietnam was again ready to face the threat by going on the offensive, and it did in late 1977. The hidden conflict in Cambodia burst into the open on New Year's Day of 1978, as Radio Phnom Penh told the world that it was the victim of "Vietnamese aggression." Within five months the fire spread north. With a massive exodus of ethnic Chinese from Vietnam, Peking too lifted the veil of secrecy and denounced Hanoi's "persecution" of the Chinese and its drive for "hegemony" in Indochina. Vietnam's growing alliance with Moscow conjured up for China a historic nightmare—a simultaneous threat from "barbarians" in the north as well as the south. Since the summer of 1978 China had been planning a punitive blow against the "ingrate" Vietnamese, who had enjoyed Peking's support for three decades. When its Khmer Rouge allies were overthrown in a full-scale Vietnamese invasion in 1979, China was ready to deliver its punishment.

The conflict in Indochina became closely intertwined with the Soviet-American rivalry and a growing Sino-American alliance. While Democratic Kampuchea under the Khmer Rouge hermetically sealed its border and relied on China, from 1975 Hanoi tried to develop an independent foreign policy based on a balanced relation between the two superpowers. In the summer of 1977 Vietnam came close to establishing diplomatic ties with the United States, when its persistent demand for reconstruction aid aborted that move. A year later, as its conflict with Cambodia and China was about to burst into open war, Vietnam desperately wanted ties with Washington and dropped the aid demand. By then, the international wheel of fortune had turned. Unknown to the Vietnamese, Peking had decided to "teach Vietnam a lesson" and had intensified its effort to establish full diplomatic relations with the United States before undertaking that venture. The Chinese design meshed well with that of Jimmy Carter and his national security adviser, seeking China's partnership in a global anti-Soviet alliance. They decided to shelve normalization with Vietnam and secretly push for establishing ties with Peking. Three decades after going to war in Vietnam to fight "Chinese expansionism," the United States became a silent partner in Peking's war against Vietnam. In February 1979, fresh from his triumphant tour of the United States, China's vice-chairman, Deng Xiaoping, launched a punitive strike against Vietnam.

The Vietnamese occupation of Cambodia and the Chinese invasion climaxed the conflict that had quietly grown since 1975, but they brought no resolution. In early 1986 some 180,000 Vietnamese troops were still in Cambodia battling the Khmer Rouge guerrillas. Chinese gunners continued to pulverize Vietnam's northern border, and infantrymen mounted periodic raids. Though ousted from Phnom Penh, a Khmer Rouge coalition government of Democratic Kampuchea was still the recognized government of Cambodia. While the Third Indochina War ground on, the international context changed dramatically. Thanks to the Sino-Vietnamese war, Moscow acquired prized military facilities in Vietnam to extend its power in the Pacific. The hope of an anti-Soviet alliance that led Washington to support China against Vietnam, however, was abandoned as China switched to an independent policy and began normalization talks with Moscow. In a full turning of the cycle, a militarily strong but isolated and economically battered Vietnam again began pursuing the elusive ties with America.

This is the story of the historic struggle in Indochina and the bigpower diplomacy that surrounded it. Events in Indochina, since the last American helicopter lifted off the embassy rooftop in Saigon, demonstrate clearly how erroneous the premise for American intervention in Vietnam was. Instead of being the cutting edge of Chinese Communist expansion in Asia that U.S. planners had anticipated, Vietnam has proved to be China's most bitter foe and rival. The Khmer Rouge, long believed to be Hanoi's tool, revealed themselves to be Vietnam's mortal enemy. The story of the last decade should serve as an object lesson: history and nationalism—not ideology— shape the future of this volatile region. Whatever may be the appearance, it is very hard to find real puppets in Indochina.

1   Old Enemies, New War

AFTER A frenetic month, quiet had returned to Indochina in May 1975. The aircraft that had crisscrossed the sky, plucking people out to safety, were all gone. The last frenzy of rescue by the Seventh Fleet and hundreds of refugee boats steaming out of Vietnam had died down. At least, so one thought. But on the morning of May 15, as a calm dawn broke over the emerald-green island of Koh Tang in the Gulf of Thailand, the unmistakable sounds of war returned. Eleven helicopters appeared over the still-dark western horizon, heading toward the Cambodian island. The object of the attack for the marines aboard U.S. Air Force Jolly Green Giant and Knife helicopters was a battered, old American container ship, the *Mayaguez*, anchored offshore at Koh Tang. On May 12 a Cambodian gunboat carrying boyish black-clad soldiers had seized the ship off Puolo Wai Island, farther to the south.[1] The ship's Mayday call had brought in the response. President Gerald Ford ordered an air force helicopter unit at Utapao in Thailand and marines from the Seventh Fleet ships to rescue the *Mayaguez* and its thirty-nine crew members. When, in the predawn darkness, the marines attempted to storm the island, they had no knowledge that the crew of the *Mayaguez*

9

had already been moved to the port of Kompong Som on the mainland. Nor did the planners realize how stiff a defense the rescuers would face from ill-equipped peasant soldiers. Barely had one Knife settled on a sandy beach and marines in combat gear begun leaping out when the dark tree line above came to life with blazing machine gun and rifle fire. They "looked like a string of Christmas tree lights," reported an awestruck helicopter pilot.[2] Within an hour two Knifes were hit and crashed on the beach. Although there was no crew on the island to be rescued, the marines themselves, pinned down as they were by intense Cambodian fire, needed rescuers. For the next fourteen hours American shore-based aircraft and ships of the Seventh Fleet let loose awesome firepower over the area.

Stunned by the show of might, the Khmer Rouge quickly released the crew. But the fight to rescue the marines from Koh Tang Island was not over, Ford argued in justification of the massive bombing that pulverized Cambodia's coastal installations. At the end of the day-long war, fifteen Americans lay dead, as did countless Khmers. And Cambodia's only oil refinery and its small fleet of aircraft lay in ruins. For Ford, the *Mayaguez* affair was an opportunity to boost America's sagging morale after the humiliating retreat from Phnom Penh and Saigon. The show of American power over *Mayaguez*, Ford said, "was a spark that set off a whole new sense of confidence." The United States had gone through a very difficult time, and "this sort of turned the corner and changed the course," he later said.[3] America could now turn its attention to healing its wounds; it could return Indochina to obscurity.

The *Mayaguez* episode disappeared from the front pages, and few noticed that the incident was merely an inadvertent sideshow to a more portentous conflict: a long-suspended struggle for living space between two old neighbors. This last fling of American power in Indochina helped to hide the making of a new war between the erstwhile comrades and brothers who had once fought the Americans hand in hand. The seizure of *Mayaguez* had come in the wake of Khmer Rouge attacks on Vietnamese-held islands in the gulf. The angry young Khmer Rouge soldiers who had boarded the *Mayaguez* with only their AK-47 assault rifles had actually been trying to assert their newly gained control along the edges of the country's territorial waters.

Battle for Islands

In some ways it was natural, almost inevitable, that at the conclusion of a successful national struggle against foreign domination the victors would try to consolidate control over territories considered to be national patrimony. But in the case of Cambodia and Vietnam, that process meant bringing out into the open rivalry and conflict that had long been hidden behind the facade of comradely solidarity.

As the Vietnamese victory in the South drew closer, one of Hanoi's first acts was to "liberate" Spratlys Islands in the South China Sea from the Thieu regime and publicly stake its claim to the Chinese-occupied Paracel Islands. Within weeks of the capture of Phnom Penh, the Khmer Rouge units had fanned out to secure their land and sea border. Troops were dispatched to the Gulf of Thailand to take control of the islands that the old regime controlled or claimed.

The imperative was not just territorial. The drive to establish their authority over the whole territory also amounted to raising banners of independence vis-à-vis their respective wartime patrons. Time had come for the Vietnamese and Cambodian revolutionaries to follow their divergent political paths uninhibited by the wartime considerations of unity and cooperation. With the war over, the Vietnamese were no longer hesitant to assert their territorial claims against China, nor were the Cambodians reluctant to press theirs against Vietnam. The long historical struggle between China and Vietnam and between Vietnam and Cambodia that had been frozen by the French colonial rule and American intervention had sprung back to life—surreptitiously at first, but with increasing intensity. While ready to openly stake their territorial claims, neither revolutionary regime, however, was willing at this stage to embark on a full-scale conflict. Their urgent needs to consolidate power at home and resolve myriad postwar problems called for a measured approach. With two of its top leaders—Mao Zedong and Zhou Enlai—on their deathbed, China—the other key actor in the new struggle—was also too engrossed in its internecine ideological struggle to pay full attention to the emerging problems on its southern border. The domestic preoccupation of the protagonists brought about a pause, but their deep-seated fear of and ambition against each other and

11

the logic of their sharply divergent domestic and foreign policies soon set Cambodia and China on a collision course with Vietnam.

On April 12, 1975—five days before their triumphant army marched into Phnom Penh—one of the Khmer Rouge leaders, Ieng Sary, was in Quang Tri in South Vietnam. A big-built man with small eyes set in a smooth, round face, Sary was born in a "Khmer Krom" family—a member of the Khmer minority in Vietnam's Mekong Delta. In the 1950s, while studying in Paris, he embraced Marxism and, along with Khmer students including Pol Pot, set up a Cambodian Communist cell. He later emerged as the second most powerful man in the Khmer Rouge ranks, the feared "brother number two." In an interview in 1980, Sary told me that he was on his way from Peking to Cambodia's liberated zone through the newly liberated parts of South Vietnam when he received a cable from Hanoi advising him of the American pullout from Cambodia. For Sary the trip ahead along the rough Ho Chi Minh Trail and across the fast-flowing streams of Cambodia's Rattanakiri Province was nothing new. He had lived in Hanoi for a number of years during the war and had undertaken the perilous journey to Cambodia and back many times. The news that Phnom Penh was about to fall into Khmer Rouge hands had in a flash ended the usefulness of this rugged lifeline to revolutionary Cambodia. Instead of continuing the bone-rattling jeep trek across the Annamite Mountains into Cambodia, Sary flew back to Hanoi and then to Peking. He arrived in Phnom Penh on April 24 aboard a Chinese Boeing 707—the first foreign aircraft to land in new Cambodia and to put an end to the era of the Ho Chi Minh Trail.

What Sary did not tell me in that interview was that during his short stay in Peking he discussed with Chinese leaders the question of building up the Cambodian armed forces. He requested that his hosts stop delivering weapons and other supplies through the normal conduit—the Vietnamese. Several weeks later, Chinese freighters carrying rice, fuel, and consumer goods docked at Kompong Som Port.

But before the Chinese ships arrived, symbolically ending the isolation of revolutionary Cambodia, the Khmer Rouge had challenged the Vietnamese control of islands in the Gulf of Thailand. To revive an old claim to Phu Quoc Island (called *Koh Tral* in Khmer), the Khmer Rouge launched a seaborne ground assault on the island on May 4. Six days later, Khmer troops landed on Poulo Panjang Island (*Tho Chu* in Vietnamese and *Koh Krachak Ses* in Khmer) and evacuated at gunpoint five hundred Vietnamese inhabitants, who were never heard of again. Nguyen Van Tot, a South Vietnamese soldier who was in Rach Gia at the time of the attack, lost his entire family of twelve. When he returned to Poulo Panjang four months later, his home was in ruins and the island littered with skulls. Two weeks after the Khmer Rouge landing, the Vietnamese launched a counterattack, killing many Khmer soldiers and taking about three hundred prisoners.[4]

Ieng Sary told a group of sympathetic Americans that the seizure of the *Mayaguez* on May 12 was the act of a local commander, done without authorization from Phnom Penh.[5] It is also possible that overzealous commanders stretched the directive of defending Cambodian territory too far and attacked Vietnamese islands. But, more probably, it was the result of a high-level directive. The Khmer Rouge leaders perhaps thought that actual occupation was the strongest argument in any territorial dispute. Khmers had never been reconciled to the loss of those coastal islands to French Cochin China and later to the successor Republic of Vietnam. In 1960 the then head of state of Cambodia, Prince Norodom Sihanouk, had tried in vain to recover Phu Quoc from South Vietnamese control through diplomacy. "The loss of the islands and the territorial waters surrounding them would lead to the stifling of the port of [Kompong Som] . . . and very soon to the end of our independence," Sihanouk had warned.[6]

Now with confusion prevailing in the wake of the fall of Saigon, the Khmer Rouge must have thought time was ripe to make good the claim by physical occupation. Pol Pot, the failed electrical engineering student in Paris and fanatical Marxist who had been the secretary of the Communist Party of Kampuchea (CPK) since the early 1960s, was now in a position to put into action his radical ideas and his deep antipathy toward Vietnam, the traditional enemy. Immediately after the capture of Phnom Penh he issued an eight-point directive; two of these points, tellingly, were to expel the entire Vietnamese minority population from Cambodia and to dispatch troops to the borders, particularly the Vietnamese border.[7] After seeing the ferocity of the Vietnamese reaction, however, Pol Pot must have reconsidered the wisdom of such a hasty move. When, on June 2, Vietnamese Politburo member Nguyen Van Linh drove to Phnom Penh to discuss the problem, Pol Pot pleaded guilty. In a great show of sincere regret he admitted to Linh that encroachments had taken place, but the "painful, bloody clashes," he said, were due to soldiers' "ignorance of local geography."

Le Duan Goes to Phnom Penh

The Vietnamese clearly did not buy that explanation. While saying that Pol Pot was welcome to visit Hanoi, they dispatched their troops to mount a combined air and naval assault on the Cambodian island of Puolo Wai. When Pol Pot, accompanied by Ieng Sary, deputy party secretary Nuon Chea, and other officials, arrived in Hanoi on June 12 for his "fraternal visit," the Vietnamese had already subjugated the Cambodian garrison at Puolo Wai and raised their flag over the island. On June 14 The New York Times quoted U.S. intelligence sources as reporting the Vietnamese seizure of the island. But the story of the Pol Pot delegation's ironically timed visit to Hanoi was to remain hidden for nearly three years.

Some years later, Ieng Sary told me that the Cambodians had, during the trip, tried in vain to raise the issue of the border dispute with the Vietnamese. The Cambodians, he said, wanted to reach a settlement on the basis of the 1967 declaration of the Democratic Republic of Vietnam (DRV) recognizing the "present borders" of Cambodia. But the Vietnamese refused to discuss the question. According to a later Vietnamese account, although the Cambodians wanted to sign a treaty of friendship encompassing such problems as trade, consular issues, and border demarcation, they requested no immediate negotiations on the border problem. The idea of a treaty of friendship was perhaps raised by the Khmers to soften up the Vietnamese and get them to formally accept Cambodia's border. It was never broached again.[8]

On August 2, Vietnamese party secretary Le Duan, Politburo

member Pham Hung, and the veteran Vietnamese negotiator at the Paris Peace Talks, Xuan Thuy, flew to Phnom Penh for a short visit. Having given the Cambodians a taste of their military might, the Vietnamese now showed some flexibility. Sixty-seven-year-old Duan, a tall, somber-looking man, had been an original member of the Indochinese Communist Party. Before assuming the secretary-ship of the Vietnamese party in 1960, he had spent a decade in jail and a number of years leading the revolution in South Vietnam. But unlike his associate Pham Hung, a portly southerner who had long been in charge of the struggle in the South and maintained contact with the Khmer Rouge leaders across the border, Duan was making his first trip to Cambodia. The purpose of the visit was clearly not tourism. The Vietnamese guests were not taken out of Phnom Penh, which had become a ghost city after the brutal evacuation of its entire population in April. And, at the request of the Cambodians, reports about the visit were kept to a minimum.[9] Despite the exceptionally cool reception, Duan was conciliatory. He conceded that Puolo Wai was indeed Cambodian territory and promised its early return. A joint communiqué was signed, pledging to settle differences peacefully, but it was never published. Neither was there any banquet or speech. Only a terse report on the visit broadcast by both Radio Hanoi and Radio Phnom Penh on August 3 announced that "cordial talks were held between the Vietnamese and a Cambodian delegation in a fraternal atmosphere on questions of mutual interest. There was unanimity of views on all questions raised."[10]

Although cordiality was a pretense, the atmosphere improved marginally when Puolo Wai was returned. On August 10, Nguyen Van Linh met Nuon Chea, one of Cambodia's top party leaders, to inform him that Vietnamese troops had been withdrawn from the island. Chea thanked Vietnam for its decision and said that all this was due to "unawareness of the border problem."[11] In fact, it was the overawareness of the border problem and the intense nationalism of both sides that had produced the bloody scramble after the victory.

Neither side was ready to carry the battle through. The Vietnamese in particular were anxious to keep the conflict out of the public view. While trying to iron out the problems by force as well as diplomacy, Hanoi was determined to maintain the facade of militant solidarity with Phnom Penh. In July, after two and a half months in "liberated Saigon," I flew to Hanoi on my way out of Vietnam. During an interview with Hoang Tung, the editor of the Vietnamese party daily *Nhan Dan*, I asked about the state of relations with Cambodia. "Normal," he replied promptly and then after a pause added, "generally normal." He denied Western press reports of a Cambodia-Vietnam clash in the Gulf of Thailand.

By the time I talked with Tung in his dimly lit office overlooking the Hoan Kiem Lake in Hanoi, thousands of Vietnamese men, women, and children had been driven out of Cambodia and into the Mekong Delta area of South Vietnam. As they crossed the border, Vietnamese army units escorted them to makeshift camps set up by the government. Several hundred Cambodian refugees of Vietnamese and Chinese origin managed to install themselves in a pagoda in Cholon. The Agence France-Presse correspondent in Saigon, Charles-Antoine de Nerciat, thought he had hit upon a minor scoop when he located refugees from fraternal revolutionary Cambodia being sheltered in liberated Saigon. But, thanks to the vigilance of the Vietnamese censors, his dispatch of June 12 was never transmitted. In an ironic coincidence, he filed his story the day Pol Pot arrived in Hanoi for an unpublicized visit. Whether the censors were aware of that visit or not, the Vietnamese were not interested in letting bourgeois journalists recount sad tales of refugees and thereby complicate its relations with Cambodia. It was not until 1978 that the full story began to emerge. During a trip to the border provinces of Vietnam in March 1978, I learned how, during the first five months after the "liberation" of Phnom Penh, more than 150,000 destitute Vietnamese had flooded into Dong Thap, An Giang, and Tay Ninh provinces. The Vietnamese were allowed to stay, but refugees of Chinese and Khmer descent were forced back to Cambodia.

Vietnam's need for caution toward Cambodia was underlined by the fact that Phnom Penh had a powerful friend. After Hanoi the next stop in Pol Pot's secret journey was Peking. On June 21 Pol Pot got a hero's welcome from his ideological mentor, Mao. "You have achieved in one stroke what we failed with all our masses," Mao told his beaming disciple.[12] As Mao spoke, hundreds of thousands of citizens in Cambodia were brutally evicted from urban centers to the vast countrywide gulags.

Mao fully endorsed Pol Pot's revolutionary plans for Cambodia and his policy of steering a course independent of Vietnam. The meeting was not reported until two years later, when Pol Pot shed his cloak of anonymity to acknowledge his role as the party secretary. The Vietnamese, of course, were fully aware of the deep admiration in which Mao held the Khmer Rouge. In 1975, Mao advised a Vietnamese leader to "learn from the Khmer Rouge how to carry out a revolution."[13]

The friendship between Mao's China and Democratic Kampuchea was based on ideology and, more importantly, on identity of national interest. The Pol Pot group not only had boundless admiration for Mao's theory of class struggle and uninterrupted revolution, they also shared China's fear and loathing of the Soviet Union. As opposition to the Vietnamese domination of the Indochinese peninsula became the primary concern of the Pol Pot group, they naturally turned out to be China's key ally in its traditional strategy of preventing the emergence of a strong power on its southern border.

Not surprisingly, in August 1975, as a bedridden Zhou was explaining China's inability to help Vietnam to the top Vietnamese planner, Le Thanh Nghi, Peking was giving a grand welcome to the Cambodian deputy premiers Khieu Samphan and Ieng Sary and promising them $1 billion of aid over a five-year period. Some $20 million of this was to be an outright grant.

While Samphan and Sary's triumphant visit, and the pledge of economic assistance, was a public demonstration of China's total support for Cambodia, secret negotiations on Chinese arms aid had begun in June—when Pol Pot made his unpublicized trip to China. In August and October, teams of experts from China's defense ministry conducted an extensive survey in Cambodia to assess defense needs, and, on October 12, submitted a draft aid plan to Phnom Penh for its approval.

On February 6, 1976, the day the Chinese embassy in Hanoi lodged its first official complaint about the forced naturalization of the ethnic Chinese in South Vietnam, a top Chinese army official was secretly visiting Phnom Penh to finalize a military aid agreement. Wang Shangrong, deputy chief of the People's Liberation Army (PLA) General Staff, told Democratic Kampuchea's defense minister, Son Sen, about China's decision to deliver artillery pieces, patrol boats, and air-defense equipment on a priority basis. A total of five hundred Chinese advisers were to train soldiers to use the equipment. Wang also listed the weapons systems to be delivered in 1977 and 1978. On February 10, the agreement for nonrefundable military aid to Cambodia was signed by Wang and Sen.[14]

While military cooperation was conducted in utmost secrecy in order not to alarm Thailand or Vietnam, the original Chinese motivation seems to have been to support a legitimate Cambodian desire to transform its guerrilla army into regular armed forces equipped for the new task of defending the country. Although Peking no doubt wished to redress the dramatic imbalance between Vietnam's large and well-equipped fighting machine, which had inherited $5 billion worth of weapons from the South Vietnamese arsenal, and the poorly armed Khmer force, it had neither the means nor apparently the desire to push the Khmer Rouge to a military confrontation with Vietnam. Mao's China wanted the Khmer Rouge to have enough muscle that they would not be cowed by Vietnam.

China's arms relations with Cambodia were naturally hidden, but China's message of support was delivered loudly. On April 17, 1976, Peking celebrated with fanfare the first anniversary of the "liberation" of Cambodia. In a joint message to Pol Pot on that occasion, Mao, Zhu De, and Hua Guofeng hailed him for resolutely defending Cambodia's independence, sovereignty, and territorial integrity and for bringing about "profound revolutionary changes." Although the country that threatened Cambodia's independence and integrity was not specified, the warning could not have been missed in Hanoi. The leaders also assured Pol Pot that the Chinese people would "fight shoulder to shoulder and march forward" with the people of Cambodia.[15]

By the spring of 1976 Cambodia had emerged as a major element of tension between Vietnam and China, but the quiet deterioration of their relationship had begun years before. Since Hanoi's victory in the South, specific bilateral irritants had been added to the strategic and political differences.

18

A Rush to the Spratlys

Almost three weeks before Communist flags were hoisted in Saigon, later renamed Ho Chi Minh City,* the North Vietnamese navy had taken over islands in the Spratly group that were held by South Vietnamese garrisons. Hanoi foresaw a period of transition and confusion as it seized the South and did not want to give Peking any chance of grabbing the islands, to which both states laid claim. On May 5, Radio Hanoi announced that in the days after April 11 the "liberation army and navy" had completely "liberated" six islands of the Spratly archipelago. Two days later, the official daily *Saigon Giai Phong* (Liberated Saigon) printed a color map of Vietnam showing not only the Spratlys but also the Chinese-occupied Paracel Islands as Vietnamese territory.

Peking maintained a stony silence about the incident. Years later, I learned how the Chinese really felt. "When we were about to leave Hanoi for a tour of liberated South Vietnam we heard the news of the capture of the Nansha [Spratly] Islands. I tasted ash in my mouth," Ling Dequan, a correspondent for the Chinese news agency, Xinhua, told me. Ling served several years in the Xinhua bureau in Hanoi and joined the first group of Hanoi-based Communist journalists to visit the South in May 1975. He said Vietnamese seizure of the islands had come as a shock since Vietnam had earlier recognized Chinese sovereignty over the Spratlys. Ling somewhat overdramatized the surprise. Although the North Vietnamese had not until then officially contested Peking's claim to the islands, Hanoi had given ample indication of its reservation over the issue. In June 1974 Hoang Tung had told a Thai journalist, "Southeast Asia belongs to the Southeast Asian people. . . . China is not a Southeast Asian country, so China should not have such big territorial waters as it claims."[16]

When Tung made this statement, Hanoi did not foresee taking over the South so rapidly. But once the Thieu army began to crumble, Hanoi could hardly be expected to stand idly by and watch China occupy the Spratlys in the same manner as it had the Paracels the year before.

---

* I refer to the city as Saigon when the events described take place before April 30, 1975.

The Paracel and Spratly archipelagos in the South China Sea are made up of 150 specks of land, coral reef, and sandbanks. The area has been known to Vietnamese, Chinese, and Filipino fishermen for centuries for guano (used as fertilizer) and for that Chinese gourmet's delight—bird's nest. Those islets acquired a new value in the early 1970s, when the search for offshore oil began in earnest in Southeast Asia. The question of their ownership had been a complicated affair, with China's claiming all of them on the basis of archeological evidence and occasional visits. Neither China nor Vietnam nor the Philippines had, however, effectively occupied them for any length of time. Until the late 1950s, when the South Vietnamese government did not contest China's claims to the islands, North Vietnam—an ideological ally and a recipient of Chinese aid— thought it only wise to accept Chinese rights as well. But after 1959, when the first incident erupted between Saigon and Peking over the Spratlys and Paracels, Hanoi consistently avoided backing China by simply staying silent on the issue.

The First Act of War

In 1972, when the Thieu government began contracting out offshore blocks to foreign oil companies for exploration, the islands resurfaced as a major subject of Chinese concern. China quietly established its presence on the Amphitrite chain of the Paracel Islands while the South Vietnamese maintained small garrisons on some islands of the Crescent chain. In April 1972, in a move that in retrospect appears to have been designed to secure American acquiescence to its claim in the wake of Nixon's historic trip to China two months earlier, Peking protested against the intrusion of American vessels into territorial waters around the Paracel Islands. Judging by his memoirs, former U.S. secretary of state Henry Kissinger did not question China's claims to the Paracels, despite the opposing South Vietnamese claims to, and actual occupation of, part of the islands. Kissinger informed the Chinese that "without prejudice to our legal position on territorial waters our Navy would be instructed to stay at a distance of twelve miles from the islands."[17]

Hanoi, and most probably Saigon, too, was unaware of Kissinger's commitment to keep the U.S. fleet away from the islands. On December 26, 1973, Hanoi notified the Chinese government of its plan to begin negotiation with an Italian oil company for oil explorations in the Gulf of Tonkin. On January 11, Peking issued a statement that claimed all the islands in the South China Sea. Four days later Chinese troops were grouped on the Crescent. A South Vietnamese attempt to remove the Chinese brought a carefully planned response by Peking. A Chinese air-naval operation on January 19 ousted the South Vietnamese reinforcements from the islands and established full Chinese control. The Thieu government reportedly requested U.S. help, only to be politely declined. The Pentagon said it was unaware of any request for help, and the U.S. Seventh Fleet stayed clear of the area of conflict. One U.S. adviser with the South Vietnamese naval units, who was captured by the Chinese, was quietly repatriated to Hongkong a few weeks after the event. A day before the Chinese riposte, Peking informed Hanoi that it would negotiate with Vietnam the issue of territorial waters, but that no prospecting should be undertaken.

Several years later, the Vietnamese ambassador in Paris, Mai Van Bo, told me that the January 1974 Paracels operation was China's "first act of armed aggression against Vietnam." But at the time, Hanoi simply stated that complex disputes over territories between neighbors frequently demand careful examination. "Countries involved should settle such disputes," it said, "by negotiation and in a spirit of equality, mutual respect, and good-neighborliness."[18]

Coming as it did after China's armed seizure of the Paracels, this statement was implicit criticism. But, given the need for Chinese economic and military assistance in fighting the war in the South, Hanoi could not afford to go any further. A year later, with total victory in the South in sight, the time had finally come for the Vietnamese Communists to assert openly their position against China by announcing the "liberation" of six islands in the Spratly chain (*Truong Sa* in Vietnamese). Since the mid-1950s there had been disagreement over certain sections of the Sino-Vietnamese land border, but that had not posed any problem. After Nixon's 1972 visit to China, and with the end of American bombing in the North and the signing of the Paris Agreement, Hanoi began assuming a more assertive posture on territorial issues. Unbeknownst to the world, minor clashes had started on the border. According to later Chinese revelations, one hundred clashes took place in 1974, and following Hanoi's victory in the South the number increased fourfold.[19]

Fear of a Base

One of the great ironies of history was that more than the United States it was China who lost the Vietnam War. The American pull-out in 1975 seemed to bring about all the Chinese policymakers' nightmares about Vietnam—a strong, reunified Vietnam challenging China from the south in cahoots with China's bitter enemy in the north.

The dramatic collapse of American power in Indochina—symbolized by photographs of the American ambassador to Cambodia, John Gunther Dean, leaving the country with the Stars and Stripes stashed away in a plastic bag, and of U.S. helicopters being thrown into the sea from overcrowded naval vessels after the evacuation from Saigon—had come at a time when Peking was obsessed with Soviet "social imperialists' " extending their influence in Asia. Since Nixon's China visit Peking had looked benignly at the U.S. presence in Asia, with the exception, of course, of Taiwan. The Chinese were now worried that a precipitate U.S. withdrawal from Southeast Asia would only encourage Moscow—Vietnam's principal supplier of military hardware—to step into the vacuum. On April 29, when Operation Frequent Wind was pulling out the last fragments of the American presence from Vietnam, the main item of foreign news in the Xinhua News Agency bulletin was about a worldwide Soviet naval exercise. After noting the Soviet naval presence in different parts of the world, including "frantic penetration into the Straits of Malacca," to the south of Vietnam, the agency expressed the hope that Moscow's latest naval maneuver would heighten vigilance "against the dangers of social-imperialist aggression and expansion."[20]

Chairman Mao, Zhu De, and Zhou, of course, sent a congratulatory message to Hanoi about "these glad tidings," but they also pointed out that the victory of the Vietnamese people was another demonstration of the invincibility of people's war, a concept originated and upheld by China. A *People's Daily* commentary on May 1 made a clearer attempt to deny the Soviets any credit for the Vietnamese victory. "The great Vietnamese victory has proved once again," the paper said, that "what is decisive for victory or defeat is the people and their support, and not sophisticated weapons." In other words, it was not Soviet tanks and missiles that brought Vietnamese success; it was the support of the people.

Such discreet warnings were necessary because Peking suspected that Vietnamese "revisionists" might now be tempted by potential aid to provide the Soviets base facilities. China noted with concern the arrival of a Soviet military delegation in Hanoi barely a week after the fall of Saigon and the beginning of a steady stream of Soviet commercial vessels to South Vietnamese ports. Barely three weeks after the fall of Saigon, China sounded its first public warning by telling a visiting Japanese delegation that the Soviets had "demanded" of the Provisional Revolutionary Government of South Vietnam that it "be allowed to use former U.S. military bases in that country."[21]

In July 1975 I asked Ngo Dien, a suave Vietnamese diplomat in charge of the press department of the Foreign Ministry (who was later to become ambassador to Cambodia), whether the Soviets had indeed asked for bases. He seemed almost indignant. "Do you think it is possible for the Soviets to ask for bases in our country?" he asked rhetorically. "Before you ask anything of a friend you must know what his feelings are about it. How can the Soviets ask for a 'base'—with all its imperialist odor?" But he added that, if needed, Soviet ships would enjoy facilities at Cam Ranh Bay similar to those available to ships of other friendly countries. As I was to discover years later, Dien's protest was essentially a quibble over the word *base*, because other Vietnamese diplomats admitted to me six years later that in 1975 Moscow indeed had unsuccessfully pressed for military facilities—something they would not get for four more years, with the deepening of Vietnam's conflict with China.

Even without Soviet bases, what was worrying to China was the sudden shift in the balance of power in Southeast Asia. With its large and battle tested army and the enormous booty of American war materiel in the south, Hanoi had emerged as a preeminent power in Indochina, in its own words, ready to claim the mantle of revolutionary vanguard in the region. Almost mocking the Chinese warnings about danger posed by the new vacuum in Southeast Asia, a *Nhan Dan* editorial on May 21 gloated over the collapse of the U.S. defense line in Southeast Asia. "The epoch-making victory of the Vietnamese people," the editorial said, "has contributed to bringing about an important change in the world balance of forces. . . . The peoples in this region are having very favorable conditions for breaking away from their dependence on the imperialists. . . ."[22] Seen from Peking, this was tantamount to Hanoi's claiming the leadership of Southeast Asian revolution.

I had a taste of Hanoi's euphoric mood during a visit in the summer of 1975. It was not a city bristling with guns and screaming billboards calling for world revolution. Hanoi was quietly exultant. Compared with the tension, noise, and anarchy I had left behind in Saigon, the Northern capital was a study in contrasts. Little had changed in Hanoi since the French had left Indochina twenty-one years before. The city had aged gracefully: with its tree-shaded boulevards and placid lakes, with the tranquillity of the streets disturbed only by the gentle whirring of bicycles, Hanoi had a quiet air of confidence. Talking to me in the colonial-style Foreign Ministry building, Ngo Dien recited a fifteenth-century poem written after the last of the Ming invaders had been driven out of Vietnam:

There are no more sharks in the sea,
There are no more beasts on earth,
The sky is serene,
Time is now to build peace for ten thousand years.

The Vietnamese were still in a daze at their feat. During the dark days of the war, when American B-52s rained death over the North, and tens of thousands of boys left home to fight in the South never to come back, few had hoped to be alive to see the victory that Ho Chi Minh predicted. After going through the ordeal of fire and defeating the most powerful nation on earth, everything seemed feasible. Vietnam was now ready to take its place in the world, stand up to friends and foe, and speak its mind.

A worried China seized the occasion of North Vietnam's thirtieth anniversary to express its concern directly to the Vietnamese leadership. It sent Politburo member Gen. Chen Xilian to attend the celebration in Hanoi. Chen, the burly commander of the Peking Military Region, had personally led Chinese forces during the 1969 border clash with the Soviets and was in a position to warn Hanoi about the dangers that Moscow posed to Asia. Addressing a meeting at the Chinese-built Thai Nguyen steel mill, which was bombed during the war and rebuilt with Peking's help, Chen praised the "antihegemonic" (China's code word for anti-Soviet) struggle in the world. He warned that "superpower contention for hegemony"— that is, the Soviet attempt to fill in the vacuum—was getting more fierce and factors for war were increasing. When Chen arrived in Hanoi on August 31, Premier Pham Van Dong climbed the ramp of the plane to embrace him—a tradition from the days of militant solidarity. But Hanoi media did not let politeness stand in the way of its political independence: they deleted Chen's references to hegemony when they reported his speech. Not to miss the chance of scoring a point over Peking, Radio Moscow took Chen to task for what it called his "uncivil act of political provocation." The Vietnamese people, the broadcast said, "know the difference between friend and foe," and they are aware of "invaluable and unselfish support" from Moscow.[23]

Such an open tussle between Moscow and Peking over Hanoi's loyalty did not augur well for the Vietnamese policy of trying to steer clear of big brothers' disputes while continuing to seek their help. When, on September 22, Le Duan and Le Thanh Nghi left for a thanks-giving and aid-seeking trip to Peking, it was clear that the visit was going to be a test of Vietnamese skill. The day before their departure, a report from Peking gave a foretaste of what the Chinese leaders wanted to hear from Le Duan. After a meeting with Mao and Deng, former British prime minister Edward Heath told a press conference that Moscow was "lovesick" in its desire to have military bases in Vietnam. But he got the impression that China did not think Moscow would succeed "in the long term" in exerting a lasting influence on Vietnam; nor would it manage to set up naval bases there. Through Heath, China gave its clearest signal to Hanoi. It was now up to Duan to reassure China that its cautious optimism was well founded.

No Time for a Banquet

Though Le Duan's reception in Peking was less lavish than the one laid out for Cambodia's Khieu Samphan and Ieng Sary the previous month, it was nonetheless warm. After being received by Deng Xiaoping and scores of other top leaders at the steps of his aircraft, Duan was given the traditional guard of honor by the People's Liberation Army and a welcoming dance and flowers by Peking youth groups. The seventy-one-year-old Deng, who was once reviled by the Red Guards as a "top capitalist roader" and had spent four years cleaning mess halls, was rehabilitated by Zhou Enlai in 1973. Receiving Le Duan proved to be his last major public appearance before his political fortunes dipped again. Peking's Tien An Men Square was decked with red and gold lanterns, flags, and banners proclaiming friendship. But the temperature fell when, at the welcoming banquet, Deng turned his welcoming speech into a homily on the evils of "hegemonism." In deference to Vietnam's friendship with the Soviet Union, he avoided any direct reference to the Soviets, talking generally, instead, of superpowers. "The superpowers are the biggest international exploiters and oppressors of today," he reminded the Vietnamese guests. Then, in a barely concealed appeal to Vietnam to join China in opposing the Soviets, Deng said, "More and more people have come to see now that to combat superpower hegemonism is a vital task facing the people of all countries." In a pointed reminder of the changed times, Deng referred to China and Vietnam not in the traditional terms—as close as "lips and teeth"—but in a more businesslike fashion, speaking of them as "fraternal Socialist neighbors." And he reminded Duan that the preservation and development of their friendship was in line with their fundamental interests.[24]

Duan had attended many such banquets in the chandelier-festooned Great Hall of the People. But this was the first time he had come to Peking not simply to solicit aid but to assert the position of a unified and independent Vietnam. Duan profusely praised China's success in building socialism and said Vietnam had "the warmest sentiments and heartfelt and most profound gratitude" for China's help, but in a politely firm way, he discarded the Chinese view of the world. Noting that Vietnam's victory could not have been possible without the sympathy and the "great and valuable" assistance of other fraternal Socialist countries—that is, the Soviet bloc—Duan went on to say, "For this reason, it is a common victory of the forces of socialism, national independence, democracy, and peace in the common struggle against imperialism, with U.S. imperialism as its ringleader." Vietnam, he said in so many words, would not join China in its anti-Soviet crusade. But, in spite of this political divergence, he still pressed for aid. The Vietnamese people, he reminded his hosts, "are firmly convinced that in the new stage, as in the past, they will enjoy the continued warmth and great support and assistance" of China.[25] In Hanoi, the Vietnam news agency's report on the speeches excised all Deng's references to superpower hegemonism.

Duan's refusal to pay heed to China meant a hardening of Peking's position on aid. Five weeks before Le Duan's visit, Le Thanh Nghi, whom the Chinese had nicknamed "the Beggar" because of his frequent aid-seeking trips to Peking, had traveled to the Chinese capital to ask for China's assistance.[26] When, in June of 1973, Zhou had asked Duan to stop fighting in the south for two years, he had promised to give Vietnam aid at the 1973 level for five more years. But on August 13, 1975, when Nghi went to see a then-dying Zhou, he heard a different tune. According to a later account in the *Peking Review*, Zhou told the Vietnamese visitor: "During the war, when you were in the worst need, we took many things from our own army to give to you. We made a very great effort to help you. The sum of our aid to Vietnam still ranks first among our aid to foreign countries. You should let us have a respite and regain strength."[27]

Now Duan found the Chinese leaders firm in their position of ending grants-in-aid and all food assistance promised in the past. Now that the war was over, they said, Vietnam should feed itself. During his meeting with Mao, Nghi tried to ingratiate himself by saying that "without China as our vast rear area, without the line you have provided us, and without your aid, we cannot possibly succeed. . . . We have always held that it is China, not the Soviet Union, that can provide us with the most direct and most significant assistance at the crucial moment when our fate hangs in the balance."[28] Such praise did not bring anything more than an interest-free loan to finance Vietnamese imports of oil and consumer goods. The only other indication that Peking had not yet written off Vietnam was its readiness not to slam the door on the question of the Paracels and Spratlys. In his talks with Duan on September 24, Deng did not take the Chinese propaganda line that the islands were "sacred Chinese territory" and thus nonnegotiable. He admitted that there were disputes on the island questions that would have to be settled through discussion.[29]

But the political differences between the two sides were now too great and Duan's disappointment too heavy for him to paper these over in a joint communiqué. Not only did Duan refuse to draw up a joint communiqué—as he had during his last official trip in 1973—he also canceled the customary return banquet for his hosts, something that a Chinese official later termed "an extraordinary act for a fraternal party leader."[30] On September 25, Duan left for Tientsin by train on his journey home. Postwar Vietnam had delivered its first public snub to Peking.

A second snub followed a month later, when Duan traveled to Moscow to receive a promise of long-term Soviet aid and sign a joint communiqué endorsing Soviet foreign policy positions. As a Chinese official told me later, the Soviet-Vietnamese joint communiqué on October 30 was "Vietnam's surrender to hegemonism."[31]

Internal developments in Vietnam, too, seemed to confirm China's worst fears. Despite China's verbal support for Hanoi's goal of reunification, it viewed with misgivings the prospect of the political and administrative union of the two parts, which would drastically alter the balance in Indochina. In its message of congratulation to Vietnam after the victory, Peking subtly alluded to this concern. "We sincerely wish," the Chinese said, "that the South Vietnamese people will ceaselessly win new and greater victories in their continued struggle to carry through their national and democratic revolution."[32] Apart from perpetuating the myth that the victory essentially was the work of the South Vietnamese people and not of North

Vietnamese armor and men, the Chinese clearly stated their preference for a social system in the South separate from that of the Socialist North.

In the first few months after the victory the Vietnamese leadership gave the impression that at least for five years the South would retain a separate social and economic system before merging with the Socialist North.[33] In his Victory Day speech on May 15, Le Duan declared that the South should build a "national democratic regime"—in Marxist parlance, a pre-Socialist state. The South Vietnamese Provisional Revolutionary Government also applied for a separate seat at the United Nations. But after six months of experience in running the affairs in the South, the Vietnamese party leaders concluded that disadvantages of a delayed reunification outweighed the advantages. While a rapid dismantling of the capitalist system in the South could provoke unrest and resistance, maintaining a free enterprise system in the absence of a sufficient number of competent cadres could create a chaotic situation and, more serious, strengthen separatist tendencies in the South. The Vietnamese leaders were wary of Peking's direct lines of communication to Southern Communists through the network in Chinese-dominated Cholon and Peking's strong ties with neighboring Cambodia. The fact that China was also keen to maintain a separate existence of the South provided an additional argument for a rapid unification, if only to foil possible Chinese maneuver.

In a surprise move, a simultaneous broadcast over Radio Hanoi and Radio Ho Chi Minh City on November 9 announced the impending North-South "consultative conference" to prepare for the reunification of the two governments. When the conference announced its decision a few weeks later, China was conspicuously absent from the Socialist countries that poured congratulatory messages to Hanoi.

China's growing irritation with Vietnam was expressed on November 24, three days after the "consultative conference" in Ho Chi Minh City had closed its deliberations. China broke its silence over the Spratlys, which Hanoi forces had "liberated" in April. A lengthy article in *Guangming Daily* on China's ancient ownership of the Paracels and Spratlys put Vietnam on notice. Reversing Deng's Septem-

29

ber position, which had considered them a disputed area, the *Guangming Daily* now announced them to be "sacred territory of China." It declared ominously that "all the islands belonging to China will definitely return to the embrace of the motherland." [34]

Undeterred by China's implicit threat, Hanoi had proceeded with its own agenda of consolidating its control over the South, including its 1.5 million Chinese population. In February 1976, in preparation for the forthcoming nationwide general elections, a census, in which citizens were asked to declare their nationality, was taken. Because a claim to foreign nationality would automatically deprive a person of all citizenship rights, including food rations, a vast majority of the ethnic Chinese in the South were obliged to become Vietnamese nationals.

To Peking, this was a violation not only of the 1955 verbal agreement between China and North Vietnam to allow Chinese residents to become Vietnamese citizens "voluntarily," but also of a similar policy announced by the South Vietnam National Liberation Front. China protested privately against what it called the "forced naturalization" of Chinese nationals in Vietnam. But three secret meetings held to discuss the issue in February and April 1976 proved fruitless. The Vietnamese continued to hold, as Vietnam's ambassador to Peking, Nguyen Trong Vinh, explained to me three years later, that there was no mention of the term *voluntarily* in the 1955 agreement. Two years later Hanoi's treatment of the ethnic Chinese would produce the spark to ignite Sino-Vietnamese confrontation.

About the same time that Vietnam began taking the census and preparing the elections for a unified national assembly, it also stepped up its effort to strengthen its position in Indochina by drawing Laos into a closer alliance and seeking to patch up territorial disputes with Cambodia. Hanoi leaders had decided that a unified government and planning apparatus at home and closer ties with its Indochina neighbor were essential conditions for embarking upon the enormous task of rebuilding the war-ravaged country and bringing about Socialist transformation. Ironically, however, this policy helped to give Vietnam's bilateral conflict with China and Cambodia a common focus. While both China and Cambodia had their own reasons to quarrel with Vietnam, they were united in their common opposition to the emergence of a strong Vietnam that would dominate Indochina.

Whether by design or coincidence, two days after the secret Sino-Khmer military agreement in Phnom Penh, the Vietnamese took the first step toward forming an Indochina alliance. The prime minister of the Lao People's Democratic Republic and secretary-general of the Lao People's Revolutionary Party (LPRP), Kaysone Phomvihane, a longtime ally of the Vietnamese, arrived in Hanoi on an official visit. A joint communiqué signed by Kaysone and Duan in Hanoi on February 12, 1976, declared that a "special relationship" existed between their two countries for long-term cooperation and mutual aid and coordination of action against "imperialism and the reactionaries in its pay." The communiqué also promised to "increase solidarity between Laos, Cambodia, and Vietnam." While symbolizing Vietnam's intention to ensure that Laos would be oriented primarily toward Vietnam, as one close observer later noted, "The use of this term [special relationship] may also have been a warning to China and the Pol Pot group that Hanoi would not tolerate Kampuchea aligning itself with China against Vietnam."[35]

There was no immediate reaction from Peking to the launching of the "special relationship." Several weeks later, when Vietnam celebrated with fanfare the first anniversary of the "liberation" of the South, Peking greeted the occasion with a deafening silence. There was no editorial in the People's Daily, nor even any pro forma message of greetings to Hanoi leaders.

Phnom Penh, too, avoided public comment on the development. However, one can gauge the depth of Khmer Rouge opposition to a "special relationship" from an anecdote told by Cambodia's former head of state and leader of the Cambodian National United Front, Prince Norodom Sihanouk. Sihanouk recounts in his memoir, La calice jusqu'à la lie, that during their September 1975 visit to Hanoi on the occasion of the thirtieth anniversary of North Vietnam, Sihanouk and Khieu Samphan had a meeting with Premier Pham Van Dong. Dong invited them to a "family dinner" with the North Vietnamese, members of the Vietcong Provisional Revolutionary Government (PRG), and Lao leaders then present in Hanoi. To Sihanouk's surprise and dismay, Samphan "coldly refused the invitation, saying that Cambodia would like a two-party dinner." Later Samphan explained to the prince, "We should never fall into the trap of the Vietnamese who want to dominate our Cambodia and swallow it by integrating into their Indochina Federation." The idea of such a dinner, he said, was indeed very dangerous.

The bogey of the Indochina Federation that the Indochinese Communist Party wanted to set up in the 1930s continued to haunt the Khmers. Speaking on the occasion of the first anniversary of Cambodia's "liberation" on April 17, however, Ieng Sary had the "special relationship" very much in mind when he declared that "our people will absolutely not allow foreign countries to undermine Kampuchea's independence, sovereignty, and territorial integrity." In a transparent allusion to the presence of Vietnamese troops in Laos by virtue of "special relationship," he said, "A country's defense should be the work of its own people, and revolution in a country should be completed by the people of the country independently."[36]

Despite such veiled criticisms, uttered in the presence of the Vietnamese ambassador in Phnom Penh, Pham Van Ba, the Cambodians agreed to the Vietnamese suggestion of a summit meeting in June. While standing firm on political questions, Democratic Kampuchea still sought a settlement of the border problem. In fact, for Phnom Penh the Vietnamese attitude on the territorial dispute was a litmus test of Hanoi's good faith and thus an essential precondition for a summit.

The Vietnamese vice-minister of foreign affairs, Phan Hien, arrived in Phnom Penh on May 4 for two weeks of talks on the border question. The discussion immediately ran into difficulties, since the Vietnamese insisted on using pre-1954 French maps to demarcate the border, while the Cambodians, though accepting those maps as the basis for discussion, demanded the right to amend the border line. As Ieng Sary later explained, "The French map is very favorable to the Vietnamese because when it was drawn, Cochin China was a French colony. If we have to accept that map to demarcate the land border, the Vietnamese would have to accept the French-established maritime border as well."[37]

The problem was that there was no proper maritime border drawn by the French. In 1939 the Brevié line, named after Jules Brevié, the French governor-general of Indochina, was drawn to demarcate administrative and police jurisdiction over the islands between Cochin China and Cambodia. The line, drawn on maps at an angle of 140 degrees out into the Gulf of Siam from the coastal border between the two French-controlled areas, but circumscribing Phu Quoc Island by 1.5 miles to keep it within Cochin Chinese administration, served its purpose for the colonial government. However, as Brevié himself added, "the question of whose territory these islands are remains outstanding."[38]

In negotiations between Cambodia and the National Liberation Front in 1966, the Brevié line was, however, accepted as the existing border. Probably out of concern not to antagonize Prince Sihanouk by questioning the validity of the Brevié line at a time when the NLF needed his support, the Vietnamese acknowledged it as the sea boundary. During an interview in Paris in June 1977 (when the May 1976 meeting and Phan Hien's role in it were still secret), I asked Hien whether Hanoi had recognized the Brevié line. "Yes, we did," he said, "but at the time we agreed to the Brevié line, we were not aware of problems of territorial waters, continental shelf, etc.—those new phenomena." It was a clear hint that since the beginning of offshore explorations in the region in the 1970s, Hanoi had had to take a fresh look at the maritime border.

Tough Time for a Camera Crew

During the talks in Phnom Penh, Hien agreed to settle the question of ownership of the islands in accordance with the Brevié line—those to the north of the line being Cambodian and those to the south being Vietnamese. But he proposed redrawing the line on the question of territorial waters. Later in the course of the public dispute, Phnom Penh charged that the Vietnamese proposal amounted to "plans of annexation of a big part of the seas of Kampuchea." To the Khmers it was evidence of Vietnam's expansionist designs on Cambodia. The talks were adjourned *sine die*, not to be resumed again, and with that the idea of the summit too was dead. Despite the failure of the talks, however, neither side was yet willing to slam the door shut. Phan Hien returned to Hanoi, carrying with him an invitation from Ieng Sary for Vietnamese journalists to visit the hermit state of Democratic Kampuchea.

In July 1976 a delegation of Vietnamese press and television journalists led by Tran Thanh Xuan, the vice-director of the Vietnam News Agency, became the first foreign newsmen to visit Cambodia. Xuan, a wiry, bespectacled man in his fifties, was chosen because, as a student in Paris, he had known Pol Pot, Ieng Sary, and many of Cambodia's would-be Communist leaders. The mysterious Pol Pot, whose real identity was still a matter of speculation abroad, emerged from the shadows to grant an interview to Xuan and to be photographed. Reminiscing about that meeting four years later, Xuan said he found Pol Pot charming indeed. Not only was he a gracious host, but, in his first-ever interview, Pol Pot expressed Cambodia's gratitude to Vietnamese friends and brothers for their past assistance and said that friendship and solidarity between the two was "both a strategic question and a sacred feeling."

The Cambodian objective in inviting the Vietnamese press, Xuan explained during an interview in Ho Chi Minh City in January 1981, was to undo the damage caused by critical reports from the first Western ambassadors visiting Cambodia in March. Pol Pot thought the Vietnamese would be the right sort of journalists to do the job. And Pol Pot was not wrong. Although the Vietnamese were quite shocked by the state of the country, a hawk-eyed Hoang Tung made sure that none of those impressions filtered into their reporting. "Our camera crew had great difficulty in finding smiling peasants building the country," Xuan remembered. "They all looked so sullen and sad." Tung even excised a sentence Xuan wrote in a piece for *Nhan Dan* that said, "While the cities are empty, the people are working in the fields." It was better to concentrate on the damages of war caused by Lon Nol and the United States, the editor, Tung, advised. The visit was rich in dire symbolism. Only years later Tung revealed that Pol Pot had made a malevolent gesture to him by sending him as a gift an animal that ate human beings—a baby crocodile.[39] Pol Pot may, in fact, have had other symbolism in mind while choosing the gift. The Khmer Rouge propaganda later had frequently called the Vietnamese "ingrate crocodiles."

As tension was growing in Vietnam's relations with China and Cambodia, Hanoi stepped up its efforts to win friends in the non-Communist world. In the months immediately after victory, the Vietnamese had cockily denounced the anti-Communist countries of the Association of Southeast Asian Nations (ASEAN) for their past role as accomplices of the U.S. imperialists and had demanded the dismantling of U.S. bases in Thailand and the Philippines. But by the end of 1975 the Vietnamese had seen China's determined bid to woo the ASEAN countries to its anti-Soviet and anti-Vietnamese strategy. It had noted in particular Peking's effort to be a match-maker between Cambodia and Thailand. Barely a month after the fall of Saigon, China had normalized relations with Thailand. In October 1975, while Vietnam had yet to establish relations with Thailand, through China's intercession Ieng Sary had made the ice-breaking trip to Bangkok aboard a Chinese aircraft.

While Vietnam saw itself as the "outpost of socialism in Southeast Asia" and cherished the prospect of being the revolutionary Mecca for Communist movements in the region, its leaders were pragmatic enough to know that its top priority was rebuilding the shattered economy. The insurgent movements were still in their infancy, and Hanoi thus had to deal with the regimes in power. Normal relations with neighbors were needed as much for political reasons as for economic: Vietnam would have no chance of obtaining Western aid and credit if it were seen as a troublemaker in the region.

A Sullen Silence in Peking

On July 5, three days after the official reunification and renaming of the PRG and DRV governments as the Socialist Republic of Vietnam, Hanoi announced a four-point policy of establishing and developing "relations of friendship and cooperation in many fields" with Southeast Asian countries: relations were to be based on mutual respect for each other's independence; no country was to allow itself to be used as a base for a foreign country for direct or indirect aggression against others; they would follow good-neighbor policies; and they would develop cooperation "in keeping with each country's specific conditions and for the sake of independence, peace, and genuine neutrality in Southeast Asia."[40]

A week later, Phan Hien set out to visit the Philippines, Malaysia, Singapore, Indonesia, and Burma. During the trip, he explained away past attacks by Hanoi's media on ASEAN countries with an ingenious argument. "The journalists," he said, "write what they feel, but that is not the government's position!" Since no ASEAN government expected the Vietnamese to engage in self-criticism, the reaction was a polite nod. Although Singapore remained skeptical of Hanoi's desire to be a good neighbor, Hien appeared to have impressed the others with Vietnam's apparent sincerity in seeking friendship despite the ideological gulf. That Hanoi was now smiling rather than snarling at ASEAN created feelings of relief.

A senior official of the Malaysian Foreign Ministry told me after Hien's visit to Kuala Lumpur, "We get the impression that the Vietnamese are maintaining equal distance between Moscow and Peking." Hien told the Malaysians that Vietnam opposed hegemony by all big powers and said that nobody would be allowed to use the Cam Ranh Bay naval base. "It was obviously a hint at the Russians," the official noted, "and not a nice thing to tell a non-Communist country." The Malaysians also found it very interesting that, of all people, it was Soviet and East European diplomats who were the most eager to find out what the Vietnamese visitor had been telling them. Other than a joking mention of flying over "our Spratly Islands" while coming from Manila to Kuala Lumpur, Hien gave no hint of any problems with China.

China, however, watched the Vietnamese attempts to win friends in Southeast Asia in sullen silence. Xinhua News Agency, which normally reported on the important domestic and diplomatic developments in Vietnam, totally ignored Hien's tour. Several days after Hien returned, a Radio Peking commentary warned ASEAN against Soviet attempts at infiltration and expansion. "So long as the people of Southeast Asia unite as one and persist in struggle," the commentary said, "they will not only be able to drive out the tiger, but will also successfully defend their own independence and sovereignty."[41]

The timing of the broadcast left no doubt as to which country

Peking had in mind as the agent of Soviet infiltration. Although Peking refrained from denouncing Vietnam, some outspoken Vietnamese did not hide their convergence of interest with the Soviet Union against China. In an interview with Swedish journalist Eric Pierre, Hoang Tung said in July, "There is a tangibly strong Soviet interest coinciding with Vietnamese interest to reduce Chinese influence in this part of the world." This was one remark that Chinese leaders later recalled to Hanoi as an example of how Vietnam had "badly hurt the Chinese people."[42]

In the summer of 1976, China was too preoccupied with its own internal power struggles to counter the Vietnamese diplomatic thrust by anything other than veiled propaganda broadsides. Since late 1973, the Chinese Politburo had been deeply divided. On one side were those who supported the pragmatic line of Zhou, which sought to offset the Soviet threat by cooperation with the United States. Opposing them were the radicals led by Zhang Chunqiao and Wang Hongwen, who called for opposition to both superpowers and advocated support for all anti-imperialist armed struggles.[43] They were also staunch supporters of the Khmer Rouge. The radicals slowly gained ground as the restraining hand of Mao and the resistance from Zhou declined. In 1974–75, the radicals made barbed attacks on the American connection and denounced Soviet-American détente, which they claimed Zhou's policy had helped to produce.[44]

With the death of Zhou in January 1976 and the purge of his right-hand man, Deng Xiaoping, in April of that year, the factional balance in the Politburo had tipped in favor of the radicals. Hua Guofeng, a burly Hunanese who was an associate of the radicals, had been confirmed in the premiership. But this was not a decisive victory. Then, in the early hours of September 9, the great arbiter, Mao, passed from the scene. China's fate suddenly hung in the balance, as did its posture toward the world. Along with 900 million Chinese, leaders across the world, and particularly in Moscow, Washington, Hanoi, and Phnom Penh, turned their eyes to Peking and waited.

Prince Norodom Sihanouk:
The Victory

AT HIS SUMPTUOUS residence on Peking's Anti-Imperialism Street
Prince Norodom Sihanouk heard the news. Phnom Penh had surrendered. A wire-service report brought to him by a Chinese official
announced that on the morning of April 17, 1975, his allies of five
years—the Khmer Rouge—had marched into Phnom Penh.

Paraplegic General Lon Nol, who had led the coup against the
prince in 1970, was already in exile in the United States. Other
"traitors" who collaborated with Lon Nol had either fled the country
or surrendered to the Khmer Rouge. The war was over. The gamble
that the prince took in April 1970 by allying himself with his erstwhile Communist enemies had paid off. His honor had been restored. Those reactionary and venal generals and politicians who
had dragged Sihanouk's name in the mud after the coup d'état were
now in the dustbin of history. The father of Cambodia's independence did not wish to end his career in disgrace as an exiled monarch. He was realistic enough to know that the Khmer Rouge victory
could also mean an end to his role as the symbol of unity and legitimacy of Khmer resistance. When no longer of use to the Khmer
Rouge, he had told an interviewer in 1973, "they will spit me out

like a cherry pit." That was as much an expression of genuine apprehension as it was aimed at preempting such a development. As the victory celebration in Peking had died down and weeks elapsed without any call for him to go back to liberated Cambodia, Sihanouk began to wonder whether the dreaded moment had arrived.

"Let me return to Phnom Penh," he urged the Khmer Rouge representatives in Peking. "If you don't want Sihanouk to be the head of state, it is up to you. I don't want to be head of state, but I want to live in Cambodia and not be a refugee." Yes, he would go back, the Khmer Rouge had said, but not now. "For the moment we are facing many problems," they told him. "You should not be involved in those problems." Obviously the Khmer Rouge did not want to risk taking the charismatic prince back to Cambodia and having him use his magic over the population. While Sihanouk waited and wondered, the Khmer Rouge went on evacuating all towns and cities, scattering the urban population, "contaminated by imperialists and reactionaries." The "glorious revolution" had begun.

Since 1970, when the deposed ruler had struck an alliance with the Khmer Rouge, he had grown increasingly frustrated in his role as a figurehead leader in exile. His repeated request to visit the guerrilla zone had been turned down on grounds of security. Most galling to the fifty-three-year-old former God King was the constant surveillance by a man he loathed—the Khmer Rouge "brother number two," Ieng Sary, representative of the resistance in Peking. He reminded him of the French "advisers" who constantly dogged his steps in his years as the puppet king of French-ruled Cambodia. While on a trip to Hanoi in 1973, Sihanouk had almost caused a diplomatic incident by denouncing Ieng Sary. The Swedish ambassador in Hanoi, Jean-Christophe Oberg, had been to see the prince in the guesthouse. "That abominable Ieng Sary is always spying on me," the prince complained in his high-pitched voice. "Mr. Ambassador, if you look at the bottom of the curtain as you go out of the room you will see his feet. He is always standing there listening in." The embarrassed envoy did not dare to look down as he walked out of the room.

By March 1973, the Khmer Rouge had established their control over vast areas of Cambodia. After signing the Paris Peace Agreement, which brought a halt to U.S. bombing in Vietnam and made it safe to journey on the Ho Chi Minh Trail, Sihanouk had been allowed his first trip to the liberated zones in the interior of Cambodia. That visit—though a morale booster—made him aware of his increasing irrelevance in Khmer Rouge–controlled Cambodia. Throughout the trip, he and his wife, Princess Monique, were shadowed by the Khmer Rouge leaders, who successfully screened them from any direct contact with the population. All he saw was grim faces of people who had to shake their fists in rehearsed unison and shout slogans. There was no scope for Sihanouk to do his usual thing—jump into the crowd, touch the people who would press forward shouting, "Samdech Euv!" (Monseigneur Papa).

Sihanouk's friend and protector, Zhou Enlai, too, had sensed Sihanouk's frustration and shared his worry about Khmer Rouge extremism. As early as February 1973 Zhou had told Kissinger that it was "impossible for Cambodia to become completely red now. If that were attempted, it would result in even greater problems."[1] For him the solution was to put the prince back in power in Phnom Penh. His efforts to get the United States to talk to the prince and bring about a compromise solution, however, had failed. Two years later, when the United States had finally removed Lon Nol from Cambodia and asked the prince to return to his homeland, the Khmer Rouge guerrillas were close to final victory. The chief of the U.S. liaison mission in Peking, George Bush, asked him through the French embassy to take over the leadership of a neutral Cambodia. On April 11 the United States made him a formal offer to fly back to Phnom Penh on a Chinese plane and take over the leadership. His personal security was guaranteed. But with the Khmer Rouge on the outskirts of Phnom Penh, even Zhou Enlai could no longer agree to the plan. On the morning of April 12 Sihanouk turned down the American offer. Within hours, Operation Eagle Pull had begun with scores of U.S. Navy helicopters plucking out American personnel and their Cambodian allies from Phnom Penh. The game was over. "It was just too late," Sihanouk said to me, recalling the episode.

Unlike 1953, when he wrested Cambodia's independence from France, Sihanouk was no longer in a position to decide on the timing or how to maneuver. All the skills that he had learned in the thirty-four years since his ascendancy to the throne of Cambodia seemed to be useless. In 1941 the French had chosen Sihanouk, the nineteen-year-old scion of the Norodom branch of the royal family, over the rival Sisowath branch because he was believed to be rather cute. *"Qu'il est mignon, ce petit!"* Madame Decoux had exclaimed, looking at the schoolboy Sihanouk. He was invited by French Governor Admiral Jean Decoux to lunch at the governor's palace in Saigon.

The playboy prince soon took a liking to politics and began to enjoy his role. He cleverly outmaneuvered the political parties clamoring for freedom from the French protectorate to make the nationalist cause his own. From being a puppet king, he emerged as the champion of Cambodia's independence. Independence, he argued before French president Vincent Auriol and U.S. secretary of state John Foster Dulles, was the only weapon to resist the Communists who waved the banner of anticolonial struggle. He used the international press and made dramatic gestures, such as voluntarily exiling himself from Cambodia, to embarrass the French and win support for his position. Finally in November 1953 the French ceded him independence in order to concentrate their energy on fighting the Ho Chi Minh–led Vietminh.

During his seventeen years at the helm of Cambodia, the prince ruled the country in the fullest sense of the term. In order to exercise full power as a head of state rather than as a constitutional monarch, Sihanouk gave the king's crown to his father in 1960. From writing editorials in the newspapers to deciding on irrigation projects or setting up health centers in villages, nothing escaped his personal attention. He termed the right-wing, or republican, opponents of his personalized rule *Khmers Bleus* (Blue Khmers) and the leftists *Khmers Rouges* (Red Khmers), both of whom were accused of extraterritorial loyalties. He ruthlessly pursued the Khmer Rouge but also tried to co-opt them into his administration. In the early 1960s Khmer Rouge leaders such as Khieu Samphan, Hou Yuon, and Hu Nim were made ministers in his cabinet. Internally, he tried to take the wind out of the leftist sails by his exotic brand of "Buddhist socialism" which in effect was state monopoly managed by the too-often corrupt elite and hangers-on. Externally, his effort was aimed at maintaining Cambodia's independence and integrity by a delicate balancing act. But as the Vietnam war intensified and his domestic problems grew, Sihanouk was thrown off the high wire. In order to accommodate the North Vietnamese, whom he saw as the ultimate winner and the emergent power in Indochina, he bent his neutrality to allow them sanctuary along the border and arms transit through the country's ports. The crisis resulting from corruption, mismanagement of the economy, and loss of American aid caused political disaffection. Rising anger against an increased Vietnamese presence only fanned the fire. With tacit U.S. support, General Lon Nol ousted Prince Sihanouk while he was in Moscow on his way back home after a rest cure in France. Urged by the Vietnamese and the Chinese, Sihanouk lent his name to the Cambodian resistance and made Peking his second home.

In the summer of 1975 Sihanouk wondered whether Peking was going to be his permanent home as well. Not having any stashed-away funds abroad, unlike so many ousted rulers, Sihanouk had no option but to accept the hospitality of his Chinese and Korean friends. Mao and Zhou had told him he could stay in China as long as he wished. North Korean president Kim Il Sung had ordered an enormous palace built for Sihanouk overlooking Chhang Sou On Lake in Pyongyang. In September 1975 Sihanouk was in Pyongyang when the GRUNK (French acronym for Royal Government of National Union of Cambodia—the government-in-exile set up by the prince in collaboration with the Khmer Rouge) deputy prime minister Khieu Samphan and minister of information Ieng Thirith (Ieng Sary's wife) arrived with the long-awaited invitation. "Now we are ready to welcome you very warmly," Sihanouk recalled Khieu Samphan telling him. "Now we have fulfilled all the conditions to be 100 percent Communist. We can surpass even our Chinese brothers. With one giant leap forward we can reach the goal of communism and not go through stages of socialism." It was all rather disturbing, but the prince was still thrilled to be going home.

They returned to Peking together by train. From there a Chinese Boeing 707 was to fly them to Phnom Penh. Before leaving Peking, Sihanouk and Monique, accompanied by Khieu Samphan, had been to see Chairman Mao and Premier Zhou Enlai. Stricken by Parkinson's disease, the eighty-two-year-old Mao was barely comprehensible. But one of his instructions was clear. He told Khieu Samphan and Ieng Thirith, "Please do not send Prince Sihanouk and his wife to the cooperative." For Sihanouk, those words were to prove life-savers.

Terminally ill from cancer, Zhou was a shadow of his former self. In a barely audible voice he entreated Khieu Samphan, "Please go slowly toward communism. You cannot reach communism in one step, but step by step. Please take many small steps, slowly and surely." Even more striking was his prescient advice "Don't follow our bad example of the Great Leap Forward." He was referring to China's utopian campaign to build instant communism in the late 1950s that had left the economy in shambles. Samphan and Thirith smiled knowingly. Having heard the boast about bringing pure communism to Cambodia, Sihanouk knew what that smile meant.

On September 9 Peking was again in a festive mood. Tien An Men Square was decorated with flags, lanterns, flowers, and streamers to congratulate Sihanouk on what Deng Xiaoping termed Sihanouk's "return in glory." As the Chinese Boeing dipped its nose to approach Phnom Penh's Pochentong Airport, Sihanouk looked down at the tile roofs and golden spires of the sprawling city. This was the first time since January 1970 that he rested his eyes on the capital that had turned against him. Phnom Penh looked strangely lifeless under the haze of a midmorning sun. Compared with the tens of thousands of people who choked Peking's streets to bid the prince farewell, there was only a motley crowd at the tarmac of Pochentong. A handful of saffron-clad Buddhist monks were in the crowd to bless him before he rode by motorcade to a deserted city. That was one of the last concessions to tradition he was to witness in Khmer Rouge Cambodia.

Sihanouk was moved to tears looking at the haunted capital that was once the most beautiful in French Indochina. The tree-lined boulevards, the bungalows with bougainvillea, the golden spires of the royal palace, and the pagodas were all there, in mourning. The evacuation was necessary, the Khmer Rouge explained to the prince, because there was not enough food to feed the population and there were of course problems of security. They did not tell him it was the first great leap toward communism. In the massive exodus of April, Sihanouk's aged uncle, Prince Monireth, and one of his aunts too were dispatched to the countryside. His request to see them was politely turned down. "They are being well looked after. You will see them after your return from New York," he was told. But he was never to see them again. In the Khmer Rouge scheme of things, Sihanouk's three-week trip to Phnom Penh was to provide credibility to his leadership before sending him off to claim Cambodia's seat at the United Nations General Assembly. Sihanouk and his entourage were taken for boat rides on the Mekong, given sumptuous banquets, and invited to revolutionary soirees, but they never saw the people who had vanished from Phnom Penh.

Sihanouk soon learned what the Khmer Rouge thought of Zhou Enlai's advice about slow steps to socialism. Army Commander-in-Chief Son Sen and Khieu Samphan told him their Cambodia was going to prove to the world that in one grand sweep they could achieve total communism. "Thus the name of our country will be written in golden letters in world history as the first country that succeeded in communization without useless steps."

After his return to Peking in early October, Sihanouk gave his family members and associates free choice. He, as a patriot and head of state, would go back to Cambodia after representing the country in the United Nations, but they were free to choose their residence. A number of his aides were too shocked by the experience in Phnom Penh to ever dare go back. They left for France.

Sihanouk himself stopped in Paris in transit. A large crowd of Khmers came to greet him at Charles de Gaulle Airport. Later, many of them gathered at the Cambodian ambassador's residence to hear from the prince firsthand about life under the Khmer Rouge. They were surprised at how cautious the normally ebullient prince was. One asked him what happened to the Lon Nol soldiers? He said the Angkar (the almighty Communist party organization) had given each of them a mat and a mosquito net and sent them to grow rice. He added that they had got what they deserved. Sitting next to him, a smiling Ieng Sary and other Khmer Rouge leaders nodded in agreement.[2] None of Sihanouk's old friends succeeded in penetrating the Khmer Rouge security net to have a private meeting. Sihanouk had a foretaste of what was coming. But his pride, his sense of obligation, were too much to call it quits. In December of 1975 Sihanouk, accompanied by his wife, Monique, mother-in-law, Madame Pom, and twenty-two of his children and grandchildren, took the journey back to Phnom Penh.

2

Silkworms and Mice

AT THE BEST of times Hanoi is an inward-looking city. It is quiet, withdrawn, and engrossed in itself. With a bone-biting cold driving its poorly clad citizens indoors, the tree-lined, aging city looks even more desolate and sad. People pedal slowly, hunched over their bicycles, mufflers wrapped around their heads in an effort to protect themselves against the wind—a small compensation for the threadbare jackets or pullovers covering their bodies. I felt awkward joining that silent, shivering traffic of Hanoi residents in my well-padded jacket and gloves, riding a sleek Raleigh bike I had borrowed from a diplomat. Inside a car, one does not feel so conspicuously dressed. I had dispensed with the gray Volga sedan, rented from the Hanoi tourist office, that I was obliged to use for making official calls. I sent my Foreign Ministry guide back, saying that I had no appointment that afternoon. My discreet rendezvous was on November 23, 1977, with someone that the Vietnamese Foreign Ministry would not be enthusiastic about.

As the sun shone weakly that windy afternoon, I slipped out of the back entrance of Thong Nhat Hotel and headed for the embassy of Democratic Kampuchea. Vietnam and Cambodia continued to exchange polite greetings on each other's national day, but relations had clearly deteriorated Pol Pot's Peking trip in October and his thinly veiled attacks against Vietnam had been the first public confirmation of trouble. During a stopover at the Lao capital, Vientiane, en route to Hanoi, I heard for the first time, from a Vietnamese diplomat, about brutal Khmer Rouge assaults on Vietnam in recent months. I was thus keen to hear from the Khmer Rouge their version of the conflict. A Mexican diplomat friendly with the Khmer Rouge had arranged for me to meet In Sivouth, political counselor at the Democratic Kampuchean embassy. One could see from a distance the bloodred flag of the embassy flapping in the wind against the backdrop of a stucco colonial-style bungalow. All the windows of the building were firmly shut. There was no sign of life there other than a Vietnamese policeman in beige uniform and pith helmet standing by the entrance. He barely noticed as I dismounted from my bicycle and went to the gate. His job, like that of all guards outside foreign embassies in Hanoi, was to keep Vietnamese citizens away. Despite my bike, I was too obviously a foreigner and therefore not worthy of his attention.

Moments after I had rung the bell, the wooden door of the embassy was cautiously opened an inch. A pair of eyes peered through the crack. "Monsieur Chanda?" a voice inquired almost in a whisper. The door quickly opened to let me in and then just as quickly shut behind me. As my eyes adjusted to the dimly lit hallway, I saw In Sivouth. Inside the embassy it was already evening. A lamp hanging from the ceiling cast a circle of light in his dark office, which had all the windows shut and curtains drawn. Sivouth, a small, lean man in his early forties, smiled nervously. "All this is necessary," he explained in polished French, "to prevent the Vietnamese from eavesdropping." Sivouth was a rather unlikely Khmer Rouge. He had never been to the jungle. While in Paris as a student he became a Communist and joined the Khmer Rouge organization. In his long years in Paris he had learned a lot about the CIA and its capabilities. He knew they could pick up conversations from a distance by bouncing back signals from the window panes. He was certain that the "evil" Vietnamese had obtained similar gadgets to engage in electronic snooping of the Kampuchean embassy. Dressed in a dark

Mao suit, Sivouth sat erect on a large divan, telling me in whispers the story of Vietnamese "betrayal" of Cambodia. "In 1973 [when the Vietnamese signed the Paris Agreement with the United States] the Vietnamese tried to force us to negotiate with Lon Nol. The price of rejecting that advice," Sivouth recalled with a bitter smile, "was Vietnam's agreement with the Americans. The B-52s that bombed Vietnam were all sent to pulverize Cambodia for five and a half months."

Before his Hanoi assignment, Sivouth had spent several years in Peking in the GRUNK embassy. Since the Khmer Rouge victory, Sivouth had not had a chance to return to Cambodia together with his wife and child. He acknowledged that in the year and a half that had elapsed, he had not heard from his wife. His knowledge of what was happening in Cambodia came, he told me with embarrassment, essentially from listening to Radio Phnom Penh. But his lack of facts was amply made up by his seemingly boundless faith in the justice of Cambodia's revolutionary policies. By emptying the cities, by putting everybody to work in the fields, the Angkar had taken the hard but sure path of self-reliance. "The Vietnamese would no longer be able to subjugate us," he added with a smile of disdain. "Cambodia is not Laos." He was convinced that the Lao-Vietnamese treaty of friendship signed in July was the first step toward colonization of Laos. "You want to see what is already happening?" he asked, and then picked up from the side table a Lao tabloid newspaper. The "proof" was in a picture of Lao farmers transplanting rice seedlings. "The Vietnamese are already taking over their rice fields," Sivouth said, pointing to a figure in the picture who had on a conical hat typically worn by Vietnamese farmers. The fact that the conical straw hat could be the typical but not exclusive attire of Vietnamese peasants was immaterial to him. As far as he was concerned, Vietnamese designs on Indochina were a self-evident truth. The lone conical hat among the row of Lao peasants that he spotted in the photograph was only necessary proof for skeptical foreigners.

After a while all the arguments and evidence about Vietnamese "greed" and Vietnamese "perfidy" blended into an assertion of faith about the "evil" nature of the Vietnamese and the inevitability of a clash in the Khmer struggle for survival. The picture which Sivouth painted that afternoon while sitting in his darkened office was a stark reminder of how little things had changed. Beneath the veneer of his urbanity and Marxist-sounding speech lay a Khmer soul soaked in bitter historical memories and racial prejudices.

From Fence-State to Federation

At the root of the racial antagonism between the Khmers and the Vietnamese lie almost a thousand years of contact, the last three hundred of them characterized by struggle between an advancing Vietnamese empire and a shrinking Cambodia.

Nam Tien—the Vietnamese march toward the south—has been a central theme of Vietnam's history since it shook off the Chinese colonial yoke in the tenth century. "Vietnamese history," a French scholar noted, "has flowed across Indochina like a flood carrying off other peoples wherever they occupied a lowland rice field or where it could be put under rice."[1] In the Red River delta—the original heartland of the Vietnamese—population pressure, thrusts from nearby China, and political instability led to a spontaneous popular movement in search of new lands.[2] The southern direction of this movement was decided by the facts of power and geography: to the north lay the giant, China; to the west, the inhospitable Annamite mountain range; and to the east, the South China Sea.

The Vietnamese trek to the south, which has gone on for centuries, involved the conquest not only of distance and terrain but also of other peoples. First to fall to the Vietnamese were the Chams, a Hinduized (later Muslim) people ethnically close to the Indonesians whose kingdom, Champa, was once a rival of Vietnam's.

But a succession of wars against Champa and Vietnamese annexations of its territory, coupled with slow and steady migrations, wiped the Hinduized kingdom off the map by the end of the seventeenth century. The majority of Chams were killed, driven off their land or assimilated—so much so that of an estimated eleventh-century population of 30,000 families (perhaps 240–300,000 people), only 65,000 Chams are left in what is now Vietnam.[3] Many thousands fled to Cambodia and were eventually killed by the Pol Pot regime for their Islamic faith.

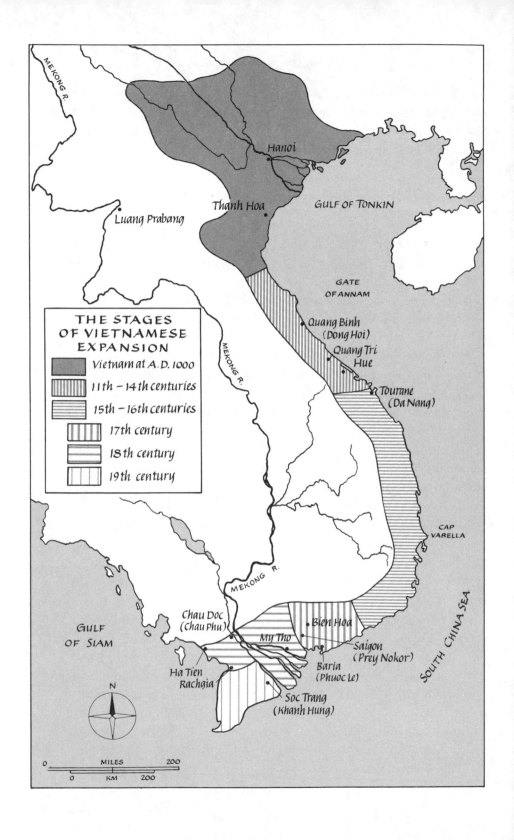

THE STAGES
OF VIETNAMESE
EXPANSION

Vietnam at A.D. 1000

11th – 14th centuries

15th – 16th centuries

17th century

18th century

19th century

MEKONG R.

Luang Prabang

Hanoi

Thanh Hoa

GULF OF TONKIN

GATE
OF ANNAM

Quang Binh
(Dong Hoi)

Quang Tri
Hue

MEKONG R.

Tourane
(Da Nang)

CAP
VARELLA

MEKONG R.

SOUTH CHINA SEA

Chau Doc
(Chau Phu)

Bien Hoa

My Tho

GULF
OF SIAM

Saigon
(Prey Nokor)

Ha Tien
Rachgia

Baria
(Phuoc Le)

Soc Trang
(Khanh Hung)

N

0   MILES   200

0   KM   200

Well before the Vietnamese empire totally absorbed Champa, Vietnamese settlers started to establish villages in forested Cambodian territory around what is now the Bien Hoa–Ba Ria area. The exhaustion of Khmer people through misrule and long decline of the Khmer monarchy, which had once ruled a vast empire extending from the Malay Peninsula to central Laos, coincided with the expansion of a rejuvenated Vietnam. Frequent factional strife within the Khmer court, coupled with attempts by Siam (Thailand, Cambodia's increasingly strong neighbor to the west) to establish a vassal state in Cambodia, provided ideal opportunities for the Vietnamese to intervene in Cambodia. The price of such intervention, whether it was to defend an incumbent ruler or to install a claimant to the Cambodian throne, was invariably the ceding of further Khmer territory to Vietnam. An eighteenth-century Vietnamese general described this tactic of slow territorial absorption of Cambodia under the pretext of supporting the Khmer throne as "the policy of slowly eating silkworms."[4] The Vietnamese had a vast appetite for silkworms, and in the course of a hundred years (1650–1750), the whole of the Vam Co River basin and the Mekong Delta, including the Cambodian fishing village of Prey Nokor (later known as Saigon), became Vietnamese territory.

With Vietnam having occupied the fertile south, the defense of that territory against the Thais became the principal concern of the Vietnamese emperor in Hue. Since Cambodia would be the gateway to an invading Thai army marching toward Saigon, the Vietnamese had a perfect excuse for turning it into a protectorate. "Chan-Lap [Cambodia] is our fence-state," Emperor Minh Mang wrote in 1831. "It cannot be allowed to collapse."[5]

Following an unsuccessful Thai attempt to bring Cambodia under their control in 1833–34, the Vietnamese embarked on a process that, unchecked, might well have led to the disappearance of Cambodia altogether. Fortresses were built throughout the country, and a garrison was installed in Phnom Penh. Independent Cambodia was turned into Vietnam's "overlordship of the pacified west." Minh Mang launched a vigorous campaign to bring the "barbaric" Khmers into the civilized world. Vietnamese teachers were sent in to teach "the [Confucian] way" to Cambodian officials. The Vietnamese em-

51

peror tried to impose the Vietnamese style of dressing the hair and Vietnamese attire on the Khmers, to introduce a system of taxation modeled on Vietnam's, and even to force peasants to grow the same crops as were grown in Vietnam. Severe punishments were meted out to those who refused to accept the new order.

Resentment against the Vietnamese generated a number of uprisings. Harsh rule and corvée labor provoked one of the early rebellions in 1820, led by a monk named Kai. The rebels slaughtered Vietnamese residents in eastern Cambodia before being subdued by superior forces sent by the Vietnamese governor in the south.[6] The most serious revolt broke out in 1840 when, with the arrest of senior Khmer officials and the deportation of the reigning queen to Vietnam, Khmers began to fear for the continued existence of an independent Cambodia. In 1840, a high Cambodian official named Prom wrote, "We are happy killing Vietnamese; we no longer fear them, however powerful they may be." He told his followers to kill all the Vietnamese they could find, "from the northern part of the country to the southern border." In a letter to Thai officials he announced, "I propose to continue killing Vietnamese."[7] It was a declaration that would have endeared Prom to a later ruler of Cambodia—Pol Pot.

Memories of Khmer uprisings in the early nineteenth century and accounts of Vietnamese ruthlessness in putting them down have survived in Cambodian chronicles and folklore. Khmer mothers often used to frighten wayward children by telling them, "If you go far playing in the bush, *Yuon* (Khmer pejorative word literally meaning savage) will get you!" The Vinh Te Canal—a twenty-five-mile waterway linking the Gulf of Thailand with the Vinh Te River dug in 1820 by the Vietnamese using Khmer forced labor—is a vivid scar on the Cambodian memory. A story I have heard countless times in pre– and post–Pol Pot Cambodia tells how the Vietnamese punished three Khmers for not working hard enough on the canal site. The Vietnamese buried the hapless Khmers to their necks, so the story runs, and used their heads to support a kettle for boiling water. When the victims writhed in pain and spilled water from the kettle, the Vietnamese warned, "Don't spoil the master's tea." That story later became a part of the Khmer Rouge propaganda repertoire to arouse the "revolutionary hatred" toward the Vietnamese enemy.[8]

The feelings of racial hostility and prejudice that the Khmers developed toward the Vietnamese were not unreciprocated. A millennium of Chinese rule over Vietnam had left a deep impression on Vietnamese thought. The Vietnamese saw their country as a mini–Middle Kingdom surrounded by barbarians. Although officially no longer in use, ordinary Vietnamese still resort to the Chinese term *cao mien,* or highland barbarians, when referring to the Cambodians. Today many are perhaps unaware of the Chinese origin of the word, thinking it to be a Vietnamized pronunciation of "Khmer." The Nguyen dynasty, emperors of a unified and strong Vietnam, considered that the gods had chosen them to bring the light of civilization to the Hinduized and relatively feeble kingdom of Cambodia. Contemptuous of the Khmers' inability to assimilate the Sino-Vietnamese culture, a Vietnamese emperor described them as "monkeys in pens and birds in cages." In 1840 Emperor Minh Mang was furious about the Cambodian rebellion against Vietnam's civilizing mission. Shocked at the Khmers' actions, which he considered treacherous, he wrote to his commander in chief in Cambodia, "We helped them when they were suffering, and lifted them out of the mud. . . . Now they are rebellious. I am so angry that my hair stands upright. . . . Hundreds of knives should be used against them, to chop them up, to dismember them." Another Vietnamese account of the 1840 rebellion expressed frustration at the hit-and-run tactics adopted by the Khmer guerrillas, who fled "like rats and mice" when facing superior Vietnamese forces.[9]

While many Cambodians continue to harbor the traditional view of the Vietnamese as a cunning race and "swallowers of Khmer soil," the Vietnamese today do not seem to have any strong feelings against the Khmers. This is not surprising, because it is the Khmers as a nation who have suffered the most from the long period of contact. The Vietnamese residents in Cambodia did suffer a great deal from time to time, but that does not seem to have affected general Vietnamese perception. However, in many conversations with official and nonofficial Vietnamese, their feelings of superiority over the Khmers—in political education, organization, and leadership ability—can be clearly sensed. When charitable, the Vietnamese tend to view the Khmers as children who need guidance. But often Vietnamese fail to conceal their exasperation with the turbulent, factious Khmers and the problems that they create for the Vietnamese.

The intangible, abstract nature of folk memory and "traditional antipathy" renders them useless as scientific tools for social or historical analysis. But these feelings are so palpable to anyone who has spent any time in Cambodia that it is impossible to ignore them in understanding recent events. During his rule, Prince Sihanouk had kept the popular memory alive by constantly harping on the history of Vietnamese encroachments on Cambodia. Partly out of a conviction about the unchanged "expansionist" nature of the Vietnamese and partly due to political expediency, the Democratic Kampuchean leaders have also chosen to explain their conflict with Vietnam in terms not of class but of race. The *Black Book* published by the Pol Pot regime in September 1978—several months after I heard the litany of complaints from In Sivouth—bluntly stated: "The acts of aggression and annexation of territory perpetrated by the Vietnamese in the past as well as at present have clearly shown the true nature of the Vietnamese and Vietnam: that is, a nature of aggressor, annexationist and swallower of other countries' territories." Whether under the feudal, colonial, or Communist party's rule, the book affirmed, the Vietnamese are the same. Later the Pol Pot group even claimed that the Communist Party of Kampuchea was founded in 1960 "in order to fight the Vietnamese"—an objective very different from the one envisioned by the founding fathers of communism.[10]

The establishment of a French protectorate in 1863 saved Cambodia from being carved up any more by Vietnam and Thailand. But the fact that neighboring Cochin China—southern Vietnam—was a full-fledged French colony was to Cambodia's disadvantage when border lines were drawn by the French. The French frontier demarcations were made on the basis of geography and of what would be convenient to the colonial administration of Cochin China rather than on the basis of historic, linguistic, or ethnic considerations. In successive border delimitations made by the French, the Pakse region (now in southern Laos), Darlac Province, and areas of Song Be, Tay Ninh, Go Dau Ha, and Ha Tien—all presently part of Vietnam—were chipped away from Cambodia. In a doctoral dissertation published in 1966, Sarin Chhak, who was to become the for-

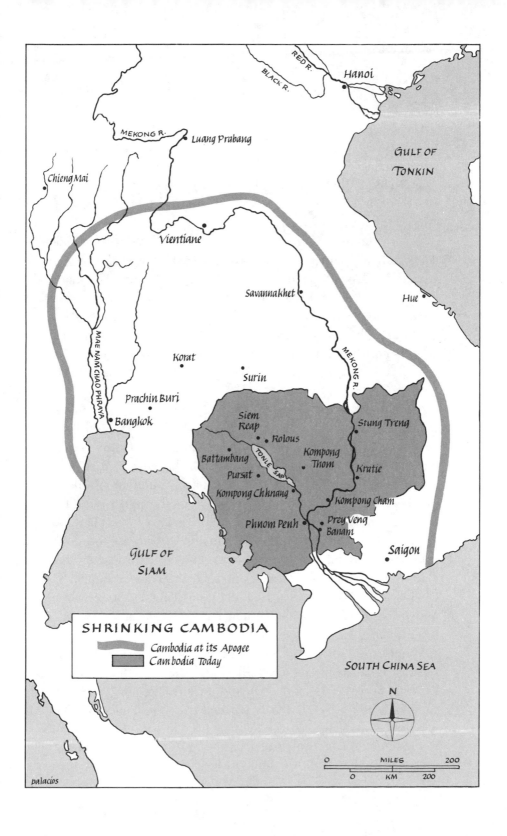

GULF OF
TONKIN

HANOI

RED R.

BLACK R.

MEKONG R.

Luang Prabang

Chieng Mai

Vientiane

Savannakhet

Hue

MAE NAM CHAO PHRAYA

Korat

Surin

MEKONG R.

Prachin Buri

Siem
Reap

Stung Treng

Bangkok

Rolous

Battambang

TONLE SAP

Kompong
Thom

Kratie

Pursat

Kompong Chhnang

kompong Cham

Phnom Penh

Prey Veng
Banam

Saigon

GULF OF
SIAM

SHRINKING CAMBODIA

Cambodia at its Apogee

Cambodia Today

SOUTH CHINA SEA

N

0   MILES   200

0   KM   200

palacios

eign minister of the GRUNK in 1970, underlined these territorial losses and appealed to Vietnam to negotiate a just border.[11]

Cambodian rulers—from King Ang Duong (1848–60) to Pol Pot—never ceased to complain about the loss of territory to the Vietnamese. In a letter to the French emperor, Napoleon III, in 1856, King Ang Duong pathetically urged him not to accept the Khmer territories recently taken by the Vietnamese if "by chance the Annamites offered them to Your Excellency." In 1949, when the French colony of Cochin China was recognized as part of a united (if still-dependent) state of Vietnam, Phnom Penh lodged an official protest. Even after the independence of the Indochinese states in 1954, Cambodia continued for several years to claim Kampuchea Krom (the Mekong Delta that was once lower Cambodia) and coastal islands such as Koh Tral (Phu Quoc) from the South Vietnamese government. The situation of the Khmer Krom living in Vietnam also remained a subject of concern and occasional protest by the Sihanouk government.[12]

Vietnamese migration into Cambodia continued apace under European control. The French considered the Vietnamese to be better workers and more dynamic than the Khmers and thus better tools for the economic exploitation of Cambodia. By 1921 Vietnamese constituted some 7 percent of Cambodia's population. While a large number of impoverished Vietnamese from the north were brought into Cambodia as contract workers on French rubber plantations (a job very few Khmers would do), many Vietnamese peasants and fishermen also quit Cochin China to compete with Khmers for good land and fishing grounds in Cambodia. Vietnamese Roman Catholics in particular, protected by French missionaries, were well placed to deprive the Cambodians of their land.[13] This caused considerable resentment.

What especially hurt Khmer feelings, however, was the fact that the vast majority of low-level officials in the French colonial administration were Vietnamese. During an anti-French insurrection in Cambodia in 1885–86, rebels recalled past Vietnamese attempts to wipe out Cambodia and condemned French use of the Vietnamese to break down Cambodian society and culture. This does not, however, mean that the two communities have always been at loggerheads. Many Vietnamese joined the Khmers in the anticolonial uprisings. Despite tensions and mutual dislike, the two communities lived in peace for long periods, but crises or external factors invariably brought latent prejudices to the surface.

Even the growth of the supposedly internationalist Communist movement in Cambodia was not immune from the racial prejudices. In fact, the way the Communist movement was born and developed in Cambodia helped to feed anti-Vietnamese Khmer chauvinism.

Both in Laos and Cambodia, Vietnamese immigrants provided the hard-core of Indochinese Communist Party (ICP) cells. Khmers were very gradually drawn into the politics of independence, and, by 1950, the Khmer Issarak (Khmer independence) movement had come under ICP influence. However, Ho Chi Minh was fully aware of the anti-Vietnamese sentiments harbored by the Khmers and the Lao. This was one of the reasons why he decided in 1951 to break the ICP into three national parties. Explaining the move, an internal document of the Vietnam Workers Party (VWP), the Vietnamese successor to the ICP, said, "The nationalist elements of Laos and Cambodia might have suspected Vietnam of wishing to control Cambodia and Laos. The band of imperialists and puppets would have been able to launch counter-propaganda designed to separate Vietnam from Cambodia and Laos, fomenting troubles among the Cambodian and Lao people." [14]

While the division of the ICP into three national parties presented a sop to the nationalists and provided a counter to the French policy of divide and rule, the political leadership of the Communist movement in Indochina still remained in Vietnamese hands. A confidential Vietnamese party directive in June 1952 ordered the Vietnamese and Chinese residents in Cambodia to join the VWP rather than the Khmer People's Revolutionary Party (KPRP), which was "not the vanguard of the working class, but the vanguard party of the nation gathering together all the patriotic and progressive elements of the Khmer population." [15] Even so, the provisional executive committee of the KPRP set up in September 1951 was composed mainly of Vietnamese members—1,800 locally born Vietnamese for only 150 Khmers.

Between the Imperialists and the Prince

In January 1953 Saloth Sar returned to Phnom Penh after three years in Paris. The twenty-five-year-old revolutionary later earned notoriety under his *nom de guerre*, Pol Pot. His application to join the embryonic KPRP was vetted by a Vietnamese cadre. That short and stocky Vietnamese was Pham Van Ba, a longtime ICP cadre living in Phnom Penh under various covers, including that of a journalist. In the late 1950s he disappeared from Phnom Penh to surface as a Vietcong diplomat. After serving as the chief of the PRG mission in Paris until 1975, Ba became the first Vietnamese ambassador to Pol Pot's Cambodia.

Seven years after I had first met Ba in the PRG office in Paris, I saw him again in Ho Chi Minh City in January 1981. He told me, relishing my surprise, what he could not have revealed before the break with the Khmer Rouge: "I was then the secretary of the [clandestine] administration bureau of the ICP in Phnom Penh." He continued, "Pol Pot contacted me, asking to join the party. He had a membership card of the French Communist party (PCF). He said he had joined the Cambodian section of the PCF while studying in the École de Radio-Électricité in Paris. I sent a message to the party headquarters in Bac Bo [North Vietnam] asking them to check it out with the PCF. Some time later I received a Morse-code message from Hoang Van Hoan in Bangkok, where he ran the overseas Vietnamese section of the party, confirming that Pol Pot was indeed a party member. So I let him join the party."

The direct Vietnamese supervision of the KPRP, however, stopped a year later with the end of the First Indochina War. Under pressure from the Chinese and Soviet delegates to the Geneva Conference (1954), the Vietnamese Communists were forced to accept the temporary partition of Vietnam and give up the claims of Khmer Issarak–liberated areas to the Royal Government of Cambodia. Unlike the Lao resistance, which received recognition in Geneva and was allowed to regroup in two provinces bordering Vietnam and China (thus securing rear areas), the Khmer Issarak was ordered to disband. The young king Sihanouk, who had launched a personal pressure campaign for independence to forestall the Vietminh-backed

Issarak, emerged a victor at the Geneva Conference. In accordance with the Geneva Agreement, Vietminh troops and some two thousand Khmer resistance fighters, hidden among Vietnamese ranks, were withdrawn to North Vietnam to wait for a better day. "We never thought that the French would fully apply the Geneva Agreements," Ba explained, "so we had to prepare." It was indeed a farsighted move. Despite the liquidation of a majority of Hanoi-trained Cambodians by the Pol Pot group in 1972–75, some survivors emerged years later to take charge of a pro-Vietnamese government in Cambodia.

While some veteran Khmer Issarak leaders accepted the setback with resignation, the younger, foreign-educated militants were bitter. Ultranationalistic Communists such as Pol Pot, Ieng Sary, and Son Sen, who had returned from Paris, accused the Vietnamese of sacrificing the gains made by the Khmers during the anti-French resistance. But the withdrawal from Cambodia of the vast majority of combatants and leading figures who had worked closely with the Vietminh, and the defection and death of others, left the field open for the Pol Pot group to develop its own political line.

When Son Ngoc Minh, the Communist leader of the Khmer Issarak movement, chose to stay on in Hanoi after the Geneva Conference, the party in Cambodia came under the leadership of Sieu Heng. He turned out to be a traitor. After several years of secret collaboration with the state police—which led to the decimation of most of the party cells—Heng defected to the Sihanouk government in 1959. At a clandestine party congress held in Phnom Penh's railway yard on September 28–30, 1960, a monk-turned-Communist, Tou Samouth (who had close ties with the Vietnamese), was named party secretary.[16]

Pol Pot, then a schoolteacher in Phnom Penh, was elected to be the deputy secretary in 1961. Following Samouth's mysterious disappearance in July 1962, Pol Pot took over the responsibilities of the secretary of the clandestine party. Soon after, Pol Pot, his brother-in-law Ieng Sary, Son Sen, and others fled to the jungle to reorganize the clandestine party. They were not heard of again until 1970.

During those years, the differences grew sharper between the radical, chauvinistic line of the Pol Pot group and the relatively moderate line stressing collaboration with Sihanouk's anti-American government and the Vietnamese. During a trip to Hanoi in March 1978 I was invited to an extraordinary dinner briefing by a senior official. After denying for years that there was any serious problem with Cambodia, Vietnamese vice–foreign minister Vo Dong Giang told me that evening of a conflict that went back over two decades— a deep division between the Vietnamese party and the Pol Pot faction in the Cambodian party. He said that right from the beginning the Vietnamese had sided with the "correct line" in the Cambodian party against the Pol Pot group. He sarcastically referred to them as "the Parisians, who had no record of active participation in the anti-French resistance." Their policy of bringing revolution, Giang said, was pure infantile communism. "Because the banner against U.S. imperialism was held high by Prince Sihanouk, his prestige among the people was overwhelming. So the Communists who knew how to use Sihanouk's influence against U.S. imperialism gained popularity. The prestige among the Cambodian people belonged first to Sihanouk and then to the political line [within the Cambodian party] that united the people against the enemy, and not to Pol Pot." The policy of uniting the various forces to fight the enemy and of promoting solidarity between the three Indochinese peoples has been "the line of our revolution from the earliest time to now," Giang said. However, as Pol Pot managed to maneuver the party along the radical path of the Cambodian revolution, it faced a most "difficult time" in 1967–69—Giang's euphemism for Sihanouk's repression of the Communists.

Giang was right in emphasizing the popularity Sihanouk had gained as the person who led Cambodia to independence, but he failed to recall that before 1954 the Vietminh and Khmer Issarak treated Sihanouk as a lackey of the French. By focusing on Sihanouk's anti-U.S. foreign policy of the 1960s, Giang also sidestepped the question of the prince's suppression of the Left. The Vietnamese advice to the Khmer Communists in the 1960s amounted to a call for freezing class struggle in Cambodia so as not to rock Sihanouk's boat and jeopardize Hanoi's relations with the prince.

What Giang chose not to mention was Hanoi's paramount need to keep its relations with Sihanouk sweet. With the intensification of the war in Vietnam after 1965, the Vietcong and North Vietnamese troops needed sanctuaries in Cambodia and safe supply routes more than ever—a need that Prince Sihanouk was willing to satisfy discreetly under the pretext of neutrality. Although Sihanouk dealt with the Khmer Rouge with an iron hand, he claimed to sympathize with the Vietnamese Communists. While he dismissed the local Communists as agents of Hanoi and Peking, he viewed the Vietnam War as essentially a nationalist struggle against unjust foreign intervention. As he later admitted in his memoirs, he closed his eyes to the installation of Vietnamese rest camps, hospitals, and provision centers in Cambodia. He also authorized vessels of China, the Soviet Union, Czechoslovakia, and other Socialist countries to unload supplies for the Vietcong at Sihanoukville Port, from where they were discreetly transported to the Vietnamese border after a percentage was retained for the Cambodian army.[17]

Sihanouk's willingness to help the Vietnamese Communists was based on a shrewd calculation that it would be advantageous to keep on good terms with the likely victor. "The reason I decided to cooperate with the Vietnamese," Sihanouk later said, "was to put Communist Vietnam in Kampuchea's debt in such a way that it would never again dare raise a hand, so to speak, against our country and our people, its benefactors."[18]

Perhaps he also feared the North Vietnamese ability to move against him if he opposed their struggle. He was convinced that China and Vietnam would be the dominant factors in Asia when the Americans went home. In August 1963 Sihanouk severed diplomatic ties with South Vietnam, and later that year he rejected U.S. economic and military aid to Cambodia. In May 1965 Cambodia broke off diplomatic ties with Washington—an act that earned Sihanouk praise from Peking and Hanoi—and in June of the same year Sihanouk followed up by expressing his support for the South Vietnam National Liberation Front with a gift of medical aid. He confidently told an interviewer in November 1965, "The Americans can murder 10 to 20 million Vietnamese. But sooner or later, they will be forced to abandon Vietnam to the survivors. . . . The United States has launched itself into an adventure which will inevitably end in defeat."[19]

The Vietnamese were grateful for Sihanouk's support, and it was not surprising that when, in the summer of 1965, Pol Pot paid a secret visit to Hanoi on his way to China, they advised him to support Sihanouk's anti-imperialist foreign policy. If the CPK launched an armed struggle against the prince's government, it would harm Vietnam's strategy. Hanoi did not consider this to be a selfish subordination of the Cambodian struggle to the needs of the Vietnamese, because it believed that Cambodia was not ripe for launching armed class warfare. Moreover, Hanoi held that the victory of the Vietnamese in the South would eventually provide ideal conditions for a successful struggle against the Sihanouk regime.

Armed Struggle Begins

The Pol Pot group, however, rejected the course advocated for Cambodia by the Vietnamese. The five months that Pol Pot spent in China in late 1965 and early 1966—a time when the Cultural Revolution's anti-imperialist, antirevisionist fervor was catching on— must have helped to drive him toward the path of armed struggle against, as opposed to collaboration with, a feudal regime. Even if there were no overt support for an anti-Sihanouk struggle, China, increasingly concerned about Vietnamese-Soviet cooperation, might have backed Pol Pot in his differences with the Vietnamese.[20]

The *Black Book* later claimed that by 1966 it had become clear that "there was a fundamental contradiction between the Cambodian revolution and the Vietnamese revolution. The Vietnamese wanted to put the Cambodian revolution under their thumb." The expression probably meant that the Cambodian revolution was given lower priority rather than that the Vietnamese sought to control the Khmer movement. It is, however, true that in order not to totally alienate the Khmer Rouge, and also perhaps to exercise a restraining hand over them, Hanoi eventually agreed to provide military training and assistance. A well-placed Vietnamese Communist defector told U.S. interrogators in 1973 that in 1966 the Vietnamese had organized a unit designated as P-36 to support the Cambodian party. Even before Sihanouk's overthrow in 1970, the P-36 had reportedly begun training Khmers and ethnic Vietnamese born in Cambodia.[21]

It is not clear whether this mysterious P-36 had any role in initiating the insurgency in Cambodia, but it did predate that insurgency. Following a spontaneous peasant uprising against land grabbing by an officially sponsored youth group in March–April 1967 in Samlaut, Pol Pot decided to found a revolutionary army and to begin an armed struggle against the Sihanouk regime. On January 17, 1968, Khmer Rouge guerrillas began a sporadic campaign of ambushing, kidnapping, and executing government forces and civilian officials. Although the Vietnamese party was most embarrassed and annoyed by this development, Sihanouk, who was unaware of the tactical rift between the two parties, blamed Hanoi and Peking for fomenting the conflict. "The more successful the CPK became," a leading historian of the Cambodian Communist movement noted, "the more vulnerable were the Vietnamese supply lines and sanctuaries in Kampuchea. Whether or not this tempted the Vietnamese to try to sabotage the CPK's struggle, it certainly must have increased tensions and suspicions between the two parties."[22]

Sihanouk responded to the peasant uprisings by stepping up the repression of the Left, the result of which was further polarization of the political situation. The Sorbonne-educated economists, Khieu Samphan and Hou Yuon, and other Communist intellectuals, like Hu Nim, who had so long managed to work within the Sihanouk system took to the jungle. On the other hand, right-wing politicians and generals, who had opposed Sihanouk's anti-U.S. policy and in particular his rejection of American aid in 1963, held him responsible for the existence of Vietcong sanctuaries in Cambodia and the growing threat from the CPK. By 1968 Sihanouk had grown doubtful about the certainty of Chinese support. The excesses of the Chinese Cultural Revolution, which at one stage even spilled over into Cambodia, shook him. If the Chinese could get rid of their revered head of state, Liu Shaoqi, for ideological reasons, Sihanouk reportedly wondered, how could he be secure about his own fate?[23] Sihanouk was also getting nervous about the growing Vietcong use of Khmer territory. The massive American buildup in Vietnam under Lyndon Johnson also led him to revise his earlier view about an inevitable Communist victory. Sihanouk not only moved to restore diplomatic relations with Washington in 1969 but also quietly signaled the United States that he would "shut [his] eyes" if Americans bombed Vietcong sanctuaries in underpopulated areas of Cambodia.[24]

Sihanouk's newfound respect for American power only helped to confirm for General Lon Nol and Prince Sirik Matak, the leading non-Communist opponents of the regime, that their criticisms of Sihanouk had been right all along. Things were further complicated by serious deterioration in the economic situation. In the growing restiveness in the spring of 1970 the rightists found an ideal opportunity to move against Sihanouk and his policy of buying insurance from the Vietcong and the North Vietnamese. The rightists' anxieties dovetailed neatly with the American concern about clearing up the Vietcong sanctuaries in Cambodia in order to win the war in South Vietnam. Although no hard evidence has been found for direct and high-level U.S. involvement in the anti-Sihanouk plot, Washington nonetheless was aware of it and did nothing to stop it. While the United States appreciated Sihanouk's discreet help against the Vietnamese Communists, the memory of conflict with him was too strong to permit intervention in his favor. When finally the staunchly anti-Vietnamese and pro-American group moved against Sihanouk, a former CIA analyst, Frank Snepp, noted, "We were in a position to rub our hands and take advantage of it."[25]

In the wake of anti-Vietnamese demonstrations in Phnom Penh and the ransacking of the North Vietnamese embassy by a student mob, the right wing–dominated National Assembly deposed the prince (March 18, 1970) and gave power to the prime minister and defense minister, General Lon Nol. Sihanouk, who was then in Moscow, flew into Peking. It was to become his second home.

The coup against Sihanouk threatened both Cambodia's domestic Left and the Vietcong sanctuaries and supply lines. By a single stroke it forced the Vietnamese and the Khmer Rouge into an uneasy alliance against their common enemy, the U.S.–backed Lon Nol government. The important hinge in this new alliance was the deposed prince. While the Khmer Rouge needed his name to provide a mantle of international legitimacy and to attract peasant support for their cause within the country, the Vietnamese saw the prince not only as a pillar of the resistance against the United States and Lon Nol but also as insurance against the domination of the movement by the Pol Pot group.

In contrast China's position was more ambiguous. Sihanouk denies the theory—vigorously propounded by Hanoi and espoused by some Western analysts—that the Chinese were initially hesitant in supporting him. "From our first meeting [on March 19] at my residence," Sihanouk says, "Zhou Enlai and I agreed that the fait accompli established by the putschists should never be accepted and that the 'legality' of the new Khmer regime should be opposed to the end." However, Zhou did not try to push Sihanouk into joining the Khmer Rouge. According to Sihanouk, he conveyed a message from Chairman Mao which said in effect that:

> Peking would scrupulously respect whatever decision Prince Norodom Sihanouk makes; if he wishes to put an end to his political career in consequence of yesterday's coup d'état, China will bow to that decision; but if Prince Sihanouk does not accept the fait accompli and decides to lead a national movement of anti-American resistance for the liberation of Cambodia, China will fully support Prince Sihanouk and will grant him all possible help.[26]

Sihanouk's account offers a partial explanation as to why Peking maintained relations for a time with the Lon Nol regime. China clearly did not want to cut off ties with Phnom Penh without being certain that the option of armed opposition would work. In particular, the coup had come at a time when, in the aftermath of its first armed clash with the Soviets, Peking was beginning to look at the possibility of improving relations with Washington. Engaging in a war against Lon Nol could further cloud those relations.

Vietnamese propaganda later claimed that Peking was colluding with Lon Nol to prevent the Vietcong from winning in South Vietnam. However, the Vietnamese party's principal spokesman, Hoang Tung, told me later that in March 1970 the Chinese were not enthusiastic about Sihanouk because of his criticism of Mao during the Cultural Revolution. "And our Communist friends in Cambodia," Tung said, "nurture a hatred against Sihanouk because of the massacres. Sihanouk had killed many Communists between 1955 and 1965.[27] . . . When Sihanouk was in Peking [March 1970], neither Zhou Enlai nor Pol Pot took any intiative to win Sihanouk to the side of resistance. It was us, the Vietnamese, who took the

65

initiative. Pham Van Dong [who led a secret Vietnamese delegation to Peking three days after the coup] had the job of persuading Zhou Enlai, while Pham Hung [a Politburo member accompanying Dong who maintained liaison with the Khmer Rouge before 1970] had to persuade Pol Pot."

Sihanouk also confirmed that he received warm backing from Dong. On March 23, the day after his lengthy meetings with Dong, Sihanouk launched an appeal for armed resistance. In a handwritten letter to the prince the following day, delivered as he left Peking, Dong expressed the Vietnamese people's "feelings of deep friendship, of admiration and respect for you, for your policies, and for the struggle you are leading at the head of the valiant Khmer people."[28] For five years after those meetings, Hanoi's leaders and Sihanouk enjoyed a relationship of warmth and even affection.

Within days of Dong's pledge of support, Vietcong units moved into villages in eastern Cambodia, distributing leaflets bearing Sihanouk's appeal and playing his taped message to the Cambodian people. Sihanouk's popularity with the peasants brought in hundreds of recruits whom the Vietnamese trained and armed, forming them into a Sihanoukist army known as Khmer Rumdo (Liberation Khmers). North Vietnamese instructors also set up a military school in the northeastern province of Kratie to train Khmer recruits. Under what Sihanouk called the "indisputably effective and heroic shield" provided by the North Vietnamese, the Khmer resistance forces swelled from some four thousand in March 1970 to some thirty thousand in 1975. Vietnamese artillery, tanks, and infantry divisions blunted Lon Nol's military campaigns aimed at relieving towns besieged by the Khmer Rouge. By late 1972, when the Khmer Rouge and Khmer Rumdo units began to operate on their own, the back of the Lon Nol army had already been broken by Hanoi regulars, and a vast area of Cambodia had come under insurgent control.

A Poisonous Alliance

The very success of the resistance meant the beginning of the end of CPK-Hanoi alliance. Despite the dramatic improvement in their relations after March 1970, the Pol Pot group continued to be wary of the Vietnamese. Sihanouk describes in his memoirs an episode in 1970–71 when ministers of the Khmer resistance government, while visiting Hanoi, talked among themselves about "*Yuon* hypocrisy" and the "need for the Khmers in the [front] to beware of North Vietnam's desire for hegemony after [the] foreseeable joint victory over the Yankee aggressors and the traitor Lon Nol." Since walls have ears, Sihanouk notes tongue-in-cheek, these words were reported to General Vo Nguyen Giap, who bristled in anger while talking to Sihanouk the following day. Giap told him that the front leaders' "anti-Vietnamese remarks, made here in Hanoi, hurt us deeply, since every day our soldiers, far from their dear homeland and beloved families, fight and die on the sacred soil of our Khmer brothers and sisters, side by side with them against our common enemies, to save and liberate your country, Cambodia."

Giap's elaborately worded outburst most probably was due not only to the odd remark uttered in a Hanoi guesthouse but also to the frustrations that the Vietnamese were experiencing in dealing with the Khmer Rouge. During negotiations with Le Duan in Hanoi in April 1970, Pol Pot had turned down a Vietnamese suggestion that a mixed military command be set up. In the course of 1970–71 the fledgling Khmer front had taken over the administration of liberated villages from the Vietnamese. By 1971 relations between the Khmer Rouge and the Vietnamese soldiers in Cambodia had become strained. The Khmer Rouge have provided no evidence for their accusation, leveled in 1978, that the Vietnamese attempted to poison Pol Pot during a meeting in November 1970. But the charge undoubtedly reflects the tension that existed. According to a CIA report in September 1970, Khmer Rouge troops fired on Vietnamese Communist forces from behind while the latter were attacking a Lon Nol unit in Kompong Thom.[29]

Nguyen Thi Cu, a Vietnamese survivor of a Khmer Rouge raid on Tay Ninh Province, was one of many thousands of Vietnamese residents in Cambodia who felt they had to flee the Khmer Rouge zone in 1972. Her family had moved from North Vietnam to work in the French rubber plantation in Chup. Her husband and two brothers joined the Vietcong army in the late 1960s, and after the overthrow of Sihanouk they were in touch with the Khmer Rouge.

But, from the end of 1971, she told me in 1978, the Khmer Rouge started harassing the Vietnamese community in the plantation and stopped selling rice to them. "The [Vietnamese] liberation army troops did try to protect us," she said, "but it became increasingly difficult. So in 1972, my soldier brother helped our family to flee from Cambodia."

The simmering tension between the Vietnamese and the Khmer Rouge reached a crisis in late 1972 when, during the final stage of the U.S.-Vietnamese peace talks in Paris, an attempt was made to bring the Khmer Rouge into negotiation with Lon Nol. U.S. negotiator Henry Kissinger's demand to this effect was passed on to the Khmer Rouge leadership in several clandestine meetings in late 1972 and, for the last time, in a January 24–26, 1973, encounter between Vietnamese Politburo member Pham Hung and Pol Pot. The idea was rejected scornfully. Pol Pot saw that the military situation could produce a quick victory, since the isolated and discredited Lon Nol regime was on its last legs. The Vietnamese warning to the Khmer Rouge that their refusal would bring heavy punishment from the United States was seen as a blackmail attempt. The *Black Book* was to argue later that the North Vietnamese had reached the end of their tether and wanted a respite from war, but they did not want the Cambodian resistance to win on its own because then Cambodia could not be made into a Vietnamese satellite.[30]

But the Vietnamese were right about the punishment. Free from duty in the rest of the Indochinese theater, American bombers dropped 257,465 tons of bombs on Cambodia between February and August 1973—50 percent more than the total tonnage dropped on Japan during World War II. There were a great number of civilian casualties. Four years later, sitting in the bunkerlike Democratic Kampuchean embassy in Hanoi, In Sivouth bitterly recalled "the Vietnamese betrayal" in signing a separate peace with the enemy, enabling the Americans to direct their full fury at Cambodia. This accusation is a classic example of how racial prejudice and feelings of historical enmity led the Pol Pot group to blame all their woes on the Vietnamese. Clearly the Hanoi leadership did not care much about the Cambodian struggle beyond the extent it helped their own cause, but neither were the Khmer Rouge leaders eager to help the Vietnamese reunify their country. Ironically enough, if the peace agreement with the Vietnamese freed American hands in Cambodia, tacit support for the bombing, according to Kissinger, came from Zhou, who "needed our military actions in Cambodia for the effectiveness of his policy almost as much as we did." The U.S. bombing, according to him, was a bargaining chip for getting China's Khmer Rouge allies to accept a negotiated settlement with Sihanouk as the leader.[31]

The Khmer Rouge leaders most probably were unaware that long before the signing of the Paris Agreement, Zhou had told Kissinger that settling the Cambodia question was easier than settling the Vietnam question, "because no matter what happens we can say for certain that elements of the national bourgeoisie will take part in such a government; and we can be sure that in Cambodia Prince Sihanouk will be the head of state."[32]

Seven months later, even after the Khmers had rejected negotiation with Lon Nol and made considerable military advances, Zhou was still interested in a negotiated settlement with Lon Nol. Having failed to persuade the Khmer Rouge to come to the negotiating table, the Vietnamese suggested to Kissinger in February 1973 that he should talk to Sihanouk. Writing about it eight years later, Kissinger dismissed this Vietnamese suggestion as "offhand" compared with Zhou's more serious concern of bringing Sihanouk back to power.[33] There is, however, ample evidence that the Vietnamese were seriously examining the Sihanouk card and had, in any case, a freer hand than Zhou in dealing with the Maoist-inclined Khmer Rouge.

Some observers, however, doubt whether Zhou really wanted the prince to return to power or whether he was just making use of Sihanouk's popularity and international standing to ensure victory for China's ideological allies, the Khmer Rouge. It is also possible that the terminally ill premier, who was facing strong opposition from the radicals led by Mao's wife, Jiang Qing, became increasingly unable in 1973 to promote Sihanouk's interests against those of the Khmer Rouge. In late 1974, when the French undertook a secret diplomatic initiative in collaboration with Washington to restore Sihanouk to power as the head of an enlarged coalition, the Chinese adopted an ambiguous position.[34]

Although the prince was grateful for Zhou's friendship and the protection offered him against the Khmer Rouge radicals, he had, nevertheless, moments of doubt. "I think the Chinese knew right from the beginning that the Khmer Rouge would get rid of me," the prince told me with some sadness. During a lengthy conversation at his sumptuous Peking residence in April 1980, he recalled the years that followed his overthrow. Beginning in 1971, Sihanouk continually asked Zhou to prevail on the Khmer Rouge to let him visit Cambodia's liberated zone. Living in exile in Peking, he reasoned, he would have little credibility as the head of a resistance government. But his appeals were in vain. "What hurts me a little," he said, "is that China did not back me at all [in his attempt to visit Cambodia] from the beginning." Zhou refused to let him make the trip, citing security risks. The only route to liberated Cambodia was via the Ho Chi Minh Trail—a permanent bombing target. After the signing of the Paris Peace Agreement, Sihanouk asked Ieng Sary (who lived in Peking from August 1971 until April 1975 as liaison with the Chinese party and also as the Khmer Rouge watchdog of the volatile prince) if he could now visit the motherland. The answer was a blunt no. Sihanouk tried his luck again in Hanoi. Since the time he took up residence in Peking, he had regularly visited Hanoi every lunar new year, when the Vietnamese celebrate Tet. This was one way for the prince to show solidarity with the Vietnamese. During his Tet visit in February 1973, Sihanouk pleaded with Pham Van Dong to intercede on his behalf with the Khmer Rouge. "You have a means of pressure on the Khmer Rouge," he said. "They cannot continue to fight if you don't transport the supplies given by China. You tell the Khmer Rouge that Sihanouk must return to Cambodia, otherwise he cannot represent his country with honor and dignity at the nonaligned meeting in Algiers." After that, Dong held a lengthy meeting with Sary, arguing with him the importance of letting Sihanouk visit the liberated zone. But Sary would not budge. Finally, Dong spoke to the Chinese. And that worked. "After I had returned to China," Sihanouk recalled, "Ieng Sary came to tell me that I had the permission of the 'interior' [to visit Cambodia]. It was Pham Van Dong's success."[35]

Sihanouk's historic return to Cambodia three years after his overthrow may well have been brought about by Hanoi's pressure, but the trip made him aware of the growing tension between the Khmer Rouge and their so-called comrades in Vietnam. In March 1973 the prince flew to Hanoi and then, aboard a Vietnamese air force Antonov 26 transport, to Dong Hoi on the southern edge of North Vietnam. Accompanied by the Vietnamese ambassador accredited to Cambodia, Nguyen Thuong, and, of course, by his shadow, Ieng Sary, Sihanouk and his wife, Monique, drove down the Ho Chi Minh Trail to Cambodia in a command car. During his month-long stay in the Khmer Rouge–controlled north and northeast, he heard accusations that the Vietnamese were trying to "nip Khmer Rouge power in the bud." The Vietnamese soldiers, Son Sen told him, had been stealing from Cambodian villagers, raping Cambodian women, installing bases inside Cambodia without authorization, recruiting Khmers to serve as auxiliaries to the Vietnamese army, and diverting Chinese military supplies for Cambodia to their own army. Khieu Samphan told him that the Vietnamese were preparing to put a government in power that would be Cambodian in appearance but in reality subservient to Vietnam.

While Sihanouk learned about the secrets of the comrades, Pol Pot (who followed the prince from the shadows) and his friends were able to see the enduring popularity of the deposed ruler. Despite the wall of security that surrounded Sihanouk in his restricted meetings with the people, there was no mistaking the loyalty and emotion that he aroused. Barely had the prince finished his trip when the Pol Pot group stepped up a campaign to denigrate Sihanouk and redoubled its efforts to eliminate Vietnam's influence. Khmer Rouge cadres who had long worked among the people as Sihanoukists began to show their true colors by denouncing the prince in public meetings. "Before, they [the Khmer Rouge] wanted all of us to say 'we want Sihanouk,' but now no more," a refugee reported in 1973. "Before, you can say anything about Sihanouk, but now you cannot show his picture." No one dared to question this policy, she explained, because it might mean death.[36] They were preparing for the day when the party, and not Sihanouk, would take charge of the country. In mid-1973, to strengthen the party's territorial and economic control, private ownership of land and the use of money were abolished, agricultural cooperatives were introduced, and Viet-

71

namese traders and fishermen were driven out of Cambodia. Those Vietnamese residents who remained in Cambodia were regrouped into cooperatives that, according to Sihanouk, "quickly turned into virtual concentration camps."

By the end of 1973 reports of armed clashes between the Khmer Rumdo and the Khmer Rouge started filtering out. In one instance in November 1973, a firefight erupted in Kandal Province after the Khmer Rumdo refused to accept Khmer Rouge demands to stop cooperating with the Vietcong and the North Vietnamese. Ken Quinn, an official at the U.S. consulate in Cantho, reported to Washington on February 24, 1974, "The KR [Khmer Rumdo], supported by a nearby VC/NVA [Vietcong/North Vietnamese Army] unit, killed 42 KK [Khmer Krahom, or Red Khmer] and drove the rest off. Since that time the KK and the KR have conducted raids across the Mekong into each other's territory."[37]

By 1974, implementation of the Khmer Rouge's radical economic policies—collectivization of agriculture and abolition of trade—began to be accompanied by purges of real or suspected opponents of these policies. In August 1974, seventy-one Hanoi-trained cadres in eastern Cambodia were assembled for a "study course" at which they were berated for taking refuge in Vietnam. Ten of them disappeared. The remaining cadres were put to work in the fields under surveillance. One of them, Hem Samin, perhaps now the lone survivor of the group, fled to Vietnam. In southwestern Cambodia, ninety of one hundred cadres returned from Hanoi were executed in September 1974.[38] One of the survivors, Yos Por, escaped execution and fled to Vietnam. Both Samin and Por were later to emerge as leaders of the Hanoi-backed anti–Pol Pot front.

The Paris Agreement in 1973 also marked the beginning of Khmer Rouge attacks on Vietnamese arms depots, hospitals, and base camps inside Cambodia—attacks that were explained away by the Pol Pot group as stemming from misunderstanding and unruly conduct by lower-level soldiers. Two correspondents of the Vietnam News Agency (VNA) were killed "by error" while visiting Kompong Cham Province in October. In February 1975 an entire NLF cultural troupe from My Tho died in an ambush while passing through Cambodian territory to visit liberated areas of Tay Ninh Province. When Vietcong leaders asked for an explanation, the Cambodians said the attack was mounted by what they called undisciplined soldiers. Tran Thanh Xuan, deputy director of the VNA, told me that in 1973 officials, at least at his level, did not think that these killings of Vietnamese in Cambodia were the work of the Cambodian party. "We regarded them as inevitable casualties of war," he said. It is, however, impossible to believe that the Vietnamese Politburo did not understand what was happening. Unwilling to pick a quarrel with Pol Pot because sanctuaries in Cambodia were still needed, Hanoi pretended to accept the Khmer Rouge explanations. The Vietnamese also believed that a "correct line" would emerge in Cambodia that would reject Pol Pot's chauvinism. Hanoi's principal task was to liberate the South, not to exacerbate a conflict with wayward allies. Thus, despite growing tension between the two, the Vietnamese played along. In response to a Khmer Rouge request, they sent sapper and artillery units that helped to finally strangle Phnom Penh.

Pol Pot, too, continued to maintain appearances. On October 3, 1974, he wrote a letter to thank the Vietnamese party, remarking, "The victories we have won are victories for the solidarity and mutual assistance between the parties and people of our two countries." These words were penned after thousands of Vietnamese had been driven out of Cambodia, Hanoi-trained cadres had been executed, and Vietnamese bases had been attacked. The charade's script also included other missives, including one in which Pol Pot assured Le Duc Tho, "in all sincerity and from the bottom of my heart," that he would always remain faithful to the line of "great solidarity and of fraternal and revolutionary friendship between Cambodia and Vietnam."[39] Neither the balance of forces within the CPK nor the domestic or international situation yet permitted an open confrontation with Vietnam. Three more years were to pass before that day arrived.

3

The Peking Debut

FOR DEMOCRATIC Kampuchea's deputy premier, Ieng Sary, the news of October 13, 1976, was a bolt from the blue. He had hardly settled down in his Belgrade guesthouse after a tiring flight from New York when it arrived. Dusan Gaspari, director of the Asia department of the Yugoslav Foreign Ministry and Sary's principal contact in Belgrade, walked, grim-faced, into the salon. "Your Excellency," Gaspari announced, "I have been instructed to inform you about the latest developments in China. The Chinese Foreign Ministry has confirmed that Madame Jiang Qing, Zhang Chunqiao, Yao Wenyuan, and Wang Hongwen have been arrested for antiparty and antistate activities." Gaspari later recalled how the color had drained from Sary's stunned face. "No, it can't be true! They are good people," Sary had muttered in a barely audible voice.[1]

Since the autumn of 1971, when he took up residence in Peking as the representative of the Communist Party of Kampuchea to the Chinese party, Sary had been friends with the radicals. Those young firebrand members had shot into prominence during the tumultuous days of the Cultural Revolution, when Mao had called upon the Red Guards to "bombard the headquarters" of the Communist party and purge it of revisionist ills. One in particular, Yao Wenyuan, who had risen from obscurity as literary critic in Shanghai to a position in the Politburo in 1969, had become a close friend of Sary's. Among other points, they shared a dislike of Prince Sihanouk as a "through-and-through reactionary."[2] That friendship was especially valuable because Yao effectively ran the External Affairs Commission of the Chinese party's Central Committee. The Khmer Rouge leaders knew they could be sure of Chinese support for their radical course as long as Yao and his kind were in charge of Chinese policy.

The arrest of his close friends and supporters, as Sary found out later, came two days after he had left Peking for New York to address the annual meeting of the United Nations General Assembly. On the night of October 6, three weeks after Chairman Mao's death, the special military unit 2341, under the command of Mao's former bodyguard, Wang Dongxing, had swiftly rounded up Mao's widow and three of her radical associates. Their names soon collectively entered China's political lexicon as the "Gang of Four." Acting Premier Hua Guofeng and the veteran defense minister Marshal Yeh Jianyiang, who had plotted the coup with Wang, had personally monitored part of the operation on a closed-circuit TV.

But neither during his three-day stopover in Peking nor during his talks at the UN with his Chinese counterpart, Qiao Guanhua, did Sary have an inkling of what was brewing in Peking. Only two days earlier, before he left New York for Belgrade, Sary had been the guest of honor at a banquet given by Qiao. Although a close associate of the radicals, Qiao had not even hinted at a problem. Now, suddenly, the ground seemed to fall from under Sary's feet.

In his last few visits to China, Sary had sensed that, despite their proximity to the dying Mao through Jiang Qing, everything was not going well for the radicals. After the death of Premier Zhou Enlai in January 1976, the radicals had secured Mao's support in ousting Zhou's protégé, the pragmatic Deng Xiaoping. But Mao clearly did not want Jiang Qing and her group to take over. He had ignored the candidature of Zhang Chunqiao, chief theoretician of the radicals, and had chosen Hua Guofeng, a Left-leaning party functionary who was then minister of public security, to be the acting premier.[3] After Mao's death Hua also assumed the mantle of chairman of the Communist party. There was clearly some concern among Cambodian Communists, such as Pol Pot and Sary, that Mao's death should not tilt the balance in China in favor of the Right. Before leaving Phnom Penh on September 30 for New York, Sary had helped draft a message of greetings to Acting Premier Hua on the occasion of China's national day. The message had pointedly praised China's Cultural Revolution and also the Chinese party's success in smashing the "anti-Socialist and counterrevolutionary headquarters of Liu Shaoqi and Deng Xiaoping." The implicit message was that the Cambodian party would welcome Hua to the extent he followed a Left revolutionary line.

The bloodless coup in Peking only presaged a swing to the Right, and perhaps even the return of the twice-purged Deng. Sary's concern at the turn of events in China could be guessed from his rather unusual behavior in the following weeks. After brief stops in Yugoslavia and Romania, Sary was reported by the Romanian and Chinese news agencies to have left Bucharest on October 16. Then he dropped out of sight, resurfacing in Phnom Penh twenty-five days later. The normal course for him would have been to take the Romanian airline, Tarom, to Peking and then take the fortnightly Chinese flight between Peking and Phnom Penh. On his previous passages through Peking, Sary was routinely received by a vice–foreign minister at the airport, and if the transit was longer than a day, he was entertained at a banquet by a Chinese Politburo member. And all this cordiality was duly reported by the Xinhua News Agency. This time neither the Chinese nor the Cambodian media mentioned Sary's whereabouts after his departure from Bucharest. On November 12 Radio Phnom Penh reported that he had received three ambassadors accredited to Cambodia. That he had not resumed his duties in Phnom Penh until November 8 was indicated by official references to Defense Minister Son Sen as acting foreign minister.[4]

Where had he been? Years later I asked that question of Sary's wife, Ieng Thirith. Sary had met her during his student days in Paris. Pol Pot had fallen in love with Thirith's sister, Khieu Ponnary, who was also a student in Paris. The two sisters and their husbands emerged as the most powerful couples in Cambodia, in Sihanouk's words "Cambodia's gang of four." Thirith's bland reply was that she did not know. "You know, we used to live separately," she told me. From all available indications Sary appears to have spent at least three weeks in China. The silence of the Chinese media was presumably due to the private nature of his stay. Or perhaps it was in accordance with Sary's desire to maintain a low profile because China was in a period of turmoil and uncertainty. He probably spent the time assessing the situation in the wake of the most important political earthquake in China and seeking guarantees from the new leaders that the death of Mao and the purge of radicals would not weaken Peking's support for Cambodia.

Ieng Sary's concern about the Chinese support was based on ideological considerations. It was a legitimate fear. In almost one decade of Cultural Revolution that coincided with the emergence of armed struggle in Cambodia and the growth of the Khmer Rouge, ideology was at the driving seat. Now that Sary's ideological peers had been ousted from power in Peking, how could Cambodia count on the support from a rightist China? But the Khmer Rouge leadership soon found out that China's national interest was more important than its ideology. China's desire to curb Vietnamese power and resist the Soviets far outweighed any ideological qualms its new leadership might have about Pol Pot's Cambodia. Within less than a year Cambodian-Chinese friendship had been reaffirmed, and Pol Pot had emerged from the shadows of anonymity to make his international debut in Peking.

Concern in Phnom Penh

Out of such concerns, Sary's colleagues back home had promptly sent a message of greetings to Hua after his nomination as chairman of the Chinese Communist party. Most other fraternal parties did not want to take sides in China's internal squabble. They congratulated Hua without reference to the fallen radicals. But the Cambodian need for Chinese support was too crucial for its loyalty to the Peking leadership to be left in doubt. Their message also warmly acclaimed Hua for his victory in "smashing the counterrevolutionary Gang of Four antiparty clique." This was a remarkable volte-face, because less than a month before, a message from Phnom Penh had strongly supported the line of the very group it now denounced as counterrevolutionary.

Although promptly reassuring Peking that the Cambodian leadership was not beholden to the Gang of Four, Pol Pot obviously considered the news of the developments in China too dangerous to be diffused internally: It might give ideas to those in the party who thought that Pol Pot–Ieng Sary radicalism had gone too far. The message sent to Hua was not broadcast by Radio Phnom Penh, the sole source of information for the Cambodian people, dispersed in isolated work camps. It was not until December 2, 1976, barely a week before the arrival of a delegation of Chinese journalists, that Radio Phnom Penh revealed to its listeners the news of the appointment of Hua as chairman of the Chinese party and the arrest of the Gang of Four. That news, too, was presented without giving any clue as to who the "gang" members were and what the nature of their alleged crime was.

A Cambodian economic and trade delegation happened to be in China at the time of the dramatic shake-up. They received assurances from their Chinese hosts that Peking would "always remain a reliable friend of the government and people of Democratic Kampuchea."[5] Still, the possible negative effect of the anti-Left swing in China on the level of its support for Cambodia and, more so, on the morale of the Cambodian party obviously worried Pol Pot. Henceforth at every opportunity the Cambodians would make a point of reminding China that the "gains of the Cultural Revolution" (that is, all the ultraleftist measures taken during the 1966–71 period) should be preserved and expanded, and that class struggle was the "key link" in building the country. At a banquet on December 10, welcoming a Xinhua News Agency delegation to Phnom Penh, Information Minister Hu Nim praised the smashing of the Gang of Four but pointedly announced that the Chinese people were "not allowing revisionism or the capitalist class to rear their heads"—an expression more of their concern than of conviction.

Chill Winds from Peking

What was the attitude of the Chinese leadership toward the Khmer Rouge? "Judging by the published account of remarks made by

Chinese officials visiting Phnom Penh in December, China was less than enthusiastic in its support." They politely ignored Cambodian remarks about the need for China to carry on class struggle. Neither did they offer their habitual support for Cambodia's "struggle in defending its independence and territorial integrity"—an indirect expression of backing for Cambodia against Vietnam. Their reticence to engage in ideological discussion and to give even veiled support may in part have been intended to warn Phnom Penh to stay out of Chinese politics. In any case, on his return from Cambodia Fang Yi, China's minister of economic relations with foreign countries, told the Romanian ambassador in Peking of his dislike of what he had seen in Cambodia. "They have gone too far in promoting self-reliance," he said. Talking to his Western colleagues during the same period, China's ambassador in Hanoi did not hide his astonishment at the extent of the Khmer Rouge drive for self-reliance. The Cambodians, he told a European ambassador, had not even made use of the commodity aid grant—the equivalent of $20 million—that China had provided in 1975.[6]

Private criticisms of the Khmer Rouge that diplomats and journalists heard from Chinese officials in the spring of 1977 clearly reflected sweeping changes taking place in China in the wake of the ouster of the radicals. In 1974, when the ultraleftist star was in the ascendant in China, an inner-party document had described the Cambodian Communists as the most brilliant upholders of Mao's thought abroad. But since 1975 the story of massacres and brutality brought out by Cambodian refugees had earned the Khmer Rouge worldwide notoriety. Western governments estimated that the Khmer Rouge were responsible for the death of more than a million of their countrymen since coming to power. By the end of 1976, with the Chinese media denouncing daily the myriad crimes of the Gang of Four in repressing the people, Peking officials were somewhat embarrassed at being seen abroad as the ideological mentors of the Khmer Rouge. One editor of a Chinese Communist newspaper in Hongkong told me in early 1977: "We cannot criticize them [Khmer Rouge] because it is not China's policy to interfere in the internal affairs of other countries. But we feel they have gone rather too far in practicing egalitarianism and self-reliance." He was particularly critical of the Khmer Rouge decision to abolish money, markets, and private property. Nor did he like the Khmer Rouge refusal to acknowledge the existence of the Communist Party of Kampuchea and to follow the classical Marxist-Leninist path of Socialist revolution by stages. Another Chinese official privately admitted to me how embarrassing it had been for China to turn a deaf ear to the plea of ethnic Chinese refugees from Cambodia for Peking's intervention to stop the killings. But China, he argued, could not meddle in Cambodia's internal affairs. Later events, however, were to prove that neither moral repugnance nor ideological disapproval would shake China's support for the Khmer Rouge—support based on the solid grounds of realpolitik.

An Anniversary to Kill

By a strange coincidence, while the inner-party struggle against the radicals was reaching its climax in China with the death of Mao and the arrest of the Gang of Four, the tide was flowing in the opposite direction in Cambodia. At the end of August 1976, the core of the Cambodian party leadership around Pol Pot held a three-day meeting at which they decided to totally collectivize agriculture and industry and to introduce nationwide communal kitchens. The building of communism, Pol Pot believed, had to be hurried in order to confront the Vietnamese with greater strength. As an article in the restricted party journal *Tung Padevat* (Revolutionary Flag) in June 1976 explained, "We want to build socialism quickly, we want to transform our country quickly, we want our people to be glorious quickly. This is especially to prevent the enemy from harming us."[7] The path to this "glory" was paved with the blood and tears of tens of thousands of people, who were forced to work in the field as beasts of burden, given scant meals at communal kitchens, and often punished with death for complaining about hard work. The work regime was particularly harsh for the "new people"—former city dwellers who were considered tainted by bourgeois ideology. They were to be cleansed through backbreaking manual labor. Those who were too weak to perform their tasks were of no use to revolutionary Cambodia. "To have them [urban population] is no gain, to lose them is no loss" was a chilling aphorism that Khmer Rouge cadres frequently repeated to their subjects.

Pol Pot also calculated that the heat of revolution would help to flush out opponents of his line within the party. As an internal party document stated in late 1976, "Evil microbes inside the party" will emerge, pushed out by the true nature of Socialist revolution.[8] Those who opposed or questioned this brutal course could only be, in Pol Pot's view, imperialists or Vietnamese agents bent on sabotaging Cambodia's great leap forward. The fact that by mid-1976 assassination attempts were made against Pol Pot perhaps provided added urgency to the search for potential opponents.

At least one of the many assassination plots against Pol Pot recounted in Democratic Kampuchea's *Black Book* was confirmed by a Khmer Rouge defector. After fleeing to Thailand, he told U.S. officials of a plot in mid-1976 to kill Pol Pot by poisoning his food. The attempt was foiled when one of Pol Pot's guards inadvertently sampled the poisoned food and died immediately. According to the defector, the plotters—a Khmer Rouge military commander, Chan Krey, and his associates—were motivated by the "hardships" that the people were made to endure.[9] It would not be surprising if the plotters also resented Pol Pot's virulent anti-Vietnamese policy, but there has been no evidence to support the claim of the *Black Book* that the Vietnamese were involved in it.

However, the beginning of systematic purges of party members in September 1976 was directly linked to the question of the Cambodian party's relations with Vietnam. Until then, the accepted date of the foundation of the Cambodian party was September 30, 1951— the date that made it a direct descendant of the Indochinese Communist Party founded by Ho Chi Minh in 1930. During the anti-French struggle (1946–54) there was close cooperation among the Vietnamese, Lao, and Cambodian movements, and many Cambodians came to value this partnership.

Veteran Cambodian Communist Keo Meas was one such leader, who wanted to reassert his party's Vietnamese origins by celebrating its twenty-fifth anniversary. Vietnam's domestic policy too appeared to be more in line with orthodox Marxism than with the radical Cambodian line. Meas perhaps felt the urgency to act in view of the radical plans adopted in August and Pol Pot's open admission of loyalty to Maoism in his eulogy of the deceased chairman. Cambodia historian David Chandler speculates that the apparent détente with

Vietnam in the middle of 1976 and the political uncertainty in China after Mao's death perhaps encouraged Meas to press for celebration of the numerologically significant twenty-fifth anniversary of the party at the end of September.[10]

Pol Pot, on the other hand, wanted to cut Cambodia loose from the perception that the Cambodian party owed its origins to the Vietnamese or that the only community of interest it shared was with the Vietnamese party. He decreed that the party's birth came not in 1951 but at the 1960 congress, when he became the deputy secretary. The rewritten history depicted the Cambodian party as beginning its "glorious" career with Pol Pot at the top and wiped out nine years of intimate—and subordinate—association with Vietnam, a period in which Pol Pot played no significant role. A special September-October issue of *Tung Padevat* was published to explain why the party's date of birth was not 1951 but 1960. "We must arrange the history of the party," an article in the journal, most probably penned by Pol Pot himself, said, "into something clean and perfect, in line with our policies of independence and self-mastery."[11]

Ten days before the anniversary was due to be celebrated, Pol Pot ordered the suspension of preparations and the arrest of Meas and another top leader, Nay Sarang. They were taken to the State Security Interrogation Center. The premises of Tuol Sleng Secondary School in Phnom Penh had been converted into a prison and interrogation center, code-named *S-21*. After a month of torture and a series of "confessions," they were put to death. In the next two years nearly twenty thousand party cadres and family members would be executed after processing through this notorious center.[12]

By disowning the historical link with Vietnam "Pol Pot was soon able to embark," Chandler notes, "as he had probably planned to do for some time, on a full-scale war against Vietnam as well as a radical program of collectivization inside Cambodia which owed nothing to Vietnamese models or advice."[13]

The *Tung Padevat* article left no doubt that the purges were also connected with opposition to the ultraleftist policies of Pol Pot, stating that some people in the party considered evacuation of cities and abolition of money and private property as "leftism." Then it asserted: "We had our reasons. And the movement has affirmed that we were right. . . . Left or no left, we must stand by the movement." It also charged that some people in the party had "opposed the movement and betrayed the revolution."[14]

On September 27, 1976, Radio Phnom Penh announced that a week earlier (the day Keo Meas was arrested, as it happened), the Central Committee of the People's Representative Assembly—Cambodia's rubber-stamp parliament—had allowed Pol Pot "temporary leave to take care of his health, which has been bad for several months," and appointed Nuon Chea as acting premier. Many observers hastily concluded that Pol Pot might have been purged. But his "sick leave" was in fact designed to give Pol Pot a free hand in curing the party of the cankers of dissent. Ken Quinn believes that Pol Pot may have decided to "go to the mattress" after surviving an assassination attempt in mid-1976.

Quinn's research led him to conclude that Pol Pot retreated to a secret, well-protected area where he would be safe from further attacks and where he could direct the effort to eliminate all of those involved in the plot to kill him. The evidence provided by refugees and survivors of the purge arriving in Thailand throughout 1977 indicated large-scale killing of "old Khmer Rouge" cadres (perhaps those sympathetic to Vietnam and favoring a moderate domestic policy, and thus Pol Pot's opponents) and suspected "reactionaries." At the time, the U.S. intelligence in Thailand also had specific information about Pol Pot's taking a direct hand in conducting the purge in northwest Cambodia.[15]

It is perhaps not surprising that throughout the latter part of 1976, while the purges began in full swing, Cambodia sought to maintain an apparent normalcy in relations with Vietnam. While the Pol Pot regime was busy cleansing its own ranks and implementing its radical program, it clearly wanted to keep Vietnam in good humor. In August a Cambodia women's delegation visited Hanoi. Pol Pot even received Ambassador Pham Van Ba to congratulate him on the occasion of the thirty-first anniversary of the Socialist Republic of Vietnam. On September 21 a ceremony was held at Phnom Penh's Pochentong Airport to mark the beginning of an Air Vietnam service to Phnom Penh from Ho Chi Minh City. The Vietnamese were most probably unaware that just the previous day one of their few Khmer friends, Keo Meas, had been taken to Tuol Sleng.

Addressing the United Nations in October, Ieng Sary made some barbed criticism of Vietnam without naming it, but he nevertheless called for its admission to the world body. Vietnam's entry to the United Nations was being blocked by U.S. veto. In Sary's absence, the acting foreign minister, Son Sen, received Ambassador Ba on October 28 for more than two hours. The subject of the conversation was not disclosed, but Radio Phnom Penh described the atmosphere as "cordial and intimate."[16]

The Cambodian party even quietly sent a delegation of seven "journalists" to attend the fourth congress of the Vietnamese party that began in Hanoi in mid-December 1976. The dispatch of the delegates and a message of the greetings from Angkar Padovat (the name used by the Cambodian Revolutionary Organization before the unveiling of the CPK) were part of an attempt to maintain the facade of normal relations. The "warmest congratulations" Phnom Penh sent to the Vietnamese party noted that Cambodia and Vietnam "already have a lasting militant revolutionary solidarity and fraternal friendship which has been tempered in the flames of revolutionary struggle."[17] The text of the message was published by Hanoi, but Radio Phnom Penh chose not to air it. At a time when Vietnam sympathizers were being hunted down by Pol Pot's security men, airing of a message like that in Cambodia would have sown confusion in the ranks.

Fear of Federation

The Vietnamese were increasingly suspicious of happenings inside the Cambodian party but did not have a clear picture. In a private conversation with a left-wing Thai visitor at the end of 1976, Vietnamese premier Pham Van Dong had expressed his concern about the safety of some "Cambodian friends." A number of former Cambodian diplomats who had served in the Sihanouk-led resistance government, he said, had written letters to friends in Hanoi before flying from Peking to Phnom Penh. But there had been no news of them since.[18]

Hanoi might not have had a clear picture of the purges within Cambodia, but it knew of the internal feud. In early March 1977 a Vietnamese diplomat in Vientiane told me of a "serious fight" within the Cambodian party between what he called the "100 percent pro-Mao Pol Pot" and those with the "correct line." The correct line was the one that called for friendship with Vietnam, he said, predicting that it "would finally emerge victorious." Dong had the same group in mind when he told the Thai visitor of his hope that "genuine revolutionaries" would emerge in Cambodia. This hope led Hanoi to play the good neighbor while looking for ways to meet the Pol Pot challenge. Perhaps it was out of the growing concern about Cambodian internal developments that the Vietnamese were ready to bend over backward to please Pol Pot. They did not want to provide him with any further pretext to worsen relations with Vietnam and corner Hanoi's friends within the party. A Vietnamese women's delegation was sent to Phnom Penh in early February 1977 to affirm solidarity. On February 15 a Vietnamese deputy foreign minister, Hoang Van Loi, arrived in Phnom Penh on an unpublicized two-day trip. His main task was to persuade the Cambodians to participate in an Indochinese summit. To sweeten the atmosphere he renewed the offer of fullest cooperation in the repatriation of Khmers who had fled from Cambodia to Vietnam in recent months.[19] At times, repatriation involved sordid business deals. In one such operation in early 1977, the Vietnamese provincial authorities allowed the Khmer Rouge to select forty-nine refugees from a camp in Moc Hoa to be taken back in exchange for one bull per person.[20]

However, the Cambodians turned down the idea of the summit, seeing the proposal as a further proof of unremitting Vietnamese efforts to bring all of Indochina under its mantle. Phnom Penh had reacted warily when, in February 1976, the term *special relationship* was used to describe Vietnam's relations with Laos. In December 1976 that wariness had turned into serious concern when Hanoi announced close permanent ties with Cambodia as its long-term objective. The resolution of the Vietnamese party congress announced that Vietnam would "preserve and develop the special relations between the Vietnamese people and the fraternal peoples of Laos and Kampuchea, strengthen the militant solidarity, mutual trust, long-term cooperation, and mutual assistance in all fields . . . so that the three countries which have been associated with one another in the struggle for national liberation will be forever associated with one another in the building and defense of their respective countries for the sake of each country's independence and prosperity."[21]

Sometime in late March 1977, after the purge begun the previous September had eliminated hundreds of cadres and put Pol Pot into firmer control of the party apparatus, a move was launched to find a Cambodian version of a "final solution" to the Vietnamese threat. Pol Pot seemed to have decided that the pretense of normalcy in the relationship with Vietnam could now be dropped. Time had come to begin a campaign to physically exterminate all ethnic Vietnamese still remaining in Cambodia and to go on the offensive in attacking Vietnam.

Ros Saroeun, a garage mechanic who survived the Pol Pot years, remembered that day vividly. It was early April 1977 in Oudong. While waiting for the Khmer Rouge district chief to arrive at his office to instruct him about cars to be repaired, Saroeun, craning his neck, noticed a letter on the desk marked "Directive from 870" dated April 1, 1977. At the time he did not know that "870" was the code for the all-powerful party Central Committee or the shadowy Angkar (organization). But the chilling message of the directive was clear: all ethnic Vietnamese in the district, and all Khmers who spoke Vietnamese or had Vietnamese friends, should be handed over to the state security service. Saroeun almost froze. As an orphan, Saroeun was raised by a Vietnamese garage owner in Phnom Penh. He not only spoke Vietnamese but was also married to a Vietnamese. Luckily she did not look Vietnamese, nor did their neighbors in the cooperative where they lived know that she was Vietnamese or that he spoke Vietnamese. After repairing the district committee's jeep, Saroeun hurried home to alert his wife. But she already knew. A Vietnamese woman in the village had been bludgeoned to death by the Khmer Rouge and buried just outside the village after they had sent her Khmer husband to cut wood in the jungle. The husband returned several days later to an empty house. Frightened neighbors would silently turn away from him. Wandering about the village, he came upon the horrible find—a hand sticking out of a freshly covered grave. He recognized the hand, but had no answer why.[22] Since March, in preparation for armed conflict with Vietnam, army units in Cambodia's Eastern Region were taken off their production duty to be combat-ready. On the night of April 30, 1977, the Khmer Rouge had mounted attacks on a string of villages and townships in An Giang Province in the Mekong Delta, killing civilians and burning down houses. The attack on Tinh Bien township alone had caused about one hundred civilian deaths. A year later I would be allowed to visit the ghost town of Tinh Bien to hear the accounts of the survivors of that fateful night of April 30. Although the Cambodians had, in fact, been raiding Vietnam's border provinces since January 1977, their choice of April 30 to launch the most vicious attack to date was rich with symbolism. It was the day when Vietnam was celebrating the second anniversary of the "liberation" of South Vietnam and preparing for the celebration of May Day—the international day of solidarity among the workers!

Hanoi Bets on Deng

There was suspense and exhilaration in Hanoi as the clattering teletype machine at the Foreign Ministry announced Mao's death. For several months since the death of Zhou Enlai in January 1976 reports from Peking had indicated an intensified power struggle in which the radicals seemed to have gained ground but were not unchallenged. Would Mao's demise toll the death knell for the Left, too? That at least was Hanoi's hope. Not to miss an opportunity to restore some cordiality in their frosty relations, the Vietnamese sent a special plane carrying wreaths to Peking. Almost the entire Vietnamese Politburo trouped into the pagoda-style Chinese embassy in Hanoi to sign the condolence book.

The Vietnamese could barely suppress their jubilation when, on October 12, they heard the news of the arrest of the "Gang of Four." An exuberant Vietnamese official told the correspondent of the French Communist party paper l'Humanité, "Maybe next year you will go to Peking to cover the developments there."[23] It was quite a bold prediction at a time when members of the pro-Soviet PCF were unwelcome in China. The Vietnamese indeed had high hopes that, with the radicals ousted, China would return to its senses and take a less chauvinistic and more pragmatic attitude in dealing with Vietnam. If the moderate line of the late Zhou Enlai and disgraced Deng Xiaoping reemerged in China, Hanoi could perhaps expect a better understanding of its independent position.

Vietnam's ambassador in China, Nguyen Trong Vinh, for one, was confident. He told some of his colleagues that if Deng returned to power a solution for the Sino-Vietnamese disputes over the South China Sea islands would be found. Vinh noted that when the Vietnamese party secretary Le Duan met Deng in September 1975 the latter acknowledged that there was a dispute and that he wanted to get it settled later. But since the beginning of the anti-Deng campaign in late 1975, Peking had hardened its position by declaring the islands as nonnegotiable "sacred territory of the motherland." A rehabilitation of Deng, the Vietnamese hoped, could bring back a more pragmatic approach.[24]

The Vietnamese were in the midst of drawing up their second five-year plan when the news of the changes in Peking came. For more than a year the Vietnamese leaders had gone around the Socialist world trying to secure aid for their plan. The only major Socialist country that had refused to make any long-term commitment was China. With the radicals ousted from the Peking leadership, Hanoi wanted to determine whether China had changed its mind. On October 15, three days after the reports of the fall of the radicals, Hanoi sent a letter to Peking requesting aid. But there had been no reply from Peking by December, when the Vietnamese party congress opened at the flag-and-banner-bedecked Ba Dinh Hall in Hanoi. Nor was there any Chinese delegate among the twenty-nine fraternal parties attending the congress. The question mark that hung over Peking inevitably left an impression of tentativeness in Vietnamese policy formulation. The party's foreign policy line focused principally on the nonaligned bloc and the Third World, leaving out the fundamental issues dividing Peking and Moscow. Although the Vietnamese party differed from the Chinese in identifying U.S. imperialism as the principal threat to world peace, it took care to praise both the Soviet Union and China for their Socialist achievements. However, the Vietnamese also made it clear that they did not believe in any universal model for revolution: each country should develop a strategy and tactics appropriate for its own specific conditions.

The suspense about China's reaction to Vietnam's nonaligned approach ended in late February 1977, when Peking finally replied to the Vietnamese letter of the previous October—one that had been written ostensibly to seek aid but really to test the waters in post-Mao China. It was a polite no. China was unable to meet the Vietnamese plea for help, Peking told a visiting Vietnamese vice-minister, because China itself was reeling from the damages caused by the Gang of Four and a severe earthquake.[25]

This was not just a pretext, nor was it an adequate explanation for China's refusal. After nearly a decade of turmoil and civil war conditions and the disastrous earthquake in Hebei Province (July 1976) that killed nearly 700,000 people and left more than a million homeless, the Chinese economy was in shambles. But this did not prevent China from dispatching Fang Yi to Phnom Penh in December to sign an aid agreement with Cambodia to provide "complete sets of equipment." The reasons for Chinese refusal to commit new aid to Vietnam perhaps lay in the political instability in Peking. The fact that Peking took more than four months to answer Vietnam's letter was indicative of controversy over the issue. The tenor of that debate may never be known, but the Vietnamese hopes for a new moderate line in Peking under Deng proved misplaced. It would not be until the end of 1978 that Deng would emerge as the unchallenged leader, and by then the changed international situation would make him the most resolute enemy of Vietnam. In the spring of 1977 neither the Maoists around Hua nor the pragmatists led by Deng were secure enough to venture new foreign policy initiatives, especially if it meant reversal of a policy followed since 1975. In view of the bitterness created by territorial dispute, Hanoi's controversial treatment of ethnic Chinese in Vietnam, and its move toward establishing preeminence in Indochina, a positive Chinese approach was not easy to obtain. The Chinese leadership would have needed vision, sophistication, and a lot of political courage to actively encourage Vietnam in its search for an independent policy and to respond to its security concerns. Instead of welcoming Vietnam's efforts to improve relations with the West as a counterbalance to Moscow, the insecure leaders of China frowned upon the move. In the end, the weight of a thousand years of checkered history and the fear of Soviet-Vietnamese collusion determined the course to be followed vis-à-vis Hanoi: It was to be stick rather than carrot. By opting for a traditional, and politically safer, approach, Peking deprived itself of the leverage it still had over Vietnam.

While the Chinese reply dashed Hanoi's expectations for a rapprochement, the latter's hope that China's new leadership would steer away from the Khmer Rouge also seemed increasingly remote. After five months of benign neglect of Southeast Asia when Peking was in turmoil, the Chinese leaders were once again turning their attention to the region. In a clear attempt to demonstrate China's break with the radical policies of the recent past, the pragmatic late premier Zhou Enlai's widow, Madame Deng Yingchao, was sent on China's first high-level mission to Burma in years. This visit was followed by others to Pakistan and Sri Lanka. After months of maintaining a low profile toward Peking, Ieng Sary was again visiting China and being entertained at banquets by high officials. Hanoi noted with concern the presence of General Wang Shangrong, a deputy chief of the General Staff of the Chinese army, at a March 31 Peking banquet for Sary given by Vice-Premier Li Xiannian. Wang's presence could only indicate that military cooperation with Cambodia was on the agenda.

China began encouraging Cambodia to come out of its petulant isolationist stance and to counter Vietnamese effort in wooing non-Communist countries in the region. Peking media, which had maintained a conspicuous silence about Vietnamese vice–foreign minister Phan Hien's trip to the ASEAN countries in July 1976 (the first since the end of the war), gave enthusiastic coverage of Ieng Sary's visit to the region. One reassuring message that Sary carried to Malaysia, Singapore, and Burma was that there was no united "Red Indochina" under Hanoi's control. "Cambodians," Sary told Singapore deputy premier Sinnathamby Rajaratnam, "do not believe in Indochina Federation." He then went on to apprise the Singaporeans of Cambodia's territorial problem with Vietnam. What Democratic Kampuchea wants, Sary said in an apparent reversal of

Cambodia's isolationist approach, is good-neighborly relations with Singapore and trade ties.[26]

As Sary continued his Southeast Asian tour, after months of silence on the subject China resumed its public claims over the South China Sea islands. A Chinese newspaper article on March 14, 1977, reminded Vietnam of China's continued desire to recover the Spratly Islands.[27] The public statements from Phnom Penh and Peking on April 17, 1977, on the occasion of the second anniversary of the Khmer Rouge victory left no doubts about Cambodia's desire to escalate the tension with Vietnam nor about China's commitment to the Pol Pot regime. At a banquet in Phnom Penh, Sary made an announcement that was a thinly disguised admission of the anti-Vietnamese purges in the country. At a banquet in Peking on the same occasion, Chinese foreign minister Huang Hua acclaimed Democratic Kampuchea for frustrating "the sabotage of foreign and domestic enemies." He assured Cambodia that China would follow Mao's foreign policy line in allying with small countries against big-power subversion, interference, or bullying. "We are confident," Huang said, "that in the future the Chinese and Cambodian peoples will unite still more closely, fight shoulder to shoulder, and advance together along the road of our common struggle."[28]

Barely two weeks after such encouraging words were uttered the Khmer Rouge had launched the first major attack on Vietnam. The Vietnamese had retaliated with aerial bombing using A-37 Dragonfly fighter bombers left behind by the United States. But neither side had reported the developments along their common border. The first unpublicized Vietnamese warning to Cambodia, in the form of a diplomatic note, was not issued until June 7—just a day before Pham Van Dong's arrival in Peking. The Vietnamese Foreign Ministry had handed over a letter to So Kheang, Democratic Kampuchean ambassador in Hanoi, proposing high-level talks to settle the border problem and put an end to the "bloody incidents"—an obvious reference to the Khmer Rouge attacks on Tinh Bien and other parts of An Giang Province. The Vietnamese also pointed an accusing finger for the first time at the leadership in Phnom Penh "The use of considerable armed forces for simultaneous operations over a large area and for such a long period," the letter said, "cannot proceed from the initiative of local Cambodian authorities." The letter then asked, "Have these actions been perpetrated by a group, a faction of ill-intentioned persons, in an attempt to sabotage the traditions of solidarity and fraternal friendship binding our two parties and peoples?"[29]

A day later the Vietnamese army daily *Quan Doi Nhan Dan* gave the first public hint of problems at the border by calling for combat-readiness to repel sudden enemy attacks. It was, however, not until 1978 that the Vietnamese population was told about the identity of the enemy or the location of the troubled border.

On June 18 Cambodia replied to the Vietnamese proposal for talks by saying that they could resume only after "a period of time" when the situation returned to normal.[30] And a week later Cambodia gave the first unambiguous public hint of its troubles with Vietnam by praising the cadres and combatants in Kampot Province, bordering Vietnam, for their "sacrifice in order to protect and maintain the territorial border, territorial waters, seas, and islands forever."[31]

Peking Bares Its Teeth

The sharp deterioration in relations with Cambodia had come while Vietnamese defense minister General Vo Nguyen Giap was on a visit to the Soviet Union and Eastern Europe. The cautious Vietnamese leaders, anxious as ever to maintain their independence of action, did not want to be seen by Peking as openly allying with Moscow. Even if their political inclinations and economic needs led them closer to Moscow, they knew China was too important to be antagonized. In June, soon after his return from Moscow, General Giap left for a "friendly official visit" to China, leading a large military delegation, diplomatically matching the size of the one he had led earlier to the Soviet Union. But the visit went badly. The Vietnamese were miffed that Giap was not received at the airport nor at a welcoming banquet by his formal host, Marshal Ye Jianying. All substantive talks were with a second-ranking leader. Giap reportedly stunned his Chinese hosts by "revealing" that Chinese advisers to the Khmer Rouge had been taken prisoner in May during an attack on Vietnam.[32]

To show displeasure at the Chinese treatment of Giap, the Vietnamese army newspaper published on its front page, alongside reports of the general's China visit, a story on the Hanoi museum that contains exhibits of Vietnam's thousand-year fight for independence against China.

On June 8, the day after Giap left Peking, Premier Pham Van Dong arrived from Moscow for a transit stop. During an earlier stop at the Chinese capital in April on his way to Paris, Dong had sought a meeting to discuss various problems. The meeting was now arranged. He sat down for a candid conversation with Vice-Premier Li Xiannian, who, as the late Premier Zhou Enlai's right-hand man in economics, had long been involved in the question of aid to Vietnam. But this time there was no question of the Vietnamese side's presenting Peking with a wish list. Li submitted to Dong a memorandum—a litany of grievances against Vietnam. He accused Vietnam of pursuing an anti-China policy in words and in action. In 1975 China had proposed negotiations on the boundary question. "But you," Li told Dong, "while stalling negotiations with us, continued to let your men enter Chinese territory illegally, claim[ing] this or that place as belonging to Vietnam. . . . They even engaged in fistfighting and other acts of violence."[33]

The number of border incidents, he charged, had jumped from one hundred in 1974 to nine hundred in 1976. After having recognized Chinese sovereignty over South China Sea islands such as the Paracels and the Spratlys for a number of years, Vietnam had invaded and occupied the Spratlys in 1975, turning them into a major subject of dispute, he said. Li also charged Hanoi with reneging on its past commitment by using coercion against the Chinese residents of Vietnam. Hanoi never revealed Dong's reaction to being put in the dock by Li. According to the Chinese, he said Vietnam's volteface on the islands was an exigency of war. Dong is reported by the Chinese to have said that, while busy fighting the Americans and needing Chinese assistance, Vietnam could not pay much attention to the islands question.

That bitter encounter between erstwhile comrades at Peking's Great Hall of the People was a watershed. Pretenses, allegorical tales, and veiled criticisms had given way to sharp words and ugly confrontation. The tensions were not public yet, but teeth had been bared.

An Offensive Friendship

General Giap's troubled China trip and Pham Van Dong's acrimonious encounter with Li Xiannian in June, just a month after
the brutal Khmer Rouge assaults on Vietnamese villages, only added
urgency to Hanoi's search for security. The events of April–June
were seen by the Vietnamese as further evidence to support their
long-held belief that their own security was tied closely with that of
Laos and Cambodia. If a power hostile to Vietnam established a
close relationship with either, Vietnamese strategists had argued,
that association would seriously threaten Vietnam's security. Shortly
after his return from China, Dong was off again, this time to Laos
to sign a treaty of friendship—the first barrier against possible Chinese
intervention in Indochina.

A measure of how close the cooperation would be between Laos
and Vietnam was given by the record number of top brass who accompanied the Vietnamese delegation to Vientiane on the morning
of July 15. Apart from the party secretary-general Le Duan and
Premier Pham Van Dong, there were two other Politburo members,
two Central Committee members, and a host of other senior officials. This was the first time Laos had received and Hanoi had ever
sent such a high-level delegation. Almost the entire Lao government—from the mustached "Red Prince" (President Souphanouvong) and Premier Kaysone to the most junior minister—had turned
out to greet the Vietnamese at the airport. The next day a mass
rally was held near That Luang—the golden-spired Buddhist pagoda
that dominates Vientiane's skyline—to give a public welcome to the
guests. Few among the citizens assembled there by the party had
understood the significance of Kaysone's remarks about smashing
"the perfidious and crafty schemes and acts of sabotage by the imperialists and their henchmen, the reactionaries" or the meaning of
his vow to "do all we can to strengthen our close unity with Socialist
Vietnam."[34]

Only later events made it clear that Kaysone was obliquely refer-
ring to the "crafty schemes" of China and the Khmer Rouge to break
Vietnam's special relations with Indochinese neighbors. The Lao-
Vietnamese response to those "schemes" was unveiled on the morn-

ing of July 18. Before departing for Hanoi the Vietnamese signed with Laos a treaty of friendship and cooperation so that the two countries could "remain united forever in national construction and defense." Article One of the twenty-five-year treaty enjoined the signatories to educate their party and people "constantly to value, protect, and foster the special Vietnam-Laos relationship so that it will remain pure and steady forever." It was a clause aimed at dispelling the traditional Lao antipathy toward the Vietnamese and preventing the emergence of chauvinism or an anti-Vietnamese paranoia of the type raging in Cambodia. Article Two said that, while national security remained the responsibility of each country, "both sides pledge to support and assist each other wholeheartedly and to cooperate closely in increasing the capability of defending and protecting independence, sovereignty, and territorial integrity [of each other's country] . . . and opposing all schemes and acts of sabotage by the imperialists and foreign reactionary forces."[35]

The treaty of friendship and other agreements laid the legal basis for close political coordination and for Vietnam's security role in Laos—which had been facts of life since the birth of the Lao republic. The treaty, however, did more than formalize a reality. It put China and Cambodia on notice that their opposition notwithstanding, Hanoi was determined to maintain its leadership in Indochina. If anything, Cambodian attacks on Vietnam had made Hanoi's search for a special relation to Laos and Cambodia a high-priority objective, not a distant dream.

For Pol Pot the Lao-Vietnamese treaty was the final confirmation of his worst fear. Vietnam had taken the plunge in erecting its long-planned Indochina Federation. He had no doubt that the Vietnamese ambition was to "take possession of the whole of Cambodia under the form of the Indochina Federation by sending every year many hundreds of thousands or millions of Vietnamese to come and install themselves in Cambodia." If the Vietnamese had their way, in thirty years or more, he told Yugoslav journalists in March 1978, "the people of Cambodia would become a national minority."[36] The Vietnamese decision to bind Laos with a treaty of special relations was, for him, an indication that it had made up its mind to annex Cambodia.[37]

Pol Pot's loathing of the treaty was not aired publicly. In a brief report on the Vietnamese visit to Laos, Radio Phnom Penh, darkly hinting at the cavalier Vietnamese disregard of Lao sovereignty, had spelled out only the consular agreement by which Lao and Vietnamese officials "could cross the border without visas."[38]

The Hubris of Victory

In a curious coincidence, on the very day—July 17, 1977—that the Vietnamese leadership was concluding its treaty-signing visit to Laos, top party cadres of Cambodia's Eastern Zone were gathered in a secret location to work out their strategy against Vietnam. The resolution adopted at that meeting came to light months later, when a copy fell into Vietnamese hands during a sweep operation into Cambodia. The resolution told the cadres that Vietnam had a "dark scheme to conquer our land and destroy the Khmer race," and so the conflict "can never be resolved politically." In a clear allusion to purged cadres who refused to follow the anti-Vietnamese line, the resolution asked, "Do we think we can solve it [the conflict with Vietnam] in accordance with the line of our party or must we solve it in accordance with the cowardly position of a group of traitors who kneel down and work as lackeys of the *yuon*? We must be determined never to be lackeys of the *yuon*."

The resolution urged the combatants to be ready to annihilate the Vietnamese if they invaded Cambodia. "We must not only stop them and annihilate them on our territory," it said, "but must cross the border to stop them and annihilate them right on their territory. This is intended to cause more difficulties to them and to increase their fear of us. Then, after some time, they will no longer dare invade our country, and it will be their turn to strive to resist us."[39]

The resolution did not elaborate what would be the Khmer objective when the Vietnamese would be on the defensive. But while exhorting the soldiers to fight Vietnam in early 1977, some Pol Pot followers had already started raising the irredentist dream of recovering Kampuchea Krom (lower Cambodia, today's Mekong Delta) and Prey Nokor (the original Khmer name for Saigon).[40]

Did Pol Pot really believe his ill-equipped, young soldiers would be able to defeat Vietnam? Like Mao, he had faith in the supremacy of men over machine and weapon. To this was added the chauvinistic pride of the Khmer Rouge in the prowess and ability of their nation. "If our people can make [the temples of] Angkor, they can make anything," Pol Pot had declared in September 1977. He had convinced himself that the Khmer Rouge had actually defeated the entire United States and had helped the Vietnamese to win their victory. Everything was possible after such an amazing feat. Soldiers of an expansionist Vietnam, Pol Pot reasoned, could never be a match for dedicated Cambodian fighters for a just national cause. The strength of Democratic Kampuchea, Pol Pot said, was the purity of its army, of its base organizations. He told a party meeting, "If we coordinate our forces well we can certainly win victory over Annam [Vietnam] because ours is a collectivist society whereas Annamite society is wracked by private property, chaos, and disorder."[41]

The "successes" achieved by his men in destroying Vietnamese villages and massacring civilians in surprise raids since April 1977 and the lack of Vietnamese response might well have boosted Pol Pot's confidence. The fact that Hanoi faced a severe food crisis, deep social malaise in the South, and armed resistance from different groups—at least one of which, the United Front for the Struggle of Oppressed Races (FULRO), received material support from the Khmer Rouge—might also have emboldened the Khmer Rouge to challenge Vietnam.

The Pol Pot regime had also come to the conclusion that a negotiated settlement of the territorial dispute with Vietnam was not feasible. Only by a show of force along the border and public assertion of its claims of territorial waters could Cambodia maintain its independence and territorial integrity. During the border talks in May 1976, Vietnamese negotiator Phan Hien had refused to accept the Brevié line as the demarcation for territorial waters. The talks adjourned at the time had not resumed, but on May 12, 1977, Hanoi had announced that its economic zone extended to two hundred miles from its shores.[42]

Although Vietnam said it was ready to "settle through negotiations with countries concerned all matters relating to the maritime zones and continental shelf of each country on the basis of mutual respect for independence and sovereignty in accordance with international law," Cambodia had no faith in such promises. The August 1977 issue of *Democratic Kampuchea Advances*, a glossy propaganda magazine for foreign consumption, published a map of Cambodia. The only noticeable feature of the small sketch was a dotted line (the Brevié line) on the Gulf of Thailand showing Cambodia's territorial waters. That was Phnom Penh's response to Vietnam's public declaration about its maritime zone.

On July 30 a Radio Phnom Penh commentary noted that in the past the "traitorous cliques in power" in Cambodia allowed imperialists to encroach upon Cambodia's territorial waters. But they could no longer do this in "the current revolutionary phase of defending and building the country." The commentary listed all the islands under Cambodian control and announced the country's determination not to tolerate "any aggression or encroachment by any enemy from near or distant lands against our territorial waters and islands."[43] The Cambodia-Vietnam conflict had reached a point when the Pol Pot regime felt the need to issue a dramatic warning to Hanoi.

Mystery Man in Peking

On September 28, 1977, there was an air of expectancy in Peking. It had been a long time since the city had seen such festivities. The year 1976 had begun with Zhou Enlai's death. It had been followed in succession by a political riot in Peking, a devastating earthquake, the demise of Chairman Mao Zedong, and a dramatic changing of guards. A benumbed China had heaved a sign of relief at the fall of the radicals but had very little else to rejoice at. The celebration of the twenty-eighth anniversary of the People's Republic on October 1 was going to be the first festival in post-Mao China. But few had guessed that it would be the world premiere for a faceless Cambodian leader and a ceremony for anointing the Sino-Khmer alliance. The Gate of Heavenly Peace—an imposing pagodalike building with a wide balcony with carved marble railings that commands the entrance to the imperial palace and the vast square in front—was decked with flags. That the decorations were not only for China's national day was obvious from the yellow-and-red flags of Democratic Kampuchea that fluttered on the balcony alongside Chinese standards. All along Changan Avenue, which runs in front of the Gate of Heavenly Peace, lampposts, with large lotuslike white lamps on top, were draped with flags of the two Asian allies. Hundreds of schoolchildren, holding colored cards, packed the viewing gallery on both sides of the gate. On cue they would hold up the cards over their heads to produce a jigsaw pattern that said *welcome* in Chinese and Khmer. A hundred thousand Peking residents were brought to line the area outside the airport and Changan Avenue to greet the exceptional Cambodian guests. Few of the assembled Chinese had any clue as to who the honored visitors were. But from the lavishness of the preparations, they knew that these were very special friends of China's. Bathed in a mild autumn sun, Peking in fact was celebrating the return to earth of Democratic Kampuchea.

The veil of mystery that shrouded the Khmer Rouge leadership was partially lifted that morning, when a smiling Khmer with crewcut hair and sporting a dark Mao-style tunic emerged from the Chinese Boeing 707. The man, the supremo of the Cambodian revolution who had never been seen in public, was Pol Pot. Since the spring of 1976, when Pol Pot was announced by Radio Phnom Penh as Democratic Kampuchea's first prime minister, there had been unending speculation about the true identity of this total unknown. The mystery had further deepened when only four months after his nomination as prime minister it was announced that he had temporarily stepped down for reasons of health. For a whole year his name was never heard again until he stepped on the red carpet in Peking Airport. The mystery man had finally appeared in flesh and blood under the glare of worldwide publicity. Grinning broadly, with his narrow eyes almost disappearing into creases, Pol Pot warmly shook hands with the Chinese premier and party chairman Hua Guofeng on the tarmac. Eight top leaders, nearly a third of the Chinese party's powerful Politburo, including freshly rehabilitated Vice-Premier Deng Xiaoping, gathered at the airport to underline the closeness of China's friendship with Democratic Kampuchea. Accompanied by Hua, Pol Pot stood in an open limousine to be driven down Changan

Avenue as the well-rehearsed crowd beat gongs, waved paper flags of Democratic Kampuchea, and released hundreds of balloons to the sky. A roar of applause followed the motorcade along its route.

At a Peking press conference for Chinese journalists Pol Pot gave a brief sketch of his revolutionary life, but he never told who he really was. Comparing the biographical details and his photographs, analysts concluded that Pol Pot was one and the same as Communist leader Saloth Sar, who had disappeared from Phnom Penh in 1963. With the exception of his Chinese and North Korean friends and a handful of foreign specialists, few realized that Pol Pot had emerged from the shadows only after conducting a year of bloody purges against his real and suspected opponents in the party. He now felt secure enough to declare to the world the existence of the Communist Party of Kampuchea, hidden so long under the cloak of the anonymous Angkar, and to undertake his first foreign trip as the secretary of the party and prime minister.

At the Chinese national day celebration on the evening of October 1, guest of honor Pol Pot stood next to Chairman Hua Guofeng on the rostrum atop the Gate of Heavenly Peace to watch the fireworks display. Among other foreign guests present that evening was Hoang Van Hoan. Though removed from the Central Committee he was still vice-chairman of the Vietnamese National Assembly. One wonders whether Hoan had a quiet meeting with Pol Pot to hear first-hand the Cambodian complaints or to confide in him the thinking of the Vietnamese leadership. The thought is particularly tantalizing because two years later Hoan would shock the world by becoming the first top Vietnamese leader to defect to China and denounce Hanoi's policy toward Cambodia.

In the banquet speeches and press conference given in Peking, Pol Pot alluded to the loss of Cambodian territory to its neighbors [Vietnam and Thailand] in the past, and, with Vietnam clearly in mind, he declared: "We will not tolerate any aggression, provocation, interference, subversion, and espionage activities by anyone against our Democratic Kampuchea and its people." The revolutionary regime in Cambodia, he said, "must defend our existing frontiers and see to it that they will never be lost."[44]

In confidential discussions with the Chinese leaders, Pol Pot, however, talked of offensive, not defensive, actions against Vietnam. He told Hua and other leaders that in his judgment the morale of the Vietnamese army was low and that it wouldn't be able to endure privations as it had in the past. "In this juncture, if the revolutionary movement in Southeast Asia intensifies its attacks, the situation will improve and we will be able to resolve our problems." He also informed the Chinese that the Cambodian party had exchanged views with the Thai, Indonesian, Malaysian, and Burmese parties on this subject and that they were all in agreement. "Although there still are some problems in executing this policy," he said, "in the north we have support of the Chinese friends and in Southeast Asia we have unanimity among friends. This strategic turn is a great encouragement to us."[45]

As purloined secret documents from Peking would reveal years later, Pol Pot was not exaggerating the extent of Chinese support. In a confidential report on the international situation delivered to a party group on July 30, 1977, Huang Hua said that the purge of Soviet revisionist infiltrators undertaken by Pol Pot was just, because it "purified its army and fortified its fighting ability." These purges, coupled with the Cambodian refusal to accept the Vietnamese as Big Brother and ideological divergences between Vietnam and antirevisionist Cambodia, he said, had led to the outbreak of fighting. The "revisionist infiltrators" referred to by Huang Hua were those who were opposed to Pol Pot's radicalism and friendly to Vietnam. Although he mentioned Soviet revisionist meddling, he clearly had Vietnam in mind when he evoked the possibility of war between Cambodia and the revisionists. "A big war sometimes determines which of the two is superior," he said, "and through a decisive war, problems are resolved. Although the loss is somewhat heavy, the solution is complete." China, he said, could not stand idly by and allow the Soviet revisionists to meddle in Cambodian sovereignty: "We firmly support the decision of the Cambodian nation and people to resist social imperialism and shall provide them with all aid which is within our power to give."[46]

It is difficult to know whether this startling willingness to back a "big war" represented a unanimous Chinese decision or was more a reflection of a leftist swing in the continued power struggle between the Maoists and pragmatists in the Chinese leadership. The fact that subsequent Chinese documents were silent about this decision and that several months later one of Peking's moderate leaders tried to restrain the Khmer Rouge adventurism against Vietnam suggests that in the fall of 1977 support for Pol Pot came essentially from the Left faction.

But the intricacies of China's internal politics concerning Cambodia were well hidden from foreigners. For the world outside, China's message was clear. No matter what the Western press said about the killings in Cambodia, China stood by its allies. "The heroic Kampuchean people are not only good at destroying the old world," Hua declared in a banquet speech, "but also good at building a new one." Using opaque jargon, he also announced Chinese blessings for Pol Pot's purges and anti-Vietnamese actions. He hailed his success in defending Cambodia's territorial integrity—in other words, his border war with Vietnam—and in smashing the "subversive and disruptive schemes of enemies at home and abroad." Hua told a beaming Pol Pot, "As your brothers and comrades-in-arms, the Chinese people are overjoyed at your brilliant victories."[47]

Pol Pot's triumphant visit to China not only dispelled the miasma of suspicion and uncertainty that had hung over Sino-Cambodian relations since fall 1976 but also helped to shore up his own position within the Cambodian party. The visit clearly showed that China's friendship for Cambodia was rooted above all in historic and geostrategic considerations. Ideological differences were not to override Peking's interest in supporting a Cambodia that would stand up to China's major regional rival—Vietnam.

Prince Norodom Sihanouk:
The Retreat

FOR SIHANOUK it was a relief of sorts to get away from the cold and smog of Peking. Phnom Penh in December has mild sunny days. There is not that oppressive humidity of summer months. After the last trace of light disappears from the mirrorlike water of the Mekong, there is even a slight nip in the air. It felt good to be back after five years' exile. But the days were very empty compared with the hectic pace he had maintained all his life—even while in exile in Peking. He had wished to become the roving ambassador of new Cambodia, going round the world to seek sympathy, support, and aid to rebuild the devastated country. But that idea was turned down by the Khmer Rouge. They could not trust the "feudal" prince to represent their fundamentalist revolution with zeal, even sympathy. In fact, for the Khmer Rouge the need of the hour was to shun the world and refashion the society in laboratorylike isolation. By remaining the titular head of the country, Sihanouk could reassure the world that all was well in Cambodia as the Khmer Rouge carried on their brutal experiments.

During a conversation with Chairman Mao in 1975 before the collapse of Phnom Penh, Sihanouk had said he would like to retire after the Khmer Rouge victory. He simply could not cooperate with them. Mao had vigorously opposed. "You should help the Khmer Rouge. Your differences with them are only two-tenths, and there are eight-tenths of mutual understanding. Forget the 20 percent." Sihanouk said, "Mr. Chairman, that's impossible," but did not engage in argument with the ailing Mao. In the end, Sihanouk went back to Cambodia. But he soon began to realize that his differences with the Khmer Rouge were not 20 percent, as Mao had said, but total.

One of the earliest indications of what an oppressive, xenophobic bunch the Khmer Rouge were was an incident at the Cuban national day reception in the state guesthouse. As was customary, Sihanouk began reading his toast in Khmer and paused for someone to translate. None of the French-trained Khmer Rouge leaders volunteered. Khieu Samphan, himself the possessor of a doctorate from the Sorbonne, could be seen nudging another French-educated intellectual, Suong Sikoeun, the former director of Khmer Press Agency. After waiting for a while, Sihanouk himself provided a French translation of his toast. In Pol Pot's Cambodia, knowledge of a foreign language was a mark of slavery that was better not to flaunt.

The few times he sat down with Khieu Samphan, Foreign Minister Ieng Sary, or Minister of Information Hu Nim, they politely turned down the smallest of his suggestions. "Why not allow the people in the cooperative at least Sunday off?" he asked. The answer was: "We cannot stop the revolutionary zeal of the people wanting to overfulfill their targets." Frustrated, Sihanouk had taken recourse to acerbic remarks and sarcasm to vent his feelings.

A few weeks after his arrival in Phnom Penh, Sihanouk invited the newly arrived Vietnamese ambassador from the South, Pham Van Ba, for lunch. The invitation in itself was ironic. In his earlier incarnation as undercover Vietnamese Communist operative in Phnom Penh, the diminutive Ba once had to flee from Sihanouk's police. Later he surfaced as the Paris representative of the Vietcong Provisional Revolutionary Government. The lunch was attended by Hu Nim, information minister of the Cambodian government, which still styled itself Royal Government of National Union—known by its groaning French acronym GRUNK. Ba offered Sihanouk a presentation on the difficulties facing the newly liberated South Vietnam. "But Cambodia too is in a bad way," Sihanouk intervened, to the visible discomfort of Hu Nim. As Ba explained to me later, he wanted to deflect Sihanouk's verbal assault. "Well," he said, "both South Vietnam and Cambodia are two sick countries left behind by U.S. imperialism. It is now time to heal them." Undeterred by Ba's moderating words, the prince retorted, "That is true, but the leaders here have applied a very strong dose of medicine." In the embarrassed silence that fell, Ba glanced at Hu Nim. He was staring at the floor.[1] A year later Hu Nim was executed on charges of being a CIA spy.

In February 1976 the first group of seven foreign envoys—from European, Arab, and African countries based in Peking—were invited to visit Phnom Penh to present their credentials. Conversations during a dinner in honor of the ambassadors gave Sihanouk another opportunity to vent his feelings through heavy irony. One of the ambassadors asked him how Cambodia could build itself when all the intellectuals have been dispatched to the countryside. "We don't lack intellectuals here," the prince quipped, moving his hand around the table. "There is Khieu Samphan, who has a doctorate in economics, there is Thioun Thioeunn, a medical doctor, there is Ieng Sary, a French-educated intellectual . . . ," he rattled off in a mock argument as the guests sat in uneasy silence. The diplomats had already seen the ghost city, its moneyless economy, the demolished National Bank, and scattered currency notes strewn about the streets, blowing in the wind. They could not have missed how terribly intellectual all this was.

The days of occasional banquets when Sihanouk could meet foreign visitors were to end soon. Successive blows to Sihanouk's fate were struck almost a week after his return to Phnom Penh. On January 5 he signed the new constitution of Democratic Kampuchea replacing that of the Kingdom of Cambodia. It was evident that the new "people's state" would have little use for him. On January 8, 1976, his friend and protector Zhou Enlai died. Within a week of Zhou's death a press campaign started in China against his chosen successor, Deng Xiaoping. This was a signal of the reemergence of the radicals in China—the soul mates of the Khmer Rouge. It was not surprising that Sihanouk's request to go to Peking to pay his last respects had been rebuffed. As the Khmer Rouge braced to announce a new government, Sihanouk thought it was now the time to call it quits. The Khmer Rouge were only too pleased to accept his resignation.

But to quietly let him retire would only create suspicion abroad. So for the first time since his return, the prince was given a chance to speak on the radio. After his resignation speech was approved by the Angkar, an official came to his residence to record it. In an emotion-choked voice, Sihanouk read his farewell message to the nation, to be broadcast on April 2, 1976:

> When the coup d'état of Lon Nol and his clique took place in Phnom Penh on 18 March 1970, I swore to myself and to the Cambodian people that after I had accompanied my countrymen to complete victory over U.S. imperialism and the traitorous clique, and after the opening of the new revolutionary era, I would retire completely and forever from the political scene, for my role would logically come to an end. . . .
>
> For the rest of my life I shall remain grateful to the Cambodian people, Cambodian heroes and heroines, and the Cambodian revolutionary Angkar for clearing my name so fully in the eyes of the world and history. It is with this sentiment and in the conviction that our people and revolutionary Angkar understand me as one of their fellows that I request them to permit me to retire today.

Two days later Radio Phnom Penh announced that the government had regretfully accepted the resignation and conferred upon Sihanouk the title of Great Patriot. The government proposed to build a monument in his honor and pay him a retirement pension of $8,000 a year. That monument was never heard of again. Years later I asked Sihanouk what he did with that $8,000 pension in cashless Cambodia. "Oh, no," he said with a mock heavy sigh, "I did not see a dollar, not even the shadow of a dollar." In fact, he had written a letter to the Angkar refusing to accept the money. The radio also reported that Sihanouk wanted to "withdraw from active life to devote himself to his family after thirty-five years of political activity." One of the first things they did to help his family life was to pack off two of his daughters, their husbands, and ten grandchildren to work in the rice paddies. The husband of his favorite daughter, Botum Bopha, was a Cambodian air force pilot who in March 1972 took his T-28 fighter to drop a bomb over Lon Nol's palace before flying to the Khmer Rouge–controlled zone. Sihanouk was never to see them again, nor was he to see a soul for a long time. He did not know that with his resignation he had begun serving an unpronounced sentence of house arrest in Phnom Penh's Khemarin Palace.

4

A Glimpse into the History

THOUGH THE Pol Pot delegation flew by jet and rode Honqi (red flag) limousines rather than horse-drawn carriages, and though they went to the Mao Mausoleum rather than to the Imperial Palace to pay homage, the Cambodian visit to Peking was in many ways a replay of history. A senior official of the Chinese Foreign Ministry had flown to Phnom Penh to escort the Cambodian visitors to the capital aboard a Chinese liner. In the old days Chinese court officials went to the border to escort the tribute-bearing ruler to the imperial capital with great pomp. However, more than in the form, the similarity lay in the strategic and political considerations that determined China's relations with its Southeast Asian neighbors.

From the third century A.D. until the end of the fifteenth century, rulers of the different kingdoms (Funan, Chen La, Champa and Cambodia) that had emerged in the area of present-day southern Vietnam and Cambodia accepted Chinese supremacy, at least symbolically, by sending tributes from time to time to the Son of Heaven. Those tribute-bearing missions were in fact a disguised form of commerce, but another principal reason for conducting them was to ensure China's protection. Those Southeast Asian kings hoped that a warning from the powerful Chinese emperor would be enough to deter any aggressive neighbors.[1]

The system worked, too, as long as the Chinese empire was powerful enough to back its threats with military might or was not preoccupied with other problems. In 1407, the Ming emperor Yongle had sent a 200,000-strong army to punish Vietnam for crimes, including an attack on Champa. The defeated Vietnamese were forced to return to Champa the territory that they had annexed.[2] However, in 1414, the Cambodian king had less luck when he sent a tribute-bearing mission to Peking to seek Chinese support against an invasion by Champa. Emperor Yongle, who was busy fighting the Mongols in the north, sent back the Cambodian envoy with due honor and the assurance that Champa, another vassal of China's, would behave. He also dispatched an envoy to Champa, urging the king to "withdraw his troops from Cambodia and leave her in peace." The missive, not backed by any threat of punishment, fell on deaf ears: armed bands from Champa continued to plunder Cambodia. Despite the fact that in the subsequent period when a declining Khmer kingdom became a prey to covetous neighbors—Vietnam and Thailand—China did not concern itself with its fate, the traditional view of China as a regional gamekeeper continued to inform Khmer strategic thinking. The first ruler of modern Cambodia, Prince Norodom Sihanouk, consciously sought Communist China's friendship in the hope that it would deter the country's potential enemies. In 1966 he went so far as to declare that China was "the synonym for Cambodia's survival with independence, peace, and territorial integrity." Clearly with Vietnam and Thailand in mind, he warned, "If we move away from China, we will be devoured by the vultures, which are the eternal swallowers of Khmer territory."[3]

Cambodia, throughout its premodern history, saw China only as a benign protector and trading partner, whereas Vietnam had a very different type of relationship. While offering protection to other vassals the Chinese court had ceaselessly attempted to subjugate Vietnam. And Vietnam, while resisting Chinese pressure, had, ironically, sought to be a good disciple of China by carving out a mini–Middle Kingdom. Since its independence, Communist Vietnam traded the old Nguyen dynasty policy of tributary relations with Laos and Cambodia for a system of alliance to ensure its security and economic preeminence. As in the old days, the Vietnamese effort at supremacy on China's southern border had now provoked unremitting opposition from its Communist rulers.

Acupuncture for the "Toe"

The origins of Vietnam remain a subject of debate among historians. According to one account, the Vietnamese people first appeared in history in the Gouandong Province area of China and in the Red River delta. And the first Vietnamese kingdom recorded in Chinese annals, Nam Viet (or in Chinese *Nan-Yueh*), was created by a renegade Chinese warlord, Trieu Da, in 208 B.C. He took a Vietnamese wife, adopted Vietnamese customs, and killed all Chinese loyal to their emperor. After a century of autonomous rule, Nam Viet was absorbed by the emerging Han dynasty and made into the Chinese provinces called *Panyu* (Canton region) and *Giao Chi* (Red River delta). During a thousand years of Chinese occupation, the Vietnamese assimilated Chinese social and political organization, adopted advanced agricultural techniques, and developed a writing system borrowed from the Chinese. This period also saw the emergence of a Sino-Vietnamese elite steeped in Chinese culture and Confucian worldview. So deep was the Vietnamese reverence for Chinese culture that answering a Chinese question about customs in Annam (meaning "pacified or quiet south"—a name China gave to Vietnam in A.D. 697), a fifteenth-century Vietnamese ruler wrote

The Quiet South [Annam] boasts polished ways.
Our king and subjects heed Han laws,
Our caps and gowns obey Tang rules.[4]

Even when the wind of nationalism had grown strong in the early part of this century, Vietnamese literati still boasted of their skill in Chinese calligraphy and their knowledge of Chinese classics. Many among Vietnam's Communist leaders, beginning with Ho Chi Minh, were steeped in Chinese culture.

However, paradoxically, assimilation with Chinese culture had also provided Vietnam with political tools and economic organization to defy the Celestial Empire. China, as one historian has remarked, "had unwittingly spawned a new nation which had successfully adopted the Chinese system to establish its own independence."[5] A nationhood that had emerged after nine hundred years of Chinese rule was honed through the thousand years of resistance to China that had followed.

Taking advantage of a period of chaos in China, the Vietnamese leader Ngo Quyen drove the Chinese garrisons and bureaucrats from Vietnam in A.D. 939 and founded an independent dynasty. The loss was not taken lightly by the Song emperor in China or by his Mongol, Ming, and Qing successors. Forty years after Vietnam's departure from the empire, when order was restored in southern China, the Song emperor sent an army to recover the rebellious Giao Chi Province. A letter that the Song emperor, Taizong, sent to the Vietnamese king before launching the invasion sums up the imperial Chinese attitude to Vietnam.

"Chinese relations with the southern barbarians," the letter stated, "is like a human body with two legs and two arms which stretch and contract at the volition of the heart; thus the heart is lord. If in an arm or leg the blood vessels are stopped up and the nerve is not peaceful, then medicine is taken for a remedy; but if no results are seen, then acupuncture is applied until health is restored." After having remedied the afflicted "arms and legs"—that is, other minority peoples in southern China—the emperor was now turning his attention to Vietnam, which was like a toe. "Does a sage ignore one sore toe? If so, the only result will be to unloose your dark stupidity which will reach out to impregnate our purity."

The letter asked the Vietnamese to submit to the Song court so that China's body could be healthy. But if they refuse to give in, "our command must be to cut up your corpses, chop your bones, and return your land to the grasses. . . . Although your seas have pearls, we will throw them into the rivers, and though your mountains produce gold, we will throw it into the dust; we do not covet your valuables. You fly and leap like savages, we have horse-drawn carriages; you drink through your noses, we have rice and wine; let us change your customs. You cut your hair, we wear hats; when you talk you sound like birds, we have examinations and books; let us teach you knowledge of the proper laws. . . . Do you want to escape from the savagery of the outer islands and gaze upon the house of civilization? Do you want to discard your garments of leaves and grass and wear flowered robes embroidered with mountains and dragons? Have you understood? Do not march out and make a mortal mistake. We are preparing chariots, horses, and soldiers. . . ."[6]

The Vietnamese monarch, Le Hoan, was unimpressed by the threat, and in 981 the invading Song army suffered an ignominious defeat. In the next one thousand years the Vietnamese fought off a score of invasions from the north.

Scholars analyzing traditional Chinese relations with their neighbors generally agree that the Chinese sense of superiority, which lay at the root of the system of tribute, was cultural rather than political. Tributary status was granted not to a country but to a ruler—one who had acknowledged China's superiority and had begged to come to the Middle Kingdom "to be transformed." In theory, the Chinese ruler could remain indifferent about whether a barbarian recognized his supremacy, which was, after all, based on moral virtue. But in reality, China frequently sought to conquer and directly control barbarians on its periphery. In the case of Vietnam, with its difficult terrain and stubborn resistance, a tributary relationship was the only possible substitute for costly and untenable direct rule. However, the tributary system based on Confucian principles left enough doors open for Chinese intervention whenever it was feasible.

Although the Vietnamese rulers continued to accept Chinese suzerainty, successive Chinese emperors (whenever they felt militarily strong) intervened in Vietnam to restore stability and set things right according to the Confucian order. For instance, before launching the 1407 invasion, which reimposed two decades of Chinese rule over Vietnam, Emperor Yongle listed twenty main "crimes" of the Vietnamese ruler. Eight of these were moral and ideological transgressions, such as usurpation of power by assassinating the properly recognized king, ill-treatment of the people, and deceiving the Ming emperor. The next five were related to China's security and included the manner in which Vietnam had disturbed the peace among the border tribes and incited them against the emperor. Five others were acts of Vietnamese aggression against Champa. The last two "crimes" were displays of disrespect to the emperor. The list, as historian Wang Gungwu notes, "reveals the extent to which Chinese claims to suzerainty denied freedom and independence of action to the vassal states," particularly one like Vietnam that had long been a part of the Chinese empire.[7] Vietnam was not just another tributary. It was a former imperial province that had once enjoyed the blessings of Chinese civilization. A key word in Emperor Yongle's justification for his punishment of Vietnam in 1407 was that Vietnam was *mi mi*—"very closely related." In view of all the enlightenment Vietnam had obtained from China in forming a bond of kinship, the "crimes" of its rulers were particularly offensive.

"Fight to Keep Our Hair Long"

For the next two decades after the 1407 invasion the Vietnamese administration was run by senior officials brought in from China. Vietnamese texts were either destroyed or taken back to China and mostly lost—perhaps the deepest hurt for later literati. The Ming tax system was introduced, and schools were set up to teach Chinese classics. Chinese customs, traditions, hairstyle, and dress were forced upon the Vietnamese. Tattooing, teeth lacquering, and betel chewing—traditional Vietnamese practices—became illegal. As in the first period of Chinese occupation, Vietnamese forced labor was used to exploit gold, silver, copper, and iron mines; to hunt for elephant tusks and rhinocerous horns; and to collect pearls from the sea.[8]

A lengthy guerrilla campaign organized by the Vietnamese leader Le Loi ended Chinese rule in 1427. For the next four and a half centuries, until the French conquest, Vietnam remained free of foreign control. The only major threat during this period came in 1788, when the Qing dynasty sent an expeditionary corps in a fresh attempt to turn Vietnam into a protectorate. That move was defeated by a brilliant Vietnamese strategist, Nguyen Hue, and by the strong spirit of nationalism that had evolved through centuries of independence. One of the songs Nguyen Hue's men marched to had this refrain:

Fight to keep our hair long,
Fight to keep our teeth black,
Fight to destroy every enemy vehicle,
Fight to leave no enemy armor intact.
Fight to let them know the heroic southern country is its own master.[9]

The struggle against Chinese domination had become so much of a leitmotif of Vietnamese nationalism that it was elevated almost to a religion. Even during the height of war against the United States, when Chinese support was crucial to Vietnamese survival, that religion was secretly practiced. During a visit to North Vietnam in October 1972, American scholar George Kahin was curious to find out the extent of religious freedom. After he had observed a well-attended Catholic mass in the Hanoi cathedral, his Vietnamese escort asked, "Would you like to see something of *our* religion?" Kahin accepted the invitation and was taken across a bridge to a temple on an island in Hanoi's Hoan Kiem Lake. In it there were three altars—one to Buddha, one to the god of earth and water, and a central one dedicated to Tran Hung Dao, the general who defeated the Chinese-Mongol army in the thirteenth century. Upon inquiring, Kahin found that there were half a dozen other shrines in Hanoi where Vietnamese paid homage to heroes and heroines, such as Le Loi and the Trung sisters, who had fought against the Chinese invaders.[10]

While struggling for its independence in China's shadow, Vietnam developed a political style that was a mix of firmness and flexibility—firmness in defending its separate identity and independence, and flexibility in seeking a modus vivendi with China. This unique approach also reflected the ambiguities of the Vietnamese view of China, marked by love and hatred, inferiority and pride, heroic courage and pragmatism. Their claim to be masters of their own house was always tempered by the awareness of China's power and a genuine admiration for things Chinese. The Vietnamese rulers understood clearly from the very dawn of the country's independence that while the heroism of their people, favorable terrain, and good strategy could defeat an invasion, China was too populous, and its resources too vast for Vietnam to succeed in an endless confrontation. By accepting Chinese suzerainty Vietnamese rulers could avoid active Chinese intervention. In the words of a Vietnamese historian, "It was in the interest of the Vietnamese kings to surrender part of their sovereignty in return for assurance that in case of rebellion they would be protected by China and that in time of internal peace they would not be conquered or directly administered by China."[11] Invariably, after a victory over an invading Chinese army the Vietnamese ruler would send a mission to beg for pardon and offer tribute to the Son of Heaven. Invariably it was granted.

Fight Now; Pay Tribute Later

After defeating the Ming army in 1427, the Vietnamese leader Le Loi was asked by a section of the population and the army not to accept peace but to take revenge by killing the Chinese prisoners. But his close associate, the strategist and poet Nguyen Trai, opposed the demand. "In the present circumstances it is not difficult to attack the enemy and to quench our thirst with his blood. But I am afraid that that way we will incur the profound hatred of the Ming. To take their revenge, to save the prestige of a great empire, they will send a new army. For how long will the evil of war last? For the good of our two nations it is better to take advantage of this situation when the enemy is at the end of its tether to make peace with him."[12] Le Loi took Trai's advice and even gave the defeated Chinese army five hundred boats, several thousand horses, and some food for their return home.

Acutely aware of the megalomania of the Chinese emperor and the importance of face, the Vietnamese had perfected the art of flattery and feigned obedience to obtain from the emperor what they could not by use of force. In the early eighteenth century the Chinese emperor was enraged by a Vietnamese claim over an area of forty *li* (thirteen miles) along the border. But when the Vietnamese ruler expressed his abject repentance the emperor graciously bestowed the contested territory on Vietnam in perpetuity.[13] After defeating a Qing invasion in 1788 Vietnamese hero Nguyen Hue sent a letter of submission and apology to the Chinese emperor. His attack on the imperial army, he humbly explained, was an accident. To soothe the bruised ego of the Chinese emperor, Nguyen Hue said that he would personally make the tribute-bearing trip to Peking on the occasion of the emperor's eightieth anniversary. In the event, he sent a look-alike nephew to pose as the Vietnamese vassal king. Whether the Chinese emperor saw through the game or not, Nguyen Hue's double was given a lavish reception befitting a repentant, royal visitor.[14]

Although from the tenth century Vietnam pursued an independent policy in dealing with its neighbors—Champa, Cambodia, Thailand, and the Lao principalities—it often took care to keep the Chinese emperor informed of the reasons or the pretexts for its actions against other Chinese vassals. In 1044 the Vietnamese ruler Ly Thai Tong justified his invasion of Champa by quoting Confucian classics to the effect that the Chams had shown insufficient respect—the kind of explanation that might find favor at the Chinese court. In 1446 the Vietnamese appealed to the Ming court against Cham depredations on the frontier. As a result, the emperor warned the Cham king not to violate the Vietnamese border. Twenty-three years later, before delivering the most serious blow to Champa, the Vietnamese emperor Thanh Tong sent an envoy to the Ming court to explain the reasons for the planned invasion of Champa, so as not to provoke Chinese wrath.[15]

In effect, Vietnamese monarchs, while accepting Chinese suzerainty, tried to develop a Chinese-style tributary system of their own. The rulers would call themselves *vuong* (king) when communicating with the Chinese but *hoang de* (emperor) when addressing their own subjects or other rulers in Southeast Asia. In trying to ape China, the Vietnamese rulers called their country "Middle Kingdom" and built an imperial palace in Hue modeled on Peking's Forbidden City—complete with moats and gates. In the early eleventh century the court at Hue even sent the Cambodian king—a supposed vassal—a gilded seal embossed with a camel, an exact replica of one that it had received from Peking as a token of recognition. The "strange" creature on the seal caused some curiosity in Phnom Penh, where it came to be known as a Chinese lion.[16]

In remaining faithful to the Chinese system of political organization, Alexander Woodside points out, the Vietnamese emperor and his bureaucracy were compelled to believe that "they were the cultural cynosures of a society surrounded by subversive 'barbarians.' "[17] The Vietnamese court's cultural pretensions were as great as China's, but, unlike China, Vietnam was surrounded by countries with equally developed cultures. This fact denied the Vietnamese the self-confidence of the Chinese. The result was tension and insecurity as exemplified by Emperor Minh Mang's disastrous attempt to Vietnamize Cambodia in the 1830s.

Aside from their cultural pretensions, the Vietnamese justified extending their tutelage over Cambodia and Lao principalities by security considerations. Nguyen Tri Phuong, a mandarin in the court of Hue, wrote in 1835, "Vietnam is in a position that is extremely dangerous. It is stuck to a large country that has a population several dozen times as large, has a warlike spirit, and is forever wanting to expand to the adjoining country they consider barbarian—that is China. To the west and south it joins with races who also are expansionist and intrude on our territory. . . . They [Vietnamese] must always oppose the aggression of the people and tribes in order to preserve itself and progress. . . . Cambodia is weak and always afflicted by internal rebellion and aggression from Siamese army which terrorizes the masses. Because of this many times they requested our forces to come and restore security and order for their country."[18] Under the guise of protecting it from Siamese intervention the court of Hue established control over Cambodia. In 1827, under the pretext of helping a tributary Lao prince against a Siamese threat, Vietnam occupied large tracts of north and central Laos, including Sam Neua (an area that was to become, 125 years later, the bastion of the Vietnamese-backed Pathet Lao movement). When in the late nineteenth century France established control over Laos, Cambodia, and Vietnam, it not only ended a thousand-year-long Chinese suzerainty over these countries but also fashioned out of them a political and strategic unit—the Indochinese Union—that the Nguyen emperors seemed on the verge of realizing for Vietnam.

Comradely Domination

A quarter-century after the French Union of Indochina was dismantled to create the independent states of Laos, Cambodia, and Vietnam the idea of an "Indochinese solidarity bloc" under Hanoi surfaced again. Were the Vietnamese Communists trying to succeed to colonial frontiers and thus "fulfill age-old Vietnamese cultural and political goals?"[19] Was the notion of an "Indochinese Federation" invoked by the Vietnamese Communists in the 1930s a modern-day version of the Nguyen dynasty empire? A study of the evolution of the Vietnamese policy toward Indochina in the last fifty years indicates a remarkable continuity of their strategic thinking—reinforced by recent experience. But it also shows an appreciation of the force of nationalism and geopolitical balance that makes drawing of a simple parallel between current Hanoi policy and that of imperial Vietnam untenable.

Contrary to popular myth about Ho Chi Minh's dream of building an "Indochinese Federation" under Vietnamese control that supposedly led him to found the ICP, the notion of a broader Vietnamese responsibility for Indochina was imposed by the Moscow-based Communist International, or Comintern. Recent researchers have shown that in the 1930s Vietnamese Communists had little interest in promoting revolution in Laos and Cambodia. When in February 1930 Vietnamese Communist groups assembled in Hongkong to form a party they named it the Vietnamese Communist Party (VCP). The decision drew a stinging rebuke from the Comintern for following narrow national chauvinism and ignoring proletarian internationalism. On the Comintern order the name was later changed to *Indochinese Communist Party* (ICP). It had argued that France's colonial rule was the single common enemy of all the people of Indochina and thus necessitated formation of a united organization to fight it. "Although the three countries [Laos, Cambodia, Vietnam] are made of three different races, with different languages, different traditions, different behaviour patterns," an ICP magazine explained in 1932, "in reality they form only one country. . . . It is not possible to make a revolution separately for Vietnam, Cambodia, and Laos. In order to oppose the enemy of the revolution which has a united concentration of force in the entire Indochina, the communist party will have to concentrate the forces of the Indochinese proletariat in a united front, under the leadership of the Indochinese proletariat [represented by the ICP]."[20]

Despite such directives, however, the Vietnamese made only

halfhearted efforts to mobilize the virtually nonexistent "Indo-chinese proletariat" or recruit Lao or Khmer members into the party. Apart from the fact that the Vietnamese did not see much revolutionary potential in the Lao and Cambodian backwaters, they had a low opinion of those peoples' abilities. The ICP was a Vietnamese party in all but name, and even in Laos and Cambodia migrant Vietnamese formed the bulk of the ICP cells. The predominant internationalist philosophy of the Comintern and its faith in a Soviet-style federated state, nevertheless, led the ICP to adopt a resolution during the first congress of the party in March 1935 invoking the possibility of a federation. "After driving the French imperialists out of Indochina," the resolution said, "every nation will have the right to self-determination; it may join the Indochinese Federation or set up a separate state; it is free to join or leave the Federation; it may follow whichever system it likes."[21] By the early forties the Vietnamese had become more aware of the national aspirations of Lao and Khmer people, especially the increasing appeal of the Khmer Issarak. An ICP resolution in 1941 stressed the need to "correctly carry out the policy of national self-determination" after the French left Indochina. "It is up to the peoples living in Indochina to either organize themselves into a Federation of Democratic Republics or remain separate national states."[22] Ten years later even that hesitant notion of political federation was abandoned. Anxious not to provide the French a lever to fan anti-Vietnamese feeling among the Lao and the Khmer, the ICP was broken up into three national parties, and the idea of federation was never mentioned again. But the idea of a Vietnamese ideological leadership over the independence struggle in Indochina had struck roots. It was further nourished by the experience of the anti-French war.

Just as the Vietnamese were moving away from the Comintern-inspired federation concept their military experience was, in fact, driving them in the opposite direction—toward a greater appreciation of Indochina as a unified strategic theater. The Vietnamese were able to modernize their military tradition, learning from their heroes in long-gone struggles against China and tempering that knowledge with the concepts of a people's war developed by Mao. But, unlike the Chinese Communists, the Vietnamese did not have

a vast territory in which they could retreat, lick their wounds, and
build base areas before challenging the superior enemy. They could
not trade space for time. That weakness was brought home by the
fact that France used the whole of Indochinese space. In 1947 the
French launched major attacks on Vietminh strongholds from Laos
and Cambodia. "This experience," notes military historian William
Turley, "forced the Vietnamese to see the virtue of revolution in
Laos and Cambodia as means to attack and tie down the French
from the rear." [23]

In 1950, as the Vietminh prepared for their counteroffensive against
the French, General Giap, their military commander, wrote a pam-
phlet that proved to be a seminal work on the Vietnamese strategic
perspective on Indochina. "Indochina is a single strategic unit, a
single battlefield," Giap wrote.

> For this reason, and especially because of the strategic terrain,
> we cannot consider Vietnam to be independent so long as Cam-
> bodia and Laos are under imperialist domination, just as we can-
> not consider Cambodia and Laos to be independent so long as
> Vietnam is under imperialist rule.
>
> The colonialists used Cambodia to attack Vietnam. Laos and
> Cambodia temporarily have become the secure rear areas of the
> enemy and simultaneously their most vulnerable area in the en-
> tire Indochina theatre. Therefore, we need to open the Lao-Cam-
> bodia battlefield resolutely and energetically. [24]

And this is exactly what the Vietminh did. Before catching the
French in an elaborately laid trap at Dien Bien Phu (in a valley
bordering Laos and Vietnam), Vietminh forces struck successively
in north, central, and south Laos and in central Vietnam while a
small Vietnamese force and their Khmer Issarak allies harassed the
French in Cambodia. When the French garrison at Dien Bien Phu
raised the white flag of surrender it was a signal for their departure
not just from Vietnam but from the whole of Indochina.

Although the French were now eliminated as the common enemy
of nationalists in the Indochinese theater, the course of the subsequent Vietnamese struggle for reunification seemed to reinforce the

validity of Giap's thesis. Those who opposed Vietnam's unity needed the territory of neighboring Laos and Cambodia to foil the Communist drive as surely as Hanoi required them to succeed in its effort. As Turley points out, even before the Second Indochina War got under way, the United States with Thai connivance took advantage of the instability in Laos to secure a foothold in the same lowland from which the French had attacked the Vietminh. The temporary partition of Vietnam at Geneva along the seventeenth parallel also virtually forced the ruling Vietnam Workers' Party of North Vietnam to use the Lao corridor to maintain contact with its organization in the south. With the guerrilla war in South Vietnam gathering momentum, a network of jungle trails leading through the mountainous Laotian panhandle into northeastern Cambodia developed to become the famous Ho Chi Minh Trail—a complex system of motorable roads totaling some eight thousand miles. As the Trail became the Communist lifeline to the south, the United States stepped up its covert war against the Vietnamese by equipping supposedly neutral Royal Lao Army and tribal mercenaries. Facing increasing danger in the south, the Vietcong started using sanctuaries and base camps across the border in neutral Cambodia.

The March 1970 coup d'état in Phnom Penh against Prince Sihanouk, and the American invasion of Cambodia that followed, finally removed the last barriers. The whole of Indochina had again become one strategic theater with the battle for reunification of Vietnam being fought in the jungles of Cambodia and hills of Laos. By defeating a major U.S.–South Vietnamese invasion of Laos to cut the Ho Chi Minh Trail in February 1971 and by routing two of Lon Nol's ambitious operations in Cambodia during the same year, the North Vietnamese secured an unchallenged position in Indochina. Thanks to massive Vietnamese participation, training, and help the Pathet Lao and the Khmer Rouge also gained strength that they could never have achieved single-handed. The ground was firmly laid for the final assault in the spring of 1975. Twenty-five years after Giap developed his thesis his description of Indochina as "a single battlefield" proved prophetic. In the course of just five months revolutionary movements triumphed in all the three countries.

While the strategic element had been paramount in the Vietnamese thinking on Indochina—in some ways a continuation of the Nguyen dynasty military doctrine—in the phase of postwar reconstruction and consolidation the question of ideology and economic policies assumed new importance. Now that peace had been achieved, Vietnam sought to build under the guise of a special relationship an alliance structure that would not only ensure Vietnam's security but also enable long-range economic cooperation among the three countries based on a common ideological approach. Awareness about the intense nationalism of the Khmer Rouge, their increasingly hostile stand toward Vietnam in the last years of the war, and their radicalism made Hanoi even more eager to patch up with Cambodia and promote closer ties. If Cambodia broke ranks with Vietnam and its enemies were allowed a foothold there, the threat that Nguyen Tri Phuong and Vo Nguyen Giap worried about would be revived. A radically different Cambodian development strategy would also upset Vietnamese plans for economic cooperation and resource sharing.

In explaining the special relationship, the Vietnamese initially stressed the brotherhood built on common struggle rather than their economic or security concern. In view of the sacrifice Vietnamese had made in Indochina battlefields it was almost a "blood debt" for the Lao and Khmers to stay close to Vietnam. "We insist on a special relationship," Vo Dong Giang, Vietnamese vice-minister of foreign affairs, told me in 1978, "because in the entire history of the world there has never been a relation like this in which the three peoples shared grains of rice and salt and cartridges in a common struggle." That close cooperation should continue in building and defending their respective countries.

The Vietnamese have never mentioned publicly the idea of resource sharing in Indochina—other than cooperation in the use of the Mekong River. It would, however, be reasonable to think that Hanoi planners view Indochina not only as a vital strategic space but an economic one as well. With some 60 million people inhabiting a narrow strip of largely mountainous territory (with a total of 6 million hectares under cultivation), the ratio of arable land to population in Vietnam is one of the lowest in Southeast Asia. By the year 2000 Vietnam will have 90 million people. Hanoi must view economic cooperation with its thinly populated but richly endowed Indochinese neighbors as a necessity. Vietnam's industrial and technical base is relatively well developed, and the agricultural and mineral resources in Laos and Cambodia make the three economies complementary.

In a cryptic reference to planning on an Indochinese scale, a senior Vietnamese planning official, Che Viet Tan, wrote in early 1980, "In a firm strategic position in which Vietnam, Laos, and Cambodia are interdependent it is necessary to combine the disposition of strategic regions with economic regions and to regulate and distribute the work force and the population for building grain production bases, industrial zones, infrastructures. . . ."[25]

It was only after Vietnam-China tension had erupted in public that Hanoi brought out the strategic rationale for a special relationship. The Vietnamese army daily, *Quan Doi Nhan Dan*, claimed in April 1979: "For more than a century now, history has always linked the destinies of Vietnam, Laos, and Cambodia. When one of them is invaded or annexed, the independence and freedom of the rest are also endangered, making it impossible for them to live in peace. Therefore, the enemy of one country is also the enemy of all three countries. To maintain unity among themselves and to join one another in fighting and winning victories—this is the law for success of the revolutions of the three countries." In a further elaboration of the theme, the Vietnamese claimed that historical experience also showed a "law"—an inevitability—in the way enemies threatened Indochina. Just as unity guaranteed the independence of the three countries outside powers on their part sought control of all three, first by creating division among them and then by occupying them one by one. "In their plots to annex Indochina and expand into Southeast Asia," a Vietnamese general claimed in 1984, "the Peking reactionaries cannot help but follow this law."[26]

Keeping Peace among Southern Barbarians

While the elaboration of these Indochinese "laws" is a self-serving Vietnamese exercise, history and geopolitics, nevertheless, point to a certain inevitability in the Chinese opposition to the Vietnamese bid for hegemony in Indochina. One feature that stands out in the history of China's contacts with the Southeast Asian mainland is its view of itself as an impartial protector of order and stability in the region. It is true that with the exception of the 1407 Ming invasion of Vietnam and of the Chinese naval expeditions through Southeast Asian waters in the early fifteenth century, China had not used its military might to play the gendarme. But time and again tributary kingdoms in the region appealed to China to restrain aggressive neighbors, and the imperial court invariably sent reprimands to the offending vassal.

In a typically Confucian, paternal admonishment, Emperor Yongle conveyed to the Siamese king the accusations of aggressive acts brought by Champa, Malacca (a kingdom on the Malay Peninsula), and Sumatra and ordered, "From now on obey the law, follow the right principles, keep your boundary, be honest to your neighbors, that you may enjoy eternally the blessings of the great peace."[27]

Behind this role of an impartial suzerain lay China's desire for an untroubled south—a balance of power among the smaller states that posed no threat to its own stability. These particular imperial reprimands did not halt the Vietnamese annexation of Champa or the Thai attacks on Malacca, but the territorial expansion of the southern tributaries did not threaten China's security or place in doubt China's predominance. Whatever the tributaries might do to each other, they mollified the Middle Kingdom by making apologies and excuses in due form and by sending tribute.

One important reason why China often refrained from military intervention in the south was that its attention was frequently focused on the northwest. For centuries, Central Asian nomads—Mongols and Khitans—and later Russians presented the most serious threat to China. In fact, Hongwu, the founder of the Ming dynasty after the defeat of the Mongols, enjoined his successors not to invade without due cause small barbarian countries across oceans or in the fastness of the mountains. "If they do not trouble China," he wrote in 1371, "we will definitely not attack them. As for the barbarians on the northwest, who have for generations been a danger to China, there cannot but be careful preparations against them."[28]

One such test, when a Chinese ruler had to decide between the threat from the north and from the south, came in the late nineteenth century. In 1882 a Chinese document described Vietnam as a "barrier of the Middle Kingdom" that protected southern China. Although it is situated outside the kingdom, "we cannot abandon it," the document said. But two years later, facing French pressure from the south through Vietnam and threat of a Russo-Japanese war from the north, the weak Qing court abdicated its Confucian obligation to protect the vassal Vietnamese king. "In the present conflict [between China and France over Vietnam]," a Qing official wrote in 1884, "the protection of a tributary is a small matter; the firming of the defenses of the empire is a big matter."[29] For the sake of its own security, China, which feared at the time a Russo-Japanese attack on the north, signed the Treaty of Tientsin (1885) with France and gave up its suzerainty over Vietnam.

With the birth of the People's Republic of China (PRC) in 1949, China was not only ushered into the modern age of equal relationships, but, as a Marxist state, was also obliged to uphold the notion of "proletarian internationalism." However, in the actual running of foreign policy, the weight of history and the age-old concern about China's security have made a greater impact then the newfangled Marxist ideology imported from the West. Behind China's revolutionary rhetoric lies a remarkable continuity in the approach to security, an approach inherited from feudal times. Ideological affinity between Communist China and North Vietnam has worked only to the extent that it has been compatible with their national interests during a given period.

From the beginning of the Communist movement in Vietnam, Ho Chi Minh and his comrades maintained close links with the Chinese party. A large number of Vietnamese leaders received political and military training in China and spent time with Mao's liberation army. Shortly after the founding of the PRC, Peking recognized Ho's jungle-based government as the Democratic Republic of Vietnam. For the second time in history (the first was the Chinese Black Flag Bands' intervention in the 1880s against the French) Chinese arms and military men crossed the border into Vietnam to help the Vietnamese fight a foreign enemy. Significant Chinese arms supplies helped Giap to win his historic victory over the French at Dien Bien Phu (1954). Later, Peking would claim that senior Chinese military advisers like General Chen Kang were responsible for the planning of the Dien Bien Phu battle—a claim that was laughed off by the Vietnamese. Whatever might have been the actual Chinese role in the battle, later events proved that China's cooperation stemmed as much (if not more) from concern about its own security along the southern border as from its feelings of ideological brotherhood with the Vietminh.

With the release of some of the confidential documents of the Geneva conference on Indochina (1954)—which marked the first appearance of Mao's China on the international stage—it is now possible to see how strikingly traditional Communist China's approach to Indochina has been from the very beginning. Paul Mus, a renowned Vietnam scholar and former adviser to the French high commissioner in Indochina, said in 1965 that China made concessions to the French in Geneva in order to deny the Vietnamese full mastery over Indochina. Fourteen years after Mus advanced that interpretation, in the first account of China's role in Geneva, based on French archival material, historian François Joyaux has reached a similar conclusion.

A Confucian in Geneva

One of the earliest deadlocks at the conference was broken when the Chinese pressured Vietnam into withdrawing its support for the claims of the Khmer and Lao resistance governments, which Vietnam had helped to set up, to take part in the conference. Not only did the leader of the Chinese delegation, Zhou Enlai, fail to support the Vietnamese view that these resistance governments were the true representatives of the Lao and Khmer people, but he also dissuaded Hanoi from launching attacks in Cambodia in order to strengthen the Khmer resistance position.[30] Zhou's principal concern was to prevent a U.S. intervention in Indochina that might drag China into a wider conflict. When that danger had receded Chinese diplomacy was directed at preventing American presence in Indochina. Zhou privately told the French about China's acceptance of the existing pro-Western administrations. "If the current monarchical regime [in Laos and Cambodia] has popular approval," he told French diplomats, "I do not see why it should not be maintained." He said that China would like these two kingdoms to become peaceful, democratic countries like Indonesia, Burma, and India. They could even join the French Union. "But," he warned, "we would not like to see Laos and Cambodia become American bases. . . . That will be a threat to China's security. How could we not interest ourselves in this?"[31]

It was, however, not just the desire to keep a threatening American presence away from China's borders that led Zhou to recognize the kingdoms of Laos and Cambodia and to push for a Vietminh troop withdrawal from those countries. Although the Geneva agreements failed to satisfy the Vietminh's desire for total independence by temporarily dividing Vietnam pending national elections, Zhou made it clear to his French interlocutors that China favored the prolonged existence of two Vietnams and, generally, wanted a multiplicity of states on its border. In an extraordinary gesture, which reflected the paternal impartiality of a Confucian ruler rather than proletarian internationalism, Zhou invited the DRV premier, Pham Van Dong, to a dinner party with other Indochinese delegates, including the representative of the American- and French-backed Bao Dai regime. In the course of the dinner Zhou even asked the South Vietnamese delegate to set up a legation in Peking. Seeing the startled look on Dong's face at this suggestion, Zhou explained, "Of course, Pham Van Dong is closer to us by ideology, but that does not exclude a southern representation. After all, aren't you both Vietnamese and aren't we all Asians?"

In the two decades since Geneva, Peking has consistently followed the policy of maintaining by all the means at its disposal a fragmented Indochina free of the major powers. These means included quiet diplomacy, economic persuasion, and, of course, use of its military might. Until the beginning of direct American intervention in Laos in 1963, Peking tried to promote not its Pathet Lao comrades, but a neutral coalition government that would provide a buffer in the south. China, like the Soviet Union, was also unenthusiastic about using armed struggle as a tool for reunification in South Vietnam.[32]

Peking's military backing for Hanoi's war efforts in Laos and South

Vietnam grew out of its concern to keep the Americans out of Indochina and also to compete with Moscow for the hearts and minds of the Indochinese Communists, particularly the Vietnamese. As the self-proclaimed champion of national liberation struggles against U.S. imperialism and its lackeys, China was also duty-bound to support the Vietnamese fight. With the beginning of the American bombing of North Vietnam in 1964, the establishment of a string of American military bases, and the introduction of 500,000 American troops into South Vietnam in succeeding years, one of the principal rationales for China's moderate posture at Geneva vanished. Faced with the threat of an American ground invasion of North Vietnam and with aerial bombardments close to its borders, Peking not only was ready to make enormous sacrifices to back the DRV but was also willing to let Hanoi play a leading role in Indochina.

With the intensification of the war in Vietnam that Washington fought in the name of stopping "Chinese expansionism" in Southeast Asia, the danger of a direct attack on China increased dramatically. China's support of the Vietnamese Communists' struggle was more than a comradely duty; it was an imperative for its national security. "If the North Vietnamese did not fight," Mao's wife, Jiang Qing, told her American biographer, "then the enemy would attack the Chinese."[33]

An American Insurance Policy for Peking

Not only did Peking see its help to Hanoi in bleeding the Americans as one sure means of weakening the imperialist enemy, but it even appeared to "welcome" the American troops' presence close to its border as a guarantee against an American nuclear attack. Talking to Egyptian president Gamal Abdel Nasser in Cairo in June 1965, Premier Zhou Enlai said, "We are afraid that some American militarists may press for a nuclear attack on China, and we think that the American involvement in Indochina is an insurance policy against such an attack because we will have a lot of their flesh close to our nails. The more troops the United States sends to Vietnam, the happier we will be, for we feel we will have them in our power, we can have their blood."[34]

Between 1965 and 1968 the Chinese sent a total of 320,000 soldiers, workers, and technicians to keep open the railway line between China and Vietnam, man air defenses, and perform other technical advisory functions. Their presence was a calculated ploy to deter America from invading North Vietnam or threatening southern China. Peking also provided transport for Vietnamese party cadres and military advisers going to Laos via China, supplied the Vietnamese with a total of thirty thousand trucks to carry tens of thousands of tons of Chinese arms down the Ho Chi Minh Trail, and even arranged with Sihanouk for the shipment of arms and food to the Vietcong through Cambodia.

In April 1980 I went to Peking to interview Han Nianlong, the Chinese vice–foreign minister, right-hand man of the late Premier Zhou Enlai, and one of the architects of Chinese policy in Indochina. I asked him why China, after having supported the Vietnamese presence in Laos and Cambodia during the war, now opposed that presence. Visibly agitated, Han said that there was a great difference between then and now. "At that time they [the Vietnamese] had taken the route through both Laos and Cambodia as a route in their struggle against U.S. imperialism. Of course we supported them then. . . . One thing we did not expect was that a country bullied by an imperialist power in the past would start to bully other fraternal countries when the victory finally came."

Han went on to make the astonishing claim that the Chinese had "never heard Ho Chi Minh say anything about an Indochina Federation." In its attempt to portray the present Vietnamese leadership as "betraying" Ho's genuinely Marxist line, Peking officially traces Vietnamese designs for hegemony over Indochina only from 1975. But, privately, Chinese officials, including Wang Guangmei, Liu Shaoqi's widow, are critical of Ho for his commitment to an Indochina Federation.[35]

Discussing the old Vietnamese ambition to dominate Indochina, a senior official of China's Xinhua News Agency quoted to me in March 1982 a paragraph about forming an Indochina Federation from the VWP's 1951 program. "Even during the anti-U.S war," he said, "the Vietnamese [then led by Ho Chi Minh] never dropped the idea. They were always preparing to set up the Indochina Federation. . . . Under the pretext of defending the Ho Chi Minh Trail, they sent troops to lower Laos and Cambodia. But, after the war ended, instead of withdrawing those troops, they sent more to other areas, such as upper Laos."

This Peking view of the Vietnamese role in Indochina is not simply a rewriting of history. China may not have foreseen, as Han claimed, an open Vietnamese attempt at domination. But there is ample evidence that, while continuing its massive aid to Vietnam during the war, Peking worried about Vietnam's future role in Indochina. From the mid-1960s, China started building a strategic road from Yunnan Province to northern Laos and for that purpose stationed in Laos about twenty thousand soldiers from its engineering corps and protected them with antiaircraft batteries. Those troops were not only China's forward defense against a possible American attack but an attempt to balance the Vietnamese presence in Laos. After discussing the status of the road with Zhou Enlai in 1974, Henry Kissinger concluded with obvious satisfaction that the Chinese presence in Laos amounted to a foothold "on the flank of the advancing Vietnamese to counter the possible domination of its presumed ally over all Indochina."[36]

China's attempt in the late 1960s and early 1970s to prize some Pathet Lao elements from the thrall of the Vietnamese led to strife and the assassination of at least one pro-Peking Lao.[37] Cambodian party leader Pol Pot visited China in late 1965 and received Mao's support for his policy of independence vis-à-vis Hanoi. But the March 1970 coup d'état in Phnom Penh created a new situation, in which cooperation between the three Indochinese parties became imperative.

Primarily at the initiative of the deposed Prince Sihanouk, an Indochinese summit conference was held in Canton in April 1970. At the summit, attended by Sihanouk, Pham Van Dong, Prince Souphanouvong of the Pathet Lao, and Nguyen Huu Tho of the NLF, a declaration that advised against domination by any one party was issued. "Proceeding from the principle that the liberation and defense of each country are the business of its people," the declaration said, "the various parties pledge to do all they can to give one another reciprocal support according to the desire of the party concerned and on the basis of mutual respect." It also stressed that future cooperation in the building of each country would be "according to its own way." Despite this cautious wording, composed at the insistence of the Khmer Rouge and the Chinese, the idea of formalized Indochinese cooperation had a short life. Prince Sihanouk told me during an interview in Peking in April 1979 that his Khmer Rouge partners and the Chinese shot down his suggestion that a second Indochina summit be held in Hanoi in 1971 as part of regular consultations to strengthen the alliance. One reason for China's reluctance was its desire not to hamper the budding détente with Washington. Kissinger made his secret trip to Peking in July 1971 to prepare for President Richard Nixon's historic journey the following year. But most of all, China wanted to avoid another gathering that would boost Hanoi's pivotal military position in Indochina.

Speaking to former French premier Pierre Mendès-France in Peking in December 1971, Sihanouk said that after the end of the war Indochina should not be allowed to fall under one power—that is, Hanoi. The consequent disequilibrium would not be advantageous for anyone. "I discussed this with Zhou Enlai, who agrees with me. The former Indochinese states should remain quite independent and the Chinese will help to ensure this," Sihanouk told Mendès-France.[38]

The French leader himself talked with Zhou, his old interlocutor from the Geneva Conference, and with other senior Chinese leaders and concluded, "It is clear that China does not wish any power in which the North Vietnamese are preponderant or dominant to spread over the whole of Indochina; they speak of the independence of each political unit, not only of Laos and Cambodia but that of South Vietnam as well."[39]

For the Chinese, the Paris Agreement of January 1973 was a guarantee against Vietnamese hegemony. Talking to French ambassador Etienne Manac'h in early 1973, Zhou stressed the importance that Peking attached to Article Twenty of the agreement, which provided for "withdrawal of all foreign forces" from Cambodia and Laos. "We will not go [to Cambodia], but we can't accept anybody else going there."[40]

By 1972, the United States had also become convinced that Peking wanted to see a "balkanized Indochina" in much the same way as Washington did—an understanding that made Sino-American détente easier.[41]

According to a Vietnamese story, recounted after Hanoi's conflict with China burst into the open, Mao advised Pham Van Dong to accept the separate existence of South Vietnam. Mao is alleged to have told Dong in November 1972, "One cannot sweep very far if the handle of the broom is too short. Taiwan is too far away for our broom to reach. Thieu in South Vietnam is also out of reach of your broom, comrade. We must resign ourselves to this situation." Dong reportedly assured the chairman that the Vietnamese broom has a very long handle.[42] Without specifically denying the anecdote, Peking later explained that, in its judgment, Hanoi in 1973 should have waited awhile before launching the struggle for reunification because then it would have been difficult for the United States to intervene yet again.

Wanted: Two or Three Vietnams

Whatever may have been the Chinese position on the reunification of Vietnam, Peking definitely tried to cultivate independent relations with the NLF in the South. The Chinese arrangement to supply arms, food, and money to the NLF via Cambodia was not only based on reasons of safety but probably also aimed at maintaining a direct channel of contact with the South Vietnamese revolutionaries. After the Chinese Cultural Revolution in 1966–67, Hanoi had clamped down on the distribution of Chinese literature in the North, but, through clandestine networks, Peking maintained the supply to a section of the Communists in the South.

In fact, notes one U.S. analyst, as the war progressed in a more satisfactory way for Hanoi, and the United States began to withdraw its combat forces under the guise of the Nixon Doctrine, China stepped up its effort to have a direct relationship with not only Laos and Cambodia but the Southern revolutionaries as well.[43]

Truong Nhu Tang, the former minister of justice of the South Vietnamese Provisional Revolutionary Government, who fled Vietnam in 1979, told me that China maintained a "very intimate" relationship with the PRG. According to him, "The Chinese suspected from the beginning that the North might impose its views on the South. That's why they supported the PRG. It was the Chinese who insisted on the inclusion of the right of self-determination for the South in the Paris Agreement."[44]

Giving an example of the Chinese respect for Southern identity, Tang said that during a visit to Peking in February 1975, not only was the PRG delegation, which he led, lodged in a separate guest-house from the DRV delegation, but the Chinese also held a separate, and more sumptuous, reception for the PRG. Tang's analysis of the Chinese position (with which he is now in full agreement) lends some credence to a report made by François Missoffe, a special envoy of the French Foreign Ministry. After a trip to Peking in early 1976, during which he had high-level meetings, Missoffe said, "It does not matter whether there are two or three Vietnams, the Chinese say, but there should not be one."[45]

Four years after the event, the Vietnamese claimed that Peking urged Hanoi in April 1975 not to launch the final offensive on Saigon. That claim, like so many others put out by the Vietnamese since their open break with China, could have been treated as propaganda. But Philippe Richer, who served as French ambassador to Hanoi in 1973–75, later confirmed that on April 20, 1975—nine days before the capture of Saigon—Peking did indeed warn Hanoi of the danger of "stretching the broom too far," using the metaphor that Mao used in 1972.[46]

In any case, there is no doubt about the long-standing Chinese opposition to Vietnamese hegemony over Indochina. China's traditional concern about a balance of power among the small states on its periphery and its anxiety, since 1954, to keep hostile powers out of Indochina have led it down a road of confrontation with Hanoi.

Vietnamese attitude, too, changed over the years. While unrelentingly pursuing Vietnam's national interest, Ho Chi Minh maintained the form of the traditional relationship. He wrote letters of thanks to Mao in Chinese in his own hand, and the Vietnamese were "properly" deferential to China in their public utterances. The Vietnamese, perhaps more consciously than the Chinese, cultivated a relationship that cast China as a big brother for a long time. François Joyaux notes that in the early 1960s the Vietnamese leaders used the same epithets for Mao as were used by previous Vietnamese kings in addressing the Chinese emperor. Following the old tributary practice, Ho sent senior officials to accompany Chinese dignitaries when they visited Vietnam. The view that China behaved toward Vietnam as a suzerain, Joyaux says, is one-sided. "The phenomenon is more complex than that. It is, in fact, possible to recall a number of instances when Vietnamese leaders spontaneously behaved like 'vassals.' "[47] While challenging China in order to defend their own national interests, the Vietnamese held to the old form.

However, the mere form slowly disappeared with the intensification of the Sino-Soviet conflict and especially after Nixon's historic trip to China—seen by the Vietnamese as a rank betrayal. China and the Soviet Union, Hanoi declared in 1972 without naming them, were "pitifully bogged down on the dark, muddy road of compromise."[48]

After its stunning victory in 1975 a militarily powerful and self-confident Vietnam not only was unwilling to compromise what it viewed as its national interests in order to please China but was also determined to "modernize" its relations with China by giving up its formal, though largely empty, show of respect to the northern giant. Vietnam had come of age and was ready to make a bid for the leadership of Southeast Asian revolution.

However, the most dramatic demonstration of Vietnam's defiant independence came only in September 1975, when Vietnamese party secretary Le Duan ended his Peking trip without offering the customary return banquet. It would be an exaggeration to say that China's Communist rulers expect a tributary relationship with Vietnam, but the intense emotion that was generated in China about the "ungrateful black heart" of the Vietnamese and their "swollen-headed arrogance" since the beginning of the open conflict suggest a relationship that is not of the twentieth century. Those emotive words revealed as much Chinese frustration at the small neighbor's defiance as Vietnamese "misdeeds." Hanoi's claim to the Paracel Islands in the South China Sea (occupied by China since 1974), its mistreatment of ethnic Chinese residents of Vietnam, and its attempt to dominate Indochina were all viewed by Peking as examples of Vietnamese insolence. Peking was particularly upset about the Vietnamese flouting of Chinese feelings and views because, as Emperor Yongle noted over five hundred years ago, Vietnam was so "very closely related" to China.

An important reason for Chinese opposition to any Vietnamese domination of Indochina—an opposition more determined and aggressive than at any time in the past—was that Hanoi compounded its defiance of China by courting the friendship of China's enemy, the Soviet Union. With its seemingly close political ties and economic and military dependence on Moscow, Vietnam created a threat that China had never faced since 1949. Emperor Hongwu could advise his successors not to invade a southern barbarian without sufficient reason because the main threat to China always came from the north. But, as the Second Indochina War ended in 1975 with the unceremonious exit of American power, China found itself faced with a totally new kind of threat. Along with fifty Soviet infantry divisions and vast arrays of missiles and aircraft deployed to the North, there was now the prospect of a Soviet-Vietnamese alliance at China's southern doorstep. Years later a Vietnamese official would explain Vietnam's alliance with Moscow as the only likely defense against China. "In all of history," he said, "we have been secure from China in only two conditions. One is when China is weak and internally divided. The other is when she has been threatened by barbarians from the north. In the present era, the Russians are our barbarians."[49]

A Soviet-backed Vietnamese domination of Indochina was a threat to China and a challenge to its "natural" sphere of influence in Southeast Asia. Opening of Sino-American relations in 1972 had finally removed the "wolf" of U.S. imperialism from China's door, but in 1978 the Soviet "tiger," which had been growling at China from the north, was, in Peking's view, about to secure a lair in the south as well. In such a strategic context few Chinese rulers could have ignored the cry for help from a southern tributary that faced the same threat as the Middle Kingdom. Despite ideological affinities with Mao's China, the prickly Democratic Kampuchea was of course no vassal. China's past experience and present fears, however, dictated that it continue to look at Vietnam and Cambodia in much the same way as its emperors had for centuries.

135

5

Window to the West

MARCH 16, 1977. As the silver-and-blue Starlifter jet of the U.S. Air Force tipped its wings to begin the descent over the pastel green Red River delta, Ambassador Leonard Woodcock peered through the window. Below lay rain-drenched rice paddies crisscrossed by narrow dikes and canals. For Woodcock, the bespectacled, professional labor leader, this was the first trip ever to Vietnam—South or North. But as he looked at the large round pools dotting the landscape, he knew they were bomb craters. A heavy rain had filled those gaping holes left behind by U.S. air power. But there were many more wounds to heal, many more loose knots to be tied before that inglorious chapter of the American war in Vietnam could be closed.

The president of the United Auto Workers Union and four distinguished Americans were on board the C-141 just to begin the business of winding down that chapter. Newly elected President Jimmy Carter had named Woodcock to head the first presidential mission to Hanoi and Vientiane to resolve the question of American servicemen missing in action in Indochina. As he felt the plane bank over an impoverished land with its pitiful shacks and bamboo thickets to approach Gia Lam Airport, he wondered what kind of reception awaited his party at the "enemy" capital. He knew that his host in substantive talks would be one of Vietnam's most polished diplomats—Deputy Foreign Minister Phan Hien. But he wondered whether some low-level functionaries would be at the airport.

The warm and moist air hit him in the face as soon as he stepped out onto the landing ramp. When the engines were finally cut, the silence was deafening. He was in Hanoi. Less than five years ago it had been an inferno. Thousands of civilians were killed and Hanoi's largest hospital turned to rubble during the Christmas of 1972 when Richard Nixon had sent waves of B-52s over Hanoi in a last paroxysm of violence.[1] Vietnamese antiaircraft batteries had spewed fire at the unseen giant bombers flying miles above. But now in front of him was a tiny terminal building and a small crowd of people with bouquets of flowers at the foot of the ramp. His job was to get the fullest possible accounting of missing servicemen, including the crews of the B-52s that were brought down over Vietnam. As president of the United Auto Workers Union, Woodcock had dealt with powerful men across the negotiating table. But the people he was about to encounter in order to secure an agreement of cooperation were a different breed from the executives of General Motors and Chrysler. They were the associates of Ho Chi Minh who had fought relentlessly for thirty years to win their objective. Would he succeed? Would he be able to resolve the issues of the past and pave the way for a new relationship with an old adversary?

As he stepped onto the tarmac, Woodcock found that the man extending his hand was no junior officer from the Foreign Ministry but a smiling Phan Hien himself. A short man, Hien looked every inch a mandarin—polite and self-confident. After a brief welcoming ceremony Woodcock and his associates—Senator Mike Mansfield, Ambassador Charles Yost, Congressman Sonny Montgomery, and human rights activist Marian Edelman—along with a small pool of newsmen, set off in a motorcade for the short ride to Hanoi. The ride turned out to be not that short after all. After crawling through a stream of pedestrians, the motorcade reached the famous Long Bien Bridge. A traffic of oxcarts, trucks, and hundreds of cyclists seemed to go into a snarl as it approached the bridge. For seemingly inexplicable reasons, the right-hand driving rules changed, forcing traffic to go in a loop and take the left lane in the prehistoric-looking bridge. Hien told Woodcock how that bridge over the Red River— originally built by the French—had been bombed during the war and not yet repaired. His host did not bother to explain how the traffic lane switch on the bridge too was the result of the war.

At the height of the war the port of Haiphong east of Hanoi was the country's principal lifeline. Thousands of tons of war material and food were unloaded at Haiphong and brought into Hanoi and to the south over this bridge. Over the years, the side of the bridge used by trucks returning from Haiphong started to tilt, endangering North Vietnam's most strategic link. While Chinese and Russian engineers wondered how to strengthen the leaning bridge, the Vietnamese found a peasant solution. Balancing vegetables on a bamboo pole across the shoulder, the peasant shifts the weight from one shoulder to the other when it begins to hurt. The Vietnamese simply changed the traffic rule on the bridge, making the loaded trucks from Haiphong use the left lane—earlier used by empty trucks heading out of Hanoi. The simple solution had worked.

Despite death, destruction, and suffering wrought by war, the man on the street showed no visible animosity toward the Americans. The Vietnamese officials showing Woodcock and his group to the government guesthouse warned them, obviously for effect, that for Americans it was very dangerous to go out on the streets without escorts. And certainly they should not go out alone. The people, they said, were still "very angry" at the Americans. But once the officials had left, some of the group slipped out of the guesthouse. Walking down the streets, they were surprised how relaxed and friendly people were. Next morning Woodcock and Senator Mike Mansfield went out for a stroll around Hoan Kiem (Restored Sword) Lake, just behind the guesthouse. Woodcock was struck by the similarity of the Vietnamese legend about the lake and its magic sword and the legend of King Arthur. According to the Vietnamese version, a sword emerging from the lake enabled a famous hero to defeat the Chinese invaders. After the victory, in a dazzling show of supernatural power the magic sword soared on its own into the sky and then dropped on a turtle in the lake.

It had rained the night before. Trees on the other side of the lake looked misty. Some Vietnamese were doing their morning calisthenics—*t'ai chi*—while others sat on the benches gazing at the water. Woodcock saw two little girls squatting on the ground watching something in a puddle of water. Suddenly one of them noticed the foreigners and sounded the alarm. They both stood up. Woodcock recalled later that as one of them turned, he saw the pretty face had a large scar. "It didn't disfigure her at that time," he recalled with sorrow, "it would later, I'm sure."

Woodcock remembered the incident as he sat across the table from Phan Hien, seeking solutions for closing that painful chapter. The evening before, he had had a surprise meeting with the Vietnamese foreign minister, Nguyen Duy Trinh. The minister had shown up at the guesthouse to welcome the delegation. Adding a personal touch, he remembered to wish Senator Mansfield a happy birthday. "I hope," Woodcock told Trinh, "by the end of our visit we have laid a basis for a closer relationship." But the foreign minister, a small man with narrow, fishlike lips and intense eyes, was tough. He basically told Woodcock no money, no accounting of the missing. Americans would have to agree to pay reparations as laid down in the Paris Agreement before the Vietnamese kept their part of the bargain to search for the missing Americans.[2]

Woodcock was equally tough. The Paris Agreement was dead, he said. The issue had to be resolved on humanitarian grounds. "We did not come halfway around the world to engage in idle polemics," Woodcock told Trinh. The meeting ended in disagreement.

The American delegation's formal session with Phan Hien did not seem to go any better. Woodcock read out the prepared statement calling for a humanitarian resolution of the MIA issue, and Hien stuck to the demand for reparations. During a tea break Woodcock had proposed an informal one-to-one meeting with Hien with only one Vietnamese interpreter. If the ice had to be broken, Woodcock and Mansfield had decided earlier, it would be through a frank and private tête-à-tête. The meeting would be entirely off-the-record. "If nothing came of it, the meeting just didn't happen," Woodcock had explained to the Vietnamese interpreter. Once face to face with Hien, Woodcock told him bluntly that with this delegation sent by President Carter, Vietnam had a unique opportunity to move forward toward normalization. "You'll never get a better commission than this one," Woodcock recalls telling Phan Hien. "You know where I stood on the war. You know where Mansfield stood on the war. You know where [Charles] Yost stood on the war. You know where Marian Edelman stood. The only one [in the delegation] who had a different position is Congressman Sonny Montgomery, but you also know where he stands firmly. If we go back with a negative report, you can forget about normalization for the next ten or twelve years." This, he said, was a golden opportunity to erase the tragedies of the recent past. He recounted to Hien how moved they had been that morning by the scar on the little girl's face—a scar that was probably caused by an American bomb. "This morning may decide if this sort of thing can happen again." As Woodcock spoke he was surprised to see tears rolling down the cheeks of the interpreter. Hien simply said, "You have been very frank. What should we do? Go back to the table?" "That's what we came for," Woodcock replied hopefully.[3]

Back at the green-baize table Hien waited for a briefcase of papers to arrive from the Foreign Ministry. When it arrived, he took out three folders and said, "Okay, there are three issues—MIAs, normalization, and economic contributions. They are separate issues but closely interrelated." This was the line of reasoning Woodcock was ready to accept. Hien announced that the delegation could take back twelve sets of MIA remains identified by the Vietnamese. He informed Woodcock that a special office had been set up to seek information on MIAs and recover remains. Vietnam, he said, would give the United States, "as soon as possible," all available information and remains as soon as they were discovered. Since the Vietnamese cooperation on the MIA question was also a humanitarian act, Hien emphasized, in fairness the United States should act humanely to repair some of the destruction caused during the war. From the point of view of reciprocity, too, Washington should take some steps to address the concerns of the Vietnamese. Aid, he said, was "an obligation to be fulfilled with all your conscience and all your sense of responsibility." As to the form U.S. aid might take, Hien assured Woodcock, the Vietnamese were flexible.[4]

Woodcock found it a reasonable position. There was no longer a demand for reparations under the Paris Agreement. "We wanted them to do this for humanitarian reasons, the same kind of reasons that said that we should help them, help them establish the nation," Woodcock recalled.

As Phan Hien told me two months later, Woodcock had discussed the possibility of U.S. humanitarian assistance to Vietnam. Although there was a ban on direct assistance, Woodcock reportedly told Hien, the President had a lot of power to give aid to Vietnam and later get a congressional approval.

Vietnam was keen to establish diplomatic relations with the United States, Hien told Woodcock, but the effort would depend on the U.S. attitude—"whether it would give up its erroneous policies of the past," such as the trade embargo and the veto of Vietnam's entry to the United Nations.

The Woodcock delegation's last engagement before departure was a courtesy call on Prime Minister Pham Van Dong. When the delegation drove into the presidential palace grounds, Dong, the "ascetic revolutionary," was waiting at the portico. His broad forehead, swept-back gray hair, tightly pursed lips, and gray tunic usually gave Dong a dignified and sad look. But this morning his eyes were smiling.

After a warm handshake Dong ushered the guests into the reception room. Under the gaze of the late President Ho Chi Minh, whose marble bust dominated the room, Woodcock sat on a sofa next to Dong, the erstwhile "enemy." They smiled as a camera rolled. For the Vietnamese it was the final hour of triumph. The envoy of the defeated powerful enemy had come to seek a new relationship. Would the United States, like the defeated former enemy France, now become a privileged partner? The mood in Hanoi was that of an ill-concealed euphoria. Dong told Woodcock, "I understand President Carter's wish [is] to solve our problems in a new spirit. And if so, I see no obstacle to our resolving the problems." Woodcock, too, manifested the new spirit by praising the "proud and courageous" Vietnamese people. "Too long," he said, "have tragic events kept our countries apart."[5] Later he told a press conference in Hanoi that the positive and constructive talks had "started a process which will improve the prospects for normalizing U.S.–Vietnamese relations."

In the friendly atmosphere that developed in the two days, Wood-cock felt free enough to ask hosts for an unconventional favor. As the delegation watched the twelve metal coffins bearing the remains of the U.S. servicemen being loaded into the aircraft, Woodcock took Phan Hien aside and asked for his help. Could he assist in reuniting a member of his delegation, Colonel Paul Mather? Wood-cock learned from aide Ken Quinn that Mather's Vietnamese fian-cée was left behind in Saigon in 1975. Hien took the particulars and said he would see what he could do. Within a few months, she was out of Vietnam and married to Mather.[6] Despite the euphoria over a new relationship with Vietnam, however, the only lasting conse-quences of Woodcock's trip turned out to be Mather's reunion with his lost fiancée and the return of the remains of twelve missing Americans.

Waiting for the Dollar Rain

Not long after the spring of 1975, when American television had presented images of the frantic flight of refugees and American of-ficials before the Communist advance on Saigon, Washington devel-oped amnesia about Indochina. It froze $150 million of Vietnamese assets in the United States and slapped a trade embargo on Cam-bodia and Vietnam. After a short-lived flutter over the *Mayaguez* in May Indochina sank below the horizon of American consciousness.[7]

U.S. disgust at and lack of interest in Indochina was almost in reverse proportion to the Vietnamese eagerness to establish ties with the former adversary. Even before the end of the war, Hanoi had decided that solidifying relations with the West, and particularly with the United States, was a crucial step toward the next phase of reconstruction.

A few days after the Communist victory in Saigon I asked a sol-dier guarding the U.S. Embassy why there was not an NLF flag over the building, since they were raised over other "liberated" Western embassies. "We are not authorized to raise one," he re-plied. This was not simply a bureaucratic oversight. Hanoi was ju-bilant at having won the war, but it was more concerned about winning the peace. In July 1975 in Hanoi I asked party daily *Nhan*

Dan editor Hoang Tung when he was going to publish the "Saigon papers"—the enormous quantity of secret American documents seized in Saigon. Among the confidential documents were the computer tapes on the CIA operations in Vietnam that were left behind by the fleeing officials of its Vietnamese counterpart—the Central Intelligence Office (CIO) of South Vietnam. Tung was very firm in his response. Vietnam, he said, had no desire to drag those things out and rub salt in the American wounds. He recalled what Ho Chi Minh had told him in 1954. After the French defeat at Dien Bien Phu, Ho had ordered Tung, who was already the editor of the party daily, not to gloat over the victory. "In the new phase we want the French friendship and cooperation," Ho had explained.

At the time, Tung did not tell me that a very important reason Vietnam was so keen in reestablishing civil relations with the United States was the hope of obtaining $4.7 billion in economic aid that Richard Nixon had secretly promised while signing the Paris Agreement. While waiting for the Americans to fulfill that pledge, Vietnam had begun wooing American bankers and businessmen. Barely two months after the fall of Saigon, representatives of the Bank of America and First National City Bank were invited to Vietnam to explore possibilities of trade and financial relations. Also within two months of the fall of Saigon the Vietnamese had made it known that American oil companies that had explored in Vietnamese waters would be welcome back.

Addressing the National Assembly on June 3, only a month after the fall of Saigon, Pham Van Dong extended a formal invitation to the United States to normalize relations with Vietnam and to honor the Paris Peace Agreement by giving reconstruction aid to Vietnam. That call was rejected by Washington. "At festive occasions in Vietnam we have wrestling games; at the end we embrace. Vietnam is ready, but Ford is not," Hoang Tung told a group of American visitors in November 1975.

In a move that raised hopes momentarily, Secretary of State Henry Kissinger responded in November 1975 to Hanoi's release of nine Americans (captured in South Vietnam in March) by allowing religious and humanitarian groups to send relief supplies to Vietnam. On November 24 Kissinger announced that U.S. relations with

Vietnam "will not be determined by the past; we are prepared to respond to gestures of goodwill." If the Indochinese governments "show understanding" for America's and their neighbors' concerns and are "constructive" on the question of accounting for 832 missing soldiers and returning the remains, the United States would be "ready to reciprocate."

"This is a commendable beginning of a new flexibility toward the Communist regimes in Indochina," a *New York Times* editorial noted, "but there is still a long way to go."[8] It suggested that the United States stop using its veto, which it had applied in August, to keep Vietnam out of the United Nations.

But the mood in Washington was for forgetting Vietnam, not forgiving it. And with the approaching presidential elections and Gerald Ford's facing a right-wing challenger, Ronald Reagan, in the primaries, politically there was no chance that Vietnamese preconditions of assistance would be accepted. In an obvious hardening of the U.S. position Kissinger announced halfway through the primaries that the return of MIA remains, as well as a full accounting of MIAs not found, "is the absolute precondition without which we cannot consider the normalization of relations." Kissinger even privately told the House Select Committee on Missing Persons in Southeast Asia that the concern about MIAs was an obstacle in forcing Hanoi to drop its aid demand. "If it were not for the MIAs, they would be driven toward us," Kissinger said. "The more anxious we are, the tougher they get."[9]

Hanoi, however, never gave up hope of gaining U.S. dollars and diplomatic ties. While arguing that it could not respect the article of the Paris Agreement concerning accounting for the Americans missing in action unless the United States honored its pledge to give aid, Vietnam nevertheless released the remains of three American servicemen in December 1975. It also had returned the remains of the last two marines killed in the South and released the names of twelve MIAs. Its hopeful calculation that Washington would reciprocate with aid had not been met. Nor did it succeed in its tactics of prizing open the American door by dangling the possibility of oil-drilling contracts in Vietnam's offshore waters. Before the fall of Saigon, nearly a score of American companies had invested an estimated $100 million in exploration off South Vietnam. Mobil and Shell had both struck oil, but the South Vietnamese collapse came before they could ascertain if the finds were exploitable commercially. Since July 1975, American oil company representatives had been having unpublicized meetings with Vietnamese officials in Paris for the resumption of exploration. In February 1976, some of them were invited to visit Hanoi to submit proposals.[10] But nothing came of this maneuver because, despite pressure from the oil lobby, the Ford administration refused to lift the trade embargo without a full Vietnamese accounting of the MIAs.

In the autumn of 1976, while Cambodia was in the throes of bloody purges and China was going through an epochal transition, a presidential election campaign was heating up in the United States. Democratic party candidate Jimmy Carter made a sharp attack on President Ford for a "most embarrassing failure" in not sending a fact-finding mission to look for the U.S. servicemen missing in action in Indochina or to talk to Hanoi. Carter's concern for the MIAs was not only good politics (with the United States still suffering from the trauma of Vietnam, it was an emotion-charged issue and a vote getter), it was also the opening gambit for a fresh policy approach to Vietnam.

Wrong Signals to Hanoi

Carter chose Cyrus Vance to be his secretary of state and Richard Holbrooke as assistant secretary of state for East Asia and the Pacific. Both men had been involved in efforts to find a peace settlement in Vietnam. From his experience of the Vietnamese, Vance believed that normalization of relations with Hanoi would help to reduce its dependence on Moscow and Peking. Holbrooke too felt that establishment of U.S. ties with Vietnam was essential to bring about a constructive relationship between Vietnam and the Association of Southeast Asian Nations. Discussing with President-elect Carter why he was interested in a job involving Asia, Holbrooke said, "The Far East is where America has had its great problem over the last thirty years. Our last three wars have started out there, and we've had the greatest domestic battles over who lost China and

Korea, Vietnam and Cambodia. And I think that your [Carter's] administration could be the turning point. We could put back together a coherent policy that ended this and built a logical position in Asia."[11]

Carter, who as governor of Georgia had never taken a position on the Vietnam War, was not moved by great strategic theories about a new order in Asia. "I don't think," Holbrooke told me, "that Carter had the slightest feeling on the issue. Carter's only interest in Vietnam was its symbolic importance, because one of the reasons he had been elected was the feeling that he was our post-Vietnam candidate. He was very interested in normalizing relations with Vietnam as a symbol; he was also very interested in normalizing with China and Cuba. He wanted to normalize with everybody." As the first post-Vietnam President his job was to heal the division at home and restore the tarnished image of the United States abroad. In a bid to put Vietnam behind, one of his first acts as President was to issue a blanket pardon to the draft dodgers. Another important means of forgetting the painful past was to get an accounting for twenty-five hundred men lost in Indochina, of whom eight hundred were listed as missing in action.[12]

By insisting on an unrealistic demand for a full accounting before normalization, the Ford administration had virtually shelved the issue. During the election campaign, Ford had wrapped himself with that demand to fight charges of softheadedness. Carter's task however was rendered easier by a report prepared by the House Select Committee on Missing Persons in Southeast Asia headed by Republican Congressman Sonny Montgomery. The report not only concluded that "no Americans are still being held alive as prisoners in Indochina or elsewhere, as a result of the war in Indochina," but also stated that "a total accounting by the Indochinese governments is not possible and should not be expected."[13]

Of all the foreign-policy agenda of the new administration, closing the chapter on the Vietnam War seemed to be the simplest. Since the United States no longer expected a full accounting of the MIAs but only the fullest "possible" one, Hanoi was thought likely to be cooperative, especially with the carrot of humanitarian aid dangling in front of it. In a memo on the foreign-policy initiatives of the new President, Vance suggested in October 1976 that a presidential envoy be sent to Indochina to discuss the MIA issue. During the visit to Hanoi the envoy would be authorized to say, Vance wrote, "that the U.S. would be prepared to put to the Congress a program of humanitarian assistance in such areas as housing, health, and food, once there was an accounting for the MIAs."[14]

And that turned out to be the first foreign-policy move by Carter. Three months after the inauguration, a presidential mission led by Leonard Woodcock was off to Hanoi. "The whole point of the Woodcock commission's trip," a State Department official said in private, "was to declare that the MIAs are all dead." It was not just a humanitarian question; it was a question of money as well. The Pentagon had to keep the lost men on the payroll and give them periodic promotions until they were declared dead.

Carter was happy with the results. Understandably eager to present his first foreign-policy success, he called the Vietnamese response to the Woodcock mission "very favorable" and expressed satisfaction about what the Vietnamese had done so far on the MIA issue. "I think this is about all they can do," he said. "I don't have any way [to] prove that they have accounted for all those about whom they have information. But I think so far as I can discern, they have acted in good faith."[15]

Vietnamese willingness to cooperate shone even more in contrast with the insult that Carter got from the Khmer Rouge. The Woodcock mission had not received any reply from the Cambodians about its request to visit Phnom Penh. While in the Lao capital, Vientiane, on its way back from Vietnam, the Woodcock delegation made one last attempt. A State Department official traveling with the delegation went to the embassy of Democratic Kampuchea to try to obtain permission to visit the country. But like Cambodia itself, the embassy seemed hermetically sealed. After half an hour of banging on the door, the ambassador's wife, who also served as the first secretary, opened the door to receive a written communication from Woodcock. "The ambassador is not here," she said through the half-open door before banging it shut. Phnom Penh's reply came in a radio broadcast. "The class anger of the Cambodian people against the U.S. imperialists and their running dogs is still boiling," it said.

"As the Cambodian people love their independence, sovereignty, and liberty," the broadcast announced, they "cannot accept the request of the U.S. imperialists to send a U.S. delegation for a visit to Democratic Kampuchea and cannot hold any meeting at any place."

Not surprisingly, Carter was pleased with what he considered to be Vietnam's new moderation. In the past, he remarked, the Vietnamese had said they would not negotiate nor give additional information about the MIAs until the United States agreed to pay reparations. But the Vietnamese now suggested a new round of negotiations in Paris without any preconditions. According to Carter, the Vietnamese told the United States, "We are not going to pursue past agreements and past disagreements. We are eager to look to the future." In a complete misreading of the Vietnamese position, Carter interpreted that Hanoi was ready to forget its past demands for U.S. reconstruction aid. Woodcock's own report, however, clearly indicated that although not specifically making aid a precondition for normalization, the Vietnamese had left no doubt about the linkage.

Hanoi was quick to challenge Carter's suggestion that aid was no longer a prerequisite for normalization. Three days after the Carter remarks, Phan Hien indirectly rebutted them in an interview with the Vietnam News Agency. Hien said he had indeed told the Woodcock mission that Vietnam was ready to look to the future in its relations with the United States but that "it was impossible to completely sever the future from the past." Several obstacles left by the past on the road to normalization had to be cleared, he said.[16]

If Carter misunderstood the Vietnamese readiness to leave the past behind, he himself uttered words liable to misinterpretation by the Vietnamese. Although denying that the United States had any obligation to help Vietnam, Carter still held out the possibility: "If, in normalization of relationships, there evolves trade, normal aid processes, then I would respond well," he said.

The fact that the U.S. President did not categorically say aid could come only "after" normalization encouraged the leadership in Hanoi to press for aid as a part of normalization. Carter's victory and his appointments of moderate antiwar personalities had inspired hopes in Hanoi. By sending there a delegation composed of such personalities, Carter seemed to reconfirm the Vietnamese view that the United States ought to expiate its crimes.[17] In his public statement after the return of the Woodcock delegation Carter, of course, denied any moral obligation. "I don't feel we ought to apologize or to castigate ourselves," he said. "I don't feel we owe a debt."

But the way the delegation was sent and the impressions the Vietnamese got from their talks with Woodcock did not dispel their notion that the United States had a moral obligation to heal the wounds of war. Carter's decision to send a presidential commission to Vietnam so soon after the inaugural also helped to reinforce Hanoi's view that Vietnam was still central to U.S. policy and that Washington would be willing to pay a price to begin a new relationship. Being Marxists, Vietnamese leaders had always attached great importance to the economic motivations behind the American imperialists' intervention in their country. They were convinced that the lure of Vietnam's economic potential—its natural resources and skilled labor—would now bring back American capitalists. Wouldn't giving aid to Vietnam also help American industry? The United States–Vietnam Joint Economic Commission had reached a draft agreement in 1973 under which Vietnam would purchase from the United States 85 percent of the goods financed by a $1.5 billion U.S. commodity aid program. In addition to the capitalist greed for profit, Hanoi could also count on the innate American generosity and sense of guilt toward Vietnam. The Vietnamese hoped that thousands of peace marchers and dozens of congressional leaders who had opposed the war could now be counted upon to push for normalization and reconstruction aid.

In fact, Carter officials had not fully grasped how dearly Vietnam hung on to the hope of massive U.S. assistance, not as a reward for cooperation on the MIA issue but as an act of moral obligation. And certainly nobody ever considered that the Vietnamese were counting on American bounty—given through some sort of a new Marshall Plan—to rebuild the ravaged country. A senior Vietnamese official confirmed to me that, while drafting their first postwar economic plan just after Carter's victory, the Vietnamese had, in fact, counted on the 1973 promise of $4.7 billion in aid. Another Vietnamese official told me that "pressures from economic planners like Le Thanh Nghi led us to be so adamant in demanding aid as a precondition for normalizing relations with the United States."[18]

Years later when I mentioned to Richard Holbrooke the Vietnamese plans about money promised by Nixon, he was astonished. "They must be out of their mind," he said.

Thirty-six-year-old Holbrooke, whiz kid of the U.S. foreign-policy establishment, was one of those bitten by the Vietnam bug. His first foreign-service posting had been three years in Vietnam. That experience haunted him.

When Carter and Cyrus Vance chose him as the assistant secretary of state for East Asia, Holbrooke saw the chance to hammer out a realistic American policy toward Asia.[19] Normalization with Vietnam and China were to be the first steps in the new approach. Patching up relations with Vietnam was top priority. "Dick was obsessed with Vietnam," a State Department colleague said later. "He wanted to go down in history as the one who brought about reconciliation with Vietnam and formally closed a painful chapter in American foreign policy."

There were also practical reasons for the Carter administration's seeking normalization with Vietnam. Talking about Vietnam, President Carter himself noted the substantial natural resources, including oil, that Vietnam possessed. American bankers, businessmen, and oil companies were also pressing for a removal of the trade embargo. They did not want to be beaten by European and Japanese companies to the opportunities that Vietnam offered. On April 18, 1977, Hanoi published its strikingly liberal code for private foreign investment—a draft of which had been shown to American bankers a few months earlier.

The economic ties were related to broader diplomatic considerations. Vance and Holbrooke had no doubts that the fiercely independent Vietnamese would prefer to have balanced relations with the superpowers rather than be wholly dependent on the Soviets. They saw the absence of an American diplomatic presence in Vietnam as an important factor inhibiting U.S. ability to counter Soviet influence in Southeast Asia. "I felt," Vance later wrote in his memoirs, "that normal diplomatic relations with Hanoi, strongly supported by our Asian friends, could increase our influence with Vietnam and offer it alternatives to excessive political and military dependence on the Soviet Union or China."[20] Only Zbigniew Brzezinski, the President's national security adviser, was unenthusiastic about what he called "such peripheral issues as Vietnam." This difference of approach was to have serious consequences.[21]

From Paris, with Chagrin

A month after Woodcock's return from Vietnam, Paris was again a venue for talks between the Vietnamese and the Americans—this time to discuss a wider range of issues with the erstwhile adversary including normalization of relations. May in Paris was gorgeous, and the omens for success looked encouraging. Despite the U.S. trade embargo against Vietnam, the Carter administration had granted licenses for $5 million worth of private humanitarian aid. In January it had reversed Ford administration policy and did not oppose a United Nations development project loan. In an interview just before his departure from Washington, Holbrooke had left open the possibility that the United States could provide indirect aid to Vietnam. The first-ever visit to Hanoi by an International Monetary Fund (IMF) team in December 1976 and by a World Bank team in January 1977 had also raised Vietnamese hopes of getting American aid channeled through those institutions, both heavily controlled by the United States. A confidential World Bank report drafted after the visit praised the Vietnamese government's efforts to mobilize its resources and tap its vast potential. It urged donors to give "substantial assistance" on concessional terms. Vietnam had greater claim to such terms, the report said, because of the "fact that the country is still in a reconstruction phase, following a lengthy war, and needs a breathing space in which to reorient its economy to peacetime objectives."[22]

On April 27, the U.S. ambassador to Thailand cabled Washington about Hanoi's high hopes. Quoting the Belgian ambassador to Hanoi, he had reported that the Vietnamese expected to get U.S. aid after normalization and "looked forward to the establishment of a small U.S. mission in Hanoi at the end of 1977."[23] In another cable, the U.S. embassy quoted an informant as saying that Premier Pham Van Dong was "very enthusiastic" over prospects for U.S.–Vietnamese relations.

But the two-day talks (May 3–4) at the former Vietcong mission in Paris dampened those high hopes. Phan Hien brought up the issue of Nixon's 1973 letter to Pham Van Dong, in which the U.S. President had promised $3.25 billion in reconstruction aid in addition to commodity aid in the range of $1.5 billion. The Carter administration's response was that it was unable to fulfill that commitment. "My instruction was to propose to the Vietnamese mutual recognition without preconditions and convey our desire to see Vietnam as a part of a stable and peaceful Southeast Asia," Holbrooke told me later. He expressed his sympathy to Hien for the plight of the Vietnamese ravaged by war but refused to undertake any commitment of aid to Vietnam. He said it might be possible after the establishment of diplomatic relations but not before. His assurance that Washington would no longer veto Vietnam's entry to the UN did not thrill the Vietnamese negotiator either because Hanoi had taken that for granted.

As Ken Quinn, then Holbrooke's special assistant, recalled, at one point during the talks Holbrooke leaned across the table and said "Mr. Minister, let's leave aside the issues that divide us. Let us go outside and jointly declare to the press that we have decided to normalize relations." Hien said no, there must be a U.S. contribution for healing the wounds of war. Quinn felt that the Vietnamese stuck stubbornly to their aid demand out of a sense of moral victory. Their victory in 1975 had vindicated the correctness of the party's line for forty years, and other vanquished nations like Japan and France had acknowledged this by paying reparations. "It was as if the justness of the Vietnamese struggle would not be fully recognized if the Americans were allowed to come back to Vietnam without paying some reparations," Quinn said.

Things took a sharp turn for the worse the day the first round of talks ended in Paris. The Vietnamese claim that Nixon had secretly pledged them aid, and the more recent suggestion of possible indirect U.S. aid had touched many a raw nerve in the U.S. Congress and revived emotions that Vance and Holbrooke had not anticipated. Although Carter had consulted the Congress before sending Holbrooke to Paris, there was considerable conservative opposition to any move seen as leading toward normalization. The House of Representatives was in the midst of debating the foreign aid bill when the report of Hien's remarks about America's aid obligation to Viet nam at the May 4 press conference in Paris clattered on the teletype machine of the House Foreign Affairs Committee. Republican Congressman William Ashbrook waved a copy of the wire service report to call for a measure to stay the hand of the State Department. His amendment prohibiting the U.S. administration from "negotiating reparations, aid, or any other form of payment" to Vietnam was passed on the same day by 266 votes to 131. Bowing to the anti-Vietnam mood of the Congress, Vance announced, "We made clear to Vietnam that we won't pay any reparations."[24]

When, on June 2, Hien drove to the U.S. embassy on Avenue Gabriel in Paris for the second round of talks with Holbrooke, the mood had changed considerably. The fact that this was the first time a Hanoi official had ever entered an American embassy did not bring any particular sense of accomplishment to the Vietnamese. All they could see was their hope of massive American aid receding even further. On May 19 Hanoi released the secret Nixon letter. "The government of the United States of America will contribute to postwar reconstruction in North Vietnam without any political conditions," Nixon wrote to Pham Van Dong on February 1, 1973. He indicated that the U.S. contribution "will fall in the range of $3.25 billion in grant aid over five years." Hanoi considered this to be its trump card in winning American aid. But those who had marched on the Pentagon calling for peace were not there now to demand help for Vietnam. Most important, the military occupation of the South, continued refugee flow out of the country, and reports of incarceration of tens of thousands of political opponents had turned the legislators against Vietnam. A secret promise made by a discredited President before the fall of Saigon had no value at all.

While Holbrooke sat across the table from Phan Hien, an invisible new curtain of suspicion and ill-feeling came down between the two. Frank Sieverts, the State Department official responsible for MIAs, who had participated in the May and June talks, was surprised to find the generally gregarious Holbrooke rather reserved and cautious in talking to the Vietnamese. "I wondered if Dick was acting according to a different marching order. Only later I understood why." Just before leaving Washington for Paris, Holbrooke had learned from the FBI that a spy in the government, possibly in the State Department, had been passing on classified cables to the Vietnamese. "We did not know how much the Vietnamese knew," Ken Quinn recalled, "but we had that strange feeling that the Vietnamese sitting across the table may well have seen our negotiating instructions." He, however, felt that other than making Holbrooke more cautious and secretive, the knowledge about spying did not alter his approach, because the Americans concluded that "if the Vietnamese had seen the briefing papers, they would know that we had nothing more to offer than what Dick had told them."

And what Holbrooke had to offer—a vague promise of indirect aid after normalization—was not what Hien wished to hear. The Vietnamese had given new information about twenty MIAs, hoping for some reciprocity from the Americans. "How can I go back to Hanoi empty-handed?" Hien had said to Holbrooke. "The research department that gave me the list of twenty MIAs will ask me what have I come back with." He rejected Holbrooke's argument that his government's hands were tied by congressional legislation. "What would you do if I said the Vietnamese National Assembly had passed a law prohibiting searches for the MIAs?" he asked. The Vietnamese were prepared to be flexible about the amount and mode of payment. "For us, the Vietnamese, a dollar is a dollar," Hien told Holbrooke. "We don't want to know where it is coming from." Holbrooke said, "We are going to help you through different international organizations." "But when I asked him to specify the sum, he kept quiet." As Hien told me this during a background chat in Paris after the talks, his frustration and bitterness were visible despite his calm and smile. Holbrooke, Hien said, had reassured him that the White House and the Congress were two different things and one should not conclude anything from the congressional vote. All this was fine, he said, but "the State Department has not had the courage to tell the Congress or the public what they think about aid to Vietnam."[25]

The failure of the two rounds of talks in Paris to bring about agreement on normalization and the emotions it provoked among the conservatives virtually meant the end of Carter's first foreign-policy initiative. As Woodcock would admit to me later, the administration simply had not gauged how deep was the feeling among congressional leaders, even among liberals, against giving money to Vietnam. In June the House of Representatives overwhelmingly approved an amendment to the foreign aid bill, introduced by Democratic Congressman Lester Wolf, to formally renounce Nixon's promise of $3.25 billion to Vietnam. At the start of the debate Carter wrote a letter to the Speaker of the House urging him not to adopt any amendment that would limit the ability of international banks to extend loans to Hanoi. But by a massive vote the House repudiated the President and adopted an amendment that barred U.S. funds from going "directly or indirectly" to Vietnam (as well as Cambodia, Laos, and Uganda).

Although Holbrooke and Vance were still interested in normalization with Vietnam, they were not committed enough to go to Capitol Hill to fight even for humanitarian aid. Moreover, in August Carter signed the controversial Panama Canal treaty. He had no intention of antagonizing the potential supporters for the treaty in the Congress by pushing the unpopular issue of Vietnam.

By the time Holbrooke and his team went to meet Phan Hien again on December 19, 1977, the Vietnamese spy affair had cast a long shadow over the issue of normalization. Working in part on a tip from Ken Quinn in the summer, the FBI had identified the American official passing secret cables to the Vietnamese and put him under wiretap. When in June the FBI first laid before Holbrooke photocopies of the purloined State Department cables, Quinn had a hunch that the man doing this might be someone with family or sentimental ties to Vietnam who was being blackmailed by Hanoi. He thought of Ronald Humphrey, an employee assigned to the United States Information Agency's (USIA) operation center, who had come to him in March requesting his help in getting his girlfriend out of Vietnam. Quinn was then preparing to leave for Hanoi with Woodcock. Unlike Woodcock, who had personally raised the case of Colonel Paul Mather's fiancée with the Vietnamese, Quinn had gone to the Swedish embassy to push the migration application of Humphrey's girlfriend. The FBI ran a check on Humphrey, and it turned out positive. While he was still under FBI watch, Humphrey would occasionally come to see Quinn to talk about his girl and ask about the progress in normalization with Vietnam. "I had great difficulty in dealing with him as if nothing had happened," Quinn recalled. An unsuspecting Humphrey had continued to copy low-classification State Department cables that passed through the USIA operation center which he passed to David Truong. Truong, an antiwar activist and son of the jailed presidential candidate Tran Dinh Dzu, sought to send them to the Vietnamese mission at the United Nations, and to the Vietnamese embassy in Paris.

By December 1977 the Vietnamese had become reconciled to the idea that no money could be expected before normalization. But unaware that their amateurish spying effort in the United States was under FBI surveillance, the Vietnamese still pressed on for a U.S. aid commitment. When Hien sat down for the third round of talks with Holbrooke in early December, he had made only a pro forma demand for economic aid. During a tea break, when he was able to talk to Holbrooke directly in French without any aide or notetaker present, Hien asked him whether he remembered the Phase A and Phase B arrangement discussed by U.S. and Vietnamese negotiators in 1966. Phase A was to involve a halt to U.S. bombing over Vietnam, and during Phase B both sides were to do certain things without formal announcement. Hien suggested that in a new Phase A, the United States and Vietnam would normalize relations, and in a new Phase B—that is, after normalization—the United States would independently announce some aid to Vietnam. What the Vietnamese wanted was a private U.S. commitment about Phase B. "You just whisper in my ear the amount you'll offer, and that is enough," Holbrooke recalled Hien as pleading. "I said, 'I am sorry. I have no authority to do that.' " Holbrooke had also turned down Hien's proposal that the United States remove the trade embargo as a first step toward normalization. Hanoi, which had issued a foreign investment code in April, was keen to get the American companies into joint ventures in developing the Vietnamese economy. "The Vietnamese looked surprised when Holbrooke told them it was impossible," a U.S. official present at the meeting later reported.[26]

The only fresh offer Holbrooke had was that the two countries should establish liaison missions in each other's capital pending a solution of other problems and the establishment of full diplomatic relations. "We will never do what the Chinese did," Hien told Holbrooke. He was referring to the setting up of liaison missions in Peking and Washington in February 1973. The fact that full normalization between the United States and China was still unaccomplished four years after the establishment of the missions clearly did not encourage the Vietnamese. This refusal would haunt the Vietnamese when within a year Sino-American normalization efforts picked up steam.

Vietnamese Communists clearly had not realized how the trauma of Watergate, once a blessing for them, had turned into a bane. It was the political turmoil and weakening of the presidency in the wake of Nixon's resignation that had given the Hanoi leaders a golden opportunity to launch with impunity their blitzkrieg campaign in the South in the spring of 1975. Now it was the same weakness of the presidency, as well as the assertiveness of Congress, that stood as the greatest obstacle to obtaining aid from Washington. The Vietnamese had failed to realize that after the trauma of Watergate and military defeat in Indochina, they could no longer expect secret deals à la Nixon-Kissinger. Nixon could defy public opinion by sending B-52s over Hanoi, but he could also make secret promises of aid. The Vietnamese kept hoping Carter would play a pacifist Nixon. To their dismay, they discovered that Vietnam no longer occupied center stage in American thinking and that, in the face of congressional opposition, Carter had even pulled back from his earlier commitment, made through Woodcock, for humanitarian aid. Vietnam had only two choices: swallow its desire to establish ties with the defeated enemy on its own terms or abandon its hopes for American dollars and technology, and turn to Moscow.

Vietnamese failure to achieve normalization with the United States, even to open trade relations, was accompanied by disappointments on other fronts. With the exception of an IMF loan of $35 million and a UN development project loan of $49 million, Hanoi had little to show for its open-door policy.

An American banker visiting Hanoi in the spring of 1977 told me he was "amazed at how flexible and pragmatic" the Vietnamese officials were in negotiating with Western businessmen. However, notwithstanding the pragmatism and liberalism of its investment code, there was no stampede of foreign investors to Hanoi. Those who came were discouraged by the Vietnamese bureaucracy and the wall of suspicion created by security people. Vietnam's hope of quickly establishing friendship and cooperation with Western Europe met with apathy and rejection.

To dramatize the opening of its doors to the West, Vietnam had planned the first foreign trip by the premier after the party congress to be a visit to France. To make it a more broad-based move Hanoi later tried to include other Western European countries in the itinerary. But, because of domestic reasons or simply not wanting to move before the Americans, who were yet to normalize relations, most Western European countries, with the exception of Denmark, Norway, and Finland, politely refused to receive Dong after his visit to France. Even those who received him had little to offer. Typical of their responses was that of the Danish Development Agency, which said it could only meet Vietnam's "wishes to a limited extent." [27]

Even Dong's historic trip to France was rich more in symbolism and emotional reunions than in commitment of aid. President Valéry Giscard d'Estaing honored the old revolutionary in a glittering reception at Élysée Palace, and two minor agreements of economic and cultural cooperation were signed. But the bounty of the West that Hanoi expected was nowhere to be seen. The Vietnamese, as a French diplomat in Hanoi wrote later, were bitter. "Their disappointment was proportional to their expectations." [28]

The buildup of Vietnamese expectations about ties with the United States and the subsequent disappointment came at a crucial juncture of economic crisis and intense political debate between ideologues and pragmatists in Vietnam. The year 1977 had all the markings of one of those times when everything seems to go badly. In February the crop in the North was blighted by a bitter cold. This was followed by months of severe drought and then heavy floods, resulting in a massive food shortage. In March 1977 Vietnam made appeals to the United Nations and friendly countries for emergency assistance—without much response. Because of the shortage of fuel and spare parts, industry was in a bad way.

No outsider will probably ever know the way the Vietnamese Politburo debated its foreign and domestic policy options. But perceptive observers in Hanoi could not miss the signs of push and pull among the policymakers.[29] Inside the Vietnamese party followers of two political lines were engaged in a serious debate. Moderates led by Premier Pham Van Dong favored close cooperation with Western industrialized countries and gradual transformation of South Vietnam, which would permit better utilization of capital and management resources. Followers of the other line, whose most prominent spokesman was theoretician Truong Chinh, were more concerned about building socialism, maintaining ideological purity, and protecting the social system from "enemy infiltration and sabotage." This group was opposed to liberalization and opening up to the West. It also resented the slow pace of Socialist transformation of the newly liberated southern Vietnam—the source of infections of corruption and decadence that were spreading north. While Dong was away on his European trip, Truong Chinh launched a blistering attack on the disastrous orientation of the bureaucratic line and called for disciplining the government organs. The fact that the United States stubbornly refused to admit any moral responsibility for the devastation of Vietnam, that Japan and France engaged in "petty" squabbles with the Vietnamese for the settlement of old debts and minor compensations, only helped to confirm the hardliners in their view of the innate hostility of the West. The hope that a new pragmatic China would take a more friendly posture toward Vietnam was also dashed in early June when Pham Van Dong returned from Peking after an acrimonious encounter.

"In the midst of the year 1977," a perceptive French observer in Hanoi noted, "a new general line had been agreed upon. As usual in Vietnam, it was achieved in a quiet manner without any need for dramatic statements or public condemnations of the losers. It implied a hardening of the domestic line. On the external front, the new line reflected a growing indifference toward the West and a narrowing of all links with the Socialist camp."[30]

In late June 1977, the Central Committee of the Vietnamese Communist party met in a plenary session to adopt a program of agricultural collectivization and to intensify their ideological work.[31]

Under the plan, the establishment of Socialist agriculture would be completed in the South by the beginning of the 1980s. This move was soon to be followed by drastic steps toward eliminating capitalist trade and industry in the South. The window opened to let the West wind in seemed shut.

Vietnam News Agency photo

Planning the siege at Dien Bien Phu, August 1954. Pham Van Dong is second from left, Ho Chi Minh is center, and Truong Chinh and General Vo Nguyen Giap are to the right.

Xinhua News Agency photo

Mao Zedong, Hoang Van Hoan, Zhu De, and Ho Chi Minh at the Peking airport, July 21, 1955.

Xinhua News Agency photo

Ho Chi Minh and Zhou Enlai in happier times (December 6, 1960). Deng Xiaoping is in the background.

Pol Pot, Prime Minister of
Democratic Kampuchea.

Propaganda photo of Pol Pot in June 1979. He is followed by his personal
bodyguard, Nuon Chea, and a band of Khmer Rouge guerrillas.

Ieng Sary, Vice Premier and Foreign
Minister of Democratic Kampuchea.

Heng Samrin, President of the
People's Republic of Kampuchea.

Hun Sen.

Heng Samkai.

The Vietnamese Politburo member
Hoang Van Hoan in Peking, after his
defection.

Nguyen Co Thac, Vietnamese foreign
minister.

Pham Van Dong, Prime Minister of
Vietnam.

General Tran Van Tra, deputy
commander of Communist forces in
South Vietnam.

Hoang Tung, editor of the Vietnamese Party daily.

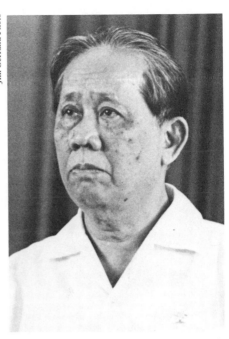

Le Duan, former General-Secretary of Vietnam's Communist Party.

Van Tien Dung, Vietnamese defense minister.

General Vo Nguyen Giap, chief strategist in the war against the United States and South Vietnam.

Souphanouvong, President of Lao
People's Democratic Republic.

Ngo Dien.

Prince Norodom Sihanouk with the author in Pyongyang, February 1981.

Sihanouk in July 1982.

Princess Monique Sihanouk.

Richard Holbrooke (*first on left*), Leonard Woodcock (*second from left, hidden*), Cyrus Vance (*third from left*), Philip Habib (*fourth from left, hidden*), Hodding Carter (*fifth from left*), William Gleysteen (*sixth from left*), Huang Hua (*first on right*). Vance talks about US-China normalization with Huang Hua in Peking, August 23, 1977.

NSC Advisor Zbigniew Brzezinski (*fourth from left*) and Richard Holbrooke (*extreme right*) by the Great Wall in China. Mrs. Brzezinski is third from left.

6 East Wind Prevails

IN THE YEAR that followed the end of the war—in fact, in all the time since the French had left—Hanoi had only two major architectural additions. One was the gray marble and sandstone Ho Chi Minh Mausoleum dominating Ba Dinh Square—the Vietnamese equivalent of Moscow's Red Square—and the other, less grandiose, a hotel on the banks of a lake. When Ho died in 1969, the Vietnamese had rejected the Soviet suggestion that his body be taken to Moscow for embalming and storage until the end of the American bombing. They could not accept that another nation, however close a friend it might be, would become custodian of the remains of the venerated leader. Instead, Russian morticians were flown in to help in embalming the body. It was then moved to a deep tunnel under a hill until the American bombers left the skies. With Russian help, the mausoleum was erected right on time for the victory celebrations in 1975. It has since become the most frequented of temples in the nation.

If the Ho Chi Minh Mausoleum was erected to mark the end of an era, the Cuban-built Thang Loi (Victory) Hotel was to propel Vietnam's hotel industry into the modern age. Compared with the prime hotel in Hanoi—the old French Metropole, since renamed Thong Nhat (reunification)—Thang Loi, with its boxlike air-conditioned rooms, modern furnishings, and glass-paneled banquet hall overlooking the lake, was the sleekest place in town. It was thus a fitting venue for the Soviet embassy reception on the anniversary of the Bolshevik Revolution.

For diplomats engaged in tea-leaf reading to sense which way the wind was blowing in Hanoi, receptions given by the Chinese and Soviet embassies were never-to-be-missed occasions. With the Chinese and Soviets vying for friendship and loyalty and the Vietnamese engaged in a constant balancing act, watching for a Hanoi swing was an absorbing occupation. The diplomats would dutifully measure the column inches devoted in the Vietnamese party daily to a report on the Soviet Union or China and determine which one had a better display. They would compare the original Soviet and Chinese commentaries with the version reproduced in the Vietnamese paper to gauge the ideological differences. When in September 1975 Chinese Politburo member General Chen Xilian went to Hanoi and denounced "hegemonism," the Vietnamese papers deleted those references. The diplomats had drawn their conclusions and cabled home.

Soviet and Chinese receptions in the capital also provided a valuable occasion to measure the varying degree of warmth in Vietnam's relations with those Socialist brothers. Diplomats would not only note the rank of the Vietnamese guests but also keep an eye on their watches to calculate how long the Vietnamese leaders stayed for the party. This was to check whether they had deviated from the established policy of spending exactly the same length of time at a Soviet or a Chinese reception.

The clock-watching technique became useless on the evening of November 6, 1976. The Chinese embassy had canceled its national day celebration the previous October to mourn the death of Mao Zedong. Hence there was no frame of reference against which the time spent by the Vietnamese leaders at the Soviet reception could be measured. But as it turned out, the diplomatic watchers were not to be disappointed. Premier Pham Van Dong, the chief guest at the reception, surprised the assembled diplomatic corps by delivering a public snub to Moscow. Hardly had they drunk toasts to the victory of the Bolshevik Revolution before Dong left the table. He had sent an aide to ask the French ambassador, Charles Malo, to join him in an adjoining room for a private chat. While Dong stayed closeted with Malo for twenty minutes, his host, Ambassador B. N. Chaplin, sat stolidly staring at his glass of champagne. "The prime minister told me how much he was looking forward to his trip to France," Malo later recounted to a colleague. According to the ambassador, nothing serious or urgent had been discussed. Dong's planned visit to France was still months away. Clearly that was not the reason that Dong stayed away from his Soviet host that long. Malo, in fact, noted with some amusement that Dong did not seem to be in a particular hurry to end the conversation and return to the table. Having finished his conversation with Malo, the premier said good night to Chaplin and left the hall.

This extraordinary act, diplomats concluded, could only have been planned by the Politburo to deliver a message. The simple message that evening was that Vietnam attached more importance to its relationship with France, perhaps with the West as a whole, than with Moscow. Sometime later, information through the diplomatic grapevine made it clear that Dong's unusual conduct that evening was also a Vietnamese response to subtle pressures from Moscow. Vietnam was a friend of the Soviet Union's, but not a surrogate to be bullied.[1]

That episode at the Thang Loi Hotel was a reminder of how much change had come in Vietnam's relations with Moscow since the late 1950s, when the Vietnamese viewed the Soviet Union almost reverentially as the beacon of the Socialist camp. Not only have the Vietnamese lost their ideological naïveté vis-à-vis their Socialist big brothers, but with the dream of reunification realized and with opportunities appearing to open up for a broad-based foreign policy, they were also ready to be more assertive toward Moscow. But the new sense of freedom did not last long. As its trouble with China and Cambodia grew, its economy was in a deepening crisis, and its opening to the West floundered, Vietnam saw its margin of maneuverability narrowing steadily, until it was time to swallow its pride and turn again to Moscow.

The Day Ho Wept with Joy

Vietnam's fascination with the Soviet Union dates back to the early part of the twentieth century, when through the window opened by French colonial rule Vietnamese nationalists had first learned of the Bolshevik Revolution. Until the arrival of the French, the universe of Vietnamese intellectuals revolved around China. Chinese scholars had provided the Vietnamese frame of reference, philosophy, political and social thought. The French opened a window not only on Europe but on the world. Reading Lenin in a tiny apartment room in Paris in 1920, Ho Chi Minh had his first Communist inspiration. "What emotion, enthusiasm, clear-sightedness, and confidence it instilled in me! I was overjoyed to tears," Ho reminisced forty years later. "Though sitting alone in my room, I shouted aloud as if addressing large crowds: 'Dear martyrs, compatriots! This is what we need, this is what we need, this is the path to our liberation.' "[2]

Four years later Ho, the international revolutionary, was in Moscow. He missed seeing his hero Lenin, who died shortly before his arrival. He studied and taught at the University of the East in Moscow and came to know Joseph Stalin, and other stalwarts such as Radek, Zinovyev, and Dimitrov. There began a relationship with the Soviet Communist party and revolution that was to prove momentous not only for the French colony of Indochina but for the Soviet Union as well. At the end of 1924 Ho traveled from Moscow to Canton to be a Communist International official in the Far East spreading the fire of revolution. Six years later he founded the ICP. The rest is history.[3]

Although geographical distance separated the Soviet Union from the clandestine ICP operating in southern China and in Vietnam, for twenty years after Ho's first visit to Moscow the Soviet Union remained the polestar of Vietnamese revolutionaries. They were ready to give unstinted support to Soviet foreign policy because, as an ICP document noted in 1935, the Soviet Union was "the wall and moat protecting the world revolution," whose destruction by the imperialists would "set back the world movement by dozens of years."

Vietnamese Communist idealism received its first jolt in 1945, when the world capital of revolution failed the Vietnamese at a crucial juncture In August 1945, taking advantage of the collapse of the French in Indochina before the advancing Japanese, Vietnamese Communists seized power in Hanoi and formed the Democratic Republic of Vietnam. But like American President Harry Truman, Soviet leader Stalin too ignored Ho Chi Minh's appeal for recognition and support. Moscow was more interested in the parliamentary gains by French Communists and its own influence in postwar Europe than in the success of Vietnamese revolution.[4] It was only after there was no longer hope for the PCF's acceding to power that the party itself began condemning the "imperialist war" in Indochina and that Moscow too found Vietnamese struggle a cause worthy of support. Even then the Soviet Union was not in a great hurry to confer recognition on the DRV. In January 1950 it unenthusiastically followed the initiative of the newly formed People's Republic of China in recognizing Ho's jungle-based government.[5]

Despite the recognition, however, Moscow and Peking were more interested in a compromise with the French than in backing Vietnam to a total victory. They argued that they could not guarantee support to Ho Chi Minh in the event of U.S. intervention in Indochina. Stalin, in fact, had struck a deal with France. Moscow would facilitate a settlement of the Indochina war at the expense of Vietnamese Communists in return for French opposition to the European Defense Community. Under intense Chinese and Soviet pressure at the 1954 Geneva Conference, the Vietnamese relinquished the gains of Vietminh troops, and their Lao and Khmer allies recognized the legitimacy of the anti-Communist regimes in Laos and Cambodia. They were also forced to accept a temporary partition of Vietnam along the seventeenth parallel—a division that was to last twenty-one years.[6] In 1980 I had interrupted a Vietnamese ambassador's account of Chinese perfidy at Geneva to ask him whether the Soviet Union did not bear some responsibility. "Ah, those things are here," pointing in a symbolic gesture to a closed drawer. "We will take them out when it is time." The world had to wait twenty-five years before the Vietnamese opened their file of complaint against China's role at Geneva in 1954.

In the years since Geneva, revolutionary rhetoric could not hide the fact that Moscow cared very little about Vietnam unless developments there affected the Soviet Union's position in Europe or its relations with the United States or China. Although Moscow began providing North Vietnam with limited economic and military assistance, it had failed to press for compliance with the article of the Geneva accord that called for reunification elections in 1956. It had been distinctly cool to the idea of armed struggle in the South. An adventure of that sort against a U.S. ally, Soviet leader Nikita Khrushchev felt, could place his attempt at détente with the United States in jeopardy. "A guerrilla war spark," he had told the shocked Vietnamese, "could give rise to world war."[7]

Khrushchev's recommendation about "peaceful transition" to socialism and national reunification was increasingly ignored by the Vietnamese. In the face of serious repression mounted by President Ngo Dinh Diem the Southern Communists had begun spontaneous armed struggle. To the chagrin of Moscow, full-scale guerrilla war was launched in 1960 with the blessings of the Communist party Central Committee in Hanoi. The Vietnamese were upset by the unilateral Soviet commitment in the 1963 Geneva Agreements that Laos would not be used for transit to South Vietnam—precisely at the moment when Hanoi was stepping up its use of the Ho Chi Minh Trail to help the struggle in the South. However, the escalation of the war—with U.S. bombing in the North and landing of U.S. troops in the South in 1965—and its own growing conflict with China almost forced Moscow to increase its support for Hanoi. Khrushchev's ouster from power in the fall of 1964 also facilitated a change in approach.

Defending themselves against the Chinese charges of revisionism and collusion with the United States, the new Soviet leaders had to prove their Socialist bona fides by helping Vietnam. Even then Soviet arms supply was aimed more at defending North Vietnam against U.S. air attacks than at bolstering guerrilla war in the South. Throughout the war Moscow constantly tried to restrain the conflict and use its arms supplier role to seek détente with Washington and score points over Peking. In monetary terms 75 percent of the military hardware used by the Vietnamese was supplied by Moscow, but it took care not to give them a weapon system that could risk enlarging the conflict. A captured North Vietnamese general complained that while the Soviets had given anti-ship missiles "to Nasser and Ben Bella, they never gave them to us to use against Yankee Station and Dixie Station [the two U.S. naval task forces] off Vietnam."[8] One story I have heard many times from proud Vietnamese but have been unable to verify, claims that it was Vietnamese technicians who recalibrated the guidance system of the Soviet-supplied missiles to shoot down the first American B-52. The Soviets, anxious not to provoke the Americans, had given them missiles supposedly unable to hit B-52 and were aghast at the Vietnamese feat. That story may well be apocryphal, but it does express Vietnamese cynicism about Soviet assistance and pride in their own ingenuity.

A leading scholar of Soviet policies, Donald Zagoria, described Moscow's predicament in Vietnam in the mid-1960s: "The Soviet Union . . . views the war not as an Armageddon but rather as a potentially dangerous nuisance-like intrusion that only complicates its foreign policy, and adds to its dilemmas. . . . Its goal there is shaped not by its own ambitions, but by the goals of its two adversaries—China and the United States. Russia wants neither an American nor a Chinese victory, either of which would undermine Soviet prestige. The best outcome for Russia is a draw."[9]

While the Vietnamese pushed the Soviets to be less cautious vis-à-vis Washington by playing upon Moscow's claim to be the leader of the Socialist camp, the growing Sino-Soviet quarrel posed a serious problem for Hanoi. Despite their occasional difficulties with Moscow and Peking, the Vietnamese leaders firmly believed in the need for solidarity within the Socialist ranks and were concerned that the disunity would only help the "imperialists" and, more specifically, harm Vietnam's struggle. Ho Chi Minh had made repeated attempts to effect a reconciliation between the two giants, but by 1966 the Vietnamese seemed to have given up any hopes of Socialist unity. Instead they turned to making the best of the Sino-Soviet rivalry by staying in the middle and drawing maximum support from both.

Moscow: Caution to Opportunism

Ho Chi Minh was drawn to Marxism-Leninism and toward the Soviet Union because they seemed to promise independence for his country. The same single-minded determination about reuniting the country under Communist rule guided Vietnam's post-Geneva approach to its Socialist brothers. Despite varying ideological inclinations among its leading members the Vietnamese party was never pro-Moscow or pro-Peking, only staunchly pro-Vietnamese. With the exception of the "Hoang Minh Chinh affair" in 1967, when Chinh, the director of the party school, and some other cadres were arrested on the charge of spying for the Soviet Union, the Vietnamese party had known no case of purge on grounds of foreign loyalty. The purge of the alleged pro-Chinese elements from the party would come only after 1975.

Not that Hanoi's policy was that of a nonaligned middle path. But it swung to Moscow or Peking on the basis of the effect its relations with them could have on achieving its supreme objective.[10] In 1963 when Khrushchev argued against liberation war as endangering world peace Vietnam sided with China in denouncing détente and the nuclear nonproliferation treaty. But in 1972, when Richard Nixon visited Moscow and Peking while continuing the bombing of North Vietnam, Hanoi publicly condemned the "opportunism" of the Socialist countries in pursuing their narrow self-interest at the cost of "proletarian internationalism"—in this case, Vietnam's struggle for reunification.

Moscow, eager to preserve its détente with Washington and fearful about getting drawn into a wider conflict as a result of Vietnamese adventurism, was distinctly cool to Hanoi's 1975 spring offensive in the South. Moscow was caught between the opportunity that a reunited Vietnam offered and the risk that a military campaign entailed. It did not want to see the return of American power in Vietnam that would confront it with the unpalatable choices of capitulation or escalation. When Washington approached the Soviet Union to restrain the Vietnamese, the Soviets made only halfhearted attempts at cautioning Hanoi but took advantage of the situation to assure the United States of their responsible attitude. "Vietnamese do not intend to damage the reputation of the United States," a secret Soviet message assured President Ford a week before the fall of Saigon.[11] The Vietnamese did not exactly respect that promise. By attacking Tan Son Nhut air base they had put an end to the fixed-wing aircraft evacuation and forced the Americans to make a hasty and inglorious exit by helicopter from Saigon rooftops. But not only was the Soviet press coverage temperate, Moscow's message of congratulations to Hanoi was also careful not to mention the United States so as not to rub salt into the American wound.[12]

Despite the caution, however, Moscow could not fail to see that Vietnam, with its millennium-old conflict with China, might now be swung over to the Soviet side. It could prove to be an invaluable ally in containing China and a stepping-stone to influence and power in Southeast Asia. The Russians could also look forward to access to Vietnam's harbors and to new opportunities to project its power. Within days of the fall of Saigon a steady stream of Soviet visitors arrived in Hanoi to pledge support, to claim a share of the victory. After years of hesitation and cautious support for the Vietnamese, Moscow was now ready to embrace the victor and, however reluctantly, pay the necessary price. "The trouble is," a Soviet official grumbled to the Soviet foreign minister Andrei Gromyko in September 1975, "we don't see how we can say no. These bastards are beginning to act as though they had done it all themselves and now we owe them the moon."[13]

On May 4—just four days after Soviet-made T-54 tanks had smashed into Saigon's presidential palace—the Soviet cargo vessel *Nina Sagaidah* and tanker *Komsomolets Primorya* arrived at the port of Danang in South Vietnam. Two weeks later more Soviet ships sailed into Saigon harbor carrying food and fuel. These "humanitarian acts" were not intended just to win the gratitude of the Vietnamese. They were to pave the way for a more regular and military use of Southern ports. Years later Vietnamese officials told me that shortly after the victory, Moscow had requested naval facilities in the South—only to be politely refused. Although it valued Soviet economic and technical assistance, Hanoi still wanted to chart its own course in foreign relations. Along with the request for port facilities, the Vietnamese also declined invitations to sign a treaty of friendship with Moscow.[14] Although ideologically the Vietnamese felt closer to Moscow than to Peking, they were not ready to move away from their neutral public posture in the Sino-Soviet conflict. Entering a formal alliance with Moscow, not to speak of granting port facilities, would be a provocation to China—which Vietnam had no desire to cause.

Whether the Chinese were aware of that refusal or not, they remained deeply suspicious of what the revisionist Vietnamese might do with the Soviets. Several weeks after the fall of Saigon, Chairman Mao reportedly warned the visiting Thai premier, Kukrit Pramoj, about Vietnamese plans for conquest in the region, where they would act as "the cutting edge of Soviet imperialism in Asia."[15]

If Mao indeed had said that, there could not have been a more serious misreading of the Vietnamese. The victory in Saigon was the fulfillment of a dream that had driven Ho Chi Minh and his comrades through unprecedented trials and tribulations. The Vietnamese party now felt freer than ever before in pursuing its chosen path. Nobody was so clear in airing Vietnam's pride and sense of importance as editor Hoang Tung. An associate of Ho Chi Minh's Tung had lived through the Vietminh's struggle for independence, the battle of Dien Bien Phu, and the long, dark years of the fight against the Americans. In July 1975 I went to see him at his tiny office, housed in an old apartment building in Hanoi. From the window one could get a glimpse through thick green foliage of the Hoan Kiem Lake—the lake that holds the mythological sword of a Vietnamese hero for the struggle for independence. Tung's weathered face creased into a smile as he said, "We are now much freer and more powerful than at any time in the past." The end of the war had finally removed many of the restraints on policy-making. Tung did not try to hide the fact that the final victory had come despite pressure from Peking and Moscow not to push the United States into a corner. Hanoi had won the war, he said, in the face of the heaviest odds—not only from the enemy but from friends as well.[16] In private, other officials were more candid, more openly proud to state that Hanoi had planned its final offensive in the South without fully informing the Socialist allies. In the last days of April 1975 Hanoi had ignored separate Chinese and Soviet counsel against an armed takeover of Saigon, which, they feared, might provoke a new American intervention.

Giving examples of Hanoi's newfound freedom to speak its mind, Tung said, "For instance, we openly support the Indian government against imperialist plots, even if China is not happy. We support the Portuguese Communist party against the maneuvers of the Socialist party, although several other Communist parties are critical." He was referring to Peking's opposition to the state of emergency declared in India in June and to the Chinese criticism of the Portuguese party as a Soviet tool. Other Vietnamese officials told me that they did not approve of Moscow's policy of unprincipled compromise with the United States or of its call for a collective security system in Asia that was nothing but an anti-China alliance. In another interview a year later I asked Hoang Tung what he thought of the Soviet idea, floated in 1969, of building collective security in Asia as a move to band Asian countries together in a pact against China. He curtly dismissed it: "There are great differences among the countries in Asia. How can you group them into one? How can you form a group with Suharto [of Indonesia] and Seni Pramoj [of Thailand]?"

Hanoi clearly was not ready to abandon support for revolutionary struggle in Asian countries in order to help the Soviets to draw the "reactionary" regimes into a plan of encircling China. "The Soviets," a Vietnamese journalist told me in April 1977, "have gone soft. They want détente with the United States to produce more cars and refrigerators for their citizens. Apart from opposing China, they have no interest in backing the liberation struggles in the Third World."

"Independence Is Expensive"

In the flush of a victory that had come so suddenly, Hanoi was euphoric. If a war could be won against the world's mightiest power, then nothing was impossible. Didn't Vietnam have a wealth of skilled workers; rich agriculture; all the minerals it needed, perhaps including oil; and a sea teeming with fish? Building a powerful economy on those foundations would certainly be an easier task than fighting the American Leviathan. At least this was what the leaders thought. But the euphoria began to evaporate as the economic reality began to sink in. The need for economic and technical assistance to rebuild the devastated country, along with the added burden of running a reunified nation, was putting a strain on Vietnam's newfound independence. While privately criticizing Moscow for aspects of its policy, Hanoi publicly agreed with the Soviet Union on all questions. Unlike his Peking trip in September 1975, Le Duan's October visit to Moscow produced a lengthy joint communiqué in which he stated Vietnam's "support for the foreign-policy activity" of the Soviet Union and spoke of "turning détente into an irreversible process." Détente was a dirty word not only in Peking's ears. The Vietnamese themselves had denounced it in October 1974 as a U.S. plot to divide the Communist countries and to conceal the real American objectives of "crushing movements of national liberation."[17] Months later, a Vietnamese official explained this volte-face to a sympathetic visitor. He told Peter Limqueco, editor of the *Journal of Contemporary Asia,* "Independence is very expensive. Every time we demonstrate independence, we have to tighten our belts. The volume of aid by 'fraternal' countries diminishes in proportion with our critical stance."[18]

A month after Duan's return from Moscow a Vietnamese paper sarcastically reminded its readers that victory meant an end to the generosity of friends: "During wartime, we received gratuitous aid from our friends. From now on, however, our economic relations with our brotherly friends are on these terms: Pay back what you borrowed, charge interest for your capital, and buy in order to sell— all this on the principles of mutual assistance and mutual benefit."[19]

Looking at the need for massive aid to build postwar Vietnam, the Hanoi leadership was more attracted to Western aid, which would also mean better technology than that from the Socialist bloc. However, the pursuit of a nonaligned foreign policy that Hanoi envisaged required a balanced approach. As the Vietnamese explained to Philippe Richer, the French ambassador to Hanoi, ideally they would like to strengthen their political independence by a "quadripartite" aid arrangement, with the Soviet bloc and China providing half of the aid and Western Europe, the United States, Japan, and Canada providing the other half.[20] However much it preferred to have balanced relations with both Moscow and Peking, if it had to bend its political views to get assistance, Hanoi appeared to have concluded, it would be better to bend in Moscow's direction. The Soviet Union not only was richer and more powerful than China but was willing to see the emergence of a strong Vietnam. Not surprisingly, and in contrast to the Chinese refusal to make any long-term aid commitment, Moscow promised aid for Vietnam's five-year plan (1976–80) and granted credit on easy terms. In October 1975 Moscow signed the first postwar aid agreement, committing itself to fund 60 percent—estimated at $2.1 billion—of Vietnam's 1976–80 economic plan.[21]

Moscow's generosity, of course, was provided at a price. Vietnam was expected to throw its prestige and support behind Soviet policies. Vietnam was required to support Soviet-American détente, but the Soviet leaders did not appreciate Hanoi's attempt to broaden and diversify its own relations. That could only mean reduced Soviet leverage over the independent-minded Vietnamese. All through 1976 the Soviets watched with concern Hanoi's efforts to develop economic and diplomatic ties with the West and to move toward a nonaligned position. Their initial enthusiasm for Vietnam as the "outpost of socialism" began to wane within months of signing the aid agreement.

While ideologically Hanoi found itself closer to Moscow than Peking, it had no interest in getting involved in their quarrel. As an internal Soviet report on Soviet-Vietnamese summit talks in October 1975 noted, the Vietnamese did not "consider it expedient for now to take a direct position on the differences" between China and the Soviet Union.[22] In particular, the Vietnamese leaders were anxious not to let the newly liberated South become a cockpit of Sino-Soviet rivalry. The Vietnamese invited countries such as France, Norway, India, and Japan to undertake projects in the South but systematically kept the Russians and Chinese away. Frustrated by the Vietnamese refusal to allow them to open a consulate in Ho Chi Minh City, the Soviets had even threatened not to send their ships to the Southern capital. But, in a determined show of evenhandedness, the Vietnamese refused to allow both the Soviets and Chinese to open consulates in Ho Chi Minh City and even denied them access to the South. The French, however, were allowed to keep their consulate open, and Western diplomats and journalists were given liberal access to the South.[23]

In May 1975 the Tass correspondent from Hanoi, who had visited the South with other Communist colleagues, bitterly complained about the "injustice" of letting imperialist news organs like the Agence France-Presse, Associated Press, Reuters, and United Press International operate in Ho Chi Minh City, while he was denied permission to open a bureau. "It's really pathetic the way Soviet diplomats besiege other diplomats returning from Saigon for news about the South," an Indian diplomat in Hanoi told me in the spring of 1976.

Le Duan had angered the Russians during the twenty-fifth congress of the Soviet party in March 1976 by stressing the theme of independence. The day after the Soviet ideologue Mikhail Suslov denounced the unorthodox formulation of the French Communist party, Duan had pointedly had lunch with the French leader Georges Marchais. In his own speech, Duan had stressed that Communists might find "diversified ways, forms, and methods of struggle suitable for the conditions of each country."[24]

In August 1976 Pham Van Dong represented unified Vietnam at the nonaligned summit in Colombo. In their first encounter with a large number of Third World countries, the Vietnamese were gratified by the high esteem in which they were held, but they were also struck by the unpopularity of the Soviets among those countries. "The Soviets would have to do a lot to improve their image," Ngo Dien confided to an Italian Communist after his return from Colombo.[25]

In September 1976 Hanoi was admitted to the International Monetary Fund (IMF), and the following January it withdrew $36 million in credit. Vietnam was the first Socialist nation to join the IMF—an organization considered by Moscow to be the "main instrument of imperialist exploitation of developing countries."[26]

Peking, Moscow, and the other Communist countries had stayed out of the IMF for another reason: members are obliged to reveal to the IMF their balance-of-payment accounts and foreign reserves, a system that is tantamount to sharing state secrets with the enemy.

Not surprisingly, the Soviets were critical of Vietnam's entry into the IMF and concerned about its ideological direction as it drafted a foreign investment code and appealed to Western investors. Soviet diplomats in Hanoi did not try to hide their displeasure. They bitterly predicted that Hanoi's attempt to lure Western capital to build socialism was doomed to failure. "We have seen what the Yugoslavs have done with Western investment," a Soviet diplomat wryly noted to an Indian colleague in Hanoi.[27]

Moscow's unhappiness with Vietnam was deepened by its refusal to enter the Council for Mutual Economic Assistance (CMEA), the Socialist group more commonly known as COMECON. "The Soviets insist," a Vietnamese diplomat told me in early 1977, "that all Socialist countries should join the COMECON. But other than Cuba, no other country outside Europe has done it. And we certainly do not want to. If we join, the Chinese won't be happy."[28]

By the summer of 1976 the Soviets seemed to have withdrawn their earlier offer to build an integrated steel mill and an ordnance factory in Vietnam. They suddenly discovered that the country did not possess either the coking coal or the good-grade iron ore necessary to make a steel mill a viable proposition. Supply of military spare parts, too, had become sparse. The work on a hydroelectric power station in North Vietnam undertaken by the Soviets had come to a virtual standstill. Hanoi had demonstrated its irritation by publishing an article on the Da River project without any reference to the Soviet Union. It had also quietly started sounding out the Asian Development Bank and Western countries about the possibility of obtaining aid to start its own hydroelectric project. An Australian economic mission visiting Vietnam in late 1976 was surprised by Hanoi officials' thorough questioning about the cost of building a hydroelectric power station like the ones in Australia. The Vietnamese would not say what specific project they had in mind, but it was clear that they were looking for an alternate sponsor for the Da River project. The Vietnamese were more open in seeking a substitute sponsor for the integrated steel mill project turned down by Moscow. While refraining from public comment about the Soviet refusal, they asked a French metallurgical firm, Creusot-Loire, to undertake a feasibility study.[29]

Vietnam also told Moscow that it needed immediate aid before it could begin to cooperate fully with the Socialist bloc and fulfill demands for increased export to the Soviet Union. The result of that stance was that in July 1976 Vietnamese planning chief Le Thanh Nghi returned from his lengthy trip to Moscow and Berlin without any new aid agreement.[30]

Vietnamese dissatisfaction with Moscow was frequently expressed by low-level officials stung by the shortages at home of foodstuffs and raw materials, the consequences of exportations to the Soviet Union to pay for imports. In September 1976 the Vietnamese party's journal of theory, *Hoc Tap,* had to urge people to "realize the changes in international cooperation, and, on this basis, more strongly emphasize our policy of self-reliance and make every effort to produce a large volume of export goods."[31] The Vietnamese had retaliated by reducing the number of Soviet military advisers from eighty to forty just after the Vietnamese Communist party congress in December and to only twenty-five by April 1977. Annual Soviet military assistance to Vietnam dropped to $20 million. Soviet-Vietnamese relations had reached such a stage that Soviet diplomats in Hanoi began openly complaining about the "ungrateful Vietnamese." In the spring of 1977 an Asian diplomat well plugged to the Soviets was surprised by their degree of concern about losing Vietnam to the capitalist world. More than any other country, the Japanese worried them. A potentially rich Vietnam with its raw materials and market, they feared, could considerably strengthen Japan— Moscow's main non-Communist opponent in East Asia. They also saw in closer Japanese-Vietnamese relations a danger of Hanoi's turning away from its Socialist ally to the lure of capital and technology.[32]

In late 1976 Vietnamese disappointment with the Soviet attitude was accompanied by euphoria about opportunities offered by the West. Negotiations were under way with Japan for economic aid. Officials in Hanoi and Paris were planning a state visit by Pham Van Dong. Vietnamese deputy foreign minister Phan Hien's successful trip to non-Communist Southeast Asia in July 1976, the U.S. proposal in October to begin talks with Vietnam, and finally the victory of Jimmy Carter in the presidential election had created a new mood of confidence and hope in Hanoi. This was the backdrop against which

Pham Van Dong had delivered his public snub to the Soviet ambassador at the anniversary reception.

Suslov Goes Home Early

The differences with Moscow became more apparent during the fourth congress of the Vietnam Workers Party in December 1976. During the congress it changed its name to the *Communist Party of Vietnam*. The party congress, held after a lapse of sixteen years to chart a formal course for the newly reunified nation, was a significant moment in the country's political life. It was an ideal occasion for Vietnam to demonstrate its independence. Despite strong pressure from Moscow, the Vietnamese refused to invite the pro-Soviet wing of the splintered Indian Communist movement—the Communist Party of India—to send a delegation. Instead, the independent wing, which called itself Communist Party of India (Marxist) and was critical of both Moscow and Peking—was invited. The Chinese party was invited, but, following a policy instituted during the Cultural Revolution, the Chinese stayed away from foreign party congresses. There was thus no complication in hosting the Soviets. But the Soviet delegation led by the chief Russian ideologue Mikhail Suslov was not to have the sole spotlight. Along with the Soviets, two other delegations received special privileges of separate villas— the Italian and French Communists, who were being condemned by Moscow for their heretical brand of Eurocommunism.

Right from the beginning, tension built up. In three successive meetings Suslov had failed to persuade Le Duan to become a full member of the Soviet bloc. Suslov took his pressure to the public domain. In a speech delivered to the congress, Suslov urged the Vietnamese to join COMECON, although he did so without naming the organization. "There are many new and still greater possibilities," he said, "to further deepen the relations of economic cooperation among the Socialist countries."[33] East German, Polish, and Czechoslovak delegates were more direct. Joining COMECON and forging an "unshakable alliance with the Soviet Union," they said, "was essential for success in building socialism."

The differences, however, could not be resolved. To demonstrate his irritation, Suslov cut short his visit and took his personal jet to return to Moscow before the close of the congress. In the six months that followed, Vietnam felt the bitter taste of Soviet anger. The aid Moscow had promised in 1975 started taking an inordinately long time to reach Vietnam. In a significant coincidence, by April 1977, when Pham Van Dong was about to leave for his first trip to Western Europe, shipments of vital Soviet supplies to Vietnam virtually came to a halt. Shortages of oil—the principal supplier of which was the Soviet Union—and spare parts seemed to threaten Vietnam's modest industrial life.

"The Vietnamese are ultrasensitive about their independence," a Soviet diplomat in Hanoi commented with relish to an Indian colleague, "but that has not prevented their economic failure. Their economy is in a mess. They had better repair the economy rather than talk of independence."[34] "Let the Vietnamese stew in their own juices" seemed to be the Soviet response to a growing economic crisis and foreign policy complications faced by Vietnam.

During the war, food shortages in North Vietnam had been met by free Chinese rice supplies of up to 250,000 tons. In the South, American aid helped to compensate for the deficit. Independent Vietnam had less luck. China had stopped its supply in 1975, and when the Vietnamese asked Moscow for an emergency supply, they were told that such "food cushioning" would be more easily available if Vietnam were a member of COMECON.

Security problems too began to preoccupy Vietnam. Its relations with Cambodia had worsened steadily since the beginning of 1977. A secret visit to Phnom Penh in February by Deputy Foreign Minister Hoang Van Loi to press for an Indochinese summit meeting had been refused. The elimination of ethnic Vietnamese in Cambodia and purge of suspected pro-Hanoi elements, begun in April, had culminated in large-scale Khmer Rouge attacks on the Vietnamese border. In Laos there were indications of anti-Communist groups' plotting against the Pathet Lao regime, Vietnam's ally, while Thailand maintained a hostile embargo against the landlocked country. Vietnamese hopes for improvement of relations with China seemed to dwindle in the spring of 1977. In February China had replied negatively to Hanoi's aid request and again revived the issue of sov-

ereignty over the South China Sea islands. China's public reasser-
tion of its claims, and its refusal to negotiate the issue, made military
preparation a prudent option for the Vietnamese.

Vietnam inherited massive quantities of American weapons from
the vanquished Thieu army, but without spare parts and the ability
to service them, they could not be of any long-term use. Whether
Hanoi liked it or not, the Soviet Union remained its only possible
supplier of military hardware and training.

There was a growing realization in Hanoi that while seeking better relations with the West, Vietnam could not simply allow relations with Moscow to deteriorate. The regional realities as well as
the harsh fact of Vietnam's economic and military needs dictated a
patching of relations. Nobody in Hanoi compared Pham Van Dong's
trip to the Soviet Union to the repentant Holy Roman Emperor's
journey to Canossa to seek papal forgiveness, but it was ironic that
a formal reconciliation with Moscow had to be initiated by Dong,
who had only five months earlier publicly humiliated the Soviet ambassador.

Under Soviet pressure, Dong's projected three-week trip to France
was cut down to three days.[35] Instead, he was to stop in Moscow
for five days first, go on to Paris, then return to spend over a month
in the Soviet Union—a time that was to prove a turning point in
modern Vietnam's history. On his way to Paris, Dong met with
Soviet premier Aleksey Kosygin to discuss "matters of common interest." His reception was cool. How dim a view Moscow took of
Vietnam's opening to the West was all too clear in the low level of
Soviet functionaries sent to see Dong off to Paris on April 25.

A Summer of Hard Bargaining

In early May 1977 Dong returned to the Soviet Union, and his
long sojourn there was shrouded in mystery. When he emerged from
obscurity on June 6 for a meeting with Soviet party secretary-general
Leonid Brezhnev, the cloud had passed. Vietnam and the Soviet
Union seemed poised again to embark on a partnership. How the
Vietnamese achieved reconciliation and what price the Soviets extracted from them can only be fully answered when the Soviets and

the Vietnamese tell their story. But a few bits of information that can be pieced together leave no doubt that Vietnam's growing economic crisis and the failure of its open door policy had led it to throw in its lot with Moscow.[36]

From Moscow, Pham Van Dong had followed, with obvious dismay, the unsuccessful talks on U.S.–Vietnamese normalization between Phan Hien and Richard Holbrooke in Paris (May 3–4). Not only had the Carter administration dashed Vietnam's hopes for reconstruction aid, but the U.S. Congress had voted on May 5 to prohibit the administration from even discussing "reparations, aid, or any other form of payment" to Vietnam. From Hanoi had come more bad news. On the night of April 30 the Khmer Rouge had launched a massive attack on Vietnamese border villages. The Vietnamese Politburo's leading foreign policy expert, Le Duc Tho, had secretly flown to Moscow to join Dong in wide-ranging discussions with Soviet leaders about the future of their relationship.

The news of Tho's unpublicized visit and lengthy meetings in the Soviet Union ultimately trickled out through Eastern European diplomats in Hanoi. Six years later, a senior Soviet official confirmed to me that "a significant series of meetings" in Moscow in May and June of 1977 had brought Vietnam closer to the Soviet Union. He played down, however, any suggestion that the Vietnamese tilt toward Moscow was the result of their disappointment with the United States. According to him, "the most important considerations for the Vietnamese were China and the beginning of worry about Cambodia. They had to start thinking about some options in Cambodia." Did the Vietnamese leader then discuss the idea of establishing formal treaty relations with Laos? I asked. "It would be only natural for Vietnam to consult the Soviet Union about that," he said cryptically.

Whatever may have been the tenor of discussions in Moscow, they resulted in Vietnam's being drawn closer to the Soviet bloc. In late May, Hanoi took the first step toward joining COMECON by becoming a member of the International Bank for Economic Cooperation (IBEC) and the Soviet-sponsored International Investment Bank. On June 6, four days after the second round of unsuccessful U.S.–Vietnamese normalization talks in Paris, Pham Van Dong had a formal meeting with Brezhnev. Both sides, as the Soviet media reported, observed "with satisfaction that the internationalist policy of the two Communist parties was contributing decisively to strengthening the friendship" between the two countries. There was a new warmth in Moscow's reports on Vietnam as they talked about the "great significance of all-round Soviet-Vietnamese cooperation." As if by magic, the blocked pipeline had reopened. Within a month of the Moscow meetings, Vietnam's Le Thanh Nghi traveled to Moscow in late June to be promised "big, easy-term credits" for forty projects that Moscow had agreed to build in Vietnam. The Soviets also announced their decision to "speed up industrial shipments." The negotiations in Moscow, an elated Nghi reported, were a "great success," and the agreements "vividly show the solidarity, friendship, and fraternal cooperation" between the two countries.[37]

Nothing symbolized more the dramatic reversal in Vietnamese strategic thinking than the decision to invite the Soviet military to visit the South. For a year and a half Hanoi had systematically rebuffed proposals for setting up Soviet and Chinese consulates in Ho Chi Minh City, but perhaps as a result of the talks in May and June in Moscow, in late July a twenty-one-member Soviet military delegation quietly arrived in Danang. In order to keep the visit secret the Soviet Ilyushin-62 had avoided Hanoi and flown directly to Danang—out of the reach of prying diplomatic eyes. But the Soviets were so pleased with the coup that news soon reached diplomats in Hanoi. That unpublicized visit marked the beginning of a new relationship that was to mature within two years into a full-fledged military alliance. The delegation, which consisted of all three wings of the armed forces, visited Danang, Cam Ranh Bay, Nha Trang, and several other places of military interest in the South. Their purpose: to assess Vietnam's military requirements for the next decade. They also took a first look at Vietnam's captured arsenal of American weapons—perhaps to examine the market potential of the hardware. Whether it was part of a barter arrangement with Moscow or Vietnam's own deal, from October Vietnam started quietly shipping U.S.–made armored personnel carriers to Moscow's new client, Ethiopia. As a result of the talks held during the visit, Moscow agreed to provide Vietnam with two old submarines, one destroyer, patrol boats, and four squadrons of MiG-21 fighters. With the arms agreement, the number of Soviet military advisers in Vietnam, which had been progressively reduced since 1976, began rising again as Moscow undertook to train the Vietnamese in the use of new weapons and aircraft. By the end of 1978 the total number of Soviet military advisers had climbed to six hundred and Soviet military assistance to $75 million.[38]

Hanoi soon began a public-awareness campaign to alert its population, and its enemies, about the significance of its reinforced friendship with Moscow. The sixtieth anniversary of the Bolshevik Revolution provided an ideal occasion for Hanoi to launch a "Vietnam-Soviet Union Friendship Month." Vietnamese press and television began an unprecedented campaign of praising the Soviet Union and its generous help to Vietnam. In just one month preceding the anniversary, eight Soviet delegations—from army generals to filmmakers—visited Vietnam. A Soviet Central Committee official crisscrossed the country to give lectures on the significance of the Bolshevik Revolution. Hanoi even dropped its habitual caution vis-à-vis Peking by publicizing the visit of a large Soviet military delegation led by General A. Yepishev, the chief of the political administration of the Soviet army and navy. The only event the Vietnamese did not report was that four naval experts in the delegation broke away from the main group to make a quiet inspection trip to Cam Ranh Bay and Nha Trang. The Soviets wanted to take a close look at the naval assets America had left behind. Vietnam was not yet ready to let Moscow use the facilities, but by allowing the visit, Hanoi was winking at the possibilities that lay down the road if the Soviets helped them to modernize.

In sharp contrast with the situation in the spring of 1977, when the Vietnamese media ignored Soviet aid projects, they were now lavishing Moscow with praise. "When you drink water," Le Duan announced, "you must not forget the source." The source was the Soviet Union, for whose great and valuable support he expressed "feelings of deep and true gratitude." At the end of a month-long celebration, party secretary Le Duan and Politburo number two theoretician Truong Chinh flew to Moscow to take part in the November 7 anniversary festivities. Exactly a year after the dismal anniversary reception at Hanoi's Thang Loi Hotel, Soviet-Vietnamese relations had turned full circle. One of Chairman Mao Zedong's favorite dictums had been "The East Wind prevails over the West Wind," but when that prophecy came true in Vietnam, there was no joy in Peking.

7

Calm Before the Storm

IN HIS NEW incarnation, the lanky and gaunt Hungarian Sandor Gyori was a journalist—the Hanoi correspondent of the Hungarian news agency MTI. In his preliberation persona, when I first knew him, Gyori had been a Hungarian diplomat—a member of the Hungarian delegation in the four-party International Commission for Control and Supervision (ICCS) set up by the Paris Agreement to monitor the ceasefire. The presence of Soviet bloc diplomats like Gyori in the heart of Saigon—locked in its life-and-death struggle against communism—had been one of the bizarre aspects of the war. So had been the presence of the North Vietnamese and Vietcong delegations in the barbwire compound inside the sprawling Tan Son Nhut air base. They were also part of the four-party joint military commission set up by the Paris Agreement. Unlike the Vietnamese Communist delegation that lived in tin-roofed barracks surrounded by Saigon troops, the Hungarian and Polish delegation members had more comfortable villas in the city. Gyori lived in the liveliest part of Saigon, at the Astor Hotel in downtown Tu Do Street. While he kept in touch with journalists, Gyori had also made friends with the Vietnamese delegation at Tan Son Nhut. One of his favorite people had been the plump, bespectacled Major Phuong Nam, a press officer of the Provisional Revolutionary Government delegation. An easygoing native of the Mekong Delta, Nam was always ready for a laugh. He would clutch his belt as his trousers slipped with his rippling laughter.

On a sultry September day in 1977, however, Nam was tense and worried. His job was no different—he was still a press officer—but now he worked for the unified government of Vietnam in Ho Chi Minh City. During the war he had lived in Hanoi for several years and loathed it. So, as the war ended, he opted for a life in the gentler clime of Saigon. As one of the men in charge of foreign journalists, Nam had the job of babysitting the Hungarian correspondent visiting from Hanoi. In the beginning, it seemed like a pleasurable task to accompany an old friend, share bottles of beer, and talk about old times.

Suddenly it all changed. On the morning of September 26, Nam was summoned by General Tran Van Tra, the commander of the Seventh Military Region, which covers Ho Chi Minh City and several provinces to the west bordering Cambodia. The general, a legendary military hero in the South, who had personally commanded the assault on Saigon in April 1975, was beside himself with rage. Two nights before, Khmer Rouge attackers had struck inside Tay Ninh Province, killing hundreds of civilians. This was the second time that the Khmers had mounted murderous raids on a Saturday night, when the commanders were away from their posts, many spending time with their families in Ho Chi Minh City. General Tra had ordered everybody to his post and had begun logistical preparations to launch a punitive raid against the pugnacious Khmer Rouge. He himself had visited the raided villages and been shocked by the barbarities he saw. This was something, he felt, that the world needed to see. The general had asked Nam to take the Hungarian journalist to the site of the carnage.

That Monday afternoon Gyori had gone to a church on the outskirts of the city to interview a radical Vietnamese priest, Chan Tin—an old acquaintance from preliberation days. A grim-faced Nam, who had walked into the room to interrupt the interview, asked Gyori to return to his hotel. Gyori wondered whether his questions to Chan Tin, who had turned into a critic of the Communist regime, were too provocative. Back in Gyori's hotel room Nam had only a partial explanation. "You have to get ready for a two-day trip," he announced mysteriously.

The surprise visit, Gyori learned the following morning as they left the hotel, was going to take him to a village in Tay Ninh Province. In his thirty years in the revolution, Phuong Nam had seen many deaths and scenes of violence, as had Gyori in his job with the ICCS. But neither was prepared for what they saw that day. In house after house bloated, rotting bodies of men, women, and children lay strewn about. Some were beheaded, some had their bellies ripped open, some were missing limbs, others eyes. Recalling the scene even a year later, Nam was overcome by nausea. His camera clicking away frenziedly, Gyori exhausted nearly all his supply of film. The pictures, he thought, would shock the world. Gyori also became the first foreign journalist to meet Khmer Rouge cadres who had fled to Vietnam. In unprepared encounters with some of these in the border area, he learned of the mass murders going on in Cambodia. "Until then," Gyori later admitted, "I was hesitating to accept the Cambodian holocaust because the whole question was a total taboo in Hanoi. Officially the relationship between the two countries was bright and fraternal." Now his official companions urged him to "inform the world public opinion as soon as possible."

But there were more surprises. Hardly had he returned to his hotel after a day in the dust, heat, and stench before a security official paid him a visit. His film and notes were confiscated, and he was firmly "requested" not to write anything about what he had seen, not even talk to his compatriot journalist staying in the same hotel. His telephone line was dead. Two days later, Gyori, shaken by the experience of "a discreet house arrest" flew back to Hanoi.[1]

Phuong Nam was severely reprimanded for having taken a foreign journalist to a sensitive area without authorization from the Foreign Ministry in Hanoi. Gyori and Nam were soon to learn that the Vietnamese Politburo had taken a dim view of General Tra's initiative. Not only had it ordered the suppression of all news about the Khmer Rouge attack, but also General Tra had been instructed to stop all preparations for a retaliatory attack. War with Cambodia was too serious a matter to be left in the hands of an emotional military commander. Cambodia was not alone. Behind the Khmer Rouge loomed China. Any action that Vietnam could take against Cambodia would have to be carefully weighed in terms of its military, economic, and diplomatic implications. Within a few weeks, Tra was "promoted" to vice-minister of defense—a sinecure that relegated him to an office in the Defense Ministry building in Hanoi. "In Vietnam," a Hanoi official explained in private, "one is not demoted or humiliated. If one cannot do one's job properly, one is kicked upstairs, given a fat salary and a high-sounding post!" Tra's fate was worse. A year later he was retired altogether from active duty.

On December 31, 1977, the day the Khmer Rouge publicly denounced Vietnam for "aggression," Ngo Dien called Gyori to the Foreign Ministry to return his film, cassettes, and notes. As a conciliatory gesture, Dien gave him the first official Vietnamese reaction to the new development. By then the news of Tay Ninh had become history. In the light of what had happened since the massacres in Tay Ninh, it had also become clear that it was no isolated act of madness. The attack, on the eve of Pol Pot's first official trip to China, was clearly aimed at impressing on China the seriousness of Cambodia's determination to fight Vietnam. American scholar Stephen Heder, who has perhaps interviewed more Khmer Rouge cadres and soldiers than any other Cambodia expert, believes that the September 24 attack on Tay Ninh, launched by divisions three and four of Cambodia's Eastern Zone, was a double gift. At a time when a countrywide hunt for suspected Vietnam sympathizers was on, the Eastern Zone leaders' zeal in killing Vietnamese was proof of loyalty to Pol Pot as well as an "offering" for him to carry to Peking.[2]

A Secret War

By the fall of 1977, people in Ho Chi Minh City were hearing the terrible stories from fleeing survivors. Some Vietnamese refugees escaping to Malaysia and Thailand carried stories of the border raids. But for the outside world there were only elliptical hints of trouble. Total government control of the Vietnamese media and the gagging of even friendly foreigners like Sandor Gyori helped to maintain the facade of normalcy behind which the Vietnamese Politburo could begin quiet preparations for retaliation. Four days after the Khmer Rouge attack, Radio Hanoi even broadcast a message of greetings for Pol Pot on the occasion of the public emergence of the Communist Party of Kampuchea.

After months of planning, including Giap's personal assessment on the ground, the Vietnamese Army launched its first important, but unpublicized, military operation against Cambodia, in October 1977. After driving armored columns up to fifteen miles into the bordering Cambodian province of Svay Rieng, the Vietnamese feigned retreat. As a battalion of Khmer Rouge infantry entered Vietnamese territory in hot pursuit, another waiting Vietnamese column swung from the side and caught several hundred of them in a mousetrap. However, the losses suffered by the Khmer Rouge did not seem to stop them one bit.[3]

Curiously enough, in its official indictment against Vietnam—the *Black Book* published by the Pol Pot regime in September 1978—no mention is made of the October 1977 attack by the Vietnamese. Perhaps the setback suffered by the Khmer Rouge was too embarrassing to mention. While the Vietnamese have been accused of several foiled assassination attempts against Pol Pot in the 1975–76 period, the *Black Book,* surprisingly, does not mention any coup attempt in the whole of 1977. The only significant act before the end of the year, according to the book, was a Vietnamese decision in mid-1977 to "set up a plan of large-scale attack."[4] The *Black Book* does not, however, provide any details about this alleged plan. A later, official Vietnamese account reveals that preparations for the most important coup attempt against the Pol Pot regime began in November 1977. Dissident Khmer Rouge cadres of the Eastern Zone had started building secret food reserves in the jungle. But no date was set for the uprising.[5]

Did Hanoi play any role in planning that coup? For the Vietnamese it would have been the most likely course of action. But Western intelligence analysts and scholars who have interviewed hundreds of former Khmer Rouge and Vietnamese Communist defectors and examined the voluminous confessions made by Khmer detainees in Tuol Sleng, Phnom Penh's notorious school-turned-prison, have not been able to find any evidence of direct Hanoi involvement in plots against Pol Pot. If the Vietnamese indeed succeeded in eluding the Khmer Rouge spy network and overcame the barrier of isolation to establish contact with plotters inside Cambodia, that feat still remains a closely held secret. What is certain, however, is that from October 1977 Hanoi started taking the first steps in forming an anti–Pol Pot resistance in Vietnam.

In many ways the Tay Ninh massacres and the planning leading up to them proved to be a turning point in Vietnam's relations with Cambodia and in the careers of several Khmer Rouge cadres who crossed over to the Vietnamese side. One of them was Hun Sen, a young Khmer Rouge regimental commander in charge of the border region—from Kratie to Kompong Cham. In early 1977 he received orders from the central command to ready his units for attacks of up to nine miles inside Tay Ninh Province. The ground attack by regional units, scheduled to be launched on May 30, would be supported by the artillery of Division Four. But several of the regimental and battalion commanders refused to go ahead with the plan; they were arrested and executed. Hun Sen, youngest of them all, was obviously trusted by the central command and so was given charge of the operation. "But I saw that I could not do this," Hun Sen later told Stephen Heder, "so I had no other choice but to withdraw together with a certain number of forces and go into the jungle. That was on June 20, 1977."[6] Soon thereafter he went over to the Vietnamese.

The plan of attack was finally implemented on September 24. Its "success" ironically, however, meant promotion for a Khmer Rouge commander who was destined to emerge as Vietnam's main ally in Cambodia: Heng Samrin, a short, dark, somber-looking forty-three-year-old. Heng Samrin's brothers, too, were cadres in the Khmer Rouge apparatus in the Eastern Zone. It is not known what personal role Samrin played in the brutal assault, but he was soon promoted to chairman of "Route 7 Battlefront"—at the zone bordering Vietnam—and thus effectively became deputy chairman of the Eastern Region military staff. Several months later this elevated position made him the lightning rod for Pol Pot's wrath when his divisions failed to stand up to the Vietnamese. He, too, fled to Vietnam to save his skin.[7]

The problem of Cambodia figured in the series of unpublicized meetings in Moscow that the Vietnamese leaders had in the summer of 1977. The Soviets were also kept informed of Vietnamese moves against the Pol Pot regime. In November 1977, a Soviet diplomat in Hanoi confided to an Indian colleague that an anti–Pol Pot resistance was in the making. It consisted of a group of ten to fifteen central-level leaders, at least three of whom were old members of the Vietnamese-led Indochinese Communist Party.[8] The diplomat had not clarified whether the resistance was inside Cambodia or whether it was being organized in Vietnam.

By the fall of 1977 a number of Khmer Rouge defectors, including Hun Sen, Hem Samin, and Bou Thang (who were later to play key roles in the fight against Pol Pot), had collected in Vietnam. And the brutal Khmer Rouge attack on Tay Ninh in September had finally shaken Hanoi to look at options other than the unpublicized aerial bombing and shelling attacks on Cambodia it had undertaken since May 1977.

After months of interrogations and observation, the Vietnamese concluded that the defectors from the Khmer Rouge whom they had been holding were not agents provocateurs. The Khmer Rouge assault on Tay Ninh turned out to be the clinching evidence of the truthfulness of the defectors, because some of them, especially Hun Sen, had provided the Vietnamese with details of the planned attack.[9] Either that information was not believed or inexplicably never passed on to the regional military command. When the attack finally came, Vietnamese civilians were defenseless. Sometime after the attack the Vietnamese organized a meeting of eight of the recent escapees to discuss the political future of Cambodia.[10]

Hanoi saw in their desire to go back to fight Pol Pot new levers of pressure that would complement its military muscle. However, before taking the plunge in backing yet another move to unseat a government in Cambodia—its third since its engagement against the French in the 1940s and 1950s and against the Lon Nol regime in the 1970s—the Vietnamese wanted to make one last try at separating China from Cambodia. Vietnam's message to China would be a mixture of a plea for help and a veiled warning about the consequences of support for Cambodia.

Testing the Water in Peking

As Vietnamese officials would later admit to me, until the fall of 1977 they were uncertain about the extent of Chinese backing for Pol Pot. Hoang Tung had forecast a weakening of Sino-Cambodian relations after the downfall of the Gang of Four. He had argued that the reemergence of the pragmatic leader Deng Xiaoping would lead to China's distancing itself from the ultraradical Khmer Rouge. Events since early 1977, when China formally declined to increase aid to Vietnam, had progressively discouraged the Vietnamese about the prospect of improving relations with China. But Vietnamese leaders were still unsure whether Chinese unhappiness with Vietnam would extend to backing Khmer Rouge military provocations against Vietnam. Pol Pot's grand welcome in Peking in the fall of 1977 and his ill-disguised attacks on Vietnam delivered there had raised grave concern in Hanoi. On October 3, 1977, while Pol Pot was still continuing his triumphant visit in China, Vietnam's top negotiator, Phan Hien, was secretly dispatched to Peking. Requesting China to arrange a meeting with the Cambodians was one way of finding out where Peking stood in the emerging Cambodia-Vietnam conflict. China obliged. The two sessions between Hien and the Cambodian representative in Peking, however, proved acrimonious and futile. The Cambodians violently criticized Vietnam for acts of aggression, subversion, and sabotage. They specifically accused Vietnam of mounting several abortive coups against the regime. Hien in turn condemned brutal Cambodian attacks on Vietnam but proposed talks to reduce tension along the border. The Khmer reply was that there would be no talks until Vietnam agreed to stop its subversion and sabotage. But for the Vietnamese such a proposition was intolerable; it was admitting guilt before even sitting down to talk.[11]

Hien did not have any better luck in settling Vietnam's border dispute with China. In October he began a separate series of meetings with the Chinese on the demarcation of Vietnam's 797-mile-long border with China and delineation of the Gulf of Tonkin, which both countries shared. The talks he started in Peking on October 7 continued off and on for ten months before open hostilities ended all dialogue.[12]

A week after Hien's departure for Peking in October, Hanoi issued a discreet warning by publicizing a Soviet military delegation's visit. Hanoi seemed to be saying that Chinese support for Cambodia would result in closer Vietnamese cooperation with Peking's enemy—the Soviet Union.[13]

Curiously enough, shortly before the Soviet military visit, China took a significant step in boosting the military capability of its Cambodian allies. It is tempting to speculate whether Peking had well-placed friends (like former Politburo member Hoang Van Hoan, who later defected to China) providing intelligence about Vietnam's growing ties with Moscow.[14]

Even if China did not have specific intelligence, it seems to have effectively second-guessed Vietnam in crucial moments of history. On October 5, just two days after Hien left for his talks in Peking and five days before the arrival of General Yepishev in Hanoi, the Chinese military attaché in Phnom Penh signed, on behalf of the General Staff of the Chinese Ministry of Defense, a protocol for the delivery of arms to Cambodia. This was a result of an agreement for nonrefundable military aid from China signed in February 1976. The quietly concluded protocol provided for a complete set of equipment—from walkie-talkies to jet fighters—needed to build all three branches of the Cambodian armed forces.[15]

In a more visible expression of displeasure with Vietnam, China pared down its regular air service to Hanoi. The Civil Aviation Administration of China's (CAAC) Trident service between Hanoi and Canton (which was linked by railway to Hongkong) was the principal route to the outside world for the foreign community in the Vietnamese capital and was frequently booked for weeks in advance. Obviously, China felt it more important to show its pique than to consider the commercial aspects of such a move. On the absurd pretext of slow business, the Chinese airline cut its two weekly flights to one, effective from November 1, 1977.

While raising barriers to Vietnam, Peking set out to strengthen its communication facilities with Cambodia. Chinese technicians had been at work in Phnom Penh since October to install telecommunication equipment. Until the inauguration of direct teletype and radio links with China, which were announced with great fanfare on November 10, 1977, the Chinese embassy's radio link with Peking was Phnom Penh's only link to the outside world.[16]

Ten days after his return from Moscow, Vietnamese party secretary Le Duan left again on a foreign trip, this time to Peking. It had become almost customary that the Vietnamese party leader would balance his visit to the capital of one Communist rival with a visit to the other. But Duan's November 21 visit to Peking was no exercise in tightrope walking. "Comrade Le Duan," a Vietnamese diplomat explained to me shortly after the trip, "is like our hero Ly Thuong Kiet. He has gone to confront the enemy in his own lair." (Ly Thuong Kiet, a Vietnamese monarch of the eleventh century, led a brilliant preemptive attack on China before the Chinese could invade Vietnam.)

The Vietnamese leader, however, began his talks modestly by appealing to China's pride. "We are your younger brothers, constantly standing on your side, and we would not do otherwise," he reportedly told Chinese party chairman Hua Guofeng.[17]

But Duan pointed out that despite its difference with China over broad strategic issues, Vietnam had taken care not to criticize China in public or side with Moscow in its denunciation of China. In return, however, it had not received any consideration from China. He pointedly reminded the Chinese leaders of the late Premier Zhou Enlai's remark that support for building socialism in Vietnam constituted an "international obligation" of China's. Duan expressed regret over the death of Mao Zedong, Zhou Enlai, and Zhu De and then, in a statement that bordered on the rude, reflected on China's political line. Duan said Vietnam was confident that China would "decidedly not allow any exploiting class to raise its head in an attempt to cause New China to change color."[18]

Le Duan failed to secure Chinese disengagement from the Khmer Rouge. The Chinese leaders accused Vietnam of bullying small Cambodia and trying to force it into a subordinate "special relationship." Hua even came close to publicly affirming China's support for Cambodia against Vietnam. Addressing a banquet for Le Duan, he said that China was resolved "to ally with all countries subject to imperialist and social-imperialist aggression, subversion, and interference, control, or bullying to form the broadest possible united front against superpower hegemonism."

Duan responded to the Chinese challenge by announcing that Vietnam was determined not to allow "any imperialist or reactionary forces whatsoever to encroach upon our independence and freedom."[19] Although Hua talked of "hegemonism" and Duan denounced "reactionary forces," it was clear they were taking potshots at each other.

During past visits, Duan and other Vietnamese leaders had politely rebuffed China's attempts to draw Vietnam into an anti-Soviet alliance. While praising Chinese help, they did not fail to thank other "fraternal Socialist countries"—meaning the Soviet bloc.[20] But on this occasion Duan shocked his hosts by praising the Soviet Union by name. The facade of civility that had so long covered Sino-Vietnamese tension had worn very thin. When Le Duan returned to Hanoi, the lines of a new conflict had been drawn.

The Chinese political commitment to back Cambodia, however, came after the acrimonious meetings with Le Duan in November 1977. In a confidential review of Chinese policy toward Indochina, Geng Biao, secretary general of the Communist party's military commission, noted that when talks were held with Le Duan in November 1977, "the divergence between Vietnam and Cambodia could no longer be covered up. Our efforts to prevent the contradiction between them from coming out into the open since the liberation of Cambodia in 1975 finally failed. Therefore, in December, the Party Central Committee decided to give energetic support to Cambodia, strengthening it so that it might cope with the possible new situation when negotiations fail to solve the problems."[21]

Geng Biao's remarks indicate that while being sympathetic to Cambodia and cognizant of its value as an instrument to frustrate Vietnamese hegemony, the Chinese leadership still stressed negotiation as the primary course for Cambodia and Vietnam rather than confrontation. The cautious approach, an obvious retreat from their encouragement to Pol Pot in September 1977, perhaps reflected the unresolved political struggle in the Chinese party itself. The re-emergent pragmatic leaders around Deng Xiaoping were not only critical of the procrustean policies of the Khmer Rouge but also reluctant to endorse their provocative approach toward Vietnam.[22]

Time to Hold Pol Pot's Hand

It was thus not surprising that when a week after Le Duan's Peking visit China wanted to demonstrate its support for Cambodia, the man chosen to do the job was a known radical—Vice-Premier and Politburo member Chen Yonggui. Chen had shot to prominence as leader of the Dazhai Commune in Shanxi Province by exemplifying the Maoist principle of self-reliance in agriculture. In agriculture, "learn from Dazhai" was Mao's famous slogan. Although not a political heavyweight, Chen was an obvious ideological soul mate of the Khmer Rouge and was likely to be listened to by Pol Pot.

On December 3 Chen flew into Phnom Penh for an unusually long ten-day trip. On the day of his arrival Xinhua News Agency published a commentary entitled "Sino-Cambodian Friendship Is Deep-Rooted and Thriving," which emphasized China's historic links with Cambodia and its unwavering support for the Pol Pot leadership. While Chen's promenades in sensitive border areas were publicized by Cambodia in order to impress Hanoi, in his speeches the Chinese visitor refrained from any direct reference to Cambodia's territorial conflict with Vietnam. Whether Chen had seen any evidence of a Vietnamese attack in the Parrot's Beak area on December 5 or not, he chose to announce China's support for Cambodia in more general terms.[23] "No force," he said, "can stand in the way of friendly relations between China and Cambodia, which will be comrades forever."[24]

The Cambodians were probably not entirely happy with China's reluctance to come out more openly against Vietnam. Cambodian vice-premier Vorn Vet (who was to be a victim of Pol Pot's purge several months later) declared in a banquet speech honouring Chen, "Cambodia will definitely not let itself . . . be reduced to a satellite once again nor slip back into a position of losing territories or territorial waters." He also reminded his guest that "our Chinese comrades have seen with their own eyes the determination of the . . . revolutionary army for a full and complete realization of its sacred aspiration." For all that Chen might have seen, his public remarks were notably devoid of any reference to the devotion and heroism of the army.

Chen, however, was generous in his support for Pol Pot's policy of a forced march to communism. Cambodia's agricultural cooperatives, he announced, were playing an important role "in crushing sabotage by the enemy and consolidating the dictatorship of the proletariat." Chen also gave strong endorsement of Pol Pot's domestic policies as "entirely correct."[25]

A Prince Tries for Peace

Two days after Chen Yonggui's departure from Phnom Penh, Pol Pot had another visitor—the Lao president, Prince Souphanouvong. As it turned out, this was the last attempt at mediation between Vietnam and Cambodia before Hanoi removed all stops in its attack. Although Lao leadership had allied with Vietnam for reasons of realpolitik and self-interest, it had anxiously watched Vietnam's growing tension with Cambodia. Khieu Samphan and Ieng Sary had visited the Pathet Lao liberated zone in Sam Neua in 1974. So when in November 1977 the Lao government approached the Cambodians through their embassy in Vientiane for a visit by President Souphanouvong, they could not turn down the offer of such a high-level visit.

On December 17 Prince Souphanouvong arrived at Phnom Penh's Pochentong Airport to a solemn reception. His meeting with Pol Pot immediately made it clear that there was no chance of averting an open rupture. The Cambodians did not even want to publicize the fact that Pol Pot received the Lao president. During a tense meeting at the government guesthouse overlooking the Tonle Sap River, Souphanouvong urged Pol Pot not to disrupt the unity of the three Indochinese countries forged through years of struggle against common enemies. "But Pol Pot did not want to listen to all that," a senior Lao official told me later, "and he just kept on saying all sorts

of bad things about Vietnam." Pol Pot tried to convince Souphanouvong that Laos should maintain independence vis-à-vis Vietnam.
It was a dialogue of the deaf.

But the Red Prince, whose own revolutionary career was inextricably linked with the Ho Chi Minh–led Indochinese Communist
Party, was not about to leave Phnom Penh without making his point
in public. Speaking at a reception in his honor, Souphanouvong told
his hosts that the Lao party "has pursued the glorious task of the
Indochinese Communist Party and fought shoulder to shoulder with
fraternal Cambodian and Vietnamese people." Pointedly responding
to the Cambodian criticism of the Lao-Vietnamese treaty relations,
he said that it was "an example of a policy of friendship and good-
neighborliness as well as an example of our international relations."
A Lao official present at the reception recalled that there was an
embarrassing silence in the hall as Souphanouvong read his speech.
Beads of perspiration formed on the foreheads of the assembled diplomatic corps and Khmer officials as they sat still through that sultry afternoon, exceptionally hot for December. In his speech Khieu
Samphan obliquely criticized Laos for forming an alliance with Vietnam and allowing the stationing of Vietnamese troops on its territory. He warned that relations between the two countries would
develop only if they refrained from interfering in each other's internal affairs and did not allow the use of one's territory against the
other.

Despite the tension, below the surface formal cordiality was
maintained. Ieng Sary came to attend a dinner hosted by Souphanouvong at the Lao embassy. As planned, the prince was taken aboard
a World War II–vintage DC-3 to Siemreap to visit the famous ruins
of Angkor. A Lao diplomat accompanying Souphanouvong reminisced later that it was an unforgettable journey. The pilots were
Khmer boys who had just finished training in China. "The landing
and takeoff were pretty hair-raising. It really felt nice to be back on
the ground," he recalled.[26]

On December 26, four days after Souphanouvong's return from
Cambodia, Vietnamese foreign minister Nguyen Duy Trinh stopped
in Vientiane on his way to Indonesia. Souphanouvong briefed him
about his tough exchanges with Pol Pot. Trinh listened gravely but

did not tell the prince that even as they talked, tank-led Vietnamese columns were rolling inside Cambodia. The Third Indochina War that the Lao leader hoped to avoid had already begun—out of sight of the world media.

A sizable force of the Vietnamese infantry and artillery, including the elite Ninth Infantry Division, launched a massive attack on Cambodia from half a dozen points along the border, with two principal prongs heading toward the capital. Troops on T-54 tanks and M-113 armored personnel carriers spearheaded the drive along Route 1 and Route 7 leading toward Phnom Penh. The Vietnamese purpose was, as Hoang Tung later explained to me, "first to chase them [the Khmer Rouge] from our territory and then deal a heavy blow to their divisions, to make them realize that we are not passive as they have assumed and to tell them that they have to choose the other solution—negotiations." [27]

The first of the Vietnamese objectives was achieved almost effortlessly. Vietnamese forces backed by artillery barrages had gone into Cambodia like a knife through soft butter. Hundreds of Khmer soldiers were killed and wounded in the Vietnamese search-and-destroy operation. The fortunate among the wounded were carried on stretchers to Phnom Penh. Although there were hospitals to shelter the injured, they had little else to comfort them. A campaign for donating blood was started among the small population of cadres and families who lived on the outskirts of the near-deserted capital. The sudden emergency brutally brought home the effects of the Khmer Rouge revolution. Hundreds of bourgeois doctors had been dispatched to the countryside for hard labor, and many had been executed. Hospitals were being run by paramedics—peasant boys turned "revolutionary doctors." Their attempts at blood transfusions wrought disaster. [28]

There was only desultory opposition from the regional forces overwhelmed by the Vietnamese armor and firepower. One prong of the attack had reached close to Kompong Cham—an important provincial capital on the Mekong River straddling the road to Phnom Penh. Another column had come to the outskirts of the provincial capital of Svay Rieng. Several other smaller probes had entered Cambodia blasting their way through scattered resistance. The regional units, even the Fourth Division belonging to the center—under Heng Samrin's command—had dispersed before the advancing Vietnamese columns.

The leaders in Phnom Penh had been taken aback by the scale of Vietnamese attack and shocked by the rout of the forces in the Eastern Zone. But they were not ready to sue for peace, as the Vietnamese had hoped. On December 25 a specially convened meeting of the leading Khmer Rouge cadres in Phnom Penh decided to send reinforcements to the Eastern Zone and, more important, to respond to the Vietnamese military move with political escalation. With Vietnamese forces occupying part of eastern Cambodia, the occasion was thought to be perfect to put Hanoi on the defensive by denouncing its aggression before the world. Public revelation of the conflict would be accompanied by the announcement of suspension of diplomatic relations with Vietnam. Khmer Rouge cadres did not seem to mind the military setback as they gloated over the diplomatic coup. "We got 'em first. On hearing the news, the world is going to jump," was how Khmer Rouge cadres talked about their announcement.[29]

Lifting the Veil on a Hidden War

Kieu Ming, first secretary of the Vietnamese embassy in Phnom Penh, habitually began his day by tuning in to Radio Phnom Penh. That was the only way of knowing the views of the Pol Pot regime. A mimeographed French translation of the broadcast was distributed to the embassies in the afternoon. Ming, a fluent Khmer speaker, preferred to listen to the news rather than wait for the translated text. On the morning of December 31, 1977, something strange was happening. Instead of the revolutionary music and news bulletins, the radio began its six o'clock broadcast with a special announcement. It marked the beginning of a propaganda barrage against Vietnam the like of which had never been witnessed among "fraternal" Socialist countries. The broadcast said:

Taking into consideration the ferocious and barbarous aggression launched by the Vietnamese aggressor forces against Democratic

Kampuchea and the innocent Kampuchean people; taking into consideration the unfriendly attitude and ill-will of the government of the Socialist Republic of Vietnam [SRV] . . . the government of Democratic Kampuchea decided to temporarily sever diplomatic relations with the SRV as from 31 December 1977 until the aggressor forces of the SRV withdraw from the sacred territory of Democratic Kampuchea and until the friendly atmosphere between the countries is restored.[30]

Four hours later a stern-looking messenger from the Cambodian Foreign Ministry came to deliver the eviction notice: the Vietnamese embassy staff was ordered to leave Phnom Penh within a week. On January 3 Kieu Ming and other staff members left for Ho Chi Minh City aboard a special flight. For Ming it proved to be a rather short farewell. After a year he was back in "liberated" Phnom Penh when the Vietnamese army had driven out the Pol Pot regime. The Cambodian ambassador in Hanoi had a different fate. Before his departure from Hanoi Airport on January 2 for Peking, Democratic Kampuchean ambassador So Kheang had embraced a Vietnamese diplomat. Whether as a result of that incident, observed by Chinese diplomats present at the airport, or any other alleged pro-Vietnamese act, he was executed within three months of his return to Phnom Penh.[31]

The Khmer Rouge were right. The announcement from Radio Phnom Penh did stun the world. Less than three years after the end of the Indochina war a new intra-Communist warfare had burst into the open—putting an end to months of hints and speculations about trouble between the two erstwhile allies. Suddenly the power equation in Southeast Asia changed.

The timing of the Khmer Rouge denunciation was particularly embarrassing to Hanoi because its foreign minister had just set out on a visit to non-Communist Southeast Asia trying to promote good-neighbor relations. While mounting its attack Hanoi, obviously, had not calculated on such a sharp public response from Cambodia. Previous Vietnamese counterattacks against Cambodia, including air strikes, had been quietly stomached by the Khmer Rouge. Now that the spotlight had suddenly been turned on the secret war between comrades, Vietnam quickly unleashed a no-holds-barred propaganda attack on the Khmer Rouge. In graphic language that matched Phnom Penh's sharp condemnations, Hanoi began to detail the myriad crimes of the Pol Pot regime and its repeated attacks on Vietnam that had so far been carefully hidden from the public eye.

It is unknown whether Pol Pot had consulted Peking or even given it advance notice before taking the irreversible step. Judging by the reticence of Chen Yonggui to publicly pronounce on the border conflict with Vietnam barely ten days earlier, the Cambodian decision to suspend ties with Vietnam may well have been designed to force China's hand.[32]

The Cambodian leaders could not have failed to notice how tardy China was in making good its promise of military aid. It took Peking over a year and a half to firm up what it had promised in February 1976. Neither could the Cambodians have missed Deng Xiaoping's noncommittal position on the Cambodia-Vietnam conflict. In October 1977, responding to a journalist's question on the conflict, Deng had said, "The problems will be resolved by themselves. What we want is for them to carry out good negotiations. We ourselves do not judge what is just or erroneous."[33] The fact that Deng, who was condemned by Phnom Penh as a "counterrevolutionary" only a year earlier, was strengthening his position within the Chinese Communist party might well have been an additional reason for Pol Pot to present the Chinese with a fait accompli.[34]

Chinese diplomats in Hanoi demonstrated their solidarity with Cambodia by accompanying the Cambodian embassy staff as they left for home via Peking aboard a Chinese airliner. But Peking clearly was uncomfortable with the dramatic escalation of the conflict and open rupture of relations between the two Indochinese countries. China's Xinhua News Agency reported fully the Cambodian charges but also reproduced Vietnamese counterallegations—albeit more briefly. While being implicitly sympathetic to Cambodia, Chinese coverage of the conflict seemed to favor negotiations rather than escalation. That Peking was not ready to openly pressure Vietnam was evidenced by the fact that on January 10, 1978, China signed its annual agreement on the supply of goods and payments with Vietnam. As U.S. government analysts noted, at the time the Chinese "could have delayed the agreement if they wished to demonstrate displeasure with Hanoi."[35] China also agreed to arrange another meeting between the Vietnamese and the Cambodians—which proved as futile as the previous one in October.[36]

Another Chinese visit to Cambodia was hastily arranged. This time China's message would be carried by a leader of moderate persuasion—Madame Deng Yingchao. China was not concerned only about the security of Cambodia in the face of overwhelming Vietnamese military superiority and the danger inherent in its provocative policy. Warily watching Vietnam's steadily growing ties with Moscow, China could not ignore the possibility of a greater Soviet involvement if it openly intervened in the conflict. It was clearly in Peking's interest not to allow the Indochinese conflict to get out of hand. Madame Deng, however, inspired little confidence in Phnom Penh. She was not only the widow of the late Premier Zhou Enlai, whose death brought jubilation among many Khmer Rouge, but also a close friend of the former Cambodian head of state, Prince Sihanouk, who had been put under house arrest in Phnom Penh.[37]

Tail Wags the Dog

On January 18, accompanied by a large entourage that included Chinese vice–foreign minister Han Nianlong and other Southeast Asian experts, Madame Deng arrived in Phnom Penh. But the fanfare with which she was received masked a serious failure. Since the fall of 1977 Chinese leaders had urged the Cambodians to broaden their political base and bring Sihanouk back to political life. Now Pol Pot turned down her request for a meeting with the prince. The message that she was to give him from his ballerina daughter Bopha Devi, who was living in Paris, remained undelivered.[38] Her suggestion that Cambodia should try to settle the problems with Vietnam through negotiations was also rejected. In a public speech in Phnom Penh, Deng Yingchao affirmed China's support for the Five Principles of Peaceful Coexistence as the "fundamental principles by which all countries the world over, including the Socialist countries, must abide in the effort to settle relations between countries."[39]

In his speech, People's Representative Assembly Chairman Nuon Chea assured Madame Deng that the Cambodian people "have a firm and most reasonable patriotism, have never provoked, and have no desire to provoke, anyone." However, he said, "our Cambodian people will struggle resolutely against the acts of sabotage and subversion from within aimed at staging a coup d'état to topple Democratic Kampuchea, against the nibbling acts in the border area, and all acts of aggression and expansion from without."[40]

As if the oblique refutation of the Chinese suggestion were not enough, Phnom Penh took the unusual step of airing a thinly veiled criticism of China while Deng Yingchao was still in Cambodia. On the afternoon of January 20, just after Madame Deng had left the capital for a visit to Angkor on her way home, Radio Phnom Penh broadcast a commentary entitled "The Cambodian People Firmly Adhere to the Stands of Independence, Mastery, and Self-Reliance and Clearly Distinguish Friends and Foes the World Over."

"Cambodia is a small and poor country, its population sparse. However," the commentary affirmed, "the Cambodian people under the leadership of the Kampuchean Communist party are extremely courageous." It downplayed the significance of Chinese aid to Cambodia by claiming that Cambodians were fighting "mainly by relying on [their] own efforts." Facing Vietnamese aggression and annexation, Cambodia needed friends, it said, but only those who treated Cambodia on the basis of equality. The radio darkly hinted at bullying by a powerful friend. "We distinguish between good and bad friends. We respect and love friends who are good to us, who respect the independence, sovereignty, and territorial integrity of Cambodia, and who deal with us on an equal footing. But our friend-making criterion is not based on whether this or that friend can provide material aid. It is based on the principles of equality, mutual respect, and mutual benefit, on sentiments of solidarity in accordance with the principle of respecting and protecting the right of each country, be it large or small, to manage its own destiny. . . ."[41]

Pol Pot's defiance narrowed Peking's options. In the winter of 1977 China was concerned by what it considered to be a weak-kneed "appeasement" policy followed by the Carter administration toward Moscow. Peking did not want to unnecessarily provoke Moscow by openly backing Cambodia against Vietnam. But, as the Cambodian reaction made clear, that cautious approach ran the risk of alienating its most important ally in Southeast Asia. China decided to forgo the tactical gain in order to retain its strategic advantage. Possibly, left-wing elements in the Chinese party were also reluctant to pressure a revolutionary ally for a tactical difference.

Other considerations—such as stepped-up Soviet-Vietnamese collaboration, the Soviet propaganda offensive against China for its Cambodia policy, and the growing problem with the Chinese residents in Vietnam—must have argued for abandoning Peking's public stance of neutrality. Soviet Politburo member Grigory Romanov had made an unscheduled trip to Hanoi and Ho Chi Minh City in mid-February. This was followed on February 21 by a Vietnamese statement that came close to publicly denouncing China. A Radio Hanoi commentary charged that an unnamed power had used Cambodia to attack Vietnam. Using the newly coined code words for China, it said that "imperialists and international reactionaries have helped them [the Cambodians] build up and equip overnight a dozen divisions armed with long-range artillery and warplanes which Cambodia did not have before."[42]

Whether giving in to Pol Pot's blackmail or proceeding from its own reassessment of Vietnam's military plans, Peking quickly dropped its efforts at a negotiated settlement. While Chinese ships started unloading 130-millimeter long-range artillery, assorted antitank weapons, and amphibious vehicles at Kompong Som Port, Peking shed its public neutral posture.[43] In a speech on February 26, Premier Hua Guofeng formally abandoned the attempt to promote settlement through the Five Principles of Peaceful Coexistence. "No country," he said, clearly with Vietnam in mind, "should seek hegemony in any region or impose its will on another. Whether a country treats others on an equal footing or seeks hegemony is a major criterion by which we will tell whether or not it follows the five principles of coexistence. . . ."[44]

In early January 1978, while the war of the airwaves was joined in earnest by Phnom Penh and Hanoi, elements of three central divisions under the command of three stalwarts of the Khmer Rouge government—Defense Minister Son Sen, Commander of the Central Zone Ke Pauk, and Commander of the Southwestern Zone Ta Mok—began to move toward the Eastern Zone. But before the divisions could confront Hanoi's troops, they turned back and headed home.

To hide its initial defeat, the Khmer Rouge began an intense propaganda campaign to present the voluntary Vietnamese withdrawal as a "great historic victory." January 6 was declared to have gone into history as a red-letter day when an invasion by mighty Vietnam was cut to pieces by the Khmers. To celebrate the victory, an extra plate of rice was served in the communal kitchen for cadres in Phnom Penh. In mass meetings stories were told depicting how the heroic combatants destroyed Vietnamese tanks by the dozens and melted them all into plates for food.[45]

The victory celebrations, however, were soon followed by a new wave of killing. If the Vietnamese had succeeded in penetrating up to twenty-five miles inside Cambodia and thousands of Khmers had fled to Vietnam with them, then the Eastern Zone administration had to be full of traitors, the central leadership reasoned. Shortly after the Vietnamese invasion the commander of the Fourth Division was shot dead by a regional security official loyal to Pol Pot.[46]

Dispensing with the habitually oblique language, Radio Phnom Penh announced that a new task now was to defend "offices and departments by exterminating both the enemy remnants planted within and the enemy aggressors coming from without." The people would have to "eliminate at all costs from their minds . . . all the vestiges left behind by the society of the imperialists, reactionary feudal capitalists, and all other oppressor classes . . . do away with all irresponsible views . . . eliminate all kinds of private, individualist concepts . . . and build the country at an extremely rapid speed. . . ."[47] Implementation of this policy meant longer work hours, less food, and an intensified witch-hunt for people with wrong ideas. Hardest hit were the provinces penetrated by the Vietnamese.

The new and ferocious wave of purges—mostly against suspect Khmer Rouge cadres and families—begun in January 1978 would culminate in an abortive uprising in May and even greater massacres. The chief executor of the extermination campaign was Pol

Pot's most trusted lieutenant, the veteran Communist leader Ta Mok, a lanky and baldish peasant with piercing eyes. His name struck terror in the hearts of people and his troops were the cruelest of all. Under his command his *Nirdey* [Southwestern Zone] troops struck a killing spree in the east that would later be taken all over the land as the increasingly beleaguered regime continued its hunt for hidden enemies.[48]

While the Pol Pot leadership began its preparations for a showdown by purging its ranks and building and equipping its armed forces, Vietnamese leaders quietly went about their own preparations.

Hanoi Plans for Cambodia

Every winter since the reunification of the country in 1975, top Vietnamese leaders would leave the cold and mist of Hanoi to travel to the sunny South. They would visit factories, cooperatives, and army units to bring the Vietnamese New Year's greetings and deliver a little pep talk on the "glorious task of building socialism." Those visits also offered them a holiday in more hospitable climes. But 1978 was different. The South was not only a warmer retreat but also where the action was. By the end of January 1978 the members of the Vietnamese Politburo had quietly assembled in Ho Chi Minh City for what turned out to be a momentous series of meetings. The Khmer Rouge decision to break relations had shocked the Vietnamese. The conflict that the Vietnamese so assiduously kept secret was out on the front pages of the world press, and all of a sudden Vietnam was in the dock, accused of "swallowing" its smaller neighbor. The hero of yesterday's "anti-imperialist" fight was now cast in the role of a mini-imperialist.

The Politburo's leaders met in total secrecy and assessed the result of their December (1977) invasion. They had badly mauled the Khmer Rouge, but there was no evidence that their victory had had any repercussions for Pol Pot's leadership. The Vietnamese military success had neither provoked a coup nor challenged his leadership. But the Vietnamese had succeeded in bringing back with them nearly sixty thousand Khmers. Since 1975 some three hundred thousand

Khmers, Vietnamese, and Chinese refugees had escaped to Vietnam from Cambodia. Hanoi had kept quiet about it. But now the army-assisted exodus was presented to the world as additional evidence of people fleeing Pol Pot's Cambodia. The United Nations High Commissioner of Refugees (UNHCR) was asked to assist these displaced Cambodians.

In March 1978 I visited a refugee camp—Ben Sanh—for newly arrived Khmers in Vietnam's Tay Ninh Province. The "camp" was a dusty and barren stretch of land with a cluster of makeshift bamboo and straw-roofed huts. From my unmonitored conversations with the Cambodians there, it was clear that they were a different kind of refugee. And Vietnam had something different in mind than humanitarian concern in giving them asylum. "Would you go back to Cambodia?" I asked a young teacher presented by the Vietnamese to talk to the press about the atrocities in Cambodia. "Yes, when the whole of the country is liberated," she answered in halting French. Liberated by whom? To the obvious discomfort of the Vietnamese officials she said, "Why, the Vietnamese army." She had perhaps been asked not to mention the formation of a Khmer resistance army in Vietnam. Other Khmers in the camp, however, privately told me of the recruitment of some two thousand men and women from the Ben Sanh camp to fight against Pol Pot in Cambodia. So while the UNHCR began a program of feeding the residents of the camp, the Vietnamese army took charge of the able-bodied Khmers. The Vietnamese had clearly improved upon Mao Zedong's theory of people's war in which the guerrilla was to be like a fish in the water of a supportive population!

In the January meeting Le Duc Tho, Politburo's "Old Cambodia hand," took the lead in discussing the next steps in Vietnam's confrontation with Cambodia. The tough talks with the Chinese leaders in November 1977 had convinced Le Duan that they—as Vietnam's foreign minister Nguyen Co Thach, a participant in the talks, told me later—"will use Pol Pot against us." The Khmer Rouge decision to sever ties with Vietnam only two weeks after the visit to Cambodia of a Chinese Politburo member had convinced the Vietnamese to prepare for a bigger intervention. "When Pol Pot broke diplomatic relations with us," Thach said, "we knew the Chinese were preparing for war. So we had to reconsider all our options." The options were military preparations and diplomatic fence-mending with the United States and non-Communist Southeast Asia. Time had come for Vietnam to combine military pressure with an open call for rebellion against Pol Pot. Active preparation would begin for setting up a Khmer resistance army while Vietnam would try to recover the diplomatic initiative from Cambodia.

The proposal the Vietnamese drafted was announced two weeks later. On February 5, 1978, Radio Hanoi aired its three-point proposal to Cambodia calling for mutual withdrawal of approximately three miles, signing of a nonaggression treaty, and international supervision of the border. "We knew," a Vietnamese official later admitted to me, "that the Khmer Rouge would never accept that proposal, but at least the blame of rejection would be on them." The Vietnamese proposal was given the widest publicity, and the Soviet bloc countries issued statements supporting it as "reasonable." As expected, Phnom Penh scornfully rejected the offer, calling it an attempt at intimidating Cambodia and swaying international opinion.

In late January 1978, General Grigoriyevich Pavlovskiy, commander in chief of the Soviet ground forces, arrived in neighboring Laos in his special Aeroflot jetliner for a "friendly visit." Vietnamese minister of defense General Vo Nguyen Giap flew to Vieng Say in northern Laos for an unpublicized meeting with the Soviet general to review the Cambodian situation. Pavlovskiy's advice, a Vietnamese official told me years later, was: "Do a Czechoslovakia." The Chinese were powerless to come to the aid of their Khmer friends, the general argued, so the Vietnamese should simply drive their armored columns to Phnom Penh and remove Pol Pot from power the way the Soviet army removed Alexander Dubček in Prague in 1968. Giap balked at the suggestion. The Vietnamese, he reportedly said, would solve the problem in "their own appropriate way."

Birth of a Khmer "Liberation Army"

The Vietnamese Politburo met again in mid-February in the outskirts of Ho Chi Minh City at the secluded compound of what used to be the police training school of the fallen Thieu regime. The meeting studied the nuts and bolts of the plan for setting up a Cambodian Communist party and a resistance organization. Shortly after the meeting, Le Duan and Le Duc Tho met separately with Cambodian party cadres who had lived in exile in Vietnam since 1954 and the ones who had escaped from Pol Pot's purges to seek asylum in Vietnam.[49]

Of some one thousand Khmers who had regrouped in Hanoi in 1954 under the Geneva Agreement, only a handful had stayed behind in North Vietnam. The majority had returned to Cambodia to join the anti–U.S. resistance, and few of them survived the war and the purges. So the Khmer candidates for leadership in February composed a small group whose main achievement was survival. There was Pen Sovan, a forty-year-old cadre who had come to North Vietnam in 1954, along with one thousand others, and who had been educated in the party and army schools in Hanoi and made a major in the Vietnamese army. There were Chan Si and Khang Sarin, majors in the Vietnamese army; Tang Saroem, another Khmer exile, who was working as a labor supervisor in Vietnam's Hon Gai coal mines; Keo Chanda, the Khmer language newsreader from Radio Hanoi; Chea Soth, a news editor from the Vietnam News Agency. And with them were escapees from Cambodia, political cadres like Hem Samin, Yos Por, Hun Sen, and Bou Thang.

Dragged out of their nondescript offices and refugee barracks, they were suddenly presented to the top Vietnamese leaders whom they had previously known only in pictures. By a turn of fortune they too were to be leaders in a new Cambodia still in the womb of the future. Le Duc Tho told them that the time had come to restore the ties of cooperation that had existed between Vietnamese and Cambodian Communists. Each was to develop the political and military structures of the new resistance movement.[50]

During the March 1978 visit to the Khmer refugee camp, I met one such leader without realizing the role he played in the Vietnamese strategy. As a television crew filmed a Khmer woman talking about life under Pol Pot and hundreds of her compatriots thronged around, I slipped out to talk to some Khmers without my Vietnamese escort. Thong Pak, a former Lon Nol official, whispered to me about the political lecture sessions in the evening to prepare for a fight against Pol Pot. He pointed to a short, stubby man wearing a Vietnamese army pith helmet: "That's him, 'Mr. Duc.' He gives the political lecture."

Dressed in a white sleeveless shirt, khaki trousers, and plastic sandals, the roundfaced "Mr. Duc" was a bit shy when I approached him for his life story. He was uncertain how much he should tell a stranger. Despite his Vietnamese alias and his typical North Vietnamese cadre outfit, he was a full-blooded Khmer, a veteran cadre of Cambodia's People's Revolutionary Party. Like thousands of other party members, he went to Hanoi in 1954 as part of the Geneva Agreement. In 1971 he had returned to Cambodia to join the resistance against the Lon Nol regime, but within three years he had had to flee back to Vietnam to escape Pol Pot's purges. After three years of life as a farmer in a Mekong Delta village, "Duc" said, he was again brought back to his revolutionary calling. His new job was to recruit and train Khmer cadres from among the refugees to fight Pol Pot. I was to discover three years later in Phnom Penh that Yos Por, the leader of the new Kampuchean National United Front for National Salvation (KNUFNS), the man with an assured smile, wearing shiny acrylic clothes and a large gold watch, was none other than "Mr. Duc" from Ben Sanh camp, and contrary to his claim of being a farmer in the delta, he had spent three years in Hanoi before taking charge of the camp.

Within four months of the rupture in Vietnam's diplomatic relations with Cambodia, a string of secret camps had sprung up in South Vietnam to recruit and train a guerrilla army. Leaders in Hanoi had begun doing what they knew best. It was ironic that in preparing for the second "liberation" of Cambodia they were making full use of what their erstwhile enemies—the United States and the Thieu regime—had left behind. The former police training school in Thu Duc, isolated by a high wall and barbwire in the suburbs of Ho Chi Minh City, had become the main base of the still-secret but fledgling Khmer Communist party. Former U.S. military bases at Xuan Loc and Long Giao near Ho Chi Minh City and a helicopter base at Vi Thanh, in the Mekong Delta, were secretly transformed into new bases to launch a clandestine war against Pol Pot.[51] On

April 22, 1978, the First Brigade of the Khmer dissident army was commissioned in a secret ceremony.[52] By the end of 1978 several such brigades—the actual strength of which was that of battalions—were ready to join the Vietnamese army in its push against Cambodia.

Along with the secret preparations, Hanoi also cranked up its propaganda machine. While the Vietnamese press and radio stations released a flood of reports about the misdeeds of the Khmer Rouge, the door was flung wide open for foreign journalists. In the two years since I left Saigon I had made only two trips to Vietnam after a host of letters and cables. But now within three months of my last trip I was invited back again. Soon after my arrival in Hanoi on March 4, 1978, Vietnamese officials made it clear that the sole purpose of this trip was to enable me to understand the Cambodian problem. I was not to count on seeing Planning Commission officials or visiting a cooperative in the Red River delta. "You have to understand clearly the origins of our problems with Cambodia," Pham Van Cuong, the official in charge of the visiting group of journalists, told me.

The man chosen by Hanoi to launch the first salvo of the propaganda war was none other than Vice–Foreign Minister Vo Dong Giang. On March 5 he invited two European colleagues—Roland-Pierre Paringaux of *Le Monde* and Karel Van Wolferen of *NRC Handelsblad*—and me to a private dinner and briefing. The invitation brought back memories of Saturday morning excursions way back in 1974–75 to the heavily guarded Vietcong compound in Saigon's Tan Son Nhut air base, Camp Davis. The weekly press conferences conducted there by a green-uniformed Vietcong colonel were quaint holdovers of the 1973 Paris Agreement. Although the Vietcong's Provisional Revolutionary Government representation in Saigon hardly helped to preserve the cease-fire—its ostensible objective—it had allowed the press to keep in touch with the other side over cups of tea, soft drinks, and an occasional bottle of fiery Vietnamese rice liquor, *lua moi*. Often the man who gave the conferences and sipped the liquor was Colonel Giang, my host-to-be at dinner that evening.

With his hollow cheeks and button-bright eyes, Giang seemed

much the same: a little thinner perhaps and, in a white bush shirt, looking mellower. Fluent in French, English, and Spanish—he had once been the PRG ambassador to Cuba—Giang had a charm that concealed the toughness of a hardened revolutionary. This was clearly an occasion to convince the "old friends from the Tan Son Nhut days" about the justness of the Vietnamese cause. Lacing a three-hour monologue with sad remarks about the fratricidal conflict and with scathing sarcasm about Pol Pot and his foreign backers, he gave an account of the Cambodia-Vietnam conflict never revealed before.

In Ho Chi Minh City an official in charge of the foreign press, Bui Huu Nhan, offered an unprecedented blank check for travel: "You can go anywhere you want along the Vietnam-Cambodia border until you are satisfied that you have understood the problem." Such an open invitation, obviously cleared at the highest levels, was designed to assure skeptical pressmen that Vietnam had nothing to hide, that the reality on the ground would show it to be the victim of Khmer attacks, and that it was not, as Pol Pot's regime claimed, an expansionist neighbor.

The provincial capital Tay Ninh was clearly a nervous place. The city was pockmarked with shelters—dug under pavements, next to government buildings, and in the grounds of private houses. North of the city and a few miles from the Cambodian border was the village of Tan Lap with its rows of charred mud huts on both sides of a dirt road; standing testimony to the Khmer Rouge attack nearly six months earlier. This was the village where Sandor Gyori had taken his confiscated photographs of the massacre. Now we had no difficulty talking to Nguyen Thi Cu, one of the few survivors in Tan Lap. She sobbed as she recounted the carnage. With the exception of a brother injured in the attack, all seven other members of her family had been killed. She, like her brother, had survived by playing dead under a pile of bodies.

In place after place along the border, we saw villages in ruins, abandoned paddy fields, and hundreds of graves. From survivors we heard unprompted stories of medieval atrocities. There was no longer any doubt in my mind about the reality of this bitter conflict that the Vietnamese had kept out of public view for so long. Even given

Hanoi's oft-proven ability to manipulate the press, the evidence I had seen was too overwhelming.

But all that I saw that week did not suggest there had been any recent large-scale attacks such as those of the previous year. In fact, my suspicion was growing that the initiative was now in Vietnamese hands. Otherwise how could one explain the ease with which we got so close to the frontier? Telltale tank tracks on a dusty road near Tay Ninh's border with Cambodia and an army truck loaded with cabbages glimpsed near the border—undoubtedly carrying supplies to Vietnamese soldiers—were clear indications that the Vietnamese army had, where the terrain permitted, pushed their *cordon sanitaire* well inside Cambodia. It was the confidence born of this situation on the ground that allowed the security-conscious Vietnamese to take foreign journalists to the border to see the evidence of Khmer depredations.

The suspicion that the Vietnamese were icing their propaganda war was bolstered during a visit to An Phu village near Chau Doc. There was no doubt that the village had come under Khmer Rouge mortar and ground attack two days before our visit. The signs of damage were still fresh. Villagers were still collecting their belongings from abandoned houses to take back to their temporary shelters.

But someone must have decided that sensation-seeking bourgeois journalists should be given a piece of the action as well. Some of us were a little skeptical about the claim that the artillery shells producing the whistling sound high above us were coming from the Cambodian side. A little later my interpreter from Hanoi, Huynh Van Tam, called, "Let's go to the edge of the village. Maybe you can see some fighting." We were given binoculars and told to look at the tree line across a rice field—the border with Cambodia. One Vietnamese soldier accompanying us was standing by a bamboo grove and talking into the mouthpiece of his backpack radio. Suddenly he shouted something. A Vietnamese army officer screamed, "Get into the trenches!" Seconds later there was the thud of an outgoing artillery shell from the village behind us, followed by a whistling sound and then an explosion in the tree line that we were watching. "The Khmers are attacking," announced the officer glumly. He had not bothered to take cover. Then came a few rounds of mortar fire and the crackle of weapons. We were again asked to take cover. Another shell hissed above us and burst among the trees.

We laughed at this amateurish attempt to impress us. The official from Ho Chi Minh City who was accompanying us pulled a long face. It was too bad that Pol Pot did not oblige the Vietnamese by ordering another assault while the journalists were around! But we had spoken too soon.

Less than one hundred miles away, at another corner of the border, real combat was in progress to drive away the Khmer attackers. Three days later I was awakened in my hotel room in Ho Chi Minh City with an unusual summons. Tam informed me that journalists had to be at Tan Son Nhut Airport within an hour for a visit to an undisclosed destination.

There was a fair throng of pressmen at Tan Son Nhut. In addition to the visiting correspondents of the Western press, there were Cuban and Polish film crews and a number of Vietnamese photographers and cameramen—all bound for Ha Tien. My heart sank when I saw our transport. It looked like a prehistoric beast—a battered Chinook helicopter—its green paint faded. The only shine left on this veteran workhorse of the departed American army was the red-and-gold star of the Vietnamese air force painted on the fuselage. The two windows were gaping holes. A tangle of wires was hanging loose inside the hull. Nevertheless, the engines fired and we lifted off the tarmac. I looked down on rows of the cannibalized and blackened remains of a variety of aircraft—Uncle Sam's legacy to Socialist Vietnam.

Soon we were over the Plain of Reeds, gouged with bomb and shell craters, and the lush green Mekong Delta—crosshatched with brown canals. Blasts of cool air came through the broken windows, which provided a clearer view of the ground than did the unbroken windows with their glass smeared with oil and dust. After a refueling stop at Can Tho, capital of the Delta, the Chinook took off again for Ha Tien.

Looking at the vast Can Tho air base, one of the biggest built by the United States in Vietnam, and at the U.S.–made A37s roaring off the runway with bombs hugging their undercarriages—certainly on combat missions against Cambodia—I was struck by the irony of it all. Only three years earlier the United States was fighting the "Cambodian surrogates of Hanoi." Then U.S. secretary of state Henry Kissinger had not believed Le Duc Tho when he told him of his inability to influence the Khmer Rouge.[53] After all, was not Cambodian communism a Vietnamese creation?

Our briefings throughout the trip, including the one at Ha Tien Airport, were conducted with plastic-covered U.S. Army field maps. But the briefing officer lacked a Texas drawl, and the positions of the enemy marked in crayon were not of the VC or the KC (Khmer Communists, the official American appellation during the war) but of Pol Pot's Democratic Kampuchea. It was a new war, to be fought with old props.

The Ha Tien airstrip was nearly deserted. White smoke from a distant cement plant drifted into a serene blue sky. At the end of the strip, soft drinks and biscuits were laid out on a white tablecloth for the visiting press; in Communist Vietnam, nothing can be done without a reception by a local committee. However, under a merciless sun, even bottles of tepid orange drink were welcome.

After a briefing on the Khmer Rouge attack by Major Hoang Chau, we set out for Ha Tien. Formerly a bustling town of thirty thousand, it was now totally empty. Shops and houses were locked, and debris from the shelling lay all around. At the ferry a few stragglers were waiting with baskets, jute sacks, and plastic jerry cans hanging from shoulder poles or piled on bicycles and pushcarts. The convoy of buses and cars carrying journalists and cadres stopped at the edge of the town where the paddy fields of My Duc commune stretched out to the hills near the Cambodian border. We trekked across the parched fields kicking up a small cloud of white dust. As we neared the thatched huts at the foot of the hill, the stench hit us—the unmistakable smell of death. In a clearing a dozen sweating, silent men were digging graves. Next to a completely gutted house lay fifteen bodies—men, women, and children. Some of the staves with which they had been beaten to death still lay around. One stave was stuck between the legs of a spread-eagled naked woman. Her two children had been cut to pieces. A few bodies were headless; some were disemboweled and covered with blue flies. I felt nauseated and had to rest briefly under a tree. Then I walked again through the village. House after house presented the same gory sight. Even animals had not been spared. Carcasses of oxen and dogs lay in the roadside ditch. On a hillock near Ha Tien, where they had dug in during the attack, two of the Khmer Rouge lay dead. Those who fled had left behind a small assortment of AK-47 rifles, B-40 rockets, and Chinese-made recoilless rifles.

Twenty-five-year-old Nguyen Van Hoan and his wife had awakened in the early hours of March 14 to the Khmer shouts of "*Chone! Chone!*" (Enter! Enter!) and the screams of villagers. In the dark they managed to flee to the nearby forested hill, where they hid for two days. From his perch on the hill Hoan had seen the Khmer Rouge hauling away bags of rice and other belongings of the villagers the following morning. Looking at these mud and bamboo huts, I could not imagine that they had contained anything worth pillaging. The only plausible clue to what was behind the murderous raid was a Khmer slogan scrawled in charcoal on a door: *Ti nih srok yoong* (This is our country). Indeed some three hundred years ago the whole of the Mekong Delta, including Ha Tien, had been Cambodian territory. A large number of My Duc commune's population and many of the dead were of Khmer origin.

The experience was numbing, incomprehensible. As I searched for an answer for the carnage, I was unaware, like most of the outside world, of what had been going on in Cambodia's Eastern Zone after the Vietnamese push in December. Nor did I know of the megalomania of power that had gripped the Khmer Rouge after their so-called historic victory of January 6, 1978. Months later Ieng Sary explained to foreign reporters that because Vietnam penetrated into Cambodian territory, "we must launch offensives to push them out and push them very far into their own territory."[54]

We returned to Ho Chi Minh City, having seen the first grisly evidence of Indochinese comrades at war. I soon learned that the decision to send journalists to Ha Tien by helicopter before the corpses were buried was made by Le Duc Tho, who had taken over the responsibility of directing Hanoi's Cambodia policy. Pol Pot had handed him a propaganda coup, and he had not missed his chance. But Cambodia too had launched its own campaign to win foreign support. The day we were visiting Ha Tien, Pol Pot was entertaining a group of Yugoslav journalists in the riverside guesthouse in Phnom Penh—the first professional newsmen to be allowed into Cambodia since the Khmer Rouge victory. Cambodia was trying to solve the problem with Vietnam, he told the Yugoslavs, "in keeping with the concrete situation. If Vietnam is truly friendly toward us," he added, "there will be no difficulty in immediately solving the problem." [55]

In briefing us, Vo Dong Giang was more direct about how friendly relations could be restored. "The end to the conflict can come only in two ways," he said. "Either the Cambodian regime will change its policy or the regime will be changed by the Khmer people."

Prince Norodom Sihanouk: The Cage

FOR THE FIRST TIME in his life Prince Sihanouk had become his own private man, surrounded by a total emptiness. His residence within the high-walled old royal palace compound had become his gilded cage, guarded by dark, unsmiling peasant boys in black uniform. He could not leave the compound without the permission of the Angkar. There was no need for the retired head of state to go anywhere. Not even to buy groceries. Every morning a soldier would come on a bicycle carrying the day's provision of fish and vegetables. Along with him, his prime minister and old associate, Penn Nouth, was also retired, as was his private secretary, Madame Sao Saroth. They lived in separate houses somewhere in Phnom Penh. Since the removal of his daughters and their families from the residence, his world had shrunk to the basic family unit of Monique and their two sons—Sihamoni and Narindrapong.

"Since Monseigneur's resignation [in April 1976], we haven't seen a soul," Monique told me three years later. "They even removed the servants." For the first time in her life, Monique had to do everyday cooking to feed the family. In their five years of exile in Peking they had had one of the finest chefs in French cuisine in China. Premier

Zhou Enlai had arranged to provide the chef to satisfy the needs of the gourmet prince. Now Monique, aided by son Sihamoni, did the household chores—cleaning, cooking, and some gardening. They planted some banana trees.

For Sihanouk time was leaden, the silence stifling. The beautiful silver pagoda next to the palace stood abandoned. The golden-spired and high-columned hall where once the ballerinas of the royal troupe danced gracefully to the languid beat of the gamelan was eerily silent. The only signs of life in the palace compound were the pigeons flapping their wings. Sihanouk was determined to retain his sanity. Luckily he still had a large Grundig radio that Khieu Samphan had given to him in January. That was his window on the world, his only escape from the unrelieved monotony of long days and nights. Every morning and every evening he would tune in, one after another, to all the major radio stations of the world that he could get— BBC, Voice of America, Radio Australia, France Inter, NHK, Radio Hanoi. For hours he sat with the earphones glued to his ears, listening to every report about Cambodia, about the region, about the world.

He heard news reports about his fate with gratification and with some amusement. The world had not forgotten him. One report claimed the prince, shocked by what he had seen, had lost his speech. Another report quoted Ieng Sary as assuring a journalist that Sihanouk lived well in his palace and that he was busy writing his memoirs. Ieng Sary told a foreign journalist while visiting Malaysia in the spring of 1977 that the prince did not want to see anybody because, he is supposed to have said, "If I see foreigners I would be involved in politics." Sihanouk marveled at Ieng Sary's ability to lie.

Most precious were the dispatches of correspondents reporting from the Thai-Cambodian border and other Asian capitals bringing him news of what was happening in Cambodia beyond his secluded palace—news that could only make him sad and worried. Instinctively he knew the stories of executions, hard labor, and sufferings told by the Khmer refugees were true. The behavior of his guards had also taught him how violent and sadistic these young fanatics could be.

Sihanouk knew that no caution could be excessive in Cambodia. He would listen to the morning propaganda bulletin of Radio Phnom Penh at full volume, keeping the windows open so the Khmer Rouge guards could hear. Once that ritual was over, he would put on the earphones and listen to the world. He used to record some of the commentaries on a cassette recorder so that he could listen to them again and analyze what it all portended for his tragic country.

This habit of recording foreign commentaries was a risky business. One day in late 1976 he was told that next morning he would be taken out by Khieu Samphan for a tour of the provinces. This would have meant leaving behind the incriminating cassettes. As he recalled later, "I myself, my wife, and Prince Sihamoni spent the whole night hurriedly recording any music we could pick up on our receiver to delete the news recordings."

The tour of the provinces with Khieu Samphan brought home to Sihanouk the great leap forward the Khmer Rouge was trying to achieve. He saw gigantic work sites with thousands of men and women silently digging miles-long canals, carrying soil on shoulder poles to build dikes. The landscape was being turned into a vast checkerboard dotted with antlike men dressed in black. Did the people looking at him from a distance recognize Sihanouk? Even if they did, they were too scared to come forward to greet him as before. Only once, people were close to the road where Sihanouk's white Mercedes stopped. A number of them recognized his face framed in the car window. They shouted, "Samdech Euv!" and surged forward. An emotional Sihanouk muttered to Monique, "That's enough, I am going to talk to them," and started getting out of the car. Samphan, who sat next to the chauffeur, bolted out and told the prince, "Please be calm and go back to the car." Monique, too, beseeched the prince to restrain himself. She later told me that Khieu Samphan had meant well; that he had not wanted to see Sihanouk blurt his heart out to those people and create a potential riot. Sihanouk gave in and returned to the car, which swiftly left the scene. Monique saw people kneeling down to touch the ground where the prince had stood.

For the prince and millions of Khmers, survival was an obsession. For Sihanouk, this meant swallowing his pride and keeping his head down. He later said he did fight on for a while, "but the more resistance I offered," he said, "the more the Khmer Rouge were tightening their screws: They withdrew our whole service staff and eventually cut off all contacts. For a whole year, throughout 1977, Khieu Samphan did not pay me a single visit." Then, after a long and violent dispute with Monique over the wisdom of resistance to the Khmer Rouge, for the good of their family Sihanouk gave in. In his own words he started praising the Khmer Rouge to the skies. "This," he said, "somewhat improved our situation. But this flattery against my own convictions was the worst degradation I have ever experienced." His consolation was that this tactic probably helped save him and his family.

But more than Sihanouk's kowtowing to the Khmer Rouge, Cambodia's growing conflict with Vietnam improved his lot. Unbeknownst to him, the Khmer Rouge had begun killing citizens of Vietnamese origin and Khmers suspected of sympathy with Vietnam. In April 1977 Cambodian soldiers had begun raiding Vietnamese border villages. Some of the Chinese leaders were concerned that such adventurism could be risky when Cambodia was so isolated in the international scene. They had advised Pol Pot during his September–October 1977 visit to China to bring back Sihanouk and use his prestige and popularity to bolster Democratic Kampuchea's image abroad. To underline the concern he had for his friend, North Korean president Kim Il Sung had given a basket of apples to Pol Pot to take for the prince.

That basket of apples was a pleasant surprise. The fact that Pol Pot had them delivered suggested Sihanouk was not totally expendable. It was also gratifying that Kim Il Sung had taken care to stress his friendship with the prince by thrusting a gift in Pol Pot's hand. Sihanouk did not want to miss this opportunity to break out of the total isolation imposed on him since the beginning of 1977. He wrote messages of "heartfelt gratitude" to Pol Pot for carrying Kim Il Sung's gift, a second one greeting Pol Pot "on the occasion of the extremely glorious anniversary of the Communist Party of Kampuchea," and a third one congratulating him for "the most noble, monumental success" of his visit to China and North Korea. Those messages were soon broadcast over Radio Phnom Penh. Sihanouk was amused to hear that the radio version had changed his message to make it appear as if "the generous gift" had come from Pol Pot himself. The censors at the radio had also put words in Sihanouk's mouth praising the CPK's "sentiments filled with warm friendship and affection" for him. Sihanouk howled with laughter as he recalled the episode. But he did not mind it then. The fact that after eighteen months' silence Radio Phnom Penh mentioned his name at all was an even happier omen than Kim Il Sung's apples. He could see a thin streak of light breaking through the darkness that surrounded him.

8

The Road to War

MARCH 24, 1978. It seemed the beginning of yet another uneventful day in the life of Ho Chi Minh City. As the sun peeped from behind the trees and the now-silent shipyard across the Saigon River, middle-aged Chinese and Vietnamese clad in black pajamas and vests, moved in slow motion, practicing *t'ai chi* on the riverfront. Hundreds of pavement dwellers asleep on the sidewalks of Boulevard Nguyen Hue and on pavements outside the central market had not yet begun to stir. Before the sun pushed up into the sky was the coolest hour of the day. As pedicab drivers slowly glided down the road in search of passengers and the old lady on the corner of Le Thanh Ton Street started setting up her noodle stand, few paid attention to the revolutionary music and stream of propaganda from the government radio relayed by the loudspeakers at Lam Son Square in downtown Ho Chi Minh City. In the soft light of the morning the city still dreamed of its Saigon days.

The dream shattered suddenly as truckloads of policemen in beige uniforms, regular soldiers in green, and thousands of students wearing red armbands began fanning out through the city in the biggest military-style operation since the end of the war. A government communiqué broadcast over the radio pronounced the death sentence on bourgeois trade. While armed policemen took up positions outside shops in the downtown area, the biggest concentration was in the Chinese twin city of Cholon. Rudely awakened by the commotion, thousands of frightened Chinese residents watched as armed policemen and volunteers surrounded the area. Many thought it was a demonstration of power by the authorities, perhaps to make more arrests in connection with the troubles of four days before.

On March 20, Cholon—the business heart of Ho Chi Minh City— witnessed an unusual sight. When some soldiers arrived in a jeep to arrest a Chinese youth refusing military draft, a crowd collected. Soon the crowd erupted in a spontaneous political demonstration against the regime. Somebody held aloft a portrait of Mao Zedong, and the predominantly Chinese crowd of some two hundred paraded in the street shouting slogans. They demanded to be repatriated to the Chinese motherland rather than be sent to inhospitable New Economic Zones or have their children forced to join the army. The Chinese did not want to be cannon fodder for Vietnam's escalating border war with Cambodia. The police arrived, dispersed the demonstrators with baton charges, and arrested over a dozen people.

But it soon became clear that the mobilization of force that morning was not merely to arrest a few more Chinese malcontents but to hit at the very heart of Cholon. After the armed men had taken up positions in the street, youth volunteers began a systematic search of households and shops to look for hidden gold and to make inventories of goods to be seized by the government. While the government agents hauled away bars of gold and stacks of dollar bills found during the sweep, businessmen were forbidden to sell any of the inventoried goods now declared to be nationalized. Rumor among the average Vietnamese, who were not too displeased to see the power of Cholon crumble, was that the government seized seven tons of gold! "Ho Chi Minh City was a doomed city," a rare foreign visitor who happened to be present that day recalled. "The people were helpless, like suddenly trapped rats running about in desperation." Some eighteen distraught Chinese were reported to have committed suicide.

Although the government made no secret of its plan to take the

South to socialism by 1980, the suddenness and scale of the move had stunned the citizens. In 1975 the new Communist government in the South had introduced currency reforms that had dispossessed much of their wealth. There had also been sporadic attempts at controlling and taxing private business. But there always seemed enough loopholes for enterprising Chinese businessmen to elude control. Not so with the operation that morning. Tens of thousands of youth volunteers who had been trained in secluded camps were brought in to assist cadres to swoop down on every business establishment. The only places spared were eating houses. Suddenly thirty thousand families of businessmen—overwhelmingly Chinese—were deprived of their possessions and livelihoods. In another drastic move, on May 3 the currency of the South was abolished, and the cash holdings of the rich were wiped out. Although, theoretically, old currency could be exchanged for new, only a small amount of cash was handed out.[1]

The long-heralded Socialist transformation was finally launched in South Vietnam. Ironically, this frontal assault on capitalism also proved to be the first open salvo in Vietnam's confrontation with Socialist China.

Although Vietnam's conflict with Cambodia was public, until now Vietnam and China only shadowboxed. While Hanoi condemned "international reactionaries" as instigators of the Khmer Rouge, China announced support for Cambodia against unnamed "hegemonists." But after the attack on Cholon and the exodus of Chinese residents from Vietnam, Peking came out with an open denunciation. As the Sino-Vietnamese war of words escalated, an abortive uprising in May by an anti–Pol Pot group in Cambodia made direct Vietnamese intervention inevitable. And with Vietnam locked in an open conflict with China, there was no longer any restraint on Soviet-Vietnamese collaboration. The stage was now set for a war that would go beyond the Cambodia-Vietnam border.

The Vietnamese had planned their assault on the citadel of capitalism well. They made sure that foreign journalists who were allowed into the South to report on Cambodian provocations were safely out of the country when the attack came. I was in Ho Chi Minh City until March 20 and had visited Cholon to see families of old friends and to have fabulous meals of seafood in packed Chinese restaurants. The bustling Cholon market—gorged with goods that had been smuggled in as well as locally produced—amazed me in its contrast with the empty shelves of the pathetically poor Hanoi market. Our Foreign Ministry companions from Hanoi ogled through the shop windows at objects they had never seen before, but they shrank back in horror when told the price. I had heard complaints about the carpetbagger cadres from Hanoi and wondered how long the spartan North would resist the siren song of Cholon. "Our task," Le Quang Chan, vice-chairman of the Ho Chi Minh City People's Revolutionary Committee, told me, "is to transform a consumer city into a producer city so that it can merit the name Ho Chi Minh." He did not elaborate how that transformation would come about.

As scheduled, I returned to Hanoi to catch my flight out of Vietnam on the morning of March 24. A day later I would discover why the Vietnamese had packed us home. At a dinner hosted by the Committee for Cultural Relations with Foreign Countries on March 23, I discussed with Hong Ha, the economics editor of *Nhan Dan*, the problems of bringing socialism to South Vietnam. Three years after liberation and several currency and anticapitalist reforms later, the South's freewheeling economy was still going strong. Almost all the industry and trade of the South, particularly the strategic grain trade, was controlled by private Chinese businessmen. It was estimated that more than half the money in circulation and most of gold and dollar holdings in the South were in Cholon—a virtual economic counterpower.[2] Cholon was a "strong capitalist heart beating inside the Socialist body of Vietnam," Hong Ha observed while explaining the shortages, inflation, and black-marketing rampant in the South. "How do you plan to resolve the problem?" I asked him. He smiled slyly. "We are thinking about it," he said. But even as we talked, thousands of cadres and security forces in Ho Chi Minh City were getting ready for the next morning's operation for a "heart transplant."

As I would learn later, the preparation for an assault on capitalism and the Chinese economic power in the South had begun simultaneously with the Vietnamese planning on Cambodia. The same Politburo meeting in mid-February of 1978, which decided on set-

ting up an anti–Pol Pot resistance, also studied the security implications of Chinese economic control over southern Vietnam as the
country prepared for a bigger confrontation with Peking-backed
Cambodia. The fact that in January Peking had initiated a new
policy toward the overseas Chinese, calling on them to join in its
"antihegemonic" struggle, only added to the Vietnamese concern about
the powerful Chinese community. In the middle of March the Politburo again assembled in Ho Chi Minh City amid total secrecy to
put the final touches to their plan of assault on Cholon. That fateful
move triggered one of the biggest exoduses in the postwar period
and added a new racial dimension to the fierce nationalistic struggle
developing in Asia.

Dr. Jekyll and Mr. Hyde in Chinatown

The tension between the Chinese and the Vietnamese that erupted
in the summer of 1978 had existed in some form or other since the
very emergence of the Vietnamese nation. Chinese migration into
Vietnam started in the third century B.C. In the two millennia since
(which included nine hundred years of direct Chinese rule of northern Vietnam), successive waves of Chinese settlers—demobilized
soldiers, administrators, convicted criminals, and rebellious soldiers—had come to Vietnam. The attitude of the rulers of independent Vietnam toward the Chinese immigrants had always been
ambivalent—they were valuable assets for consolidation of the regime as well as potential liabilities. As an industrious and disci-
plined group, Chinese immigrants could be put to use in reclaiming
land, opening up new settlements, developing trade, and expanding
Vietnamese sovereignty. When in the seventeenth century several
thousand supporters of the defeated Ming dynasty fleeing from the
invading Manchus arrived in Saigon, its nominal Khmer ruler did
not know how to deal with these armed settlers. He called for assistance from the Vietnamese Nguyen dynasty ruler, who promptly put
the Chinese in order and settled them in an area near Saigon that
was later to develop into Cholon. As a price for this "assistance,"
the Cambodian ruler acknowledged the Nguyen dynasty's suzerainty
in Saigon. Yet another group of Chinese soldiers led by Mac Cu

settled in the Ha Tien area, which, in the seventeenth century, was under Cambodian control. The self-styled Chinese "King of Ha Tien," who transformed his domain into a prosperous trading post and expanded his control over surrounding provinces, transferred his loyalty to the Vietnamese emperor, thus pushing Vietnam's border to its current southernmost limit.[3]

While making use of the Chinese settlers, the Vietnamese rulers were never comfortable about their loyalty. The fact that they originally came from a large country that had from time immemorial tried to subjugate and dominate Vietnam made them objects of suspicion. At the worst point of relations, during the Tay Son rebellion against the Vietnamese emperor in the eighteenth century, ten thousand Cholon Chinese were massacred by the rebels. At better times they enjoyed freedom and prosperity. But they were always segregated from the Vietnamese population. In 1840 the Nguyen dynasty emperor Minh Mang was amazed at the liberal policy of the Siamese (Thai) court that allowed the Chinese to live with the local population. He predicted that failure to segregate the Chinese would lead to the fall of Siam.[4]

"The Chinese in Vietnam," as one perceptive Japanese scholar noted, "were a Dr. Jekyll and Mr. Hyde to Vietnam, with the harmful part to keep an eye on and the useful part to make the most of. . . . Even in the case of the Nguyen dynasty, which adopted a favorable policy toward them, they nevertheless worried continually over their relations with China. They used the Chinese in their domain to investigate the real state of affairs in China in an attempt to improve relations with her."[5]

Although the Vietnamese Communist party seems to have inherited the same basic ambivalence toward the Chinese community, its actual treatment of the Chinese was conditioned by the ideological affinity between Peking and Hanoi in the 1950s and 1960s and by the practical need for Chinese support for the Vietnamese struggle to unify the country. The fact that only 15 percent of the Chinese in Vietnam lived in the North and that the vast majority of residents there were industrial workers, miners, and fishermen made the party's task in managing them easier. Because they belonged to a fraternal Socialist country, the status of some one hundred thousand Chinese residents was not a matter of state law but the subject of an arrangement between the two parties. Under an agreement signed in 1955 by the Chinese and Vietnamese parties, the Chinese residents in Vietnam were "placed under the leadership of the Vietnam Workers Party." Thanks to the special arrangement, Chinese residents in Vietnam, unlike their compatriots in other newly independent Southeast Asian countries, were not immediately asked to choose a nationality. They could live in Vietnam and maintain their nationality with a proviso that they eventually become Vietnamese citizens.[6]

Although in the twenty-three years since that verbal agreement Hanoi made no overt attempt to impose Vietnamese nationality on its Chinese population, in 1961 China agreed to a Vietnamese proposal that, in essence, naturalized all Chinese in North Vietnam. Peking agreed to issue only tourist visas to Chinese Vietnamese planning to visit relatives in China.[7]

But in day-to-day life the immigrants existed in a convenient ambiguity that made them a privileged minority. "We had the best of both worlds," said Ke Xuan, a seventy-one-year-old former Chinese resident of Hanoi. "The Hoa [Vietnamese of Chinese descent] in the North had all the rights and privileges of Vietnamese citizenship and none of its disadvantages. From about 1970 the Vietnamese had been trying to get us to become citizens, but few of us saw it as in our best interests. We could even vote in their elections. We were regarded as Vietnamese in all respects, except that we were not subject to the military draft," he said.[8]

The latter privilege was invaluable in a country where almost every family had lost someone in the war. Like their counterparts in China, members of the Chinese business community in the North bore the brunt of Socialist reforms but were not otherwise discriminated against. In fact, a number of ethnic Chinese cadres served in sensitive party and government positions. Their brethren under the anti-Communist regime in South Vietnam prospered financially but were forced by Ngo Dinh Diem to adopt Vietnamese nationality under pain of losing their businesses. Peking protested that move, and the Hanoi-controlled National Liberation Front of South Vietnam lent its voice to the protest and promised to give the Chinese in the South freedom to choose their nationality after liberation.

The attitude of the Vietnamese Communists started to change in the late 1960s, however, when ripples from the Cultural Revolution began to affect the Chinese community in North Vietnam. While the Red Guards in China denounced Hanoi and tried to interrupt arms shipments, the Maoists among the Chinese community in North Vietnam carried on their own Cultural Revolution, accusing the Vietnamese party of revisionism.[9]

A *Paranoia Is Reborn*

A Vietnamese official later admitted to me that in the wake of the experience of the Cultural Revolution and particularly since the Nixon visit to China in 1972, the topmost echelon of the Vietnamese party became aware of the "need for vigilance" against ethnic Chinese cadres. The fabric of common ideological commitment that kept the two communities together had started wearing thin. If Peking could not be trusted anymore after the Nixon visit, neither could one rely on the cadres of Chinese origin, even if they were second-generation. With the state-level relations deteriorating, Vietnamese paranoia, rooted in two thousand years of history, started to surface. Discreetly, cadres of Chinese descent were reassigned to new jobs with less access to sensitive information.

By 1975, Vietnamese leaders were convinced that Peking did not view favorably the emergence of a reunified, strong Vietnam. Years later it was revealed that even amidst the euphoria of victory in May 1975 they had not forgotten the potential danger they faced from China. Shortly after his arrival at Saigon's Tan Son Nhut air base to an emotional welcome, Party Secretary Le Duan reportedly said that the country faced great difficulties "because we had to deal with two major threats: hunger and the Chinese reactionaries." He did not specifically mention the possibility of aggression by the Chinese, a Vietnamese Politburo member later recalled, "because such a situation did not exist, but he did mention the need to keep a vigilant eye on them."[10]

As Chinese aid to Vietnam dwindled in 1976–77 and state relations deteriorated, Hanoi saw less and less need to be accommodating to the Chinese community in Vietnam. If anything, Vietnam thought it necessary to tighten its control over the Chinese. Ever since the liberation, the Communist party entertained doubts about the loyalty of the million-strong Chinese community in the South. It had not taken kindly the gesture of Cholon residents who had flown the flag of the People's Republic of China and displayed portraits of Mao Zedong in the days immediately after liberation. For the capitalist Chinese in Cholon—who had often turned to anti-Communist Taiwan as their protector—the gesture most probably was an opportunistic act to assure the new rulers that their hearts were in the right place, perhaps also to show that they now had a powerful protector in Peking. Little did they realize how offensive that act would prove to be to the leaders in Hanoi or how much of a gulf had developed between China and Vietnam behind the official proclamations of friendship. The flags were ordered removed.

The government had no desire to implement the promise of free choice given to the Chinese by the National Liberation Front. Years later when I asked a Vietnamese ambassador in Peking about the unfulfilled promise to the Chinese in the South, he just brushed it aside. "A reality left by history is that almost all the Chinese residents in Vietnam are Vietnamese. We don't feel it necessary to reverse the situation. After all, declaration is one thing and reality another," he said. [11]

The reality of a self-confident, unified Vietnam in 1975 was certainly different from that of the early years of North Vietnam, so close to and dependent on China. Hanoi was not ready to reopen the Pandora's box of nationality nor hand over to China the control of a powerful lever in the South by acknowledging Peking's right to protect its nationals. In early 1976 all citizens of Chinese origin in the South were forced to accept Vietnamese nationality. Peking did not publicize its displeasure, but later, in a meeting with Premier Pham Van Dong on June 10, 1977, Chinese vice-premier Li Xiannian accused Vietnam of going back on its promise not to force Chinese residents to adopt Vietnamese nationality. [12] Li's complaint was not only about the treatment of Chinese in the South. In the spring of 1977 Vietnam had started clarifying the question of nationality among citizens living along Vietnam's border with China. Minority people as well as Chinese who lived in that mountainous zone had families on both sides and freely, if illegally, went back and forth for business or family visits. Hanoi, concerned about China's influence over those people, and especially about the pull of Peking's economic power, quietly started evicting those who preferred Chinese nationality.[13]

Soon, economic concern over the power of Chinese business was added to the long-term Vietnamese worry about security. Since the summer of 1977, when the Communist party adopted a program for agricultural collectivization in the South, the tempo of Socialist transformation had been stepped up. A committee was set up to enable private industry and business to draw up plans for curbing the capitalists. A calamitous drop in food production in 1977 and hoarding and black-marketing of scarce food grain added urgency to the need of a stricter control of the market. At a time when Vietnam's security was threatened by increasingly bold attacks by the Khmer Rouge as well as by the sputtering resistance from the tribal organization FULRO (Front Uni pour la Lutte des Races Opprimées [the united front for the struggle of oppressed races]) and other anti-Communist groups, the government could not afford to have economic dislocations create social unrest in the southern capital.[14]

Hanoi Twirls the Dragon's Tail

When the Vietnamese Politburo gathered in Ho Chi Minh City in mid-February 1978, they considered the implications of China's newly announced policy toward the overseas Chinese. During the radical years of the Cultural Revolution, Peking's Overseas Chinese Affairs Commission was in limbo and its policy toward overseas Chinese in disarray. But since early 1977—about the same time when Vietnam started "purifying" its border with China—Peking had begun showing increasing interest in harnessing the expertise and capital of overseas Chinese. On January 4, 1978, an article by Liao Chengzhi in the Chinese *People's Daily* unveiled Peking's new approach. Calling overseas Chinese "part of the Chinese nation . . . with their destiny closely linked with that of the motherland," the chairman of the revived Overseas Chinese Affairs Commission urged them to form a "broad patriotic united front" against "hegemonism." Not only the overseas Chinese were called upon but also "friends of foreign nationalities who are of Chinese descent." Liao declared that in addition to protecting the rights of those overseas Chinese holding Chinese citizenship, China would also "welcome and make proper arrangements for those who wish to return to China to take part in building up the motherland or to settle down." Those who had adopted the nationality of the host country were "still our kinsfolk and friends."[15]

Liao's astounding statement meant that whatever their nationality, all persons of Chinese origin had the right to participate in the struggle against Moscow and its cohorts and could count on Peking's friendship. Since the beginning of 1978, the Chinese embassy in Hanoi had explained to the Chinese community its new policy and had quietly begun issuing passports to some of the city's wealthy Chinese who had closed their shops and restaurants in order to return to China. In the face of Peking's increasingly active interest in Vietnam's Chinese community and its growing involvement in Cambodia, Hanoi concluded that the time had come for a drastic move to solve both the economic and security problems posed by Cholon.[16]

Curiously, however, the Vietnamese did not seem to expect that China would publicly condemn them for their anti-Chinese moves. "China would not damage its international prestige by openly attacking us," a Vietnamese diplomat confidently predicted in late March. "We will keep hitting each other under the table," he told me, punching the air with his hands.[17]

Hanoi seems to have calculated that Peking would not jeopardize its effort to woo non-Communist Southeast Asia by openly espousing the cause of the overseas Chinese and giving substance to the region's fear about a Chinese fifth column. Vietnam also hoped that China would be prevented from openly opposing the drive against Cholon because it was primarily an anticapitalist move. Clearly with an eye to disarming any Peking criticism, the government directive on March 24 had announced: "The policy of terminating all bourgeois tradesmen's business will be carried out in a unified manner throughout the city and all southern provinces, regardless of nationality or religion." It had also warned people to "remain vigilant against all reactionary [Peking] plots to distort this policy and to divide our working people."[18]

The Vietnamese had grossly miscalculated. Peking had seen the Vietnamese move in Cholon as an open challenge to its overseas Chinese policy and indeed to its claim as a regional power. Peking's failure to act in defense of the Chinese in Vietnam, especially after the announcement of its new policy, promised to deal a severe blow to its prestige among the fifteen million overseas Chinese in Southeast Asia. Chinese inaction could also embolden the anti-Chinese and chauvinistic politicians in the region to move in a similar direction as Vietnam.

For over a month after the operation in Cholon, Peking was silent. Behind the curtain of silence, however, tension was building as thousands of Chinese residents from northern Vietnam poured into China and many more dispossessed Chinese businessmen in the South were dispatched to New Economic Zones. With an ironic sense of timing, Peking chose the third anniversary of the end of the Vietnam War to fire its first shot across Vietnam's bow to signal the beginning of a new war. At a tea party for overseas Chinese visitors on April 30, 1978, Liao Chengzhi announced that a large number of Chinese residing in Vietnam had "suddenly returned to China." Without much drama he noted that China was concerned and was "closely following developments." In the same speech Liao added that while China encouraged overseas Chinese to adopt the nationality of their country of residence, it opposed "any attempt to compel them to change their nationality." [19]

Twelve days later China increased pressure by quietly telling Hanoi that it was suspending work on twenty-one Chinese-aided projects. It had decided instead to "divert funds and materials to make working and living arrangements for the expelled Chinese." It was an ironic replay of a Soviet move in 1960 when Moscow suddenly suspended its aid projects in China to express its anger at Peking. That episode strongly denounced by China, brought the final breach. Peking, however, waited until the loudly anti-Soviet U.S. national security adviser Zbigniew Brzezinski's China visit was over before it launched its first attack on Vietnam. A statement issued by the Overseas Chinese Affairs Office on May 24 charged Vietnam with "unwarrantedly ostracizing and persecuting Chinese residents in Vietnam, and expelling many of them back to China." Many of those expelled, the statement charged, were maltreated, robbed, and even beaten up so much so that "they had nothing left except the clothes they were wearing when they entered Chinese territory." It also accused the Vietnamese of carrying on "mass arrests and wounding and killing Chinese residents" in Ho Chi Minh City. Peking warned Hanoi that it would be responsible for the consequences arising from its "arbitrary, truculent, and illegal" actions.[20]

By the time China made its first public remark on the exodus, some seventy thousand Chinese had already crossed over from Vietnam. How did the exodus begin? Why did China open her border? Why did it wait so long to publicize it? The full story may never be known, overlaid as it is with intensely emotional charges and countercharges of brothers turned enemies. Hanoi had ostracized and persecuted Chinese residents; it was said they even physically transported them to the Chinese border. Vietnam accused China of instigating the exodus through vicious rumors meant to bring dislocation to the Vietnamese economy and exert pressure to its politics. None of the accusations provided an adequate explanation for the mass evacuation that reached 133,000 people by mid-June. This exodus from the North—although it began in March—was not directly related to the drive against capitalists in Cholon. It involved some traders but mostly workers, miners, and fishermen. The fact that Haiphong's port—North Vietnam's main outlet to the world—Vietnam's coal mines, and its fishing operations came to a standstill because of the departure of the Chinese workers implies that Hanoi's hand was probably not behind that exodus. But neither could tens of thousands of destitute fishermen and unskilled workers from Vietnam be the type of overseas Chinese that Peking would encourage to return to the motherland to contribute to the "Four Modernizations." Available evidence, in fact, suggests that although both Hanoi and Peking pushed and pulled the Chinese residents, the exodus soon developed a momentum of its own and assumed proportions that served neither. As we have seen, Vietnam had begun clearing the border region of citizens claiming Chinese nationality as part of a security measure. And as it began its clampdown on Cholon, Hanoi also started harassing the Chinese small traders and restaurant operators about their "ill-gotten wealth" and unpaid taxes.

Since February Hanoi had also celebrated two unusual anniversaries—the victories of Vietnam's national heroes Le Loi and Tran Hung Dao over Chinese invaders. Such celebrations could not have been reassuring for Chinese residents.

A Rumor of War

Beginning in early 1978, the Chinese embassy in Hanoi had started issuing passports to some Chinese residents. The main encouragement to leave, however, came from rumors of impending war between China and Vietnam, mysterious leaflets left under the door at night that either requested the Chinese to return home to build the country, or threatened punishment for those who stayed. Who was behind this rumor campaign? "Bad elements among the Hoa," said Hanoi. Peking charged it was the Vietnamese Public Security Bureau. Targets of the campaign themselves are unsure. Charles Benoit, a Chinese- and Vietnamese-speaking American scholar who interviewed many refugees from the North, concluded that "the motives of those who fled from the North were (then) fear of their fate in the increasingly likely event of war between China and Vietnam, sentimental attachment to their nationality, which they feared losing, concern regarding their ability to maintain what they considered an acceptable standard of living, and in general an increasing perception of the erosion of privileges they had enjoyed as perpetual foreign residents."[21]

Whoever may have been behind the rumor campaign, the Vietnamese certainly did not make any serious attempt to stop the exodus. Given the distance most Chinese had to travel to get to the border, lack of transport, and, most important, security restrictions over citizens' movements, such massive numbers of people could not have reached the frontier without official complicity. In any case, whatever restraint Hanoi showed in the first three months dwindled sharply as China stepped up its public attacks on Vietnam. On May 30, China announced that it was terminating an additional fifty-one of its aid projects in Vietnam, making the total of canceled projects seventy-two, a move that not only went against the stated Chinese principle of not using aid as a lever against any country but also meant that within a month of public airing of the conflict China had exhausted virtually all its nonviolent means of pressure.[22]

The withdrawal of Chinese aid would prove to be a serious blow to Vietnam's battered economy. Immediately, however, it removed the qualms that Hanoi had about joining COMECON. Since the high-level secret meetings in Moscow in the summer of 1977, Vietnam had given its agreement in principle to join COMECON at an "appropriate time." Hanoi did not want to provoke China by joining the Soviet-dominated organization as long as Peking maintained normal relations.[23] The Chinese decision now freed Vietnam to formally join COMECON on June 28. Victory in the first round of the Sino-Vietnamese match, ironically, went to Moscow.

Peking escalated the conflict by announcing on May 26 that it was sending two ships to "bring home persecuted Chinese." Hanoi condemned the unilateral Chinese decision as "gunboat diplomacy." "This is the height of arrogance," a Hanoi commentary said. "The South China Sea is not China's own pond. Haiphong and Ho Chi Minh City are not Chinese ports where Chinese ships can come and go as they please."[24]

Hanoi also would not let go the opportunity to score the contradiction between Peking's claim to protect its countrymen and its policy toward Cambodia, where hundreds of thousands of Chinese residents were suffering at the hands of the Khmer Rouge. If China wanted to repatriate any "victimized Chinese," a Hanoi broadcast taunted, "it should send ships to pick up these Chinese residents [in Cambodia] as quickly as possible."[25]

The mission to rescue Chinese from Vietnam was doomed from the beginning. China's insistence that it would repatriate only the "victimized Chinese" meant that Vietnam would not only have to admit to victimization but also go back on its claim that there were no Chinese in Vietnam, only Hoa—Vietnamese of Chinese origin. After initially condemning the move, Vietnam sought to exploit it to its own advantage by creating a catch-22 situation. China, it said, could take back all the Hoa who wished to leave Vietnam after their applications had been processed and China had given them all visas. Apart from the fact that Peking could never take back 1.2 million people by agreeing to receive Vietnamese citizens of Chinese origin,

China would open itself to charges of interference in Vietnam's internal affairs.

It is doubtful that China really expected Vietnam to acknowledge its mistreatment of Chinese by permitting them to leave aboard Chinese vessels. The fact that the two liners could only accommodate a total of twenty-two hundred passengers indicated the symbolic nature of the move. The gesture was more likely to have been designed to publicly embarrass Hanoi and demonstrate to the overseas Chinese the depth of Peking's concern about their fate.

After six weeks of diplomatic maneuvers over the method of processing returnees and the details of docking, accompanied by shrill propaganda campaigns by both sides, the move was finally abandoned in July. An advance Chinese team sent to open a consulate in Ho Chi Minh City cooled their heels in Hanoi for three months before returning to Peking. Hanoi stipulated that for security reasons they could not be allowed to go into Ho Chi Minh City. A consulate could be opened, Hanoi said, in the third quarter of 1978—well after the deadline it had set for evacuation of citizens of Chinese origin. After waiting off the coast of Vietnam for six weeks, often in heavy monsoon squalls, two Chinese ships quietly returned to Hangpu Harbor with a lot of sick seamen, broken crockery, and bruised egos. Soon, in the face of the continued and massive arrival of Chinese across its land border with Vietnam—openly promoted by Hanoi since May—Peking had to remove its "welcome home" banner that greeted the returnees. It sealed all entry points.

On the whole the ship episode proved to be an embarrassment to Peking and a propaganda bonanza for Hanoi. A Hanoi broadcast beamed toward Southeast Asia said, "In the face of China's volte-face toward Vietnam, the governments in Southeast Asia have reasons to worry. If they do not heighten vigilance, they will lose lock, stock, and barrel."[26] China indeed was concerned. The ASEAN ambassadors in Peking were given a special briefing to assure them that China's reaction to Vietnam's treatment of ethnic Chinese was a "special case," because Hanoi's action was part of a Soviet plot.

Peking's emotional and obviously ill-considered reaction left Chinese residents in Vietnam even more vulnerable. Its heady pronouncements, like "Our relatives in Vietnam have long been hoping for this day when they will be brought home,"[27] had generated false hopes, leading thousands of Chinese in the North to set out for the border and hundreds of thousands in Cholon to openly ask for repatriation. In June the office in Ho Chi Minh City registering those willing to go to China was swamped with thirty thousand applications in just one week.[28]

Most of the Chinese who opted for repatriation to China did so as a stepping-stone to migrating to another country. But in Vietnam's eye they were siding with the enemy. By showing their interest in emigrating to Communist China, where the plight of businessmen was not any better than in Vietnam, they helped to reinforce Vietnamese paranoia about a Chinese fifth column. Instead of forcing Cholon merchants into a farm life in the New Economic Zone, as it had been doing to jobless ethnic Vietnamese, the government decided to get rid of them altogether—and at a profit. The stage was set for the beginning of one of the biggest and most tragic exoduses in the postwar period. After the Chinese ships went home and the land border was sealed, Hanoi launched a cynical emigration policy. "Since we refused to go to the countryside to produce as farmers," a Cholon businessman explained, "and since sooner or later we would have fled anyway, the government decided it might as well collect our gold and let us go."[29]

In the summer of 1978 the Vietnamese Public Security Bureau set up offices in coastal towns in the South to build boats and dispatch the Chinese (or Vietnamese posing as Chinese) after collecting a hefty fee in gold and dollars.[30] The operation, dubbed by Western diplomats in Hanoi as "Rust Bucket Tours Inc.," might have been responsible for generating in two years close to a quarter million boat people, thirty to forty thousand of whom perished at sea.[31]

East Is Red

While world attention was focused on the snarling match between Asia's big and small "dragons," Cambodia was in the grip of a new paroxysm of violence that would hasten Vietnamese intervention. Even the handful of Cambodia watchers in the West who dutifully monitored Radio Phnom Penh broadcasts and interviewed refugees freshly arrived from Cambodia for clues as to what was happening inside the hermit republic could not have guessed the violent drama that was being played out in the rice paddies and rubber plantations of eastern Cambodia. On May 24, the day after Brzezinski left Peking after a successful visit, China publicly lashed out at Vietnam. On the same Wednesday, in an ironic coincidence, a different type of attack was being launched on a small Cambodian town called Suong, some two thousand miles from Peking. Central divisions sent by Pol Pot surrounded the Eastern Zone party head-quarters in a bid to arrest "traitorous" party leaders suspected of colluding with Vietnam. Some were caught, tortured to make confessions, and then executed. So Phim, the Eastern Zone party secretary and once a right-hand man of Pol Pot's, committed sui-cide. Others who could rose up against Pol Pot's troops, then es-caped to Vietnam to swell the ranks of the Khmer resistance. The ruthless killing of the Eastern Zone cadres and soldiers extinguished the last hopes of an internal coup against Pol Pot. Vietnamese fire-power was now the only alternative.

On June 25 Radio Phnom Penh startled the world by claiming that the regime had crushed a coup attempt fomented by Vietnam and the Central Intelligence Agency. While few believed claims of such an absurd partnership, simultaneous Vietnamese propaganda about uprisings in Cambodia confirmed that something very serious indeed was happening. It was not until two years after the event that details of killings and rebellion in the Eastern Zone emerged or that its full significance was understood. The impact of the abortive uprising and repression in this zone on the course of events in In-dochina is a story worth dwelling upon.

In many ways the Eastern Zone purges were the culmination of a bloody campaign for supremacy of Pol Pot's political line that had cut a swath through other zones. Democratic Kampuchea was ad-ministratively divided into seven geographic zones named after their compass directions—Northern, Northeastern, Eastern, Southwest-ern, Western, Northwestern, and Central. More or less similar di-visions were maintained by the Communist party during the years of underground existence as well as during the five years of armed struggle (1970–75). The lack of communications and concern about security had led to a certain autonomy among party units in different zones. In the four years since the seizure of power, Pol Pot's central leadership had sought to impose a vertical authority over the zonal leaders while maintaining a tight horizontal division between the zones. With the assistance of Central and Southwestern Zone forces, Pol Pot launched waves of purges in 1976–77 to eliminate Northern and Northwestern leaders. The difference of opinion essentially was over the pace of revolution and the harshness of its methods. Those who questioned Pol Pot's ultraradical line of instant communism and ruthless treatment of the urban population and his adventurist policy toward Vietnam were considered traitors deserving execution. Ironically, most of the purge victims believed that Vietnam posed a threat to Cambodia and that, unless errors were corrected, the Cambodian revolution would be destroyed and the nation left unable to defend itself against Vietnam—an accurate prognosis, as later events proved. For Pol Pot and his small band of loyalists the charge of treachery against dissenting members was the convenient way of avoiding "debate on the party line in which," as Stephen Heder points out, "not only might Pol Pot be defeated, but the whole party unravel."[32]

Of all the regions, the most serious threat to Pol Pot's leadership seemed to come from the Eastern Zone. Since the birth of the anti-French Issarak movement in the 1940s the region enjoyed close collaboration with Vietnamese Communists. Physical proximity to Vietnam and the existence of Vietnamese workers in the region's rubber plantations facilitated contacts. During the first phase of the anti–Lon Nol resistance, this was the area where Vietnamese helped to train and organize the Cambodian resistance army. The long association with the Vietnamese seems to have left an impression on the political style of the Khmer Communists in this area. While the group led by Pol Pot was most influenced by Mao and the concepts of the egalitarian and ceaseless class struggle, the Eastern Zone leaders had a more classical, "Vietnamese" approach to Socialist transformation. This approach emphasized making use of available resources—bourgeois or otherwise—to increase production. Abolishing class differences could come second.[33]

It is not known whether these differences were ever openly debated or whether the Eastern Zone leaders ever challenged Pol Pot politically. But it seems that Eastern Zone leaders were not enthusiastic in the application of some of the harsh or ultraleftist policies decided by the Center. During the first three years of Khmer Rouge rule, this zone had more food, and, in certain respects, the life of the "new people"—the dispersed urban population—was less harsh there than elsewhere in Democratic Kampuchea.[34]

This does not, however, mean that the Eastern Zone did not have its share of killings. Over sixty thousand Cham minority people— mostly in the Kompong Cham area—were massacred for their Islamic faith. Some of the most vicious killings of Vietnamese civilians were perpetrated by Eastern Zone units—of course with the Center's blessings. Nevertheless, the fact remains that, whether as a consequence of their dissent or because of Pol Pot's self-fulfilling paranoia about the Eastern Zone, this part of Cambodia produced the largest number of cadres who rose up against him or were crushed by the Center before they could do anything.[35]

"Khmer Bodies with Vietnamese Minds"

The story of the Eastern Zone is inextricably linked with the life of So Phim, a pudgy, round-faced peasant, who had led the Communist movement in the region for over a quarter of a century. In 1954 he was one of the one thousand Khmer Communists who regrouped in Hanoi. But he had clandestinely returned to Cambodia within two years to reorganize the party. In 1963 he became the only member of peasant origin to make it to the five-man party standing committee (equivalent to the Politburo), which was dominated by Pol Pot's anti-Vietnamese intellectuals. During the years of the anti–Lon Nol guerrilla war he rose to the rank of deputy chief of staff of the Khmer Rouge army. All through the 1960s and 1970s he maintained a close relationship with the Vietnamese Communists, despite occasional friction. His influence in the region was such that after 1975 he became the only member of the standing committee to remain in charge of a zone. He is credited by many for creating the relative prosperity of the Eastern Zone, but Cambodian scholars are divided over the role he played in its final destruction.

We have seen how the failure of the Eastern Zone troops to stop the Vietnamese invasion in December 1977 led to the beginning of a new wave of purges. In the confusion after the Vietnamese withdrawal, local units, which dispersed before the Vietnamese invasion, later got involved in firefights with freshly sent Central troops, creating more suspicion of complicity. One by one, middle-ranking military cadres from the Eastern Zone forces as well as from the Central divisions were called to Phnom Penh for "meetings." They never returned. The Tuol Sleng Prison's records show that by April 19, 1978, Eastern Zone personnel being held there numbered 409—ten times the number of cadres from the Northwestern Zone, the second largest figure from any other zone. All of the 28 prisoners who arrived the next day were from the Eastern Zone. The commanders of the two Central divisions stationed in the east were also arrested in April. One was Heng Samrin's brother, Heng Thal, the commander of the 290th Division.[36]

On May 10 Radio Phnom Penh broadcast the extraordinary call to exterminate the Vietnamese race and "purify" its own ranks. "In terms of numbers, one of us must kill thirty Vietnamese . . . that is to say, we lose one against thirty. We don't have to engage 8 million people [Cambodia's presumed population]. We need only 2 million troops to crush the 50 million Vietnamese, and we would still have 6 million left." Such an ambitious undertaking could be attempted only with a total commitment from the army, party, and the population. The broadcast ended with a call: "We must purify our armed forces, our party, and the masses of people in order to continue fighting the enemies in defense of Cambodian territory and the Cambodian race."[37]

As a member of the party high command, did Phim endorse this insane policy and the purges? Ben Kiernan, a Khmer-speaking Australian scholar who has spent considerable time researching recent Cambodian history, believes that So Phim was ill most of this time and unaware of the arrests. When he came to know about the arrest of the commanders of the two Eastern Zone–based Central divisions—the 280th and 290th—he "was angered," but his pathetic advice was only to "ask everyone to watch out, to be careful." According to Kiernan, So Phim was hamstrung by a sense of party discipline and by his belief that these arrests and killings could not reflect the nature of the revolution. As the purges developed, he was caught by inertia, powerless to stop them. Stephen Heder, however, believes that following the successful penetration by the Vietnamese in December, So Phim struck a deal with Pol Pot to purge the military cadres. In Democratic Kampuchea the only way for a leader to survive was by blaming his failure on the treachery of his subordinates. "So Phim did exactly that," says Heder. "But he had not realized that he himself was suspect for keeping the Eastern Zone relatively prosperous and for trying to develop zonal and sectoral forces."[38]

Whether Phim was a well-meaning but naive leader or a murderous accomplice of Pol Pot's whose time had run out, his belated attempt to push away the tightening noose only marked the beginning of a civil war that would culminate in a full-scale Vietnamese intervention.

In late May of 1978, Ke Pauk, the commander of the Central Zone dispatched by Pol Pot to conduct purges, sent his "invitation" to Phim to come to a meeting. Phim knew very well what that invitation meant. He sent three emissaries, including a senior party leader, to investigate the purpose of that meeting. They never came back.

On May 24, as reinforcements of an armored brigade arrived from Phnom Penh, Central troops surrounded the Eastern Zone party headquarters at Suong, about twenty miles from the Vietnamese border. A number of party officials were arrested and taken away for execution. But Phim had already climbed into his jeep with his wife, children, and bodyguards and slipped away hoping to go to Phnom Penh. According to Kiernan, he told his associates that Pauk and Defense Minister Son Sen, who were leading the attacks, were traitors; he would get the party high command to stop them. Heder says that Phim was still under the impression that the Central troops had simply overstepped their instructions. So he ordered the Eastern troops to resist the Central troops until he could get Pol Pot to rein in Pauk and Son Sen's men. Little did he realize that in Pol

Pot's eyes he had become the traitorous chieftain of the Eastern Zone. By May 1978, Pol Pot was convinced that So Phim was the leader of a clandestine "Workers Party of Cambodia" set up by the Vietnamese and the CIA to seize power in Cambodia.[39]

So Phim set himself up on the banks of the Mekong near Phnom Penh and waited to hear from Pol Pot. (He had sent a courier to contact Pol Pot before he entered the capital.) On June 2, a "welcoming party" of two ferryloads of Pol Pot's soldiers arrived. Phim was too highly placed not to realize what that kind of escort meant. He pulled out his pistol and put a bullet through his chest.[40]

With the operation launched on May 24, 1978, began the goriest chapter in the blood-soaked history of Democratic Kampuchea. Until then, purges of political cadres had been conducted discreetly. Victims would be called for "routine consultations," "advanced study," "emergency meetings," or a "new job" outside their village to be handed over to the State Security Bureau. In four years nearly twenty thousand such "invitees" would be tortured for confessions and killed in Tuol Sleng Prison. Given the secrecy that governed party affairs and the total isolation of one zone from another, such methods instilled fear and uncertainty, but not panic. By seizing the zonal party headquarters at Suong with armored units, Pol Pot left no doubt in the minds of surviving cadres what was in store for them. The next day battalion- and regiment-level officers of the 4th and 5th Divisions were called for a conference. As soon as they arrived, they were stripped and trussed. They were taken on a truck to a field, pushed down from the truck, and machine-gunned. Only one miraculously survived and later escaped to Vietnam to tell the story.[41]

Commander of the 4th Division Heng Samrin, who had seen his brother disappear, did not wait for his turn. With about a thousand of his loyal troops, he headed for the jungle. One middle-level cadre, Tea Sabun, led a local militia group to raid the Eastern Zone arsenal for guns and antitank rockets. They engaged the Central troops for nearly three weeks before retreating to the forest. Other zonal leaders like Chea Sim, Mat Ly, Men Chhan, Ouch Bun Chhoeun, and Sim Kar took to the jungle with some three thousand armed men and thirty thousand civilians. For nearly two months after the end of May, three provinces in the Eastern Zone—Kompong Cham,

Svay Rieng, and Prey Veng—became a battlefield for hit-and-run attacks on Central troops. As the Khmer Rouge cadres fled, many villagers destroyed communal kitchens and divided cattle and communal property among themselves.

In the face of the Chinese-made firepower and armor brought in by the Center, which by June included the dreaded *Nirdey* troops led by Ta Mok, the spontaneous resistance of the hastily organized groups did not last long. In July, after the fighting died down, the vengeance killing began. The carnage was unlike any the Eastern Zone had ever known before. In the eyes of Pol Pot and his friends, the people of the Eastern Zone had shown their colors—they were "Khmer bodies with Vietnamese minds" and had to be crushed.[42] Not only captured rebels and their families, but whole villages that had sheltered them were killed. They were driven in trucks to killing fields and hacked to death. Two years later I visited one of the killing grounds in Kompong Cham where an estimated fifty thousand people had been massacred. Under the mango trees, the skulls and bones of the old and young lay in an obscene carpet of death.

In the Eastern Zone the number of killed in response to the May uprising was probably over one hundred thousand. In order to clear it of suspects, nearly a third of the population were removed from the east to the malarial areas of western Cambodia, where half of them would later die of starvation and disease, if they had not been executed.

As the savage repression went on, the Eastern population and rebel leaders hid in the forest under torrential monsoon rains. Lacking food, medicine, clothing, and ammunition, they soon became demoralized. Time had come to make a choice between surrender, which promised sure death, and luck with Vietnam. Many deserters from the Central divisions had been involved in attacks on Vietnam and were understandably fearful of seeking refuge there. Cadres who had been brought up on a staple of anti-Vietnamese propaganda also had difficulty in shifting gears. The surviving Issarak cadres who had once enjoyed close relationships with the Vietnamese were sent as emissaries across the heavily mined border. Beginning in late June, Hanoi had begun Khmer-language broadcasts calling for an uprising. Voices of known Khmer cadres, who were believed to be dead, came over the radio and provided some assurance. The fact that Heng Samrin's elder brother, Heng Samkai, another Eastern Zone leader, had already made it to Vietnam helped in the liaison. "We had come to realize," Samkai told me in 1981, "that it was impossible to overthrow Pol Pot on our own. We had to seek Vietnamese help." As the chairman of the Eastern Zone couriers—who carried messages back and forth between party units as well as to Vietnam—he had long known the Vietnamese. Making it to the border in January 1978, he was flown to Ho Chi Minh City in a Vietnamese helicopter. He and other Khmer Rouge defectors assembled in the former police training school at Thu Duc.

The Vietnamese party had already begun training resistance fighters and putting together a resistance movement. The dismantling of the Eastern Zone party, where the Vietnamese could have expected to get some sympathy, had foreclosed the possibility of a change from within, a coup against Pol Pot. There was now little chance that the Khmers being trained in Vietnam could be slipped back into Cambodia to join with the dissidents and organize a rebellion.

Contacts were established between the Vietnamese and different rebel groups hiding in the jungle. In early September, the Vietnamese launched another tank-led operation inside Cambodia. The objective this time was to contact Heng Samrin and his followers hiding in the forest and escort them back to Vietnam. With the arrival of Heng Samrin, Chea Sim, and other Khmer Rouge survivors, the future government of a pro-Vietnamese Cambodia was assembled.[43]

Le Duc Tho flew from Hanoi. Flanked by other Khmer experts in the party, he sat down with the Khmer Rouge defectors and old Khmer residents like Pen Sovan and Chea Soth for a two-day (September 21–22) conference at Thu Duc. They decided that a decisive military push against Pol Pot would have to be made in December, when rice was ready for harvest and the ground was dry. Work began at full steam to set up the Kampuchean National United Front for National Salvation, in whose name the struggle would begin.[44]

China Sees a Plot

The summer of 1978 was action-packed, although much of that action was not visible to outside observers. With the upheaval and massacres in eastern Cambodia, with thousands of Chinese residents in Vietnam jamming the border town of Lang Son in the hope of crossing over to China, and with stepped-up Soviet military activity around China's periphery, all the gears of a large conflict meshed. Viewed from Peking, the Vietnamese treatment of the ethnic Chinese was neither part of Socialist transformation nor simple racial discrimination, but an integral part of Moscow's policy of encircling China. Vietnam's conflict with Cambodia was increasingly seen as part of a Soviet drive against Peking's regional leadership by using the "lesser hegemonists," Vietnam. The Vietnamese saw the orgy of violence inside Cambodia and the Khmer Rouge attacks on Vietnam as a part of a well-laid Chinese plan to crush Vietnam. Moscow found its long-sought cooperation with Hanoi even more crucial in the light of an emerging Sino-American connection. The view from the White House—increasingly colored by the Manichaean anti-Sovietism of Brzezinski—saw the Vietnam-Cambodia conflict as a proxy war between Moscow and Peking in which China deserved America's strategic support.

For Moscow it was a time of opportunity, but also a time of danger. The beginning of the public quarrel between China and Vietnam came as a long-awaited opportunity to draw Vietnam firmly into its embrace. Moscow took advantage of the overseas Chinese issue to belabor its favorite theory of a Chinese fifth column and win propaganda points in Southeast Asia. It twisted the knife into China by a full denunciation of Peking's "great-power hegemony" and its interference in Vietnam.

But Brzezinski's May 1978 trip to China and his anti-Soviet rhetoric in Peking alarmed Moscow, particularly the report that he had discussed military-related technology and arms transfers with the Chinese. On June 25, Soviet party secretary-general Leonid Brezhnev himself launched the sharpest attack ever on U.S. policy toward China. Those in the United States who were playing the "China card," he said, were pursuing a "short-sighted and dangerous" policy, and he warned that "its authors may bitterly regret it."[45]

Secretly, the Soviet Union stepped up its collaboration with Hanoi. The Vietnamese Politburo meeting in mid-February that had made a series of momentous decisions about Cambodia and China had also concluded that Vietnamese military involvement in Cambodia was likely to bring a Chinese riposte. In order to face the threat from China, Hanoi needed an insurance policy "We took a leaf out of India's book," a Vietnamese official would later tell the Indian ambassador in Hanoi. A Soviet proposal to sign a treaty of friendship and cooperation with a clause assuring military support had been made to India in 1969. India had sat on the proposal for two years. It had agreed to sign the treaty and obtain Soviet military protection only when it felt that, in light of its looming conflict with Pakistan and the possibility of a Chinese intervention in favor of the latter, it needed a superpower guarantor. Three months after signing the friendship treaty with Moscow, the Indian army defeated Pakistan and brought about an independent Bangladesh.

Hanoi perused its shelves and dusted off a proposal for a friendship treaty that the Soviets had made in 1975 just after the victory in the South. By early June, General Giap was off on a secret trip to Moscow to present a Vietnamese draft of the treaty and also to submit a shopping list of arms. On his way to Moscow, Giap made an unpublicized stopover in New Delhi. At an airport meeting with the Indian defense and foreign ministers, Giap made a request that India help Vietnam in setting up an ordnance factory to produce small arms. Considering its conflict with Cambodia and China was looming over the horizon, Vietnam did not want to be totally dependent on Moscow for arms. A well-placed Indian official, who related this closely guarded incident to me two years later, said that Giap's request was politely turned down on the grounds of a lack of resources. Things might have been different if the Congress government of Indira Gandhi—who had acted as midwife for the birth of Bangladesh—was in power. But the government of Morarji Desai, India's first right-wing government, was reluctant to get involved in an apparent anti-Chinese venture with a Soviet ally.

Moscow was thrilled with Vietnam's revived interest in the friendship treaty. In late June, Nikolai Firuybin, Soviet deputy foreign minister, flew to Hanoi. In the course of that unpublicized visit he smoothed out all major differences in the draft. The time when the treaty would be signed was to be decided by Hanoi. It could not be revealed prematurely, and thereby warn Peking, but it had to be announced in time to deter Peking from contemplating any military action against Vietnam. And the Vietnamese Politburo also did not want to cloud the prospect of normalization with the United States by early announcement of a military treaty with Moscow.[46]

As the text of the Soviet-Vietnam friendship treaty awaited signatures, the logistical preparations for the coming conflict continued. In August, responding to Vietnam's request, the Soviet Union began an unprecedented airlift and sea transport of arms. Huge Antonov 12 aircraft made dozens of flights to Danang to unload long-range guns, missiles, radar, and ammunition to bolster the Vietnamese defense against China. MiG-21 fighters delivered to Danang by ship were assembled and flown north, closer to the Chinese border.

As the Soviet propaganda against China grew increasingly strident, so did China's against the Soviet Union. Within three weeks of Peking's first attack on Vietnam for "ostracizing, persecuting, and expelling" its Chinese, it had begun presenting Vietnam as a Soviet surrogate. China called Vietnam a "Cuba in Asia"—an insulting allusion to Cuban soldiers fighting in Angola to advance Moscow's cause. For Peking, "Soviet social imperialism" was the "main backer and instigator" of Vietnam's anti-China policies.[47]

In the midst of a sharply escalating polemic over the treatment of the Chinese in Vietnam and Peking's cancellation of aid projects, China shed all restraint and publicly denounced Hanoi's moves against Cambodia. From mid-June, China started echoing the Khmer Rouge charges of a Vietnamese expansionist design over Cambodia. A Chinese People's Daily editorial in July charged that Hanoi's victory against the United States and its acquisition of great amounts of U.S. arms had "made the Vietnamese authorities' heads swell and their hands itch to get more." It had led Vietnam to dream of becoming the "overlord" of Southeast Asia, the first step being to "rig up an Indochina Federation" under its control.

Soon, the Peking propagandists upgraded the significance of the Vietnam-Cambodia conflict from purely regional to global significance by claiming a linkage between Vietnamese expansionism and the Soviet drive for supremacy. They no longer viewed the Cambodia or overseas Chinese issue as disputes between two Socialist countries that could be settled through negotiations. As a Chinese commentator put it, "This conflict [Vietnam-Cambodia], together with the Vietnamese authorities' anti-China acts, including the persecution and expulsion of Chinese residents in Vietnam and the using of the question of overseas Chinese to disrupt the relations between China and Southeast Asian nations, forms a component part of the whole plot. In this plot, the Soviet superpower with its own hegemonistic aims provides cover and support for the Vietnamese authorities' regional hegemonism, while the Vietnamese authorities serve as a junior partner for the Soviet Union."[48]

Time to Teach a Lesson

China's public outpouring of anger against Vietnam and the Soviet Union reflected a policy shift that was taking place in China in the early summer of 1978. The late Chairman Mao had firmly believed in the inevitability of war between China and the imperialists and exhorted his people to ideologically fortify themselves, store grain, and dig tunnels in preparation. But since the death of Mao and the overthrow of the radicals, the new Chinese leadership was cautiously moving toward a more optimistic position that saw postponement of the war as being possible if China formed an internationally backed united front against the principal threat, Moscow. Having launched an ambitious ten-year plan for modernization in March 1978, China needed a long period of peace to prepare itself for the inevitable global war. The Peking leadership argued that China could buy time by preempting the enemy plan at an early stage. "The West should break up the timetable of Soviet strategy," Chinese officials told American defense specialist Michael Pillsbury in May 1978, "by challenging Soviet influence in third countries that have strategic value; by denying allies to the Soviets; and by always keeping in mind the internal weaknesses of the Soviet society, economy, and the ethnic balance."[49] Although no specific name was mentioned as a third country "that had strategic value," they had certainly meant Vietnam. Interestingly, at about the same time China developed this new approach, Brzezinski visited China. According to the National Security Council's China specialist Michel Oksenberg, who accompanied Brzezinski to Peking, "the vehemence with which the Chinese denounced Vietnamese perfidy was the most unexpected aspect of Brzezinski's discussion."[50]

In the light of later revelations, a Japanese report saying that it was at a Politburo meeting in May 1978 that the Chinese decided "to respond by deed to Vietnam's provocations" and to "dare a showdown if Vietnam should launch a military adventure" seems entirely possible.[51] That contingency plan, if indeed it was made then, was firmed up two months later. Chinese leaders looked carefully at the military situation in Cambodia and the consequences of a Khmer Rouge collapse under Vietnamese pressure. Some of the military leaders proposed sending Chinese volunteers to Cambodia, arguing that to let Cambodia go under would deal a serious blow to China's credibility in the region. But that idea, Chinese sources told me years later, was quickly dismissed on a variety of political, military, and economic grounds. One official explained Peking's approach to Cambodia by quoting a Chinese saw: "One should not expect others to come and do one's cooking." "After all," he explained, "Chairman Mao's principle is that the defense of a country's independence and sovereignty is essentially the job of its own people." A more practical consideration was the geographical distance from Cambodia, the logistical hurdle. Another was the danger of provoking Soviet involvement in Vietnam's favor. China's direct military intervention in Cambodia would surely frighten non-Communist Southeast Asia, antagonize the West, and upset China's modernization plans. China agreed to accelerate the delivery of military supplies and send more advisers, but it concluded that Pol Pot's Cambodia would have to sink or swim on its own.

While ruling out intervention in Cambodia, the Chinese could not, however, let Vietnam threaten its only ally in Southeast Asia with impunity or defy Peking by expelling Chinese residents and cavorting with its sworn enemy. Chinese leaders, led by Deng Xiaoping, chose to do what Chinese emperors had always done to "insolent" Vietnam—punish it. In the Confucian world order of ancient China nothing was more reprehensible than lack of filial piety to the emperor—the father of the polity. For all its aid to Vietnam during the war—estimated by Peking to be worth $20 billion—Vietnam was now kicking China in the teeth. "The Vietnamese have a black heart" was the bitter remark of a Peking official who described to me their ingratitude in August 1978.

Emotion certainly played an important part in China's hostility to

Vietnam. Ironically, the man who seemed to hate the Vietnamese most passionately was Deng Xiaoping, whose reemergence had been welcomed by the Vietnamese. Perhaps it was Deng's intimate involvement in supporting Vietnam during the war years that made him feel more bitter about what he saw as Hanoi's volte-face. A Thai diplomat who had been present at many meetings with Deng recalled that "the moment the topic of Vietnam came up, one could see something change in Deng Xiaoping. His hatred [for the Vietnamese] was just visceral." He spat forcefully into his spittoon and called the Vietnamese "dogs." The Vietnamese, Deng announced at a press conference, in November 1978, were the "hooligans of the East." Sitting next to him, the Thai premier Kriangsak Chomanan cringed in embarrassment. While the emotions were clear in August 1978, China's intentions were less obvious.

Three years later, a Peking official revealed to me that during one of its regular weekly meetings in early July 1978, the Chinese Politburo decided to "teach Vietnam a lesson" for its "ungrateful and arrogant" behavior. The decision, taken in absolute secrecy, was not without some opposition, but Deng convincingly argued that limited military action against Vietnam would demonstrate to Moscow that China was ready to stand up to its bullying. If the Soviets failed to come to Vietnam's help, as he expected, it would demonstrate Moscow's unreliability as an ally and weaken the Soviet position in the Third World. According to the Chinese official, Deng argued that in order to be effective, the Chinese move had to be cast not as a national conflict but as part of China's global antihegemonic strategy serving broader interests. The Politburo deferred the timing and scope of its military action and decided to step up the effort to build closer relations with the United States, non-Communist Asia, and the West.[52]

When in the end of July 1978 Cambodian defense minister Son Sen arrived in Peking seeking China's military commitment against Vietnam, he got an earful about the merits of self-reliance. Particularly harsh in the lecturing was Deng Xiaoping—who had once been reviled by the Khmer Rouge as a "counterrevolutionary." He bluntly told Son Sen that Chinese aid would be of no use if Cambodia did not abandon its "sectarian" policies and form a united front against the enemy. The Chinese urged the Khmer Rouge to bring Prince Norodom Sihanouk back to head the government and make efforts to improve the Khmer's international image. The Chinese leaders advised Son Sen to begin preparations for a protracted guerrilla war by digging tunnels, setting up arms caches, and mobilizing the masses. If Vietnam invaded Cambodia again, there should be guerrilla resistance rather than frontal opposition. China also promised to pressure Vietnam, but Peking leaders did not explain how.[53]

Despite the advice of self-reliance China soon began an unprecedented airlift of arms and ammunition to Cambodia. In addition to its twice-weekly flights across Laos, a contingent of five Boeing 707s shuttled between Canton and Phnom Penh across the South China Sea. Along with arms and ammunition, hundreds of Chinese advisers were flown into Cambodia. According to U.S. intelligence estimates, the total number of Chinese personnel in late 1978 reached five thousand.

China's own preparations for military action against Vietnam, however, started in diplomacy. Thanks to Brzezinski's quiet encouragement to Tokyo, in August 1978 Japan signed the long-stalled Japan-China peace and friendship treaty. A controversial clause in the treaty expressing its opposition to hegemony by any power was China's first diplomatic coup against Moscow. With the arrivals of Leonard Woodcock in Peking and Chai Zemin in Washington as respective heads of the U.S. and Chinese liaison missions, a new phase began in the effort to normalize relations with the United States. And as the Chinese media launched an operation to woo the Southeast Asian neighbors (which had been long suspicious of China's revolutionary expansionism), preparations began for Deng Xiaoping's historic fence-mending visit to non-Communist Southeast Asia.

As the summer of 1978 drew to a close, both Vietnam and China secretly drew up their war plans. But before the guns boomed, it was a time for winning friends and isolating the enemy. One of the biggest prizes in the Hanoi-Peking race was the friendship and support of the very one they had so recently sought to expel from Asia entirely—Uncle Sam.

9

Yankee Come Home!

Assistant Secretary of State Richard Holbrooke operated on the principle that secrecy is best kept in a crowd. On September 27, 1978, for the second time in a week his small negotiating team had assembled at the American mission at the United Nations amid the bustle of activity surrounding the General Assembly session. The afternoon traffic on First Avenue was heavy as scores of cars carrying ministers and ambassadors jostled with the regular traffic and tourist coaches to approach the UN. Presidents, prime ministers, and foreign ministers of 140 nations had descended on Manhattan. They joined the procession of speakers addressing the General Assembly and engaged in a frenetic series of banquets, receptions, and meetings. Holbrooke had thought the setting ideal for the quiet talks with the Vietnamese to establish diplomatic relations. Since the expulsion of the Vietnamese ambassador to the UN in February on charges of involvement in espionage, building bridges with Vietnam was not a particularly popular move, and premature publicity, Holbrooke thought, could hurt President Carter.

The secret arrangements worked out as planned. The press had not got wind of his first meeting with the Vietnamese deputy foreign minister Nguyen Co Thach five days earlier. Nobody noticed when on the afternoon of September 27 Holbrooke, Frank Wisner, National Security Council staffer Michel Oksenberg, and two State Department aides set out in two taxis for their second unpublicized rendezvous with the Vietnamese. The tiny Vietnamese mission, hidden in the anonymous thirty-five story brick-and-glass Waterside Plaza apartment building overlooking the East River, was an unglamorous setting in which to make history. But Holbrooke was fairly certain that this session with Thach would finally close the painful chapter of America's Vietnam years and make a new beginning. After the success of the Camp David Agreement, signed the previous week by Menachem Begin and Anwar Sadat, normalization with Hanoi would be another feather in Carter's cap.

During his first session with Thach on September 22, Holbrooke was surprised by the tenacity with which the Vietnamese had clung to their demand for American aid as part of normalization. He had taken with him a thick file of all the Vietnamese public and private statements since July 1978 affirming the Vietnamese desire to have unconditional normalization. But once at the table Thach had started the familiar refrain about America's moral obligation toward Vietnam in providing reconstruction aid—the same sterile arguments that had led to failure of the talks in 1977. "You won't believe it, Cy. The Vietnamese are still asking for money," he had reported to his boss, Secretary of State Cyrus Vance.

But knowing the Vietnamese negotiating tactics, Holbrooke expected Thach to drop that line during the second session. Otherwise, he thought, Thach would not have asked for a second session when on September 22 Holbrooke had broken off talks, saying that it was useless to continue in that vein. Holbrooke, in fact, was so confident that Thach would finally make the offer for unconditional normalization that he had brought along Oksenberg to sit at the talks. He knew that Carter's national security adviser, Zbigniew Brzezinski, was not at all keen about establishing ties with what he considered the Soviet "surrogate," Vietnam—especially when Hanoi was at loggerheads with America's likely strategic ally, China. Holbrooke calculated that a formal Vietnamese renunciation of the aid precondition in the presence of Oksenberg, Brzezinski's Asia specialist, would make it difficult for the NSC to throw a monkey wrench into his plan to normalize with Vietnam.

The meeting was businesslike. Dressed in a blue suit, Thach welcomed them as they walked into the Vietnamese mission. After brisk handshakes, the American team sat down at a green-baize table placed in one corner of the sparsely furnished room that otherwise served as a reception area of the Vietnamese mission. For China specialist Oksenberg it was his first encounter with a Vietnamese official. He was struck by how young fifty-three-year-old Thach looked. His apparent youth and easy smile, however, hid three decades of experience in war and diplomacy. In the course of a chat during a tea break, Thach told them that he was a lieutenant colonel in the Vietminh army at the time of the historic siege of the French garrison at Dien Bien Phu in 1954. Two years later he had begun his diplomatic career as consul general in New Delhi. This was when the French-speaking Thach had taught himself European table manners and English. "Can't you smell curry in my English?" he had once asked an interviewer, sure in the knowledge that it had only Vietnamese flavor. That knowledge of English and diplomatic experience came to use in the 1970s when he served as an aide to Le Duc Tho in the protracted Paris negotiations with Henry Kissinger. Now it was his show. Thach began his presentation in Vietnamese and quickly revealed he had not changed his tune. It would be nice if the Americans came to Hanoi with something in hand, he said. Holbrooke again repeated why the United States could not make any commitment. After an hour and a half of such a sterile exchange Holbrooke collected his papers and put them back into his folder, a clear sign the session was over. "Mr. Thach, we have reached the end of the road," he said. "If this is all you have got to say, there is no point in continuing this discussion." "Should we have some tea?" Thach had suggested in response.

They left the table to go to the other corner of the room, where pots of tea and coffee, cookies, and freshly fried Vietnamese spring rolls (*cha gio*) were laid out on a table. The Vietnamese and the Americans sipped coffee and munched *cha gio* as the sky across the East River slowly turned a light shade of purple. All through the afternoon Oksenberg had sat silently with a scowl on his face. He was deeply skeptical about how serious the Vietnamese really were about normalization. To him it seemed Holbrooke was the one who wanted it badly, pressing Thach to drop the aid demand. Thach knew who Oksenberg was and perhaps sensed his lack of interest. He tried to strike up a light conversation with him in Mandarin. Oksenberg ignored that attempt and kept staring at the skyline of industrial Queens framed in the window. "I just couldn't relate to him," Oksenberg later recalled. "This was the first time I had met a Vietnamese." To break the embarrassed silence, Holbrooke picked up the thread of conversation.

Tea session over, Holbrooke was going to take leave from Thach when he said, "Let's have some more talks." Back at the green-baize table Thach was suddenly a different man. "Okay, I'll tell you what you want to hear. We will defer other problems until later. Let's normalize our relations without preconditions." Holbrooke recalled later, "Bang! In one go Thach laid it all out. Then he wanted the agreement, which could not be signed for two years, to be settled in ten minutes." Thach asked Holbrooke to sign a memorandum of understanding about normalization. "There is a typewriter here," he said. "Both our staffs can draw it up while we have some more tea," he suggested. Holbrooke was delighted. "This is a most constructive development, a significant step forward," Holbrooke had said. But he refused to put anything in writing then and there as Thach asked. "I will convey your position to the President. We will carefully consider your proposal and let you know when we can proceed." Thach was keen that the agreement at least be signed while Vietnamese foreign minister Nguyen Duy Trinh was in New York in the first week of October. But Holbrooke said it might not be possible to have a reply within that time.

That was all right, Thach said, he would be in New York until October 20. As if by magic the mood of the dreary meeting was transformed. Setting up an American embassy in Hanoi was suddenly on the horizon. Thach told Holbrooke that a building that used to be the American consulate in Hanoi in the French colonial days was ready for reoccupancy by the Americans. The old embassy of the Republic of South Vietnam in Washington is also lying vacant, a beaming Holbrooke informed him. Thach could not wait to discuss the number of diplomats to be assigned to each embassy, the arrangements for communications and diplomatic pouches. Time was now to fix the nuts and bolts of the agreement.

When a jubilant Holbrooke took leave of a broadly smiling Thach, evening was descending on New York. But it felt like a new day.

With the removal of the last obstacle to establishing ties with Vietnam, American foreign policy in Asia had reached a crossroads. It was a moment of decision. The conflicting strategies toward China and Southeast Asia pursued so far by Zbigniew Brzezinski and Cyrus Vance without public contradiction now had to be resolved. Vietnam and China, Cambodia and Vietnam, were clearly on the path of an armed confrontation with increasing danger of Soviet involvement. Should Washington side with China and its unsavory ally the Khmer Rouge for the sake of an anti-Soviet alliance—as Brzezinski advocated? Or should it regard the emerging conflict, as did Vance and Holbrooke, to be a historically rooted nationalist struggle that the United States should stay out of? Would the U.S. national interest in Asia and the world be better served by diplomatic relations with both Vietnam and China? Or should Washington spurn ties with Hanoi in order to have Peking's friendship? Asia's two leading Communist nations were beckoning the United States back to the region to be a major player. Now was the time for Jimmy Carter to decide whether the United States should return as a balancing power or as a partner of one.

Knocking on the American Door

The high-level American-Vietnamese contacts in the fall of 1978 had come after ten months of chill. During the last round of talks held by Holbrooke with Vietnamese vice–foreign minister Phan Hien in early December 1977, the Vietnamese had stopped asking for economic aid as a precondition, but Hien had insisted, nevertheless, that the United States make a private pledge about an aid package after normalization. That meeting had ended in failure.

Two months later another blow was struck. Ronald Humphrey, an employee of the U.S. Information Agency, and David Truong, his American-Vietnamese associate, were indicted on charges of espionage, and the Vietnamese ambassador to the United Nations, Dinh Ba Thi, was named as an unindicted coconspirator. Thi was expelled from the United States.

The spying case was of limited importance—the stolen cables had the lowest classification, and some were not classified at all. One of them contained the views of the Indian and Yugoslav diplomats posted in Hanoi. Another contained the Woodcock Commission's views on reconciliation with Vietnam. Yet another classified as "confidential" gave the details of the Air France flights in and out of Ho Chi Minh City over the period of a month! Not a great intelligence coup for the Vietnamese, nor a heavy blow to U.S. national security. But ironically it was precisely the limited significance of those purloined cables that made the case perfect for the FBI to take to the courtroom. For some time the FBI had been frustrated at its failure to bring to trial several espionage cases. Accused spies could not be brought to justice without divulging the secrets they had stolen. The case involving the Vietnamese was thus an ideal one to punish the offenders with no damage to national security. At least some State Department officials were surprised by the rapidity of the decision to declare the Vietnamese ambassador to the UN persona non grata as an accomplice in the spying operation. Was the haste due in part to a desire for revenge? At least the Vietnamese claimed it was. Robert Oakley, Holbrooke's deputy for Southeast Asia, says that the Vietnamese never understood why the United States acted the way it did. "But given our laws and given domestic politics and other things, there was nothing we could do [but expel the ambassador]." [1]

The case may not deserve even a footnote in the annals of East-West espionage, but it proved to be a turning point in the checkered history of U.S.–Vietnamese relations. "It just froze everything," Oakley said. Washington was totally unaware that, in an ironic coincidence, it had decided to expel the Vietnamese envoy just when the Vietnamese leadership was in the midst of a major reappraisal of its foreign policy.

Vietnam's January 1978 Politburo meeting, which had looked at the option of military preparations against China and Cambodia, had also concluded that the time had come for moving ahead on the stalled normalization talks with Washington and expanding ties with the non-Communist world even if that meant forgoing U.S. aid.[2]

The Vietnamese decision to drop the aid precondition had been painful. Not only did it mean giving up hope for sorely needed money, but it admitted to a defeat in diplomacy as well. Despite a stunning victory against the Americans, this would be the first time a defeated power had been allowed to reestablish ties without paying any reparations. But the interest of Vietnam's security outweighed everything. The course of events in late 1977 and early 1978 had made it obvious to the Vietnamese that they would have to seek increased Soviet military assistance in preparing for the conflict with China and Cambodia—a course that could seriously compromise their ambition to be an independent Socialist power in Southeast Asia. Setting up the U.S. embassy in Hanoi not only would help to balance the Soviets but could also prevent any Chinese move to isolate Vietnam in Southeast Asia.

Vietnamese plans were now suddenly clouded by the expulsion of its UN ambassador from the United States. In the recriminations that followed the scandal, a chill descended on U.S.–Vietnamese relations. A fourth round of talks between Richard Holbrooke and Phan Hien, scheduled for February, was canceled.

A Walk in Hawaii

But this was not a time for Hanoi to go into a long sulk. The Vietnamese had watched with great concern Brzezinski's China trip and his declaration to support China against "regional hegemony"— which they knew referred to Vietnam. The growing tension with China, Peking's military buildup in Cambodia, and Vietnam's own preparations for an intervention in Cambodia in the summer of 1978 made establishment of ties with Washington a matter of urgency. "The Vietnamese wanted normalization by Labor Day, or latest by Thanksgiving," State Department official Fred Brown later recalled. Waiting for a meeting with the Americans, Hanoi nevertheless put the word out. During a visit to Tokyo in early July, Phan Hien told a press conference that while the issue of U.S. aid remained to be resolved, Vietnam would not be pressing it as a precondition for normalization. He said, "A new, forward-looking attitude is being shown by the Vietnamese side." Vietnam, he said, was prepared to welcome the Americans if they came with an attitude of friendship and cooperation. But "if they come with something in their hands, they will be more welcomed than if they come with empty hands," Hien had added.[3]

After Tokyo, Phan Hien traveled to Australia. In a meeting with Australian prime minister Malcolm Fraser and foreign affairs minister Andrew Peacock, Hien repeated his earlier statement for an unconditional normalization of relations. "Before Hien arrived, I already had two, if not three, telephone conversations with Dick [Holbrooke] about Vietnam's new position," Andrew Peacock told me. "I called him again after our meeting. He was quite optimistic because they dropped the precondition."[4]

Holbrooke's optimism grew as the Vietnamese put the word directly to a U.S. official. The meeting came in July when Hanoi took up an old American invitation to send a delegation to visit the Joint Casualty Resolution Center (JCRC) in Honolulu to look at the technological wizardry used by American forensic sleuths to identify individuals from a piece of bone or a lock of hair. The United States hoped that it would help induce the Vietnamese to search for Americans missing in action. As one of the American participants recalled, the meeting was exceptionally warm and friendly. Vietnamese Foreign Ministry official Vu Hoang, on his first visit to the United States, was expansive. "I have never slept so well in my life," he told Frank Sieverts, the State Department official in charge of the MIA issue. After the visit to the JCRC and talks about cooperation, Fred Brown took Hoang to see the Marine Zoo. While watching the dolphins, Hoang quietly dropped the news to Brown. Vietnam would no longer insist on aid for normalizing relations. At long last a direct statement from the Vietnamese after various publicized hints. A pleased Brown went over to a pay phone to call Holbrooke in Washington. That's good news, Holbrooke said, adding that he looked forward to hearing it directly from the Vietnamese.

Holbrooke, however, kept his optimism to himself. While there was secret excitement among foreign service officers about the possibility of a posting in Hanoi, in public statements the State Department maintained that there was no change in the situation and the United States had not officially heard anything from the Vietnamese. Since no talks were scheduled, there was no occasion for the Vietnamese to formally put it across to the Americans. In fact, Holbrooke had turned down a Hanoi proposal for another round of normalization talks in Paris in August. Holbrooke later explained to me that he wanted to avoid the glare of publicity in Paris and asked to meet the Vietnamese quietly when the deputy foreign minister visited New York in September for the UN General Assembly. Particularly with the danger of war growing between Vietnam and China, it was not a diplomatic move to reopen publicized talks with Hanoi. The Vietnamese too, while giving public hints and private assurance about its new flexibility, clearly did not want to give away their bargaining chip before another face-to-face encounter with the American negotiator. When Congressman John P. Murtha, who accompanied a House of Representatives delegation to Hanoi to look at the MIA issue, asked whether Hanoi had really dropped the precondition, Phan Hien was cryptic: "We know how to be flexible." Pressed for details, he teased Murtha, "Leave it to the negotiators. Don't deprive Richard Holbrooke of his job."[5]

Although the Vietnamese were unhappy about the delay in scheduling the meeting with Holbrooke, they were still confident that once talks resumed in New York, normalization would come quickly. A series of American congressional visits to Hanoi in the summer only added to the euphoria. The House delegation, led by Congressman Sonny Montgomery, invited Premier Pham Van Dong and Phan Hien to visit the United States. The Vietnamese handed over to the grateful delegation the remains of fifteen missing servicemen.

Back in Washington, Montgomery recommended that the administration immediately resume negotiations to establish full diplomatic and trade ties with Vietnam. "They are anxious to resume negotiations," Congressman Murtha explained approvingly, because among other things, "they are afraid of the Chinese."[6] A group sent by Senator Edward Kennedy had come back from Hanoi with a strong recommendation to establish relations and grant extensive humanitarian aid. In a report to the Senate Judiciary Committee the group said, "Indeed, we have arrived at a historic decision point in our foreign policy . . . where we now have an opportunity to do through peaceful means what we sought to do so long through war: to protect U.S. national interests in Southeast Asia by assuring Vietnam's independence from the domination of any outside power."[7] One member of the group privately noted the irony that Pham Van Dong sounded a bit like former Secretary of State Dean Rusk when he spoke of "the need for a U.S. presence to help secure the peace and stability of Southeast Asia."[8]

Although the Vietnamese watched Brzezinski's tilt toward China warily, they were confident that in enlightened self-interest Washington would soon agree to establish diplomatic relations. And with U.S. diplomatic recognition in the bag, Hanoi could go ahead and sign the friendship treaty with Moscow. American ties and a Soviet treaty would provide Vietnam with a double guarantee against Chinese pressure and maneuvers as it prepared to mount its military push against the Pol Pot regime. Hanoi had not realized that the wind in Washington was turning against Vietnam. Unbeknownst to all but a handful of top presidential aides, a plan was drawn up in late June for establishing full diplomatic relations with China by December 1978.[9]

In a memo written on July 7, 1978, Brzezinski reminded Carter that key decisions facing him included China but not Vietnam. "Development of a relationship between our two countries [the United States and China]," he wrote, "will bring a major change in the international balance." He warned that "moving ahead on relations with Vietnam would only be an irritant to expanding our understanding with China."[10]

On July 5, six days before Hien announced the new Vietnamese line in Tokyo, talks on Sino-American normalization had begun in Peking. By delaying the talks with Hanoi, Holbrooke unknowingly narrowed the Vietnamese window of opportunity and gave China a boost in its race against Vietnam for normalization with Washington. While the anti-Chinese motivation of Vietnam's normalization drive was obvious to all and provoked some opposition, the total secrecy surrounding the U.S.–China normalization talks guarded it against any scrutiny or political opposition.

Time for an Alliance

China's relations with the United States had remained on ice since their dramatic beginning in 1971 with Henry Kissinger's secret trip and the historic visit by President Richard Nixon in February 1972. Mao, anxious to bolster China against an increasingly hostile Soviet Union, had been eager to open relations with the United States. It was part of the same "United Front" strategy of joining hands with lesser enemies against the principal foe. In early 1973, liaison missions had been set up in Washington and Peking. Trade and cultural ties were established, but domestic turmoil in the United States over the Watergate scandal and the intense power struggle in China quickly chilled the newly initiated relations. China, which had counted on building its relations with the United States as a strategic counter to Moscow, was deeply concerned by the U.S. drive for détente with the Soviet Union. It was also dismayed by the failure of the Ford administration to carry forward the momentum of the Nixon initiative to fully normalize relations with China by dropping Taiwan.

But by the beginning of 1978 a totally different situation had emerged in China to pull it toward the United States. Since the arrest of the Gang of Four in late 1976, the coalition of pragmatic and moderate leaders around Deng Xiaoping had adopted a new approach emphasizing modernization of the country's economy. Since his rehabilitation in July 1977 Deng not only began a campaign to dismantle radical domestic policies but called for a change in China's approach to the world. He charged that Peking's foreign policy was too narrowly based on class struggle.[11]

While Deng initiated purges of the radicals and slowly built support for his policies in the party, government, and the army, developments in Sino-Soviet relations and China's growing trouble with Vietnam gave him additional arguments for a pro-West foreign policy. The idea of an international united front against Moscow and its Vietnamese friends received a new boost from President Carter's national security adviser, Zbigniew Brzezinski. Brzezinski's anger and frustration over Soviet behavior in Africa and Deng's desire to punish Vietnam were pulling them toward a coalition that doomed the prospect for balanced U.S. relations with Asia's feuding Communist powers.

Although normalization of diplomatic relations with China and Vietnam was one of Carter's priority foreign-policy objectives, a year after his inauguration they both appeared far from realization. Compared with the establishment of diplomatic relations with Vietnam, the problem of forming diplomatic ties with China, in fact, appeared more complex and difficult. The United States could set up relations with Hanoi only if the Vietnamese agreed to cooperate on the search for the missing in action and dropped their aid demand. But transforming the liaison missions set up in Washington and Peking since 1973 into full embassies required concessions on the part of the Americans. The Chinese refused normalization of relations if the United States would not break its diplomatic ties with Taiwan and abrogate its defense treaty. Meeting with Carter in February 1977, the chief of the Chinese Liaison Office, General Huang Zhen, bluntly rejected Carter's invitation for a Chinese leader to visit until such time as Taiwan's embassy had been removed from Washington. A rather miffed Carter wrote in his memoirs how the Chinese "still considered themselves members of the Middle Kingdom—at the center of the civilized world—prepared simply to wait until others accepted their position on 'matters of principle.' "[12]

A White House Leak

Despite such irritation, Carter had concluded by mid-1977 that he would meet the Chinese demands—those "matters of principle"—if ways could be found to maintain unofficial relations with Taiwan and ensure a peaceful resolution of the dispute between mainland China and Taiwan. He had also decided on working slowly, step by step, to get China to accept those American concerns. In August 1977, a month after Leonard Woodcock had taken up his post as chief of the U.S. liaison office in Peking, Secretary of State Cyrus Vance arrived in Peking to try to narrow some of the differences. He offered to recognize the PRC as the sole legal government and let the U.S. defense treaty with Taiwan "lapse," but it would be necessary, Vance told Foreign Minister Huang Hua, "for U.S.

government personnel to remain on Taiwan under an informal arrangement." [13]

Although Vance's proposal seemed to be a retreat from the position taken by Ford and Kissinger (since it amounted to a "Two China" policy, with the United States maintaining an embassy in Taiwan in all but name), the Chinese did not reject it out of hand. Vance strongly hinted that it was not the final U.S. position but refrained from presenting to the Chinese the more flexible option he had with him. But he was not in a hurry and it was clear that the Chinese were not yet ready for normalization. However, the Chinese did not want to present the trip as a failure. William Gleysteen, the senior China expert of the State Department accompanying Vance, recalled the care the Chinese had taken to work out a formula for how the meeting would be characterized to the press. A news story from Washington claiming that China had shown unexpected flexibility in the talks destroyed the delicate agreement. An enraged Deng hit back by telling a group of American newspaper editors that the result of the Vance mission was a setback to Sino-American relations. This unusual public denunciation froze the normalization effort. More important, perhaps, the episode proved to be the opening shot in the fight over China policy between the head of the National Security Council, Zbigniew Brzezinki, and the State Department—a conflict that would have far-reaching consequences for Asia.

The leak from the White House that resulted in Deng's outburst was suspected by Vance to be an attempt at a deliberate sabotage of his efforts. The soft-spoken and ever-courteous Cyrus Vance betrayed emotion as he talked about what came to be known as his "failed trip" to China. "We had very successful talks," he told me three years later, "but unfortunately somebody in Washington leaked the news—it was actually somebody in the White House. I was absolutely furious. I knew that the talks with Deng Xiaoping were sensitive, and if prematurely revealed it would ruin the talks. This was what happened." [14] Brzezinski denied to me that the NSC was the source of that leak. The Chinese reacted negatively to Vance, he explained, because "they felt they were not prepared to move rapidly enough on normalization, and they felt that we were not being tough enough to the Soviets." [15]

While the leak from Washington might have provoked the public denunciation, an additional factor in Deng's harsh words was the Chinese perception that Washington, and Vance in particular, was more keen on détente with the Soviet Union and reaching agreement on limiting the arms race than on normalizing relations with China. Domestically, Deng had just been rehabilitated and had to feel his way in a complex personal and policy struggle with Mao loyalists like party chairman Hua Guofeng. By publicly denouncing the U.S. press claim of Chinese flexibility on Taiwan, Deng was also establishing his bona fides as a tough and patriotic leader before his leftist opponents.

From the end of 1977 Brzezinski, concerned by what he saw as expansionist Soviet behavior in Africa, was increasingly a proponent of normalization with China as a counter to Moscow. He had also begun to snipe at Vance and Holbrooke's continued effort at normalizing relations with Vietnam, which he considered to be of "peripheral" significance.[16] In a memo to Carter in mid-November 1977 Brzezinski warned that the public perception of his foreign policy was "soft" because of Cuba, Vietnam, SALT, and Korea.[17]

Brzezinski objected to Vance's concern about not pushing too fast on normalization with China since it could affect the prospects for achieving a SALT agreement. If Soviet misconduct elsewhere in the world could not be linked to SALT, he argued, why should the United States be excessively deferential to Moscow about normalization with China? In fact, U.S.–Chinese collaboration, in his view, could be valuable in making the Soviet Union understand the importance of restraint and reciprocity. It would be Washington's "strategic response" to what he called Moscow's "misuse of détente to improve the Soviet geopolitical and strategic position" in the Middle East and the Horn of Africa. The idea of a China card was born.

Through Michel Oksenberg, Brzezinski quietly started soliciting a Chinese invitation for himself. As Oksenberg coyly noted, the Chinese decided to "play upon the institutional rivalry between the National Security Council staff and State, about which Henry Kissinger had educated them, to prod American China policy forward. The Chinese turned to the official whose world views more closely corresponded to their own."[18]

The Chinese extended an invitation to Brzezinski in early November of 1977. It brought the latent tension between him and Vance to the surface. Vance strongly urged Carter not to let Brzezinski make the trip and thus undercut the negotiating effort by the State Department. But from his proximity to the Oval Office, Brzezinski kept steadily chipping at Carter's resistance to the idea of his visit. Brzezinski also got Secretary of Defense Harold Brown to lobby Carter to let him make the trip. Finally in mid-March Carter gave in to the pressure and overruled Vance.

Carter not only gave Brzezinski permission to draw China into a broad strategic dialogue and seek normalization of relations in that context but committed the United States to a policy course that negated the balance approach pursued by Vance. Vance had been an early proponent of normalization with China, but for its own value, not as a part of an anti-Soviet strategy. In a memorandum to the President on May 10, 1978, Vance called for normalization with China before the end of the year. His assumption was that the sensitive SALT talks then underway with the Soviets would also be wrapped up around that time. Presentation of the normalization agreement to Congress before submitting the SALT agreement, he calculated, would strengthen the administration's hand in getting ratification of the arms control agreement. The last thing Vance wanted to see was the Americans' flaunting a China card before Moscow. As he recorded in his memoirs, "I was convinced that loose talk about 'playing the China card,' always a dangerous ploy, was particularly risky, more so at a time when we were at a sensitive point in the SALT negotiations." [19]

But unbeknownst to Vance, Brzezinski had begun wooing China to become a partner in an anti-Soviet strategy. In February 1978 he had begun a series of quiet meetings with Han Xu, the acting chief of the Chinese liaison office in Washington, in which he put forward views of policy toward Moscow substantially different from those of Vance. [20]

Before leaving for Peking, Brzezinski had secured Carter's signature on a presidential instruction that he and Oksenberg had drafted. The net effect of the new position would be to internationalize the Sino-Vietnamese conflict and commit the United States to side with

China. Relations with China, the instruction said, was "a central facet of U.S. global policy." The United States and China were said to have parallel, long-term strategic concerns, the most important of which was "our common opposition to global or regional hegemony by any single power." Hidden in that arcane sentence was a signal to Peking that Washington was sympathetic to China in its troubles with the Soviet Union and Vietnam, whom Peking had accused of practicing "regional hegemony." The instruction also involved telling the Chinese that the United States was concerned by the Soviet design of "encirclement of China through Vietnam (and even perhaps someday through Taiwan)."[21]

Brzezinski Goes to the Great Wall

On May 19, two weeks after Peking had publicly expressed concern about the exodus of Chinese from Vietnam, Brzezinski and his small entourage of NSC, State Department, and Pentagon officials took off for China aboard an air force Boeing 707. Hardly had the aircraft departed when Holbrooke, who was accompanying the national security adviser, realized that this visit was going to be a one-man show for Brzezinski. He was beside himself with rage upon learning that Brzezinski planned to exclude him from the high-level talks in Peking. In a desperate bid to reserve that plan, Holbrooke cabled Woodcock at the U.S. liaison office in Peking to rush to Tokyo, where the party was stopping over. That mysterious summons to Tokyo barely twenty-four hours before the team was to arrive in Peking sparked intense speculation among the American diplomats about a major shift in policy. As they soon learned, this was yet another episode in the Vance-Brzezinski feud. Holbrooke wanted Woodcock to intercede with Carter on his behalf so that he might be allowed to sit in on the talks in Peking. Woodcock politely declined to intervene. "Holbrooke arrived in Peking," one U.S. official recalled, "in a stormy mood. He spent his time sulking in the tent." One associate of Brzezinski's later attributed the decision to bar Holbrooke to "bad chemistry between the two." William Gleysteen, himself a victim of this ban, later ascribed it to professional jealousy between the two. Both Brzezinski and Holbrooke were ac-

tive in Carter's election campaign and were important members of his foreign policy braintrust. Both aimed high, but Brzezinski had ended up higher than Holbrooke. Holbrooke, however, had excellent access to the White House and made good use of it—something that Brzezinski resented. As Gleysteen put it, Brzezinski, who considered Holbrooke "an upstart, too big for his breeches," would not simply let him share the glory of the Peking initiative.

Whatever may have been his motive, Holbrooke's exclusion from the talks must have been seen by the Chinese as a demonstration of Brzezinski's distrust for an associate of Vance's. The Chinese were soon to fully exploit to their advantage this personal and ideological cleavage within the Carter administration.

Brzezinski calculated that if the Chinese leaders were convinced of the seriousness of the Carter administration's anti-Soviet resolve, they could be expected to be flexible on the question of unofficial U.S. ties with Taiwan. Even if the Chinese were unwilling to concede on Taiwan, the attraction of security cooperation would lead them to closer effective ties with the United States without establishing full diplomatic ties. He assured Deng Xiaoping that the United States accepted the Chinese conditions on severing official ties with Taiwan—virtually the second option that Vance had in his pocket in August 1977 but did not present to the Chinese. Brzezinski also told him that Carter had made up his mind on these issues. As evidence of American seriousness in seeking cooperation with China, he brought with him "gifts" that were certain to impress.

NSC staffer Samuel Huntington, who once advised the Johnson administration on counterinsurgency in Vietnam, discussed with the Chinese the top secret "Presidential Review Memorandum 10"—a U.S. assessment of the world situation, especially with regard to Soviet power. The exercise was aimed at convincing China that Washington considered it to be a partner in an informal alliance against Moscow. Brzezinski informed the Chinese that henceforth U.S. regulations concerning the sale of "dual-use" technology to China would be relaxed and that the United States would no longer oppose arms sales to China by its alliance partners. To demonstrate the seriousness of the U.S. readiness for technology transfer and for developing security relations, Brzezinski took with him Benjamin

Huberman, an assistant to the President's science and technology adviser, and Morton Abramowitz, deputy assistant secretary of defense for international security.

Abramowitz, a Mandarin-speaking Foreign Service officer, had been long associated with American planning for military cooperation with China. He had directed one of the earliest Pentagon studies on the possibilities of establishing military ties with China and their strategic implications.[22] He was now to become the first U.S. Defense Department official to visit China. He split from the group to have a quiet meeting with a senior Chinese defense official. "It was not really talks," a participant recalled later, "it was a monologue. Abramowitz spoke for over an hour, giving the Chinese a highly classified briefing on the deployment of Soviet forces along the Chinese border." In what must have been the first act of sharing intelligence at the defense ministry level, Abramowitz provided his Chinese interlocutor information about Soviet strategic weapons. To the pleasant surprise of the Chinese official, he pulled out of his briefcase top secret reconnaissance photographs of Soviet military installations and armor facing China. Benjamin Huberman too held separate talks with the Chinese on the possibility of Sino-American cooperation in science and technology, particularly in electronic intelligence gathering about the Soviet Union. Ideas mooted during that meeting would lead a year later to installation of U.S. monitoring stations in China to watch Soviet missile tests.[23]

Even Vance, who had strong reservations about security cooperation with China, did not object to the monitoring station project because, as one of his close aides explained later, it would help monitoring of Soviet compliance with SALT and make the agreement more salable to Congress.

Brzezinski, of course, had a totally different objective in mind while pushing intelligence and security cooperation. "Zbig was trying to tantalize the Chinese," one member of his team explained later, "giving them hints that they could expect a lot more from us." On returning to Washington, William Gleysteen wrote a scathing memo attacking Brzezinski's tactics as calculated to raise Chinese expectations about obtaining the kind of support from the United States that had neither been approved nor discussed at the highest level. Vance was pleased with the memo, but Brzezinski ignored it.

In his own discussions with Huang Hua and Deng Xiaoping, Brzezinski also curried favor with the Chinese by stressing the need for closer cooperation "on such matters as Afghanistan, aid to Pakistan, and assistance to Southeast Asian efforts to check Soviet support for Vietnamese expansionism."[24] This statement came close to endorsing Chinese backing for the Khmer Rouge, because the only Southeast Asian country resisting "Vietnamese expansionism" at the time was Pol Pot's Democratic Kampuchea. In private "Zbig did not only swallow completely the Chinese line on the Soviet threat and Vietnam as a Soviet puppet," a Brzezinski associate recalled later, "he also accepted the Chinese argument that the way to remove the Soviet threat from Vietnam was to push them into closer cooperation, which would lead to eventual friction between the two and put an end to the Soviet presence."[25] Brzezinski also publicly announced the new U.S. approach by supporting China's opposition to "global and regional hegemony" in a toast at a Peking banquet. Vance was furious to hear of the toast; it had not been cleared by him. "It was a stupid thing to do. Brzezinski's speech and the things he said at the Great Wall sure pleased the Chinese," Vance remarked with a wicked twinkle in his eyes, "but [they] did not achieve anything."[26]

While visiting the Great Wall, Brzezinski challenged his Chinese interpreter, Nancy Tang: "Whoever gets to the top [of the wall] first gets to fight the Russians in Ethiopia." He made it to the top before his bemused Chinese companion. On the way down he saw some naval cadets posing for a group picture. He went right in the middle of the group to have his picture taken. "How does it feel to be standing with the greatest Soviet baiter in the world?" he had asked a puzzled cadet who did not have the slightest notion who this "long-nosed devil" was.

However annoying these antics may have been to Vance, Brzezinski's China trip gave a new boost to the normalization process. More important for the Chinese was that his support and understanding for Deng's position made him a de facto participant in the crucial Chinese Politburo meeting in July 1978 that would decide to "teach Vietnam a lesson."

A month after Brzezinski's return from China a unity of sorts was restored among Carter's policy advisers. Vance, Harold Brown,

Brzezinski, and Hamilton Jordan met with Carter to decide on a target date of mid-December for normalization with China. In early July, amid total secrecy, Woodcock in Peking began making detailed presentations to the Chinese on ways of resolving the differences over Taiwan. "Ironically, as it turned out," Vance was to write later, "the idea of using a special White House channel [code-named 'Voyager'] to communicate with Woodcock was Holbrooke's and mine."[27] They thought it would lessen the risk of leaks that could jeopardize the sensitive talks. In the end this proved to be an arrangement that would enable Brzezinski to cut the State Department out of the policy process at crucial moments.

Planning for an Embassy in Hanoi

After the September 27 meeting in New York, the Vietnam desk at the State Department organized a special working group to look at the practical details of setting up an embassy in Hanoi. Fully aware of the difficulties that the Australian, West German, and other embassies faced in Hanoi because of hasty arrangements, Holbrooke wanted to sign a detailed agreement with the Vietnamese before raising the American flag in Hanoi. Deputy Assistant Secretary Robert Oakley and desk officer for Vietnam, Laos, and Cambodia Steve Lyne made several trips to New York to thrash out with Thach's special assistant, Tran Quang Co, the details—from the number of diplomats and the route for sending diplomatic pouches to the possibility of landing a C-5A Galaxy carrying embassy effects in Hanoi's airport.

At the State Department, work began on selecting the diplomats to be sent to Hanoi. Holbrooke's special assistant, Ken Quinn, wrote him a memo recommending that for security reasons nobody with a Vietnamese wife should be chosen for the Hanoi post. Douglas Pike, a veteran Vietnam specialist with the U.S. Information Agency who had spent years in Saigon analyzing captured Vietcong documents and interrogation reports, heard of the impending normalization from his perch at the Pentagon. He submitted an application for a job at Hanoi. With few exceptions, however, diplomats were not dying to go to the backwaters of Hanoi. Steve Lyne recalled meeting a colleague in a State Department corridor. "I hear you're looking for people to go to Hanoi. Steve, forget you know me!" the colleague had said.

Preparations began for selling the Vietnam normalization to the public and Congress. Indications from public polls were favorable. In a September 29, 1978, memo to Holbrooke—two days after Thach had given up the aid precondition—Assistant Secretary for Public Affairs Hodding Carter analyzed the results of a poll taken by NBC News and concluded that "at least plurality support could probably be gained for recognition [of Vietnam] if large-scale financial aid was not made part of such 'normalization'; the limits of what such aid would involve were explained; [and] the public felt that the Vietnamese had made a significant effort to clarify the status of the MIAs."

In preparation for facing congressional leaders Holbrooke ordered his staff to prepare a brief outlining the reasons why it was now time to establish ties with Vietnam. The position paper entitled "Diplomatic Relations with Vietnam—Now" noted that Vietnam had become an arena of conflict between the Soviet Union and China and that the Soviets had increased their presence there and stepped up assistance to the Vietnamese in the conflict with Cambodia. "A U.S. presence in Hanoi would enable us better," the paper said, "to monitor this competition and to offer a visible option to alignment with either of the two Communist powers." Without relations with Vietnam, it argued, "the United States has virtually no influence, as well as almost no knowledge about Vietnamese news or likely actions." An American embassy in Hanoi "would serve us better (in seeking MIA accounting) than irregular contact in Paris and Bangkok and occasional meetings between the Vietnamese and administration officials and congressional visitors." Embassy assistance would also be helpful to U.S. companies competing with their counterparts from other countries.

Meanwhile the special working group got busy looking at the nitty-gritty of setting up an embassy in Hanoi. Did anyone know how that old U.S. consulate in Hanoi looked? Michael Eiland, the Vietnamese-speaking colonel from the Pentagon working at the Bureau of Politico-Military Affairs of the State Department, came up with a fuzzy slide he had taken of the American consulate building in Hanoi during a congressional visit two months earlier. Eiland had no difficulty in spotting the villa on Hai Ba Trung Street in downtown Hanoi. "That was the only green building in Hanoi—like a dollar," he recalled. When he had raised his camera to focus on that historic building, which the Vietnamese had freshly painted in the expectation of American occupants, a soldier had rushed out to stop him. The result was a fuzzy photograph. But that was the only one that the State Department had as planning began on the embassy layout. Eventually the special working group managed to dig up from the archives the blueprint of the building to help in planning. "During a visit to the State Department," Michel Oksenberg recalled, "I was astonished to see the voluminous materials they had prepared dealing with practical aspects of normalization—the frozen assets question, the question of embassy location, communications—the whole works."[28]

It was decided that Dennis Harter, another Vietnamese-speaking officer from the desk, would visit Hanoi in December to look at the building with the layout plan in hand.

Since the Vietnamese would be given the possession of the former South Vietnamese embassy, Harter went for an inspection tour. As he recalled, it was a journey through history. The carpets were moldy, paint was peeling off the walls, but otherwise time had stopped when in May 1975 the South Vietnamese diplomats walked out of the mission. Issues of *Time* and *Newsweek* depicting the traumatic end to South Vietnam lay on a table, as did uncleaned plates from the last meal. The Office of Foreign Buildings refused to undertake repair of the embassy despite assurances that they would recover the cost later. The office was upset that it was already paying a lot of money to keep the embassy cars in a warehouse. But as it turned out, there was no need for fresh paint or a cleanup. Unbeknownst to the State Department, a different course was being charted by the White House.

The China Card at Play

When, on the evening of September 27, the American team left the Vietnamese mission after talks with Thach, opening an American embassy in Hanoi suddenly seemed in the realm of possibility. But some were skeptical. Michel Oksenberg recalled telling Holbrooke, "Dick, the Vietnamese are teasing you; they are mocking you." Oksenberg was struck by how tenaciously Thach hung on to his demand for aid. "He dropped the precondition only at the last hour and that too as a result of Holbrooke's persistent probing," Oksenberg said. "Having done that, Thach immediately wanted to sign a memorandum of understanding. He should have known that business is not conducted that way." He was convinced that the Vietnamese were only posturing for the record—they wanted to be seen as the ones who made the gesture for normalization—but they were not serious about it. Reminiscing about that episode four years later, Oksenberg thought that in the fall of 1978 the force of events was pulling the two countries in different directions. "The hands were extended, but there was a realization that they were not going to meet."[29]

One can only speculate how much of this premonition was based on Oksenberg's knowledge of Brzezinski's opposition to Vietnam normalization. Or was he simply speaking with the benefit of hindsight? Contrary to what he felt, the Vietnamese were indeed eager, almost desperate, to get the normalization agreement. Thach's stalling tactic, as Holbrooke correctly guessed, was only a final attempt at securing an aid commitment from the United States before giving up the demand. The Vietnamese could afford to engage in a little theatrics precisely because they were convinced that once their precondition was dropped, an agreement would be concluded swiftly.

Holbrooke did not share Oksenberg's pessimism. He knew there were obstacles but did not think them insurmountable. Holbrooke was aware of Brzezinski's views. He was also concerned about the border war between the Vietnamese and the Cambodians and its big-power implications. Shortly before the meeting with Thach an American RC-135 reconnaissance plane flying close to the coast of central Vietnam had picked up military radio traffic indicating deployment of an elite Vietnamese division near Cambodia. Other intelligence pointed to a military buildup along the Cambodia-Vietnam frontier and a heating up of the border war. Raphael Iungerich, chief Indochina analyst of the State Department's Bureau of Intelligence and Research, wrote an assessment in August predicting a

Vietnamese-engineered overthrow of the Pol Pot regime in six months.[30]

There was also concern over Vietnam's increasingly close ties with Moscow as evidenced by its joining COMECON. Holbrooke made those concerns clear to Thach. "Our intention toward Cambodia is defensive," Thach assured him. That answer seemed plausible, for the United States had known for a while of the insane Khmer Rouge raids across the Vietnamese border. "In fact," Iungerich told me, "Holbrooke and all of us were sort of taking the Vietnamese side on this issue up through December 1978. It was the Vietnamese who were being ambushed within Vietnamese territory. It was happening against the Thais also that summer. So we were all looking upon this wild dog Pol Pot as the pariah of the whole region, as the original terrorist. Therefore we were very much on the Vietnamese side at this point."[31]

For Vance and Holbrooke, these tensions in the region were another reason to inject a stabilizing U.S. presence. Normalization of U.S. relations with China and Vietnam could give Washington some leverage in reducing the tension. The intra-Communist conflict in Asia posed a threat to stability but also an opportunity for a return of U.S. influence in the region. Australian foreign minister Andrew Peacock, a personal friend of Holbrooke's, fully shared the Vance-Holbrooke view. He later told me that he was so excited to hear the news of the coming normalization with Vietnam that he came up with the idea of a supplementary move. "Things were then looking very much in place," Peacock recalled, "and I suggested to them [Vance and Holbrooke] it would not be a bad idea, perhaps, if countries like Australia started talking to the Cambodians about some form of diplomatic exchange and flagging every step on that route with the Chinese. The Chinese could see that we were keeping them informed. Countries like Canada and New Zealand could be asked to do the same. We could thus play a role in containing any adverse spin-off from the U.S.–Vietnamese normalization on Sino-American relations."[32] Holbrooke later could not recall that such an idea was discussed, but he said, "I just don't remember, but if Andrew says it happened, I'm not going to dispute it."[33]

On September 27, the daily digest of world events that is sent every evening from the State Department to the President contained the summary of the Holbrooke meeting with Thach along with Secretary Vance's recommendation that steps now be taken to normalize relations with Vietnam. This seemed to be in line with Carter's own thinking, for in early September he had instructed Brzezinski to aim "at simultaneous recognition of China and Vietnam."[34]

Brzezinski opposed what he termed the attempt by Vance and Holbrooke "to insert Vietnam into the [Sino-American normalization] process, recommending that we normalize with Vietnam." In his strategic objective of countering the Russians, regional issues were of minor importance. He also could not have cared too much about the deep historic animosity between the Chinese and Vietnamese and the fear of China felt by many of its neighbors. He dismissed the regional fear about a southward push by China because, as he put it to me, "neither historically nor strategically does there seem to be reason to expect that." To him Vietnam was simply a "Soviet proxy," and the fact that China was worried about Vietnam's becoming a Soviet base was the most important U.S. consideration. "Vance and Holbrooke pushed for normalization of relations with Vietnam, which in my judgment would simply have spoiled normalization with China. It would have undermined the possibility of developing a strategic relationship with the Chinese," he said. He was convinced that it was Holbrooke, eager to normalize relations, who prodded the Vietnamese to give up their aid demand. "I think Holbrooke went there [to the Vietnamese mission in New York in September 1978] to suggest that they do that in order to facilitate normalization, and I shot it down," Brzezinski declared with obvious pride.[35]

He said he discussed with the President the negative impact of such a move, and Carter, agreeing with his analysis, decided to shelve normalization. By 1981, when Brzezinski gave me his version of events, Vietnam, with its occupation of Cambodia and its boat people, had become such a pariah nation that he sounded almost statesmanlike in claiming that he alone had nipped the chance of normalization with Hanoi. One person who could have claimed equal if not more "credit" for blocking normalization was, ironically enough, Leonard Woodcock, who had led the presidential mission to Hanoi in the spring of 1977 in a bid to clear the path to normalization.

As the chief of the U.S. liaison office in Peking and the man charged with negotiating a normalization agreement with China, Woodcock now had a very different set of priorities from what he had when he visited Hanoi. The secret negotiations with the Chinese on normalization that he had begun in Peking in July had reached a sensitive stage and needed additional care to carry them through. How touchy things were was brought home to him during a dinner offered by Chinese foreign minister Huang Hua in New York on October 3, 1978. Along with Vance, Holbrooke, and Oksenberg he had gone to the Chinese mission for a working dinner. The same evening, George Quintin held one of his fireworks extravaganzas in Central Park, a few blocks away from the Chinese mission. The loud report of the explosions vibrating the glass panes added drama to that heat-charged encounter. A combative Huang Hua had harangued Vance about U.S. stubbornness in maintaining links with Taiwan and selling arms. By ten o'clock, when they had thought of dinner, the magnificent spread of Chinese dishes laid out on the table was cold. Holbrooke wistfully recalled the long, cold dinner. "There we were. We couldn't see the fireworks, but the stuff was going off like mortar rounds, like in Saigon during the war."

Woodcock was depressed by the whole affair. But he saw a streak of hope when one of Huang's aides sidled up to him to quietly ask when he was returning to Peking so that a new round of talks could be fixed. It was a discreet Chinese signal: although they were quarreling with Vance, they were ready to be flexible with Woodcock, who they knew was working closely with Carter and Brzezinski.

So, when during a meeting with Brzezinski in the Oval Office on October 11, 1978, Carter asked Woodcock his views on moving ahead on normalization with Vietnam, his answer was a quick no. He told Carter of his strong feeling that ties with Vietnam at that juncture would have "blown normalization with China out of the water." As far as he was concerned, Woodcock later said, his position was related purely to the desire to conclude the normalization agreement with China. But did the Chinese indicate to him that they would take a dim view of the establishment of U.S.–Vietnamese ties? Woodcock told me he had never tested the Chinese on that issue.

288

Those questions, he said, were raised when somebody was visiting with the Chinese. "Once in a while somebody would say, What would you think if we normalized relations with Vietnam? The answer would usually be to the effect that it is your business, but we would think it would be unwise for this reason or that reason without saying clearly that 'it would not make us happy.' " The reason he feared a negative Chinese reaction was not that they had expressed opposition to the idea but because the issue had not been discussed at all. "I had been talking with them seriously since July," Woodcock explained, "and this was October. We were getting ready for the last push, as it were. Never having discussed Vietnam [with the Chinese] in the three-month interval, that [bringing up the issue of normalization with Hanoi with them] would have raised the question of our good faith in their mind, I thought."[36]

Brzezinski's and Woodcock's reading of Chinese reaction was diametrically opposite to that of Holbrooke. "I remember vividly," Holbrooke said, "in 1978 in the UN General Assembly meetings the Chinese saying to us, 'What you do with the Vietnamese over normalization is your affair. We do not oppose normal diplomatic relations between you and any Socialist country.' By which we all understood that though they were not enthusiastic about it, because they wanted normalization with us, they weren't going to oppose normalization between us and Vietnam."[37] But Carter agreed with Brzezinski and Woodcock that "the China move was of paramount importance" and decided to postpone the Vietnam normalization until after an agreement had been concluded with China.[38]

In the atmosphere of conspiratorial secrecy that surrounded normalization talks with China, that presidential decision taken on October 11 was to remain unknown to all but a handful at the State Department, where the machine cranked on preparing the opening of the U.S. embassy in Hanoi. Even Holbrooke and his principal assistants were not told the real reason for shelving normalization— perhaps to avoid another fight between Vance and Brzezinski. Instead of being told that keeping China humored was more important than establishing ties with Hanoi, they were given the pretext that any sign of friendliness toward Vietnam could produce domestic complications that might affect the congressional elections in early

November. As one of Holbrooke's closest aides would later admit, "Our instructions from the White House after September 27 were very clear: Do not agree [to normalize] until after the elections."[39]

Leaks in Bangkok

That the normalization of relations with Hanoi had run into some policy snag at the White House was darkly rumored in the State Department's East Asia Bureau. Staffers later recalled how tension had built up between the Vietnam desk and the China desk because of the China desk's sharp criticism of the Vietnamese and its concern about jeopardizing China relations by establishing ties with Hanoi. But the news that the White House had decided to shelve normalization of relations with Hanoi did not come to light until a ministorm broke over Holbrooke's purported remarks in Bangkok. Curiously enough, the story broke just a day after the Vietnamese had been quietly told about what amounted to new U.S. preconditions for normalization.

Robert Oakley made two trips to New York in October to talk to the Vietnamese. The working group organized to look at the specific problems of setting up embassies had continued its work. In his last meeting with Nguyen Co Thach on October 17, Oakley had found him impatient. As he recalled, "Thach kept saying hurry, hurry, hurry. We want to do it right away." He resisted the demand, saying that all the details needed to be worked out first.

But on October 30 he went to see Vietnamese diplomat Tran Quang Co with a different set of issues. Normalization would have to wait, Oakley told him, pending a satisfactory Vietnamese answer to three problems—Vietnamese hostility toward Cambodia, Soviet-Vietnamese ties, and the increasing number of boat people coming out of Vietnam. "Why the new conditions?" Pham Binh, a senior Vietnamese diplomat, asked rhetorically as he recounted the episode several years later. He also gave the answer: "Because since May 1978 [the time of Brzezinski's visit to Peking] the Chinese have openly carried on a hostile policy toward Vietnam. Now the U.S. leaders decided to collude with China."[40]

What Binh did not care to talk about was that Vietnam too had prepared its own collusion with Moscow. In Hanoi on the morning of October 30 (when it was the evening of October 29 in Washington) a Soviet Ilyushin-62 jetliner roared out of Noi Bai Airport with an unusual constellation of Vietnamese leaders on board.[41]

Almost half the Vietnamese Politburo, led by party secretary-general Le Duan, was on its way to Moscow to sign a friendship treaty that was expected to provide Vietnam insurance against Chinese attacks in its approaching conflict with Cambodia. After a full month of waiting to sign the normalization agreement, a frustrated Thach had left New York for Paris en route to Moscow. There, on November 3, he witnessed the signing ceremony of the Soviet-Vietnamese friendship treaty. The Vietnamese hope of bagging American recognition before taking on military cooperation with the Soviet Union had failed.

Did the American decision to present the Vietnamese with new preconditions stem from intelligence about the imminent signing of the Soviet-Vietnamese treaty? That a high-level Vietnamese visit to Moscow was coming was known. On October 27 Hanoi had announced that Le Duan and Premier Pham Van Dong would pay an official visit to Moscow "in the near future." But it was doubtful that anybody knew the Vietnamese were about to sign a treaty. At least so far nobody has claimed that kind of intelligence coup.

Later, the State Department tried with post facto justification to put a bold face on its failure to get normalization with Vietnam: Vietnam's treaty with Moscow and its invasion of Cambodia and the surge of boat people made diplomatic ties impossible. This explanation flies in the face of chronology. The first two developments took place well after the October 11 decision by Carter, and the boat people exodus reached crisis proportions only in the summer of 1979.[42]

In a series of interviews with me, Holbrooke repeatedly said that there was never one specific decision to postpone normalization. Contradicting the testimony of Brzezinski, Woodcock, and for that matter Carter himself, Holbrooke maintained that the decision to shelve normalization had nothing to do with China. "A lot of people think," Holbrooke said, "that there was a conscious decision made not to proceed with Vietnam and to proceed with China. Whereas what really happened was that the Vietnamese created conditions that made it possible to move forward." Holbrooke would recall three practical reasons why normalization could not be achieved. "There were three factors as far as I can make out," he said. "One was boat people, one was intelligence saying there was an invasion coming up, and the last one was the congressional elections."[43]

It certainly made sense to avoid a controversial measure like normalization with Vietnam just before congressional elections, but it did not call for indefinite postponement. Explaining the shelving of normalization, Holbrooke said that the administration was concerned that setting up an embassy in Hanoi at a time when American television networks were daily showing boat people from Vietnam arriving in Southeast Asian waters would provoke an uproar. This and an intelligence report about Vietnamese preparations against Cambodia seem, especially in retrospect, valid reasons for not going ahead with normalization. But these considerations did not seem insuperable to Holbrooke or his State Department associates all through October, when full-scale preparations to set up an embassy in Vietnam were under way.

In fact, all the elaborate justifications for not going ahead with normalization were the very opposite of arguments Holbrooke's staffers had put together in their position paper in the fall. As Oakley would come close to admitting, the new obstacles mentioned to the Vietnamese on October 30 were to cover the American retreat. The three issues he raised that day with the Vietnamese were not new discoveries. Holbrooke had raised them with Thach in September but had nevertheless recommended normalization. Who now gave the order to state these obstacles to the Vietnamese? Oakley, clearly defensive, protested, "There was no order from the White House to do it. There was no Oksenberg who suddenly discovered what was happening and had the President issue an order to Vance." He said it was his and Holbrooke's idea. "We wanted to make it very clear to them in advance where the responsibility lay for what we could see was going to be a failure."[44]

Holbrooke's memory failed when I asked him exactly when he came to know of Carter's October 11 decision to shelve normalization. All evidence points to his having learned something was amiss while traveling in Southeast Asia, when angry phone calls denying his purported remark that normalization was coming soon came from Washington. Holbrooke strongly denied that he ever told the Thais that U.S.–Vietnamese normalization would come in two months— as United Press International and the *Nation Review* reported from Bangkok on October 31. The fact that the stories appeared a week after he had met the Thai premier Kriangsak Chomanan lent credibility to the story and made Holbrooke appear as its likely originator. Knowing how keen Holbrooke was on normalization, many of his own colleagues at the State Department were willing to believe he was behind the story.

But as my later interviews with Thai and American participants in the meeting confirmed, Holbrooke indeed had not forecast any likely date. Accompanied by Abramowitz, now U.S. ambassador to Thailand, he gave Kriangsak a full briefing on his September meeting with Thach, including the Vietnamese decision not to insist on U.S. aid. Since aid precondition had so long held up normalization, the Thais simply had put 2 and 2 together and concluded that U.S. ties with Vietnam were imminent. The ASEAN countries, especially Thailand, were worried that Holbrooke, in his zeal to establish relations with Hanoi, would ignore their interests. Hoping that premature publicity would stymie the move, the Thais embellished Holbrooke's private remarks and leaked to the press. In a little twist designed to alert China, the *Nation Review* article pointedly said that U.S. normalization with Vietnam would come "certainly before" the establishment of Sino-American ties. The leak produced the desired result. Hours after the Bangkok reports hit the American wire, both the White House and State Department issued strong denials. In a subtle dig at Holbrooke, State Department spokesman Hodding Carter said, "No knowledgeable official of the U.S. government could say such a thing." Then he went on to deny it "as categorically as it is possible to deny. No decisions have been reached by the U.S. government as to when normalization might take place, and no agreements or understandings of any sort have been reached with the Vietnamese." This was certainly not the truth, but the message was delivered. Peking was assured and so were Southeast Asian allies.

Holbrooke Fights for His Job

Brzezinski was furious with the reports from Bangkok, seeing them as inspired by Holbrooke's trying to promote Vietnam normalization and throw a monkey wrench in the China normalization works. As if those reports from Bangkok were not enough, the CIA's monitoring of domestic transmissions in Communist Indochina picked up a report on October 31 that came close to ruining Holbrooke's career. In the course of his daily reading of the intelligence, Oksenberg spotted the item—an internal teletype transmission in Vietnamese from the Vietnam News Agency correspondent in Vientiane to his headquarters in Hanoi. The report quoted a "U.S. dignitary" as saying he was convinced that after the November elections in the United States "the Carter administration will be able to perform two things at the same time: normalize relations between the United States and China and between the United States and Vietnam without allowing U.S.–Chinese relations to hamper the potential normalization of relations between the United States and Vietnam." The report also mentioned that Brzezinski was "pressing the Southeast Asian policymakers of the U.S. State Department into continuing to woo China and contain Vietnam." Toward the end of the report, the VNA correspondent noted that while on a visit to Vientiane Holbrooke had "warmly received" a Vietnamese representative during a social gathering. He "delightedly said that he had just held talks with Vietnamese vice–foreign minister Nguyen Co Thach and that he had left one of his aides in New York to maintain permanent contacts." Holbrooke was further quoted as telling the Vietnamese representative that he was "very optimistic about the prospects for normalizing relations between the two countries." The VNA interpreted this as a message and a "friendly gesture" to Vietnam from Holbrooke. When Oksenberg put that report on Brzezinski's desk, he was livid. He went to Carter to demand that Holbrooke be fired.

When the trouble began, Holbrooke was in Lashio on the Burma Road making one of the State Department's periodic visits to that picturesque but isolated country. The U.S. embassy in Rangoon rushed him a cable from the State Department informing him of the Bangkok reports and Washington denials. In the cable Vance wanted to know what exactly Holbrooke had been saying. Holbrooke cabled back denying any responsibility for those reports. As he recalled later, "There was a lot of tension at that time between the State Department and the White House, and an attempt was made to hold me accountable for these stories. The first story Abramowitz denied cleanly and flatly, and Vance backed me up and talked to Carter on the phone, and there was no more problem about that. The second story, the CIA did a study on it and decided that it might be, probably was, Soviet disinformation."[45] Holbrooke, in fact, was publicly exonerated with a column by Rowland Evans and Robert Novak dismissing the VNA internal report as Soviet disinformation aimed at disrupting U.S.–Chinese relations and sowing discord in the Carter administration.[46]

Holbrooke believed both the reports from Bangkok and Vientiane to be a conspiracy. "It seemed as if somebody was trying to undermine me," he said, reminiscing about that troubled time. But if indeed these were results of conspiracy, they could not have involved the same conspirators. The leaks in Bangkok on the eve of U.S. congressional elections, which Holbrooke called "misquotes," were aimed at sabotaging U.S.–Vietnamese talks—something that served Thai and Chinese purposes. But the VNA internal report from Vientiane, which was never put out by the agency as a news item, was anti-Chinese. If it was transmitted in the hope that the Americans or the Chinese would pick it up, then it was aimed at creating Sino-American tension and dissension within the Carter administration. The interesting thing about the VNA item was the icing it put on known and probable facts. Holbrooke had indeed met the Vietnamese chargé d'affaires in Vientiane during a social function at the residence of the U.S. chargé d'affaires. "I had said hello to him, but the description 'greeted him warmly' was hardly justified," Holbrooke said. He stoutly denied having made any criticism of Brzezinski or the policy of the China card that was indirectly attributed to him.

It indeed is unbelievable that Holbrooke would say these things, whatever might have been his personal feelings, to a Vietnamese diplomat. But the story does not say that the "U.S. dignitary" made those remarks to the Vietnamese. His opinion was "voiced during a private discussion." The VNA correspondent in Vientiane, Dang Kien, regularly talked to resident American Quaker and Mennonite representatives as well as other Western reporters visiting Vientiane. It was quite possible for him to have picked up the story of the Brzezinski-Holbrooke feud from them or from the diplomatic grapevine. The fact that a Vietnamese diplomat was invited to the residence of the American chargé was significant enough for the Vietnamese to feel elated. In view of the positive picture of U.S.– Vietnamese normalization that Holbrooke gave in Bangkok prior to his visit to Laos, it seems probable that he conveyed optimism about it as he talked to the Vietnamese chargé. While the theory of Soviet disinformation cannot be discounted, the VNA dispatch most probably was just an internal report by a correspondent to his superiors. The dispatch after all was sent the day after Holbrooke left Vientiane for Burma. Whether there was a conspiracy against Holbrooke or not, the Bangkok press reports and the VNA message indicated one thing—Holbrooke did not know that normalization with Hanoi had been shelved.

Holbrooke's denial, Vance's backing, and the CIA study averted his personal crisis, but it introduced a bitterness in his relationship with Brzezinski and Oksenberg that he was never to recover from. And as it turned out, the episode also put an end to his two-year effort to build a bridge to Vietnam. When in the beginning of November Holbrooke returned to Washington, the hopes for diplomatic ties with Hanoi lay in shambles and so did the prospects of a new leadership role for the United States in Asia. America had cast its lot with Peking as the region braced for a war.

Prince Norodom Sihanouk:
The Survivor

JANUARY 1, 1978. It was a cool morning in Phnom Penh. Sihanouk had, as he did every day, switched on his Grundig radio set to listen to the news from Radio Phnom Penh. And as usual he had put it on high volume for the benefit of his guards. The act was more to assure his guardians of his patriotism than to inform himself. But that day proved to be different. Instead of the usual account of the heroic workers, peasants, and soldiers of Democratic Kampuchea harvesting a bumper crop and building a glorious Cambodia, the radio broadcast startling news. Democratic Kampuchea had decided to suspend diplomatic relations with Vietnam because of its "large-scale, unwarranted aggression." Sihanouk knew the Vietnamese too well to fail to understand what a dangerous course Pol Pot had embarked upon.

During his March 1973 visit to the liberated zones, Sihanouk had become aware of the undercurrents of tension between the Khmer Rouge and their Vietnamese "comrades." Since then Sihanouk had seen increasing evidence of differences. During a trip to Hanoi in September 1975 Vietnamese premier Pham Van Dong had told him, right in the presence of Khieu Samphan, that Vietnam had confidence *only* in him. A few weeks later, back in Phnom Penh, Khieu Samphan and Son Sen had given him a piece of their mind about Vietnam. The Vietnamese, they said, threatened the very existence of Cambodia. The threat could be eliminated only by expelling all ethnic Vietnamese from Cambodia, by building a strong Cambodia, and by engaging in armed confrontations that would force the Vietnamese to accept a "more just" land and sea border with Cambodia.

In the following weeks Radio Phnom Penh announced astoundingly great victories over the invading Vietnamese army—claims that were hard to believe. Sihanouk kept his anxiety about the perils of getting involved in a duel with the battle-hardened Vietnamese to himself. He sent a letter to Pol Pot offering his service for the defense of the nation. As he recounted later, "They rejected my offer because, they said, they had just won an even bigger victory than April 17, 1975! [the day Phnom Penh fell to the Khmer Rouge]." When he heard on the radio the news of the visit to Phnom Penh of Zhou's widow, Madame Deng Yingchao, he had half hoped to meet her. But that was not to be. She was told Sihanouk did not want to meet anybody. She was instead invited to a ladies' tea party given by the wives of the Khmer Rouge leaders, led by Pol Pot's wife, Khieu Ponnary.

The stream of invective against the Vietnamese and the boast of Cambodian prowess over Radio Phnom Penh convinced Sihanouk that Pol Pot was still not dealing with reality.

He was astonished to hear the Pol Pot version of a final solution to the Vietnam problem. In May a Radio Phnom Penh broadcast claimed that each Khmer was capable of killing thirty Vietnamese. So Cambodia did not need to use its population of 8 million to exterminate the Vietnamese. The radio comfortably concluded, "We need only 2 million troops to crush the 50 million Vietnamese, and we would still have 6 million people left."[1]

While the insanity of such claims made him laugh, he relished the news that some Khmers had started calling for an uprising against Pol Pot over Radio Hanoi. Pol Pot's black regime had at least started to shake. How shaken it was became clear in September when Sihanouk found that suddenly he was in demand. Khieu Samphan invited him for yet another visit to the provinces. Unlike in the past, one of the objectives of this visit was to bring Sihanouk closer to the population and show them how he was fully behind the regime. Both in Kompong Som Port and in Battambang the prince was taken close to the workers to be greeted with applause.

For the time being, Sihanouk was thankful for small mercies. On his return to Phnom Penh he was invited to what Khieu Samphan described as an "intimate banquet to honor patriots." Sihanouk expected to see his veteran associate Penn Nouth at the unusual party in the government guesthouse. "But I was surprised to see two more of my close collaborators—former Foreign Minister Sarin Chhak and former Minister of Armory Duong Sam Ol. They were so traumatized that they would barely look at me." Sihanouk could hardly recognize the skeletal figure of Sarin Chhak, the brilliant jurist whose thesis on the Vietnamese-Cambodian border ironically had provided Pol Pot the ammunition for pressing claims against Vietnam. And there he was, a pale cadaver, still puzzled by all the attention after years of hard labor and starvation diet. The meal served at the table was a dream. Ieng Sary and Ieng Thirith, who had sent many of the Sihanoukists and former resistance partners to death, were charming. A cameraman was also on hand to immortalize the occasion on film. A few weeks later, Ieng Sary was in New York for the UN General Assembly, and he distributed the pictures of the Phnom Penh banquet to diplomats and journalists. Photographs do not lie. Sary had proved that, despite dire rumors about his fate, Prince Sihanouk was alive and well and that along with his former associates he was a respected senior statesman of a united Cambodia.

Not only was Sihanouk suddenly back in favor, the Khmer Rouge seemed to have become unusually concerned about his security. The house in the royal palace compound where he lived was no longer considered safe. The palace grounds were wide open for enemy helicopters to bring in assassins. Sihanouk understood their real fear was that the Vietnamese might attempt to kidnap him to deprive them of an international trump card. He was removed to a smaller house surrounded by high brick walls and barbed wire. That precaution by Pol Pot was well-founded. Years later, Vietnamese foreign minister Nguyen Co Thach told me that the Vietnamese indeed were planning to "liberate" Sihanouk shortly before he was moved out of the palace.

Next to his new residence was a tall building. The Khmer Rouge had installed projector lamps on its roof and kept them trained on his house all night, which meant there was no night for him and Monique. The shaft of light coming through the translucent screens on his bedroom window flooded the room. Sihanouk often wondered whether they were being watched by Khmer Rouge guards peering at them through binoculars.

Other than listening to the radio, Sihanouk spent his time reading and trying to learn Spanish from a teach-yourself book. His own distraction in the gloomy and tense days was cooking. He had always been interested in the culinary art, and he had invented recipes that combined his Khmer taste and his deep knowledge of French cuisine. On the evening of December 24 he was in the kitchen trying out a new recipe when an excited Monique called him. She was listening to the Voice of America news bulletin. Malcolm Caldwell, a British scholar who was then visiting Cambodia along with the first two Western journalists, had been murdered in his Phnom Penh guesthouse. The Democratic Kampuchean government officials had blamed the Vietnamese for the murder. A fantastic claim, Sihanouk thought.

From his own experience Sihanouk knew how tight security was in Pol Pot's Cambodia. How could a commando succeed in breaking unnoticed through the multiple rings of Khmer Rouge soldiers, who were certainly guarding Caldwell and the two American journalists? How could they know which one of three foreigners was Caldwell and in which room he slept? If the Vietnamese could do that, he thought to himself, then Pol Pot himself could not be safe. Sihanouk concluded that the murder was ordered by Pol Pot for something that the British professor, a staunch supporter of the Khmer Rouge, had done. The incident was a telling reminder of how precarious his own life was.

He could sense that the pace of history was accelerating. Foreign radio stations reported that the Vietnamese had launched a large-scale attack on Cambodia and heavy fighting was going on. Knowing the Vietnamese, knowing the legendary General Vo Nguyen Giap, he had long felt this was inevitable. But how was it going to end? On the afternoon of January 2 a Khmer Rouge cadre came to say that Sihanouk and his family had fifteen minutes to get ready to go somewhere. "So our time has come," Sihanouk told Monique as he prepared for last prayers. Sihanouk had heard many Khmer refugee accounts from foreign radio broadcasts describing how people were taken away from their homes never to return. It was now their turn. He had decided to commit suicide rather than be taken away like a lamb to be butchered. But the Khmer Rouge cadre had come back to ask the prince to pack whatever tinned food they had. That suddenly relieved the gloom. If they want us to take provisions along, maybe this is not the journey to the execution ground, Sihanouk thought.

In the evening, Khieu Samphan arrived to see off the prince and his family as they left for the northern town of Battambang. Khieu Samphan explained that the Vietnamese aggressors were still advancing and that it would be better for their safety to leave the capital for the time being. He said he himself would soon visit Sihanouk in Battambang. As the convoy of cars rolled out of Phnom Penh in the dusk, distant sounds of explosions wafted in the air from the east. War was approaching.

Khieu Samphan did not tell the prince that in the early hours of January 2 Vietnamese commandos had made an abortive attempt to enter Phnom Penh and kidnap Sihanouk. Weeks later, when he was again a free man, Sihanouk was to hear of the failed Vietnamese attempt to liberate him and make him the head of the anti–Pol Pot opposition. In the early hours of January 2, two Vietnamese teams of *Dat Cong* (sapper commandos) crossed the Tonle Sap River on dinghies to reach the banks close to the royal palace. Most of them were killed by Khmer Rouge soldiers guarding the riverfront, but one of the few survivors managed to escape. Years later he defected to Thailand and provided Western intelligence the first detailed account of that abortive attempt.

After a bone-rattling journey along the potholed Route 5, Sihanouk was in Sisophon, the town close to the Thai border. Two days later Khieu Samphan arrived to tell him that the enemy had been pushed back and they could now return to Phnom Penh. However exhausting and nerve-wracking this shuttle to safety, it at least had proved Sihanouk's fear for his own life to have been mistaken. The Khmer Rouge did not perhaps want him dead, but he wondered how

301

secure he would be in their hands as the Vietnamese army advanced. He had quickly realized that, contrary to Khieu Samphan's claim, the Vietnamese had not been pushed back. Window panes in his residence rattled frequently as the rumble of artillery seemed to come closer.

On the evening of January 5 Sihanouk was summoned for an audience with "Brother Number One"—the Khmer Rouge supremo, Pol Pot. As evening was descending, Sihanouk was driven to the massive two-story colonial building on the the bank of Tonle Sap River that was once the residence of the French governor. In his time Sihanouk used the building as the government guesthouse. This was the first time since 1973 that Sihanouk was going to meet face to face with Pol Pot. During his visit to the liberated zones in Cambodia in March 1973, Sihanouk had met Saloth Sar. He had then found the Paris-returned Communist theoretician shy and self-effacing. All the time he stood in the background letting others talk to Sihanouk.

The aloof and shy Pol Pot was a different person that evening of January 5. During the four hours Sihanouk spent with him, Pol Pot was very much the man in charge but exceedingly gentle and polite. Years later Sihanouk reminisced about that evening. "Pol Pot is very brutal, but it seems he did not hate me very much. He was really very charming." Sihanouk was taken aback by his use of court language—the respectful form of address in Khmer that is reserved for royalty and Buddhist monks. "Ieng Sary refused to speak to me in that language. He said Sihanouk is just a citizen." Khieu Samphan was different. Despite their egalitarian theories, he spoke to the prince in the language of the court. "Surprisingly that night," Sihanouk recalled, "Pol Pot had the same behavior as Khieu Samphan. Fantastic! Incredible!"

"Pol Pot said, 'Your Highness, I apologize that Comrade Khieu Samphan had to represent me before you.' He saluted me with joined palms and did not use the word 'I' but said 'your servant'—like in the English court 'your obedient servant,' something like that. I was very surprised."

Pol Pot told the prince how much he wished him to represent Cambodia at the UN. With so many friends abroad, he could be of considerable help to Cambodia. Sihanouk said he loved the country and condemned the Vietnamese invasion. He promised to do his best to secure the support of the UN Security Council for Cambodia. Ieng Sary interrupted him to say that as there were not enough places on the plane the prince would only go with his wife. "But I beg you, Your Excellency," Sihanouk asked Pol Pot, "to allow the members of my family and my associates to accompany me." Pol Pot looked at Ieng Sary, seated next to the prince, and said, "Yes, arrange for all of them to take the plane." Suddenly Sihanouk felt lighter. He thanked Pol Pot profusely for his kindness and consideration. But he knew this kindness only showed how dangerously cornered he was. Pol Pot also spent hours in painting an optimistic picture of the war against the Vietnamese. "Within two months we will wipe out the Vietnamese," he said. Sihanouk said, "Congratulations, Mr. President! Congratulations!" With Ieng Sary vigorously nodding in agreement, Pol Pot told the prince, "From now on if you want to go to China very often, you can do that. You are free. If you come back, you will be very warmly welcomed. If you decide to spend a few days with us, it will be a great pleasure to have you." Sihanouk gaped in amazement. "Oh, really? Thank you very much."

Freedom on the wings of an airplane that seemed so near while talking to Pol Pot appeared uncertain on the morning of January 6. Vietnamese artillery sounded very close to the capital. Could the Chinese Boeing 707 approach Pochentong Airport? Once on the tarmac, could it safely take off without coming under Vietnamese fire? Ieng Sary advised that if the plane did not arrive, they would have to leave Phnom Penh for the jungle. "I prepared two bags to take to the airport," Sihanouk reminisced to me. "One suitcase had business suits for New York, and a backpack was stuffed with tinned food, khaki shirts, pajamas, *krama* [scarf], and the Ho Chi Minh sandals." (The Ho Chi Minh sandals, made of used rubber tires, had become the standard guerrilla footwear in Indochina.) Would he have to again go to the jungle in the company of the despised Khmer Rouge? The answer was hidden in the stark sky, swept by the eyes of prospective Chinese and Cambodian passengers. Their ears strained to hear the soothing drone of the Chinese Boeing over the steady thump of artillery. As a row of Chinese-built MiG-19s with Democratic Kampuchean colors sat at one end of the tarmac, immobilized by lack of pilots to fly them, and the sun steadily climbed, warming the still air at Pochentong, Sihanouk waited for the bird of freedom.

Indochinese summit in Canton in May 1970. Pictured left to right are Pham Van Dong, Sihanouk, Zhou Enlai, Souphanouvong, and Nguyen Huu Tho.

An ailing Lon Nol in his last days of power, 1972.

Liberation day in Saigon, April 30, 1975. A Vietcong tank enters the palace grounds to hoist the NLF flag.

Le Duc Tho and Huynh Tan Phat at the May 7, 1975, victory celebration in Ho Chi Minh City.

Historic photo of Chinese Li Chiang visiting Cambodia during December 1976. The front line from left to right: Ieng Sary, Khieu Samphan, Li, Pol Pot, Nuon Chea, and Vorn Vet.

Also in December 1976, Le Duan visiting with Soviet Party ideologist Mikhail Suslov.

Richard Holbrooke (*left*), Frank Sieverts (*rear center*), and Phan Hien (*right*) in Paris, May 1977.

Soviet leader Alexei Kosygin with Pham Van Dong, June 1977.

Cambodian refugees in Vietnam being recruited for the resistance army by a Vietnamese soldier.

Vietnamese survivors of September 1977 Khmer attack on border villages. The mounds in the background are graves.

Spring 1978. Scene from the Khmer Rouge massacre at Ha Tien.

Chinese Party Chairman Hua Guofeng (*right*) receiving Pol Pot (*center*), September 30, 1977. Ieng Sary is at left.

Deng Xiaoping in the White House garden with his interpreter and President Carter, January 28, 1979. Deng advised Carter of the planned invasion of Vietnam.

Vietnamese fortification near Lang Son being exploded by Chinese artillery, March 3, 1979.

Vietnamese civilians fleeing the border before the Chinese invasion in February 1979.

Bridge near Lang Son and village after invasion, February 1979.

Captured Chinese soldier being led by Vietnamese militiawoman.

Deserted center of Battambang City in April 1980.

Khmer Rouge guerrillas with Chinese-supplied B-40 rockets.

Skulls lined up in one of the mass graves of Cambodia's killing fields.

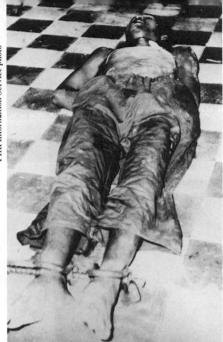

Victim of the notorious Tuol Sleng prison.

Confessions extracted from prisoners at Tuol Sleng.

Spring 1980 scene of Cambodia traders going to Thailand. A Vietnamese soldier guards a bridge on the way.

Khmer Rouge guerrillas.

Cambodian supporters of
FUNCINPEC resistance rallying to
welcome Prince Sihanouk in July
1982.

Political Commissar Ny Kon giving a
lecture to civilians at a Khmer Rouge-
controlled camp.

10

A Red
Christmas

O<small>N</small> <small>THE</small> <small>EVENING</small> of January 6, 1979, Lao ambassador Khamphan Vilachit spent a sleepless night, as did his six-member staff. War seemed to have come dangerously close. The deathly silence was shattered frequently by thunderous booms of cannon and their rolling echoes in the deserted capital. The window panes of the chancery rattled. Khamphan had seen the war coming, yet he never thought that it would reach the capital so fast.

He consoled his staff and asked them to pray to Lord Buddha. Away from family and home and in the seclusion of the embassy where they huddled together, these young men had almost become his children. However unorthodox that advice may have sounded coming from a Socialist ambassador, for him it was the most natural, and certainly the only, thing he could do under the circumstances. It was as if they were living on a desert island: Since January 2, the Lao had been a lonely group in a haunted city awaiting its last hour. At a time like this, it was not surprising they would turn to Buddha's teachings about the path of Nirvana leading from the cycle of suffering and death.

In many ways Khamphan was an unusual envoy to represent Socialist Laos in the most radical country on earth. A tall man with a long forehead and a quick, shy smile, he was chosen to be the Lao ambassador to Democratic Kampuchea not for his revolutionary credentials but for his fluency in Khmer and his serene view of life. A serenity of character was certainly the most essential quality for survival in Pol Pot's Phnom Penh. Khamphan's predecessor, a young revolutionary cadre, had almost gone around the bend after a year in the isolation of Phnom Penh. He had required emergency evacuation—a procedure that had little meaning in Khmer Rouge Cambodia, where flights to Vientiane took off only once a month. The diplomat had been sent home on a week-long boat journey up the Mekong.

Khamphan had first been to Cambodia some forty years before. As a young novice, he had studied at Phnom Penh's Institut Bouddhique. A greater part of his adult life he had spent as an administrator and mayor of the royal capital Luang Prabang, which was also the country's most important center of Buddhist learning. He had never thought he would be a diplomat and certainly not in a country that had declared war on religion. But he could not turn down the call from the Lao People's Revolutionary Party, which had shown extraordinary tolerance toward Buddhism.

After eight years of absence he was back in Cambodia. It had changed beyond recognition. Gone was the once lovely town with its French provincial flavor. With the exception of one pagoda near the royal palace, all had either been abandoned or turned into granaries and workshops to produce fish sauce. Defrocked monks had been either executed or deported to the countryside to labor. The Khmer Rouge proudly showed Khamphan a propaganda film in which former monks were harnessed like animals and ploughing the fields.

Life had been cheap in Cambodia. On that Sunday morning of January 7 life to him seemed more ephemeral than a droplet of water on a lotus leaf. He had been listening to foreign radio broadcasts and monitoring the progress of the Vietnamese invasion of Cambodia. The fast-approaching boom of guns told him the situation was more serious than the radio had reported. The danger to the Lao loomed even more ominously: theirs was the only diplomatic mission left behind in Phnom Penh. The uncertain Morse-code radio link he had with Vientiane had been dead for six days. In response to his last cable, sent on New Year's Day, about growing insecurity, the Lao Foreign Ministry in Vientiane advised them not to panic and stay put. They could do little else since there was no obvious way to get out of Phnom Penh. As he would learn later, the one radio operator in Vientiane's Foreign Ministry was down with diarrhea the very week hell was breaking lose in Phnom Penh.

On the night of January 2, Khamphan was awakened by one of his staff. "The Khmer Rouge are evacuating all embassy personnel," the nervous young diplomat reported, "but they don't seem to be asking us." It was a moonlit night. From his window Khamphan could see the commotion in the street that served as Phnom Penh's diplomatic enclave. Cambodian soldiers were busy loading personal belongings of embassy personnel onto trucks while the diplomats were readying their cars. "What's up, comrade?" a Khmer-speaking Lao asked their guard. For reasons of security the diplomatic corps would be taken to Battambang, the guard explained, adding that there was no instruction to evacuate the Lao. It was clear that Pol Pot wanted to keep the embassy of Vietnam's ally hostage in the capital to deter the onslaught.

The Khmer Rouge decision to evacuate the diplomats came out of the blue. On the morning of January 2, Yugoslav ambassador Mihailo Lompar went to see Pol Pot to hand over a gift of medicine from the Yugoslav Red Cross. Pol Pot was supremely confident that the Vietnamese invasion that had begun in late December would be defeated. But that evening a cadre of the Foreign Ministry came to hesitantly inform the ambassador that he would have to "temporarily evacuate" the capital. Lompar thought it a contingency preparation. But when the cadre said, "You'll have to leave in an hour," Lompar thought he saw panic in the Khmer's eyes. Was it then the end of Democratic Kampuchea? Within hours, a large convoy of cars and trucks carrying the members of all but one of Phnom Penh's embassies headed toward Battambang. Ambassador Lompar found his Chinese colleague, a normally mirthful Sun Hao, very disconcerted. The evacuation must have been a shock to him.

After spending a night at Battambang, the Yugoslav and Chinese embassy staff took the bone-rattling journey back to Phnom Penh. Arrangements had been made for Chinese aircraft to fly them out to Peking. On the morning of January 6, as guns boomed closer to

315

the capital, several hundred Khmers and Chinese waited for the aircraft at the Phnom Penh airport. With the notable exception of Pol Pot, almost the whole Khmer Rouge leadership was present, standing grim faced. Lompar quickly saw why they were there. He spotted the long-unseen but familiar face of Prince Sihanouk. The prince's Khmer Rouge jailers were there to give him a reluctant send-off. In the past year, Lompar's requests to see Sihanouk on behalf of the prince's old friend Josip Broz (Marshal Tito) had been politely turned down. At last his incarceration was over. Ieng Sary approached the Yugoslav ambassador apologetically. There were so many people waiting for the flight that his embassy could have only four seats, Sary told him. Both the Chinese and the Yugoslav ambassador elected to stay behind to make room for their subordinates.

At noon, the silver-and-blue Boeing 707 of China's Civil Aviation Administration touched down. Sihanouk was in tears—joyous now that his freedom seemed a reality, but distressed to be fleeing his country again. He embraced the Yugoslav ambassador and said with a choking voice, "Please give my regards to President Tito and tell him our people will never surrender." After that last flight from Phnom Penh took off, the two ambassadors left again for Battambang.

On January 7, chaos was building up around the Phnom Penh railway station since dawn. Thousands of men, women, and children—government cadres and their family members who had been living in camps on the outskirts of the capital—were arriving on trucks, motorbikes, and bicycles. But there did not seem to be enough room; the two trains at the platform were already packed with wounded soldiers and panicky civilians. A harassed Ieng Sary and his Foreign Ministry cadres were trying to calm the crowds and make room for more wounded soldiers. With the sun mercilessly beating down on Phnom Penh, the compartments were slowly turning into ovens. Shortly after 9 A.M., a messenger arrived to inform Ieng Sary that the Vietnamese columns were only three miles away. Sary gave the order to start. With hundreds of desperate people perched on rooftops and hanging from door handles, the last trains from Phnom Penh lumbered out of the station and headed toward Battambang.

Sitting on the terrace of his embassy building, Khamphan wondered how it would all end. Since daybreak, the crackle of automatic fire accompanied exploding shells. At about 10 A.M. a jeep drove into the diplomatic enclave to collect the young Khmer soldiers standing guard. Before leaving, one of them lifted his AK-47 automatic rifle and casually sprayed the Lao embassy with bullets. Nobody had been hurt—the one Lao watching from a window had ducked—but a bullet hit the portrait of Lao prime minister Kaysone and sent the wood-and-glass frame crashing to the floor.

The former ghost city was now caught in a frenzy. Occasionally, Chinese-built trucks laden with men tore down Boulevard Monivong at breakneck speed. The steady boom of cannon was drowned by the heavy thump of green helicopters with their rotors swishing through hot midmorning air. They quickly disappeared over the western horizon. Was Pol Pot in there? Khamphan wondered. Standing on the terrace of the Lao embassy, he was witnessing the end of an era. At about noon, the heavy sound of treads suddenly hit him. He looked down. At the end of the street, framed by buildings on both sides, was a visible patch of Phnom Penh's major artery, Boulevard Monivong. One tank after another flying red-and-yellow flags rumbled down the boulevard, leaving a pall of blue smoke hanging in the air. The Vietnamese had arrived. "Raise our flag!" Khamphan called out to his staff.

An hour later, the second secretary of the embassy went out into the street to beckon excitedly to a small patrol of Vietnamese troops walking down the deserted boulevard. Startled by his call, they leveled their guns at him, but he promptly threw his hands over his head. As they approached, he explained to the lone Khmer member in the group that he was a Lao diplomat and indicated the embassy. That evening a dozen Vietnamese soldiers arrived to guard the building. The nightmare was over. An elated Khamphan ordered a banquet of boiled rice and tinned meat for the "liberators."[1]

Friendship Treaty, Anyone?

As the Lao diplomats and their new guardians celebrated victory in Phnom Penh, the world reacted with astonishment. In just two weeks Vietnam had overrun its Socialist neighbor and driven out of power China's only ally in Southeast Asia. The climax came after months of intense diplomatic and military preparation by both Vietnam and China. The Soviet-Vietnamese treaty had been followed by Sino-American normalization, which in turn had been followed by the Vietnamese invasion of Cambodia and the Chinese invasion of Vietnam. In the course of three months the political map of Asia had undergone a dramatic change.

In the wake of the expulsion of overseas Chinese from Vietnam in the summer of 1978, Hanoi had stepped up its efforts to portray China as a threat to the whole of Southeast Asia. Simultaneously, the Vietnamese had made a desperate attempt to cement their own relationship with ASEAN countries and seek their understanding and support against China and Cambodia. In this, they had executed a remarkable volte-face. Hanoi had nothing but contempt for ASEAN, which had come into existence in 1967 while Vietnam battled against the United States. The Vietnamese Communist party daily then called ASEAN a "product of the U.S. imperialist policy of intervention and aggression."[2]

But in mid-1976 Hanoi had responded to the ASEAN call for normalization of relations and cooperation, though maintaining a distance.

However, its reservations about ASEAN's Western-oriented policies were quietly dropped as the Sino-Vietnamese conflict heated up. Peking and Hanoi began an intense competition for the "hearts and minds" of ASEAN. In June 1978, when Vietnam began its unpublicized aerial bombing of Cambodia, flying as many as thirty sorties a day, it announced its readiness to deal with ASEAN as an organization—something it had so far stubbornly refused. By July, Phan Hien had visited Malaysia and declared Vietnam's support for a zone of peace and neutrality.

In September, Premier Pham Van Dong set out on a historic trip to court the anti-Communist Southeast Asian countries. In an extraordinary gesture to anti-Communist Malaysia, Dong laid a wreath at a monument in Kuala Lumpur in memory of Malaysian soldiers who had died fighting Communist insurgents. He even privately apologized to Malaysian leaders for Hanoi's aid to the insurgents, which was given only because of a "flawed understanding of the situation." While in Bangkok he assured the Thais that Vietnam did not support the outlawed Communist Party of Thailand (CPT). The Vietnamese leader, in fact, insisted on signing a treaty of friendship and cooperation with ASEAN countries to formalize the new approach. That offer was politely rebuffed by the group, which had decided against rushing into any formal agreement with Vietnam. Instead they signed a less grandiose joint statement pledging friendship.

The Vietnamese attempt to draw Thailand into an implicit anti-Chinese alliance also failed. While Kriangsak and Dong signed a joint communiqué pledging to refrain from "carrying out subversion, direct or indirect, against each other and from using force or threatening to use force against each other," the Thais rebuffed attempts to include a clause against "third country" use of one's territory for hostile purposes. This was viewed as indirect criticism of China for its use of Cambodia against Vietnam.

The ASEAN refusal to sign a friendship treaty upset Hanoi's plan to diplomatically shield its Cambodia venture. The Vietnamese hoped, with surprising naïveté, that their offer of a treaty would dispel the fear of Vietnamese expansionism and be evidence of their sincere desires for friendly relations with ASEAN, notwithstanding their military involvement in Cambodia. A series of friendship treaties with their neighbors and the conclusion of a normalization agreement with the United States, Hanoi leaders had calculated, would help absorb the shock of their planned treaty with Moscow.

The fast-paced diplomacy undertaken by the Vietnamese in the fall was closely linked with their military timetable. In the late summer of 1978, when Hanoi had proposed Pham Van Dong's ASEAN visit, the countries had been surprised by the Vietnamese haste to bring it about not later than October. Many ASEAN diplomats had concluded that this was to preempt Chinese vice-chairman Deng Xiaoping's visit to Thailand and Singapore, which had been planned for November. It was not just a question of scheduling the visit. Hanoi also put enormous pressure on some ASEAN countries to agree to a treaty of friendship. Every Malaysian diplomat in Hanoi—from second secretary to ambassador—was told by his Vietnamese interlocutors that if Pham Van Dong's visit was not a success, Hanoi would have to reconsider its policy of friendship.[3] Although "success" was not clearly defined, it clearly involved signing the treaty proposed by Vietnam. Halfway around the globe, in New York, Vietnam's foreign minister, Nguyen Co Thach, urged the U.S. government to hurry up and sign a communiqué establishing diplomatic relations.

In retrospect, Vietnamese diplomatic haste was probably dictated by the decision to go into Cambodia at the beginning of the dry season in December—the ground would be hard enough for tanks, and the rice harvest would provide enough food for the Cambodian resistance that Hanoi had been training since early 1978. The target date for the invasion could not be too close to the signing of the treaty with Moscow, for it would create more of an impression of a direct and leading Soviet role in the Cambodia venture than Hanoi would like to see. It was this consideration that had probably prompted the Vietnamese to push for a treaty with Moscow by fall and to work toward a normalization agreement with Washington and treaties of friendship with ASEAN countries before that event. While seeking an umbrella of protection from the Soviets, the Vietnamese sought to ensure that other doors to the West did not slam shut as a result or that their conflict with China and Cambodia did not bring about isolation. The Vietnamese also probably calculated that a bolstered diplomatic position would strengthen their hand in dealing with the Soviet Union.

Shopping for Insurance in Moscow

By mid-October 1978, when Pham Van Dong returned to Hanoi from his Southeast Asian visit, Vietnamese plans seemed to have hit serious snags. A suspicious ASEAN had rebuffed the idea of a treaty. Back home in Vietnam, unprecedentedly heavy rains, floods, and typhoons had hit the Red River delta, central Vietnam, and the Mekong Delta in August and September. Nearly one and a half million tons of crops had been destroyed, and 20 percent of all livestock had been wiped out. Estimates of Vietnam's yawning food deficit for the year had risen dramatically to three million tons.[4]

The flood had affected not only the Ninth Military Region of Vietnam—the area in charge of operations in Cambodia—but a large part of eastern Cambodia, through which the Mekong flowed south. It promised a soggy terrain for Vietnamese tanks long after the rains had stopped. The most worrisome consideration was that there was no news from the United States. Richard Holbrooke had left for an Asian trip while Thach waited impatiently in New York to sign a normalization agreement.

As October drew to its end, the Vietnamese Politburo seemed to have concluded that despite the unfavorable situation it could no longer delay the signing of the treaty with Moscow. After two postponements, Hanoi sent its negotiators to Moscow and ordered Thach to proceed there.[5]

As a light snow covered the tarmac of Moscow's Vnukovo Airport on the evening of Wednesday, November 1, a special Aeroflot Ilyushin-62 jetliner touched down amidst a clapping of hands. In an unusual display of warmth, five members of the Soviet Politburo and nine members of the Central Committee and several dozen other senior officials had assembled at the airport. Heavily clad Soviet party secretary Leonid Brezhnev walked up to the ramp under the gaze of television cameras to hold Vietnamese leader Le Duan in a tight embrace. After the national anthems, and after Le Duan and Pham Van Dong reviewed the guard of honor, the delegation proceeded to the guesthouse along a road dressed up for the occasion: red-and-gold Vietnamese flags hung from poles beside the Soviet hammer and sickle. Banners strung across the street welcomed the "dear Vietnamese friends" and saluted the Socialist Republic of Vietnam, "the forward bastion of socialism in Southeast Asia."

The Soviets had reason to be pleased with the "forward bastion": the long-cherished Soviet dream of roping Vietnam into a military alliance against China was, at last, a reality. On November 3, the Soviet and Vietnamese leaders gathered in the Great Hall of the Kremlin to put their signatures to a twenty-five-year treaty of friendship and cooperation. Article Six of the treaty provided the insurance guarantee Vietnam had sought against possible Chinese attack. "If either side is attacked or exposed to the threat of attack," it said, "the two signatory powers will immediately confer with each other in order to remove this threat and take appropriate and effective steps to safeguard the peace and security of both countries."[6]

An elated Brezhnev did not miss the opportunity to crow about Moscow's coup and issue a thinly veiled warning to China. The treaty, he said, would displease those who view with disfavor the friendship between Vietnam and the Soviet Union and those who count on division between Socialist countries and on exacerbating their tension. "But right from now on, the treaty is a political reality and whether one likes it or not, one would have to take into account this reality."[7]

The reality, as it would become clear in a few months, was also military. The "appropriate steps" mentioned in Article Six would involve facilities for Soviet navy and air force in Vietnam. That was the price Vietnam would have to pay for Soviet insurance against China, for obtaining supplies of all the arms and equipment it needed and promise of economic assistance, including emergency food aid of 1.5 million tons of grain. In August 1978, when Hanoi still counted on normalization with Washington, Pham Van Dong had talked about the danger of relying on one power. "Whenever in our four-thousand-year history Vietnam has been dependent on one large friend," he said, "it has been a disaster for us."[8] But three months later, as Vietnam braced for a new military adventure, the country had been brought to that very position of disastrous dependence on one friend.

At a Kremlin banquet after the signing of the treaty, Le Duan declared that now Vietnam would be more inspired to accomplish with honor its "sacred national task as well as its noble internationalist duty"—in other words, to defend itself against China and to intervene in Cambodia. Deep gratitude displayed by Hanoi leaders in Moscow made observers feel as if the Vietnamese had received a "gift of life." Le Duan bowed twice to his hosts before boarding the homebound jet on November 9.

Moving the Guns to the South

During the time that the Vietnamese delegation was in Moscow, the Chinese were secretly putting finishing touches on their logistical preparations for an attack on Vietnam. As early as August 1978,

U.S. intelligence had picked up indications of contingency preparations in China's Guangzhou Military Region bordering Vietnam. American spy satellites and travelers in southern China had watched large fleets of MiG-19s and MiG-21s of the Chinese air force being moved to airports closer to Vietnam, such as Nanning and Kunming. Tanks and heavy artillery were also gradually moved south. By the beginning of November, detailed plans for the large-scale moving of troops, armor, artillery, and fuel to the Vietnamese border had been completed. There was another telltale sign picked up by U.S. intelligence: in mid-November it had observed the Chinese setting up a microwave communication relay station on a hilltop in Guangxi Province. This would enable the Chinese General Staff and the party's Military Affairs Commission to be in direct contact with the People's Liberation Army (PLA) field headquarters.[9]

One of the most interesting sources on China's preparation for war would be available to Western intelligence in early 1982 when it got hold of a deserter. A second lieutenant of a PLA battalion from Guangxi Military Region was picked up by police in the British colony of Hongkong as he tried to sneak in as an illegal immigrant. The lieutenant told American and British debriefers that in late November 1978 the commander of his unit had delivered a speech invoking the possibility of a war with Vietnam. Then, on December 11, General Wei Guoqing, head of the PLA's General Political Department, told a meeting in Nanning commemorating the twentieth anniversary of the founding of the Guangxi-Zhuang Autonomous Zone that Vietnam had taken many hostile actions against China and that Peking would "teach Vietnam a lesson." That speech by the seventy-two-year-old Zhuang minority leader—who was also a key military ally of China's emerging strongman, Deng Xiaoping—marked the beginning of the final phase of Chinese preparations for an invasion.

As leader of the Guangxi-Zhuang Autonomous Zone bordering Vietnam and as kinsman of the minorities living on the Vietnamese side of the border, Wei had been directly involved in military assistance to Vietnamese Communists. At the time of the seige of Dien Bien Phu in 1954, Wei had been one of the Chinese military advisers attached to the Vietnamese military command. During the height of the Cultural Revolution, when he had been the target of Red Guard attacks, Wei had tried to ensure a continued arms flow to Vietnam through his region. Now, twelve years later, it was Wei's job to announce to the PLA its new task against an "ingrate" Vietnam. The day after Wei's speech, the headquarters of the Guangxi Military Region was moved closer to the Vietnamese border, and the First Independent Division, to which the PLA deserter belonged, was ordered to take up a position approximately a mile from the border and begin training and exercise.[10] In mid-December a booklet printed in color was distributed to PLA units along the border. It showed drawings of the uniforms and insignias of the different branches of the Vietnamese forces.

While China's secret military preparations against Vietnam shifted into a new gear, it was Deng Xiaoping's turn to woo non-Communist Southeast Asia. In his nine-day tour through Thailand, Malaysia, and Singapore, Deng's task was to assure these countries of China's benevolent role as guardian of regional security and to enlist their support in the confrontation with Vietnam. Although China had shed its hostile stance toward the non-Communist Southeast Asian states since the early 1970s, and although by 1975 it had established diplomatic relations with all but one of the ASEAN countries, the relations had been rather cool. Trade and cultural ties had developed, but China's support for the Communist insurgents in Thailand and Malaysia left a miasma of suspicion hanging over the relationships. Peking's claim that its friendly state-to-state relations were independent of fraternal party-to-party ties did not convince anybody. Despite Chinese denials, the ASEAN governments knew that the Thai and Malay Communist radio broadcasts calling for an armed struggle actually emanated from Chinese transmitters in Yunnan, and that the arms and funds for the guerrillas came from Peking. Premier Pham Van Dong's public assurance to ASEAN a few weeks before Deng's arrival that Vietnam did not support subversion had put China in an even more awkward position. Either it could follow in Vietnam's footsteps and abandon a long-held principle, or it could maintain its stance and provide Hanoi with propaganda ammunition about a Chinese "threat" to the region.

Deng resolved the dilemma by going on the offensive. "I will not copy Pham Van Dong in lying," he told a press conference in Bangkok when asked about China's ties with Thai Communists. "Sincerity is the prerequisite for good relations among states."[11] While publicly maintaining Peking's principled stand of moral support to fraternal Communist parties, Deng privately promised Thai premier Kriangsak to stop Chinese support for the CPT. He argued that if China publicly refused to support the CPT, the Soviets would step into the breach; this was in the interest of neither China nor ASEAN.

Time to Win Friends and Influence People

But if the Vietnamese renunciation of subversion as a policy tool upstaged China, the signing of the Soviet-Vietnamese treaty two days before Deng's arrival in Thailand was a propaganda windfall. The newly announced alliance seriously shook ASEAN's confidence about Vietnam's claim to be an independent and nonaligned nation and made it more receptive to Deng's arguments about bigger Soviet "hegemonists" encouraging "smaller hegemonist" Vietnam.

In a restricted meeting on November 6, at which only one aide, an interpreter, and a notetaker assisted, Deng surprised Kriangsak with his candor and toughness. "There is a possibility," he told him, "that Phnom Penh will fall. This would not be the end of the war but the beginning."[12]

He said that China did not like the policies of Pol Pot but it would never allow such a strategic area to fall to the Vietnamese. "China will never stand idly by," he said. "We will take appropriate measures." Deng strongly hinted that the Chinese response would be military punishment of Vietnam. Several days later Deng made the same point to Singapore leaders. Singapore deputy premier Sinnathamby Rajaratnam, who sat in the meeting with Deng, said that the "Chinese never get emotional, but when the prime minister [Lee Kuan Yew] asked Deng about the Vietnamese, it was the first time I saw his eyes glint, [it was] real, I mean not simulated. 'These ungrateful people must be punished. We gave them $20 billion of aid, Chinese sweat, and blood and look what happened.'" Lee asked Deng how he would punish them. "We have ways and means,"

Deng replied cryptically. Although China's decision to "teach Vietnam a lesson" in July of 1978 had been in response to Vietnam's treatment of the ethnic Chinese, Deng now argued that it was for the sake of the security and stability of Southeast Asia, especially of Thailand, that China now opposed Vietnam. Deng had presented a scenario, with remarkable prescience as later events would prove, of a massive Vietnamese invasion and a protracted Cambodian resistance war. In that struggle against Vietnamese expansion, China and Thailand would need to cooperate closely, he urged Kriangsak. The Thai premier, a practitioner of the traditional Thai policy of balance, was chary of being drawn into an intra-Communist fight. He promised action only as the situation warranted.[13]

However, he granted the Chinese request for overflights to Phnom Penh through Thai airspace. Increasing tension between Peking and Hanoi's ally Laos had made China's usual air route to Phnom Penh insecure. And that, too, at a time when China needed to send increasing volumes of materiel and more advisers to beleaguered Cambodia.

In fact, while Deng continued his journey through Southeast Asia, another Chinese delegation, led by Politburo member Wang Dongxing, arrived in Cambodia. The visit was ostensibly planned to demonstrate China's support for the country amid growing signs of Vietnamese preparation for a large-scale attack. But as it became clear later, Wang, Mao's personal bodyguard and a political opponent of Deng's, had been chosen to relay an unpleasant message to his "fellow" leftists in Phnom Penh. Although he publicly affirmed China's support for the Cambodian people's "just struggle in defense of their independence, sovereignty, and territorial integrity," he scrupulously avoided making any specific commitment of Chinese military support. In fact, by suggesting that aggressors "may run wild for a while" but would ultimately be defeated, he seemed to be advocating a protracted guerrilla resistance rather than a quick fix with foreign help.[14]

Later revelations would show that the display of Vietnamese power in the autumn of 1978 had shaken Pol Pot's confidence about Cambodia's invincibility. He asked Wang Dongxing to send a Chinese volunteer force to fight the Vietnamese in Cambodia. An interesting bit of evidence of the Khmer Rouge surprise at China's rejection of the request was provided by French-born militant Laurence Picq, who was married to a senior Khmer Rouge cadre in the Foreign Ministry and worked in Phnom Penh as a translator and typist. Picq translated a speech that the Cambodian host was to deliver at a reception for Wang. However, shortly before the reception, her breathless husband came to ask her to delete a paragraph and retype the speech. The paragraph had said: "The government of Democratic Kampuchea and the Communist party can certainly count on the aid of the fraternal Chinese army in case of need."[15] Cambodia's cry for help as witnessed by Wang and the insane radicalism and disorganization of the society as observed by Deng Xiaoping's political allies Hu Yaobang and Yu Qiuli (who were on the Wang delegation), provided firsthand material for a key policy debate on China's role in Indochina.

Deng Takes over the Controls

Shortly after Wang and Deng returned from their trips, the Chinese Politburo met in Peking in an enlarged working conference. The agenda of the conference was China's domestic politics as well as its policy toward the United States and Indochina. The lengthy conference (November 11 to December 15) proved to be a watershed in Chinese politics, marking the establishment of Deng Xiaoping's control over what Sinologist Jurgen Domes calls the "CC switchboard"—the key levers of power in the party Central Committee.[16] Deng cleverly orchestrated a campaign in the official media, in rallies, and on wall posters as well as through his own supporters in the Central Committee, to bring about a change in the Politburo composition. Four of his backers—including Zhou Enlai's widow, Madame Deng Yingchao—were elected to the Politburo, and his closest aide, Zhao Zhiyang, was named secretary-general of the party Central Committee. A number of leaders who had advanced their careers during the Cultural Revolution and who opposed his pragmatic economic policies—party chairman Hua Guofeng, security boss Wang Dongxing, and Peking mayor Wu De—were forced to make self-criticisms and accept a diminution of real authority.[17]

Consolidation of Deng's position inside the party now enabled him to make an uncompromising push for foreign-policy issues that had earlier provoked controversy. The eclipse of the left-wing leaders—some of whom had visited Cambodia and had strongly backed the Khmer Rouge—further strengthened the Deng line of ideologically distancing China from the Khmer Rouge and building a broad coalition with non-Communist countries to curb the Vietnamese thrust. Historian King C. Chen believes that foreign-policy debate in the conference centered on the issue of "to intervene or not to intervene," and some of the members took a hawkish position. Wang Dongxing reportedly recommended that China honor Pol Pot's request for troops. First Political Commissar of the Navy Su Zhenhua suggested that China send a detachment of the East Sea Fleet to Cambodia to help it guard its territorial waters. Veteran commander of the Guangxi Military Region Xu Shiyou even wanted to lead his troops in an attack on Vietnam.[18]

But Deng and his friends strongly argued against direct Chinese intervention: not only was it against China's principles, but it was counter to China's goal of modernization. "If we send our soldiers to Cambodia," Politburo member in charge of international affairs Geng Biao argued, "what kind of impression shall we create in the eye of the Southeast Asian countries and other countries in the world? In addition to the failure in building up the united front against hegemony by uniting with the Third World countries, we shall become another new hegemonic power." He said that Moscow in fact hoped China would send troops to Cambodia. The Soviet Union would then be able to mobilize world opinion against China and so hinder its modernization.[19]

Although he decided against a dispatch of volunteers to Cambodia, Deng, however, carried the party with his plan to punish Vietnam. He reportedly argued first that a "self-defensive counterattack" on Vietnam was unlikely to provoke a large-scale Soviet attack on China. Citing U.S. military intelligence estimates of Soviet troop strength along the Chinese border, he argued that they would be unable to drive rapidly toward Peking. A small-scale attack by them could be handled by China. Second, an attack on Vietnam as an act of "self-defense," instead of an intervention in Cambodia, would not invite an unfavorable international reaction. Third, the punitive measure would not interrupt China's Four Modernizations and in fact would deter Vietnam from disturbing it in the future. He argued that if China achieved even 70 percent of its war objectives, the 30 percent failure would serve as a stimulus for military improvement. Most important, he argued, China's invasion and withdrawal from Vietnam would demonstrate to the Soviet Union and Vietnam China's determination and ability to break their encirclement. Soviet global strategy would suffer a setback in Asia, Deng concluded.[20]

Not only did the working conference back this decision, it supported Deng's policy of coalition with the United States, compromising China's stance on Taiwan. As Michel Oksenberg would later note, the contingency of military action against Vietnam "added to the attraction of completing the normalization processes with the United States. It also may have strengthened Deng's hand against potential critics of the compromises necessary to reach an agreement."[21]

Deng's emergence as the party strongman in December 1978 was directly linked to the acceptance of his pragmatic economic program, his plan to punish Vietnam, and his desire to establish full ties with Washington. In a historic coincidence, Deng's personal and Indochina policy timetables seemed to mesh perfectly with Carter's. As Oksenberg later noted, by November 2, when President Carter had sent Deng the final U.S. proposals for normalization of relations with the target date of January 1979, he "had begun to think of three spectacular successes to announce to the American people before Christmas: completion of the Camp David Accords, normalization [with China], and SALT II."[22]

Time to Get the Americans on Board

A day after Carter's proposal was communicated to Peking, the Soviet-Vietnamese military alliance was sealed, and three days later Deng set out on his tour of Southeast Asia. In an ironic twist of history, domestic political forces in Washington and Peking—namely, Brzezinski's successful bureaucratic maneuvering against Vance, and

Holbrooke and Deng's political manipulation of the Left in the Chinese party—and the evolving strategic situation seemed to converge to push for a rapid establishment of a Sino-American alliance while war clouds were building up on the horizon. "Until the November–December work conference, Hua Guofeng, for one, was opposed to normalization with the United States if it involved acceptance of unofficial U.S. ties with Taiwan," a Chinese official told me two years later. Pointing to the growing Soviet-Vietnamese threat to China and its ally Cambodia, Deng would now successfully argue for flexibility on Taiwan as a price of multifaceted cooperation with Washington.

The first Chinese hint that they might compromise on Taiwan came on December 4, 1978—just two days after Hanoi had announced the formation of a rebel front (KNUFNS) to fight Pol Pot in Cambodia. On that day when Ambassador Woodcock went for a meeting with China's then–acting foreign minister Han Nianlong to discuss the previous American proposal on normalization, he immediately noticed a change in personnel. Two aides with leftist reputations who had regularly sat in on normalization talks—Wang Hairung, Mao's niece, and Nancy Tang, the renowned interpreter—had been replaced by two professional diplomats. Han Nianlong, too, had a different tune. China so far had not only refused to rule out use of force against Taiwan but had also opposed issuance of any unilateral statement by the United States expressing hope for a peaceful future for Taiwan. But Han now told Woodcock that if the United States issued a statement about a peaceful settlement of the Taiwan issue, China would not "publicly contradict it." Han ended the meeting by saying that Vice Premier Deng would receive Woodcock soon.

When, on December 13, Leonard Woodcock walked into Peking's gigantic Great Hall of the People for his first meeting with Deng Xiaoping, the Chinese leader, unbeknownst to the United States, had already won over the Communist party's top leadership to his plan of a punitive attack on Vietnam. Establishment of full diplomatic relations with Washington and his own visit to the United States (Carter had sent him an invitation two days earlier), Deng had calculated, would give China an ideal opportunity to gain some added protection against Moscow and cement an effective united front with the United States before going to war with Vietnam. Woodcock later told me that he had seen occasional intelligence reports about Chinese troop movements near the Vietnamese border since November 1978, but he "was rather skeptical" about the possibility of Chinese attack.[23]

In any case, the handful of policymakers involved in the super-secret negotiations with Peking seemed almost sympathetic to China's military buildup, as opposed to their concern about Vietnamese preparation. What the United States wanted was China as a partner against Moscow. That China could be using the diplomatic ties with Washington in its power play in the region either did not occur to or did not bother the Americans. The U.S. failure to see how desperately China wanted the relations at the stage also meant that Washington gave in more on Taiwan that it perhaps needed to.

Unaware of China's plans, Woodcock was pleasantly surprised by how quickly Deng agreed to the U.S. proposal. "We will adopt the draft of the United States, and I accept the President's invitation to visit your country," he had told an amazed Woodcock. Deng even seemed in a hurry to visit Washington. He told Woodcock that he would like to go within a month of normalization—in January 1979.[24] Deng's agreement was particularly surprising, since the U.S. proposal he was now accepting was essentially the one that he had rejected when Vance had presented it to China in August 1977. Carter now proposed that the United States would maintain a full defense agreement with Taiwan for another year, that it would continue selective military sales to Taiwan after the expiration of the defense treaty, and that China would not contradict the U.S. statement about its expectation of a peaceful settlement of the Taiwan issue.[25]

Carter was thrilled with Deng's response. Essentials of a normalization agreement were at last in hand, but he did not want the news to leak and provoke opposition from friends of Taiwan in the Congress. Instead of waiting to announce the news on January 1, as originally planned, he decided to bring it forward immediately. As Carter said, "I decided to surprise Deng in return." On his instructions, Woodcock went to see Deng on the morning of December 14 to propose that the agreement be announced the next day. Final agreement on the communiqué had not yet been reached, yet Carter was asking for agreement to announce the yet-to-be concluded normalization statement! Deng was startled but he agreed.

This change in the scenario proved to be the last blow to Vance in his fight with Brzezinski over China policy. Vance's policy of a balanced relationship with China and Vietnam had suffered a setback when his recommendation about normalization with Vietnam had been shelved pending establishment of ties with China. Now his concern about the effect of the China card on U.S. relations with Moscow was also given short shrift. Vance had agreed to January 1, 1979, as target date for normalization with China. But he did not want it announced before his scheduled meeting with Soviet foreign minister Andrey Gromyko because it could adversely affect the long-negotiated SALT treaty. However, on December 14, Carter called him in Jerusalem to advise that normalization with China would be advanced to December 15—that is, before Vance's meeting with Gromyko. "The news came as a shock," Vance wrote in his memoirs. "At a critical moment Brzezinski had blocked [Deputy Secretary Warren] Christopher and [Assistant Secretary Richard] Holbrooke out of the decision making for about six hours, and they had been unable to inform me of what was taking place."[26]

While Vance was on his way back to Washington to be present at the time of the announcement, an excited Carter and Brzezinski suddenly got cold feet. Unaware that speeding-up normalization fitted beautifully with Chinese military plans, they wondered whether Deng's prompt agreement resulted from a misunderstanding of the U.S. position on Taiwan. Woodcock recalled the urgent message from Carter on the morning of December 15 (evening of December 14 in Washington) ordering him to seek yet another meeting with Deng to make sure that he understood the United States would continue to sell weapons to Taiwan after one year's moratorium. Woodcock checked the transcript of his conversation with Deng on the previous day. There could be no misunderstanding. But in another cable via the Voyager backchannel Carter insisted he see Deng once more. With unusual alacrity a meeting was set within an hour. Woodcock, accompanied by his deputy chief of mission, Stapleton

Roy, was on his way to the Great Hall of the People for his third encounter with Deng in twenty-four hours.

Deng was nonplussed. When Woodcock repeated to him the United States position on continued arms sale to Taiwan, he exploded, "Why are you bringing the arms sales question up again?" Woodcock himself was not sure why this meeting was necessary but tried to explain that the U.S. right to provide defensive arms to Taiwan was necessary for stability. "Deng just dumped his load on me. He hit me over the head. He was bitter," Woodcock recalled, seeming to relive the experience. Deng vehemently repeated China's position that Taiwan was a province of China, that it could not have independent arms relations with the United States after full normalization. "We will never agree to that," Deng declared with finality. Woodcock said that he was not seeking China's agreement on that; it was normalization he was after. Once normalization was achieved, things would start to change, Woodcock said. "The relationship between the mainland and Taiwan begins to change, our relationship to Taiwan begins to change. Over time, things that seem insoluble now become subject to solution." [27]

Deng calmed down a bit. "What shall we do?" he asked. Woodcock said, "I would earnestly suggest, Mr. Vice-Premier, we carry out the agreement we made." To Woodcock's relief, Deng said, "Okay." That shelved issue of arms sales to Taiwan would later vitiate the relations, but for the time being China's strongman Deng had claimed the trophy in the quiet race between China and Vietnam for America's friendship.

Getting Ready for the Final Act

If Peking's military preparations in southern China did not attract U.S. attention, the Vietnamese buildup along the Cambodian border did. By October 12, Vietnamese divisions, including some elite units, were deployed in Dac Lac, Tay Ninh, and An Giang provinces bordering Cambodia. After having used captured U.S. A-37 and F-5 fighter-bombers against the Khmer Rouge in June, the Vietnamese had evidently run into maintenance problems due to lack of spares. They began moving Soviet-built MiG-19s and

MiG-21s from the North to Chu Lai, Bien Hoa, and Can Tho air bases in the South.

Vietnamese preparedness also involved cautious measures against threats from Cambodia. They took quite seriously the possibility of a Cambodian air attack on Ho Chi Minh City—less than thirty minutes from Phnom Penh by air. A UN official, whose work frequently took him to South Vietnam, was surprised in November to see the outskirts of Ho Chi Minh City bristling with antiaircraft batteries and missiles pointing west. Trenches were being dug and bomb shelters built near important installations in the city. These preparations could, in part, have been designed to rally the public behind the government as it organized its operation against Cambodia, but the Vietnamese military planners also felt threatened by the possibility of a pincer attack—a Chinese-backed Khmer Rouge assault along the southwestern border and a direct Chinese move against the north. The fear was based on intelligence reports gathered since the spring of 1978 that China had not only stepped up its delivery of tanks, armored cars, and MiG-19 fighters to Cambodia but had also accelerated work on a new large airfield in Kompong Chhnang. The Vietnamese also believed that some ten thousand Chinese soldiers, advisers, and technicians were engaged in rapidly building up the Cambodian army for a drive against southern Vietnam.[28]

The fast-evolving political and diplomatic situation also added a new urgency to Vietnamese military planning. As the Vietnamese would later admit, they were concerned by clear signs of a moderate Khmer Rouge approach toward the world. In the fall of 1978, under Chinese prodding, Cambodia had come out of its isolationist, xenophobic cocoon and begun a campaign to improve its bloody image. All through the summer and autumn Cambodia had played host to a series of friendly delegations—from tiny U.S. Marxist-Leninist groups to Maoists from Belgium and Socialists from Japan. Some of those visitors had returned with glowing accounts of "progress" made in Cambodia and condemned press reports of killings as propaganda. One such American visitor wrote in the New York Times that while there may have been some excesses in Cambodia, which no revolution is immune to, a "genocide myth is being fabricated" in Bangkok by operators in Thailand who "paid up to $50 a shot for some refugees to tell good horror stories to foreigners."[29]

Cambodian deputy premier Ieng Sary had set out on a trip to Southeast Asia calling for closer ties, especially with Thailand. Malaysian and Thai foreign ministers visited Cambodia. Ieng Sary himself had launched the image-building operation by announcing at a press conference in New York, "We want you to see for yourself whether there are human rights violations" in Cambodia. Reversing an earlier stand of not bothering about international criticism, Cambodia had extended an invitation to UN Secretary-general Kurt Waldheim to visit the country and look at its human rights record. He was scheduled to visit Cambodia in February of 1979. In November Phnom Penh had granted permission to a Thai travel agency owned by Chatchai Choonhavan, the former Thai foreign minister and a close friend of Peking's, to begin one-day tourist trips to Angkor Wat. Only citizens of Vietnam, Israel, South Korea, Taiwan, and South Africa were barred from the tours, scheduled to begin in January.[30] "I was not concerned about profit. I just wanted Cambodia to open up, and the Chinese wanted it too," Chatchai told me.[31]

A Prince for All Seasons

Politically a matter of greater Vietnamese concern was the indication that the Khmer Rouge were moving toward an eventual political rehabilitation of Prince Sihanouk. While visiting the UN in October, Ieng Sary had distributed photographs of the prince at an "intimate banquet to honor the patriots" in Phnom Penh in September.[32]

The Vietnamese feared not only that restoration of Sihanouk would make the Khmer Rouge less of a pariah but that it would also counter Hanoi's own plan of using his name to win domestic and international support for the anti–Pol Pot resistance. In early October 1978, a member of the Vietnamese delegation to UNESCO in Paris quietly traveled to a city in the French Midi to meet one of the brightest of Sihanouk's many children—Prince Norodom Ranaridh, who taught law at the University of Aix-en-Provence. With his round head, big rolling eyes, and ready smile, Ranaridh was a young replica of his father. As he recalled, the visitor arrived with a letter of introduction from a common Vietnamese friend and identified himself as a special Vietnamese emissary. He praised Sihanouk for his role as the builder of modern Cambodia and confided that the Vietnamese hoped to "liberate" him from the Khmer Rouge so that he could again play a leading role in the resistance against the Pol Pot regime. "We want you to work for the new Cambodian resistance as a representative of Samdech Sihanouk," the Vietnamese told him. Ranaridh profusely thanked the visitor for Vietnam's concern for his father but refused to commit himself to any cooperation. "I did not know what was the condition of my father in captivity. I did not know what the Vietnamese were really up to," Ranaridh later told me, explaining his reticence. He had a better idea of what was happening when the Vietnamese emissary visited him again in mid-December. "It must have been a week or ten days before Christmas because I had just put up the Christmas tree and lights when he arrived again," he recalled. "This time the Vietnamese asked me to accept the position of a representative at large of the newly announced Cambodian national salvation front. I again declined." [33]

The failure to enlist the support of one of Sihanouk's progeny or any known non-Communist Cambodian figure to lend respectability to the Hanoi-backed resistance and Phnom Penh's public relations offensive meant a considerable narrowing of the Vietnamese window of opportunity. The time when Vietnamese intervention in Cambodia could enjoy international support or complicity was running out fast. Although Waldheim did not accept the invitation for a visit, the opening of Cambodia and the varnishing of its pariah image through a controlled exposure now threatened to complicate Vietnamese planning. If the Vietnamese army had to march in to install a guerrilla government in Cambodia, Hanoi calculated, it was now or never.

With the military alliance with Moscow sealed and diplomatic maneuvering over, the Vietnamese turned their full attention to the final preparation for the Cambodia operation. Events had moved faster than Hanoi leaders had foreseen. Some two hundred former Khmer Rouge cadres and Hanoi-trained Cambodian exiles who had gath-

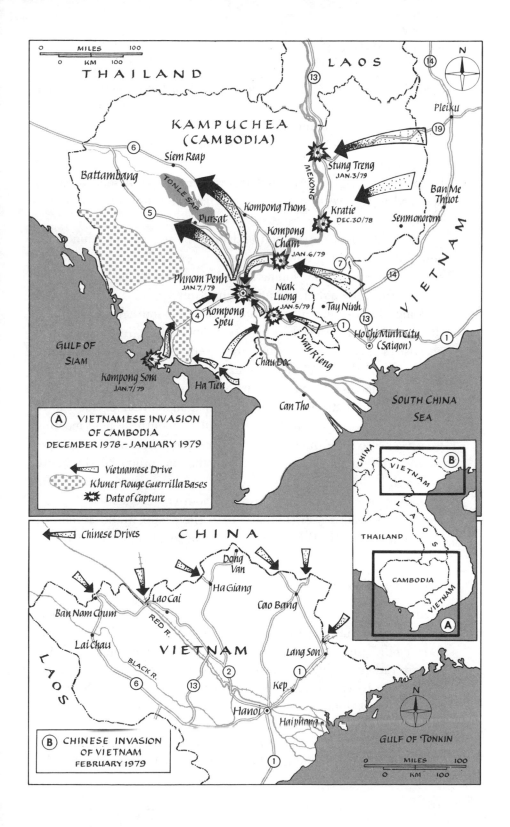

THAILAND

LAOS

N

KAMPUCHEA
(CAMBODIA)

Siem Reap

Battambang

TONLE SAP

Pursat

Kompong Thom

MEKONG

Stung Treng
JAN.3/79

Pleiku

Kratie
DEC.30/78

Senmonorom

Ban Me
Thuot

Kompong
Cham
JAN.6/79

Phnom Penh
JAN.7/79

Neak
Luong
JAN.5/79

Tay Ninh

Kompong
Speu

Chau Doc

Svay Rieng

Ho Chi Minh City
(Saigon)

VIETNAM

GULF OF
SIAM

Kompong Som
JAN.7/79

Ha Tien

Can Tho

SOUTH CHINA
SEA

A VIETNAMESE INVASION
OF CAMBODIA
DECEMBER 1978 – JANUARY 1979

Vietnamese Drive

Khmer Rouge Guerrilla Bases

Date of Capture

CHINA

B

VIETNAM

THAILAND

CAMBODIA

VIETNAM

A

Chinese Drives

CHINA

Dong
Van

Ha Giang

Cao Bang

Lao Cai

RED R.

Ban Nam Coum

Lai Chau

BLACK R.

VIETNAM

Lang Son

Kep

Hanoi

Haiphong

LAOS

B CHINESE INVASION
OF VIETNAM
FEBRUARY 1979

GULF OF TONKIN

N

MILES 100

KM 100

ered in South Vietnam were determined to fight Pol Pot but had not yet ironed out political differences in order to be able to form a new Cambodian Communist party to lead the struggle. But time was pressing. The Vietnamese could not afford to sit around until a party congress was held and a new party leadership was formed. Even without a party, a Cambodian liberation front had to be announced to the world before the Vietnamese army could move into action.

The political indoctrination and military training of Khmers begun since early 1978 now moved to a fever pitch. One way of telescoping the process and eliminating delays caused by linguistic barriers was to enlist the aid of the important Khmer minority living in the Mekong Delta—known as Khmer Krom, or southern Khmer. Although politically they had always been suspect in Hanoi's eyes, because of their bilingual ability they were seen as useful auxiliaries to be used with the Vietnamese army inside Cambodia. Major Say Pak, a Cambodian Communist who had lived in Hanoi since 1954, arrived in the delta province of Bac Lieu in November 1978 to recruit Khmer Krom youth. Every week for a month he held meetings in a pagoda to urge them to join in the Cambodian liberation movement. After total liberation of Cambodia, he promised the youth, "you will be holding responsible positions in the government." After an induction ceremony, five hundred youths were sent to Ca Mau for military training. In January 1979 the group would accompany Vietnamese units in their drive into Cambodia's Takeo Province.

A Backdoor Entry for the Front

An interesting glimpse of behind-the-scenes Vietnamese preparation for launching the Cambodian front was given by Dinh Can, a former officer in the South Vietnamese army engineering corps. Can got off rather "lightly" from the reeducation camp for old-regime officers run by Hanoi. Hanoi needed the services of this U S.–trained engineer in its 476th Engineering Division to build roads and bridges in Dac Lac, Song Be, and Tay Ninh provinces bordering Cambodia. His suspicion that the Vietnamese were planning something in Cambodia had grown since the summer of 1978 when orders had come for urgent repair work on routes leading to Cambodia. Since October, Vietnamese units had actually occupied stretches of Cambodian territory along the border. In mid-November the Vietnamese army had launched a big operation in Cambodia's Kratie Province along Route 13. The bloody battle had ended with near decimation of a Khmer Rouge division and had secured the area for use as a "liberated zone." But its intended purpose was not clear to Can until later that month when he saw a helicopter land amidst a swirl of red dust at his work headquarters near the border. To his surprise, the visitors were none other than Le Duc Tho and General Dong Van Cong, deputy commander of the Seventh Military Region. They had come to supervise the launching of the Cambodian resistance organization and the installation of a forward headquarters for the Vietnamese army.

The site chosen for unveiling the newest Cambodian liberation front—the Kampuchean National United Front for National Salvation (KNUFNS)—was two miles inside Cambodia. It was a small clearing in the middle of a rubber plantation east of the Cambodian township of Snoul. Can drove an army bulldozer to the site to level the ground. The men from the 476th Division set up a dais and a public address system. On the morning of December 2, 1978, several thousand Khmers gathered in the bright sunshine to witness the formal launching of the KNUFNS. Most of the assembled men and women had come in a convoy of trucks from Khmer refugee camps in Vietnam. Several hundred front soldiers composed of deserters from Khmer Rouge divisions as well as ones trained in Vietnam also had assembled, proudly sporting their new green uniforms and caps. A newly written national anthem was sung as dozens of newly fashioned red-and-yellow front flags fluttered in a gentle breeze.

One after another, fourteen members of the front Central Committee were given bouquets of flowers brought from Vietnam as they were introduced to the cheering crowd. Front chairman Heng Samrin read out the KNUFNS program as those assembled shouted in approval with raised fists. After the meeting, Heng Samrin walked up to thank Le Duc Tho, who had watched the ceremony from a distance like a proud mother hen. "I did not think you would have done things so perfectly," a beaming Samrin told Tho.[34]

After the meeting, resistance army units and the front leaders set out to visit villages along the border from which Khmer Rouge units had withdrawn. They explained to the population the eleven-point program of the front to oust the Pol Pot regime and restore family life, markets, money, and religion and to put an end to the border war with Vietnam.[35] A radio station in Ho Chi Minh City, calling itself "Voice of the Kampuchean People," began broadcasting the front program and reports of struggle. Thousands of leaflets calling for an uprising against the Pol Pot regime were dropped by Vietnamese aircraft over Cambodian provinces close to the border.

The founding of the front seemed like a rerun of an old movie. Twenty-eight years after the Vietnamese helped to set up the first Cambodian national liberation organization—the United Issarak Front—to fight against French rule and eight years after they joined hands with the anti–U.S. National United Front of Cambodia, the Vietnamese were back again promoting another "liberation struggle" in the neighboring country.[36] Even the Vietnamese leader in charge of training Khmer resistance cadres was the same Le Duc Tho who helped set up the United Issarak Front and had been in charge of a special Politburo office for Cambodia since 1966.[37] However, the enemy this time was neither French colonialism nor U.S. imperialism but Hanoi's onetime Communist allies.

A striking symbol of the return to the old tradition of Cambodia-Vietnam collaboration was the new flag—five yellow towers on a red background. This banner, originally used by the Khmer Issarak in the 1950s, was abandoned by the Pol Pot group in 1975 when Democratic Kampuchea adopted a three-towered red flag.

The symbolism was, however, lost on most Cambodians, whose principal concern was the life and death of families and friends still left under Khmer Rouge control. It was the common hatred for the Pol Pot regime that had brought together under Vietnamese guidance the disparate collection of survivors—middle-class refugees, escapees, defectors. Many of the assembled Khmers both on the dias and among the crowd harbored grave doubts about Vietnam's ulterior motives, but they saw no other alternative to seeking help to fight the murderous regime that seemed to threaten the existence of Cambodia. The fourteen Central Committee members presented at the meeting represented that uneasy coalition. Six of them, including Chairman Heng Samrin, were former Khmer Rouge, four were pro-Hanoi Cambodian Communists (Khmer Issarak), and the other four included urban intellectuals and a monk.[38]

While the meeting was in progress, Vietnamese regular units ringed the area and antiaircraft gunners kept a wary eye on the horizon. After the ceremony was over, Dinh Can and his men were ordered to clear a wooded area a little more than a mile inside Cambodia's Kratie Province to be used as the forward headquarters of the Vietnamese army. Aluminum container boxes, which once dotted American bases in Vietnam, were brought in, thatched houses and bunkers built, electrical generators and radio equipment set up under the trees. The headquarters, named Tien Phong, or "Vanguard," was soon to unleash a storm on Cambodia.

A Campaign Begins

The opening shot of the military campaign, however, was fired from the Central Highlands township of Ban Me Thuot. Seizure of this town in a surprise attack in March 1975 marked the beginning of the "Ho Chi Minh Campaign," which ended with the capture of Saigon. The strategically located town was again chosen for a place of pride in Vietnam's military history. At midnight of December 24, as bells chimed in the cathedral dominating the small town, General Chu Huy Man, director of the General Political Department of the Vietnam People's Army (VPA), lifted his pistol to fire a shot in the air to officially launch the campaign. General Man had come down from Hanoi for the ceremonial launching of an operation to be led by General Hoang Cam. "General Cam knows eastern Cambodia like the back of his hand," a Vietnamese official later told me, "because he led all the major military campaigns against Lon Nol in the 1970s." Under a cold, starlit sky, columns of Vietnamese T-54 tanks and trucks laden with troops began to rumble down Route 14 leading toward Cambodia. Within five days, the Vietnamese forces had routed the Khmer Rouge garrison and captured the province capital, Kratie.[39]

Kratie is one Cambodian town the Vietnamese knew well. After "liberating" it from Lon Nol hands in 1970, the Vietnamese set up a military training school where they trained hundreds of Khmer Rouge in commando operations. Now, nine years later, the Vietnamese snatched the town back from their old pupils to hand over to their newest Khmer allies.

By January 1, 1979, Vietnamese forces advancing from Laos along the Mekong captured the second provincial capital, Stung Treng. Capture of the two major towns on the Mekong had effectively cut off all four provinces in the northeast from the rest of the country. Though sparsely populated by Montagnards, the forest-covered hills of the northeast which were the anti–Lon Nol resistance base in the 1970s had again become a "liberated zone" for Cambodia's newest front.

Meanwhile, Vietnamese divisions from the Seventh and Ninth Military Regions, under the overall command of General Le Duc Anh, began a massive push along Route 1 and Route 7, both leading toward the Mekong River. For nearly a week before beginning the tank-led push, the Vietnamese air force mounted an intense bombing attack on Khmer Rouge positions. By concentrating some thirty thousand men—half of the Khmer Rouge regular force—in an arc along the Parrot's Beak and Fishhook areas near the Vietnamese border, Pol Pot made their destruction easier. These troops were decimated by a combination of artillery fire and aerial bombing after being picked up by spotter aircraft. There was surprisingly little resistance from Pol Pot's peasant army, which knew how to kill with machetes but had not had time to learn to fly fighter planes or man antiaircraft guns. Most of the Chinese advisers and instructors were quickly pulled out by sea, leaving the untrained Khmers to fend for themselves. Rows of brand-new MiG-19s painted with the Democratic Kampuchean colors sat in Pochentong Airport, some even in mothballs, when the Vietnamese reached Phnom Penh to claim the booty.

Despite the bombing raids, the ground assault was not easy. Colonel Bui Tin, who watched the battles from a helicopter and took photographs, told me that the heaviest battle of the campaign before capture of Phnom Penh was fought in the Fishhook area. Fighting raged for two days as the Vietnamese tried to go across a defense perimeter along irrigation canals and minefields. Once that hurdle was crossed, the Vietnamese moved swiftly up to the Mekong River opposite the provincial capital of Kompong Cham. The two other big battles of the operation were fought at Neak Luong, the Mekong ferry town on Route 1, and at Tani (Takeo Province) on Route 3, leading to the coast.[40] A Vietnamese commando unit managed to reach the banks of Tonle Sap River, facing Phnom Penh. Their attempt on the early morning of January 2 to cross the river and "liberate" Prince Sihanouk from his guarded residence was however foiled. "They came across the river to kidnap me, but they all got killed," Sihanouk told me with a sigh of regret. "At that time I did not know why suddenly that evening [January 2] Khieu Samphan came to tell me, 'You have fifteen minutes to get ready to leave. I was then taken to Battambang and Sisophon."[41]

By January 4 the Vietnamese had gained total control of the east bank of the Mekong, comprising seven provinces, but the prospect of putting Sihanouk at the head of the Salvation Front controlling this vast "liberated zone" had vanished.

After a day of lull the final order came from the Politburo on the night of January 4: "Go for Phnom Penh." On January 6 the Vietnamese units crossed the Mekong at Neak Luong and north of Kompong Cham. Soviet-built pontoon bridges and big U.S.–made ferryboats brought up the river from Vietnam carried tanks and troops to the western bank. Soon nine of Vietnam's twelve divisions, accompanied by three regiments of front soldiers, would close in on Phnom Penh from the southeast and the north. By the morning of January 7, Vietnamese artillery started hitting the outskirts of Phnom Penh. All of a sudden two of the capital's important accesses—Route 1 and Route 7—were blocked by the advancing Vietnamese columns.

The Party Is Over

Judging by all accounts, the scenes on the last day of Phnom Penh could have been from a Fellini film. The city's only working hospital overflowed with wounded soldiers arriving from the front. Hundreds of them lay in the courtyard and on the street outside the

343

hospital, covered with blood and flies and screaming in agony. In other parts of the city it was time for feasting and ceremony. The traditional fishing season began in late December and early January when bamboo traps set in the Tonle Sap River disgorged tons of fish. On the morning of January 6 two truckloads of fish were delivered to "Bar 30," a camp that housed junior cadres and their families. To people who had lived on a near-starvation diet for months, the sight of fish alone was heartening. Immediately, a festive atmosphere set in. Everybody in the camp got busy cleaning the fish before they could rot. The camp inmates ate their fill for lunch and got to work on the rest to prepare them for dinner and to preserve them for coming months. But suddenly the party was over. The order was given to prepare for immediate evacuation. "Leave just now?" one woman asked in disbelief. "And our fish?" A three-foot-high mountain of fish lay in the communal kitchen glistening in the light of the dim kerosene lamp as a cold panic overtook the inmates.[42]

Another party was abandoned at the Phnom Penh textile mill not far away from the camp. On the same day the Khmer Rouge had given permission to the workers to slaughter pigs and chickens for a banquet celebrating the first anniversary of the "historic victory" over Vietnam. The banquet was almost ready when the workers were ordered to immediately proceed to the railway station for evacuation.[43]

Clearly, the lull in the Vietnamese attack since the night of January 3 gave Phnom Penh a false sense of security. Even on the evening of January 5 Pol Pot confidently told Sihanouk that within two months his forces would wipe out the Vietnamese. Although on Peking's advice the Khmer Rouge had built arms caches in the Cardamom Mountains as a contingency for abandoning the capital, and although in an interview with the Chinese news agency Xinhua on December 11 Pol Pot had declared his government ready to engage the advancing Vietnamese in a "protracted war," they simply had not foreseen such a sudden collapse of their defense. By the time Pol Pot realized that there was no victory round the corner, it was too late. Within less than twenty-four hours the capital had to be abandoned, leaving behind not only unfinished meals and tons of rotting fish but also mountains of weapons and ammunition and a self-incriminating archive at Tuol Sleng prison. Even one of the most wanted men of the regime, "Deuch," who headed Tuol Sleng Prison, almost got left behind. He managed to slip out of Phnom Penh well after the Vietnamese moved in. The Chinese ambassador and several hundred advisers left Phnom Penh in time, but they abandoned almost everything. For the Vietnamese one of the most gladdening finds in the Chinese embassy was a cellar full of French cognac.

Was Phnom Penh's collapse a surprise to the Vietnamese as well? No definitive answer to that is available yet. Unlike the "Ho Chi Minh Campaign" to capture Saigon, which produced two memoirs by the generals involved,[44] none has been written so far about Vietnam's Cambodia venture.

Those memoirs about the 1975 campaign reveal that according to the original Vietnamese Politburo plan adopted in December 1974, the Vietnam People's Army was to step up the military and political struggle in 1975–76 "so that conditions will be ripe to carry out a general offensive and uprising . . . and liberate the South."[45]

But after the initial push in the Central Highlands in March 1975 the South Vietnamese regime crumbled so fast that the Politburo decided to seize the strategic opportunity and "liberate Saigon before the rainy season." Was the capture of Phnom Penh in 1979 a repeat of the seizure of Saigon four years earlier? Or did the Vietnamese set out to occupy the whole country and install a client regime? Judging by the speed with which the Vietnamese captured Phnom Penh and set up a new government, most observers concluded that this indeed was the objective. But enough indications have surfaced since to suggest that, like that of Saigon in 1975, the seizure of Phnom Penh, too, might have been the product of strategic opportunism.

One of the most interesting pieces of evidence of that hypothesis came from interviews by two Salvation Front leaders. Chea Soth, one of the founders of the front and a Politburo member of the Kampuchean People's Revolutionary Party (KPRP), admitted to Stephen Heder in 1981 that initially they did not think taking over the country was possible. He said, "We were just thinking in terms of taking over half the country, the half on one side of the Mekong, and leaving the rest to Pol Pot." That plan was changed after the initial Vietnamese military success. It was decided to capture Phnom Penh if possible and fight a protracted war. "We didn't think we were going to take over everything all at once. But then when the attack was launched and there was no resistance, they [the Pol Pot forces] just kept withdrawing, we just kept going and going. . . . When we knew that this was the situation [Phnom Penh was evacuated], we just came right in to Phnom Penh. There wasn't any point in letting it remain unoccupied!"[46]

Another KPRP Central Committee member, Hem Samin, also told Heder in a separate interview that the original plan was to attack and "take just one bank of the Mekong. But then when we attacked and pursued them and saw how easy it was, we just kept going."[47]

These remarks were also supported by clear indications of hasty preparations by the front to catch up with events. Although the offensive had begun in late December, it was not until January 6 that the front broadcast an eight-point "immediate" program to be applied in the "liberated zones" of Cambodia. The program was adopted on January 5, when after many postponements a congress was held in Mimot in Kompong Cham Province to reorganize the Communist party. The congress was still in progress in order to elect a new platform and leadership when at noon on January 7 the electrifying news came over the radio. Phnom Penh had been liberated. The newly formed party was immediately called upon to assign duties among sixty-six delegates assembled for the congress.[48]

On January 8, while the front leaders awaited the all-clear signal from the Vietnamese army to proceed to Phnom Penh, the front radio announced that after liberation of Phnom Penh by the "revolutionary armed forces and the people of Cambodia" an eight-member Revolutionary Council had been installed, headed by Heng Samrin. The former Khmer Rouge division commander who had fled to Vietnam only four months earlier was suddenly Cambodia's new head of state.

The haste with which Hanoi commandeered the services of Vietnamese civilians—technicians and bureaucrats—to take charge of things in Cambodia also indicated an uncharacteristic lack of plan-

346

ning if the Vietnamese had indeed wished to take over Cambodia. Another interesting indication that the initial Vietnamese objective may not have been full control over the country was the fact, as observed by U.S. intelligence, that Vietnamese tanks ran out of gas on their way to Kompong Thom on Route 6. As they waited for fuel, several tanks were destroyed by the retreating Khmer Rouge. It took the Vietnamese a week before the refueled armored column could finally reach Battambang.[49]

And although by the third week of January the Vietnamese army had occupied the strategic shell of Cambodia—its major towns and the highways—it was not before April 1979 that with proper reinforcements it would be able to launch a major sweep operation against the stronghold of Ta Sanh, set up by the retreating Khmer Rouge close to the Thai border.

Since the last flight had taken off from Pochentong Airport on January 6 and the last train with Ieng Sary on board had left Phnom Penh station on the morning of the seventh, Thailand's border with Cambodia became the country's only exit to the world. Weary and harassed Chinese, Yugoslav, and other Phnom Penh–based diplomats, as well as several hundred Chinese advisers and technicians, had streamed across the border to the safety of Thailand. "For China," a Thai Foreign Ministry official recalled, "it was a moment of unprecedented humiliation." Never before had an envoy of the Middle Kingdom had to flee from a former tributary country in such disgrace. Thais, of course, gave the Chinese a most courteous reception. Quiet arrangements were made for Chinese Boeing 707s to land, ironically enough, at the former U.S. air base of Utapao to pick up the Chinese evacuees from Cambodia. Only a few years earlier Peking had stridently denounced the bases as beachheads for "American imperialist aggression."

On January 11, 1979, Ieng Sary arrived at the Thai border hungry and exhausted. In the melee of the flight to the frontier he had lost his sandals. Chinese diplomats from Bangkok had taken fresh clothes and shoes for him. A Thai army helicopter secretly flew Sary and his associates, which included broadcasters from Radio Phnom Penh, to Bangkok's Don Muang Airport. There, they were put on Thai International's regular flight to Hongkong en route to China.

A *Secret Mission to Utapao*

The documents captured by the Vietnamese at Ta Sanh included transcripts of talks between the Chinese leaders and Ieng Sary held on four different occasions. At a meeting on January 13, 1979, Deng scolded Sary for "the cleansing campaign you are conducting—a campaign somewhat excessive and of too broad a scope." The Khmer Rouge purges, Deng bluntly told him, caused China inconveniences and brought "quite a few negative results." He pointed to the Chinese example of united fronts with lesser enemies, such as the one formed with Chiang Kai-shek during the anti-Japanese war, and he urged Sary to draw Prince Sihanouk into a front. "We would lose a great deal," he said, "if we failed to unite with him. So at the opportune moment and in the near future, I would ask you to reserve the post of head of state for Sihanouk. Comrade Pol Pot will be prime minister in charge of national defense and supreme commander." If the Cambodian party agreed to this suggestion the Chinese would "lend a hand." Deng had bluntly set the price. He also advised Sary to change the Khmer Rouge propaganda tune. "For the moment don't put the Communist party in the foreground; rather, emphasize patriotism, nationalism, and democracy."

Deng informed him that China had put at Cambodia's disposal a fund of $5 million, which would be replenished as soon as it was exhausted. "How shall we send you money? Via Bangkok? Via Kriangsak? Via the Bank of Thailand?" Deng asked. Sary prudently suggested, "We would rather have it deposited at the Chinese embassy in Bangkok." [50]

On January 13, within hours of attending the meeting between Deng and Sary, two of China's senior policymakers—Politburo member Geng Biao and Vice–Foreign Minister Han Nianlong— rushed to Peking airport to board a Boeing 707 of China's national carrier, CAAC, on a secret mission. The hastily arranged flight, carrying Geng, Han, and several senior members of the Chinese PLA General Staff, was bound for Utapao. Thai premier Kriangsak flew into the air base to greet the visitors. January 14 was spent in long sessions discussing the modalities of Sino-Thai cooperation in the Cambodian war. Much water had flowed down the Mekong since

Deng had raised the idea of collaboration with China in suport of the Khmer Rouge. While still maintaining his stance of neutrality, Kriangsak was now ready for a deal with Peking. As a senior Thai official revealed to me years later, it was at that secret meeting between Chinese and Thai military leaders that a foundation of de facto Sino-Thai alliance was laid.[51] After that one-day meeting Chinese officials flew back to Peking with Sun Hao, the evacuated Chinese ambassador from Phnom Penh, and one of the most important agreements in their briefcases. Kriangsak agreed to allow the use of Thai territory to supply the Khmer Rouge and provide transport and transit facilities for Cambodian personnel and materiel and also help Khmer Rouge leaders to make foreign trips through Thailand.[52] This proved to be the beginning of the most significant strategic relation developed by Peking in post-Vietnam Southeast Asia.

Two Chinese freighters, which were steaming toward Cambodia laden with arms when Phnom Penh fell, were now ordered to drop anchor at a Thai port near the Cambodian coast. Chinese aircraft also flew secret flights carrying emergency supplies to the former U.S. air base at Takhli.

On January 16—two days after the secret Thai-Chinese meeting—the Voice of Democratic Kampuchea, which had fallen silent on January 7, was back on the air with the same announcers making the habitual pledge of unrelenting struggle against the Vietnamese aggressors. The only difference was, as U.S. intelligence noted, that the Cambodian voices were beamed from transmitters inside China.

While logistical groundwork was being laid in Thailand for sustaining a guerrilla resistance movement against the Vietnamese—very much the way Deng had predicted during his trip to Thailand two months earlier—China began a massive movement of troops, armor, and aircraft closer to Vietnam. During his trip to Thailand Geng Biao in fact had tried to cheer Kriangsak in his new role as an ally of the Khmer Rouge by pointing to the forthcoming punishment of Vietnam. "It is not for the mere sake of intimidation that China has sent troops to Guangdong and Yunnan: we have anticipated all possible reactions," he told the Thai leader.[53]

Brzezinski Wins a Skirmish in Washington

The announcement of normalization of its relations with the United States and the snapping of ties between Taiwan and Washington now enabled China to transfer its divisions from provinces facing the Taiwan Strait to the Vietnamese and Soviet borders. By the end of January, some seventeen regular divisions, or about 225,000 men, were assembled near the Vietnamese border. Over seven hundred fighter aircraft and bombers—a fifth of the Chinese air force—were brought to airfields close to the frontier. On January 19, U.S. intelligence issued its second "alert memorandum" for top officials about the Chinese buildup. At least some of them, especially in the State Department, were concerned by these obvious preparations for an attack on the eve of Deng Xiaoping's visit to the United States. "We don't know what he [Deng] is trying to pull," an agitated official told the *Washington Post's* diplomatic correspondent, Don Oberdorfer. "He may be sucking us into his attack, hoping for at least an aroma of collusion."[54] Richard Holbrooke summoned Chinese ambassador Chai Zemin twice in the week before Deng's arrival to warn him that an attack on Vietnam during the visit would deeply embarrass the United States.[55]

The Chinese obliged, not because they did not want to embarrass Washington but because their timetable for attack put it at a later date. "When Vice-Chairman Deng left for Washington," a Chinese official told me in March 1979, "we had already decided on the time of attack. He did not go there to get American assent, just moral support." In the end China got more than that. In a lasting irony of history, China went to war against Vietnam with discreet American blessing. Few cared to remember that one of the original justifications for the American intervention in Vietnam was to stop "Chinese expansionism" and that the insignia of the U.S. Military Assistance Command in Vietnam (MACV) was an American sword piercing a stylized Great Wall representing China.

Deng was direct about what he wanted from his trip to the United States. He wanted support and understanding of the planned invasion of Vietnam for the benefit of Moscow and Hanoi and to impress doubters in the Chinese party. On the very first night of his arrival in Washington on January 28, he told Brzezinski that he wanted a private meeting with Carter to discuss Vietnam. At the opening session of talks at the White House the next day Deng reminded Carter that "both the United States and China had long and unpleasant contacts with the Vietnamese." In the evening, when it was almost time to prepare for the banquet, he urged Carter to meet in a smaller group to discuss a confidential matter. Carter left the Cabinet Room to retire into the Oval Office with Mondale, Vance, Harold Brown, and Brzezinski to listen to Deng outline his plans for an attack on Vietnam. Puffing on his Panda cigarette, he calmly declared that China must disrupt Soviet strategic calculations. "We consider it necessary to put a restraint on the wild ambitions of the Vietnamese and to give them an appropriate limited lesson." He assured that the attack would be limited in scope and duration. All that he asked for was America's "moral support" in the international arena.[56]

With Deng's proposing a de facto alliance against Moscow and seeking U.S. support for his Vietnam adventure, the Brzezinski-Vance struggle had reached a new peak. On the eve of Deng's visit Vance announced that the U.S. policy toward Moscow and Peking "will be balanced and there will be no tilts one way or the other."[57]

In order to avoid joining voice with China against "hegemonism" the State Department tried to avoid issuing a formal communiqué. But Brzezinski had again scored over Vance. Not only did Carter rebuff these efforts, but at Brzezinski's suggestion he even deleted from the joint statement the balancing disclaimer of two previous Sino-American statements that their ties were "not directed at other states." Prior to Deng's meeting with Carter, Brzezinski had tried to soften Carter's likely opposition to the idea of Chinese punishment. As he later wrote, "I was worried that the President might be persuaded by Vance to put maximum pressure on the Chinese not to use force, since this would simply convince the Chinese that the United States was a 'paper tiger.' "[58] It was, however, more than a desire to prove American macho. In Brzezinski's own words, he and some of his friends who had been "intimately involved in the discussions that took place prior to the Chinese attempt at giving Vietnam a 'lesson' . . . perceived potential benefits as well."[59]

Dazzle of Raw Power

Judging by Carter's and Brzezinski's accounts, both were tremendously impressed by this small, tough leader from a former enemy country talking imperiously about administering "lessons."[60] To Brzezinski, Deng's discussion of his plan to attack Vietnam was the "single most impressive demonstration of raw power politics" that he ever encountered in his four years at the White House. "I secretly wished," he later wrote, "that Deng's appreciation of the uses of power would also rub off on some of the key U.S. decision makers."[61] It is safe to assume that one decision maker he had in mind was Vance, who not only disapproved of a Chinese "lesson" but was also seriously concerned that the White House's handling of Deng's visit would lead Moscow to conclude there was Sino-American collusion.[62] But Carter had rejected what he considered to be Vance's "apologetic" approach toward a relationship with China.[63]

This meant Deng got almost all he wanted. While Deng publicly denounced the Soviet Union, questioned the value of the SALT II agreement that the United States had so patiently worked out with Moscow, and issued threats against Vietnam, Carter, the fascinated and polite host, made no effort to contradict or even dissociate himself from Chinese statements. During his restricted meeting with Deng on January 29, Carter made a halfhearted attempt to discourage the Chinese leader, but he never hinted that the contemplated Chinese action would affect Sino-American ties. He did not question the end, only the means. Carter argued that the Vietnamese were increasingly isolated in the world because of their Cambodia invasion and that a Chinese move against them might arouse sympathy. However, finding Deng unmoved in his determination to punish Vietnam, Carter proposed another meeting. On the morning of January 30 they met again in the Oval Office with only one interpreter present. Carter then did something strange. He read aloud and then handed over to Deng a handwritten letter summarizing his arguments discouraging a Chinese invasion. The purpose seems to have been to put on record his opposition while fully expecting Deng not to pay it any heed. "My impression was," Carter wrote, "that the decision had already been made. Vietnam would be punished."[64]

The contents of the letter were not disclosed, but Brzezinski later justified presenting the letter as the right approach because, as he noted with striking candor, "we could not collude formally with the Chinese in sponsoring what was tantamount to an overt military aggression. At the same time, the letter did not lock the United States into a position which could generate later pressure to condemn China in the UN."

In any case, lest the Chinese take these formal protestations seriously, in a private meeting with Chinese foreign minister Huang Hua the same day, Brzezinski indicated that the only real U.S. worry was possible Soviet reaction to the Chinese move. He tried to "encourage the Chinese to concentrate on a swift and decisive move and not undertake a prolonged engagement"—something that Deng himself had already promised Carter. As Brzezinski noted in his memoirs, "as a particular gesture of friendship, I went out to the helipad near the Washington Monument to bid good-bye to Deng personally. I wanted to underline presidential support and Deng gave me the impression of being quite pleased." If Carter had really meant to dissuade China from attacking Vietnam, Brzezinski did not serve his boss by this symbolic underlining of presidential support. In fact, Carter, torn between his Christian pacifism and the urge to be a tough-minded President, seemed to have chosen the easy way out— a formal opposition and a wink. When the much-awaited Chinese invasion began sixteen days later, Washington acted to shield Peking from Soviet retaliation by urging restraint on Moscow and by linking good Soviet behavior with the signing of SALT II.[65]

If Carter and Brzezinski went through the motions of opposing a Chinese attack on Vietnam, some of the congressional leaders were very straightforward in supporting Deng. During a meeting on Capitol Hill, House Speaker Tip O'Neill told Deng that if adventurous Vietnam was not restrained, there might be a Third World War. When the Japanese attacked Manchuria in 1931, the world did not do anything, he said, and then it found itself in the midst of the Second World War. Deng was taken aback by this somewhat strained analogy, but he told the Speaker that although Vietnam's situation was not exactly the same, it was still necessary to "teach Vietnam a lesson."[66]

Addressing a press conference in Washington at the end of his talks with the administration and congressional leaders, Deng announced, "We call the Vietnamese the Cubans of the Orient. If you don't teach them some necessary lessons, their provocations will increase. . . . But as to what action to take, we will have to wait and see. I can say two things: one, we Chinese mean what we say; and two, we do not act rashly."[67]

A Message to Moscow

Deng was being brutally honest. Hasty normalization with the United States and his private meetings and public utterances were carefully measured steps in the Chinese plan to attack Vietnam. Unlike the Vietnamese, who sought to retain an element of surprise by disclaiming any intention to invade Cambodia, the Chinese pursued a strategy that depended on disclosure. By carefully telegraphing its intention to all concerned, China tried to create an environment of understanding, if not complicity, for its pedagogical war. On his way back from the United States, Deng stopped in Tokyo. He outlined to the Japanese leaders the plan for attack on Vietnam and also China's calculations about the limited nature of the probable Soviet reaction. Deng also told them that he had already apprised President Carter of China's planned punitive action against Vietnam.[68]

This revelation and the lack of any public Washington response to the threat strengthened Japanese suspicions about Sino-American collusion. Despite their own opposition to the idea, in deference to Washington, the Japanese only expressed mild disapproval.[69]

On February 9, the day after Deng's return from Tokyo, the Chinese party Central Military Commission opened a three-day meeting under Deng's chairmanship to make the final decision. Deng told the commission about the favorable attitude among the Western nations as well as the ASEAN countries. The only thing to consider carefully was possible Soviet reaction. In his view there were three possibilities: Moscow could engage in rhetorical condemnation, launch a limited punitive raid across the border, or mount a full-scale invasion. He argued that the third was the least likely course and the first the most likely. China, he said, was prepared to face the second eventuality of a limited Soviet attack.[70]

Ironically, Deng's confidence about Soviet inaction was based on the importance Moscow attached to SALT II—the very agreement he denounced. His assumption (which proved to be right) was that Moscow was too interested in SALT to get involved in hostilities. The United States was also expected to pressure Moscow not to jeopardize the arms limitation treaty by taking military action against China. Deng had told both the Americans and the Japanese that the invasion would be limited in scope and would not last more than twenty days, and he perhaps expected that that assurance would be transmitted to the Kremlin.[71]

But Peking did not rely only on the American and Japanese channels. On February 12, a young French diplomat in Manila was surprised by a call from Xiao Fei, a Chinese colleague and cocktail-party acquaintance. He urgently wanted a meeting. Barely installed in the diplomat's office at the French embassy that afternoon, Xiao breathlessly announced the reason for the meeting. China, he solemnly declared, had reached its tether's end and would punish Vietnam very shortly. "Like our punitive attack on India in 1962, this one too would be limited in time and space," he assured. How would Moscow take it? the French diplomat had inquired. "They have assured us that they will not intervene," Xiao replied confidently. The Frenchman was intrigued by this bizarre revelation about the coming war and promptly drafted a cable for the Quai d'Orsay. As the result of some bureaucratic mixup, the young diplomat's February 12 dispatch announcing the Chinese invasion was not cabled but put in the diplomatic pouch and reached Paris two days after the "lesson" had begun.[72]

Thus Paris did not have the chance either to alert Hanoi or test Moscow's reaction to the Chinese claim, but one can safely assume that similar assurance about the limited nature of the operation had gotten through to the Soviet Union by the morning of February 17, when hundreds of Chinese guns opened up a deadly artillery barrage all along the Vietnamese border.

On the morning of February 16 Washington time, exactly six hours before the attack began, Chinese ambassador to the United

States Chai Zemin had delivered to the White House a message announcing the start of a "self-defense measure" against Vietnam. Peking had chosen its time well. Indian foreign minister Atal Behari Vajpayee was visiting China after seventeen years of frosty relations that followed the 1962 war. Few, certainly not the Vietnamese, expected China to spoil this new thaw by mounting an attack on India's friend Vietnam while Vajpayee was still in China. In fact, Hanoi was so confident that on February 16 Premier Pham Van Dong, along with Chief of Staff Van Tien Dung and other senior leaders, had left for Phnom Penh on a four-day visit to cement ties with the newborn state.[73]

New Guns, Old War

In the predawn darkness of Saturday morning, February 17, when thick mist blanketed the forested hills on the Sino-Vietnamese border, the Chinese People's Liberation Army unleashed its fury. The scale of the attack this time was different from the previous one in 1788 when the Manchu emperor Ch'ien-lung sent an expeditionary corps of cavalry and infantry to install a king of his choice in Hanoi. In an awesome display of firepower, hundreds of 130-mm and 122-mm long-range guns and 140-mm multiple-rocket launchers poured shells into Vietnam, at the rate of almost one a second. "The firing is so intense," an American reporter visiting the border region in Vietnam wrote, "that from a distance, it is merely a rumble, similar to a B-52 bombing strike." But he added that at least on one occasion the barrage lasted twenty minutes rather than the usual minute or less of an American bombing run.[74]

Then, like floodwater bursting through a dam, some eighty-five thousand Chinese soldiers, supported by armor, streamed into Vietnam through twenty-six points along the border. While the main thrust soon narrowed to five main entries leading to provincial capitals, the invading troops were thrown in a wide net to destroy Vietnamese outposts. With their celebrated "human wave" tactic, used by the PLA during the Korean War, thousands of soldiers attempted to dislodge Vietnamese militia and border guards entrenched on hilltops and precipices. As Peking would later admit, the tactic proved

356

a disaster. The Chinese had not foreseen the kind of traps the Vietnamese had laid and the maze of tunnels and bunkers they had constructed in the border region. In the first three days of fighting the Chinese suffered heavy casualties as thousands of soldiers were cut down by machine-gun fire from fortified positions, blown up by mines, and maimed by booby traps.

Peking implicitly recognized the defeat by replacing General Xu Shiyou, commander of the invasion force, with a relatively younger General Yang Dezhi, nicknamed "Ever-victorious General" for his role in the Korean War. He quickly abandoned the human wave tactic and ordered a more discriminating attack in coordination with artillery and tank support. In ten days of fighting, armor-led Chinese had slowly advanced between twenty and thirty miles inside the border, and after heavy fighting captured four provincial capitals— Lai Chau, Lao Cai, Ha Giang, and Cao Bang. With an intense artillery barrage followed by a tank assault, the Chinese had begun on February 27 the invasion of Lang Son—the only remaining provincial capital in the border region. It proved to be the toughest campaign in the whole operation. After occupying the high grounds around the sleepy, French-built city, Chinese troops had to fight house by house, bunker by bunker to dislodge the defenders. When at 2:40 P.M. on March 5 the Chinese had finally established control over Lang Son and opened the gateway to the Red River delta, the border town lay in rubble, littered with corpses of comrades turned enemies. Within a few hours Peking announced that China's frontier troops had attained their objectives. The same day they began withdrawing to Chinese territory.

The sixteen-day "pedagogical war" had left a wide swath of devastation along Vietnam's border with the northern neighbor. China, ironically, had completed the destruction of an area that was spared by American bombers during the war. For fear of inadvertently striking Chinese territory, the Americans had not touched the border towns, which remained the only urban centers besides Hanoi where brick buildings stood. After the passage of the Chinese invasion army everything was flattened. Unlike Lang Son, where destruction came in the course of the battle, most other towns occupied by the Chinese were objects of systematic destruction. During a trip to Cao Bang a few months after the invasion concluded I was struck by how methodical the Chinese sappers had been in blowing up with plastic anything that stood—from municipal buildings to post offices, schools to hospitals. Verdant, rolling hills where once Ho Chi Minh plotted revolution with his Chinese friends stood in mute testimony to the destruction. With the tiled roof blown off, the iron beams of the central market stood like a skeleton against a stark sky. A twisted sterilizer, a piece of an oxygen cylinder, and the wheels of a mobile bed stuck out of concrete and rubble, suggesting where there once was a hospital. An iron bridge on the outskirts of the town lay in the water like bended knees. There was no sign of any fighting taking place inside the town. That impression was confirmed by a Vietnamese colonel who admitted that the destruction of Cao Bang was wrought on March 10—five days after the Chinese had announced their withdrawal. The reason the Chinese had not engaged in deliberate destruction in the first stage of their occupation, he said, was that they had hoped to use the occupied territory as a bargaining chip to get the Vietnamese troops out of Cambodia.

A Wink from Washington

What were the objectives of the Chinese expedition? Peking's goals seem to have gone through some transformation after July 1978, when the Chinese Politburo first contemplated "teaching Vietnam a lesson." While the idea of punishing an "ungrateful ally" and a "disobedient pupil" by hitting Vietnam hard and forcing it to rethink its policy options remained a core objective, the evolving international situation had provided China with additional targets. Vietnam's treaty of friendship with Moscow and its invasion of Cambodia had thrown down a gauntlet to China's regional preeminence. The loss of face suffered in the collapse of the Pol Pot regime and the threat of encirclement by Moscow could be countered by a display of Chinese power. Throwing a quarter of a million men against Vietnam to "explode the myth of Vietnam's invincibility," as Deng put it, was designed not only to blunt Vietnamese pride and restore China's credibility but also to force Vietnam to withdraw some of its units from Cambodia. It was also to be a lesson for the whole Western world, which appeared to China as paralyzed in the face of Soviet adventurism. "We cannot tolerate the Cubans to go swashbuckling unchecked in Africa, the Middle East, and other areas, nor can we tolerate the Cubans of the Orient [the Vietnamese] to go swashbuckling in Laos, Kampuchea, or even in the Chinese border areas," Deng told American newsmen while the invasion was still in progress. "Now some people in the world are afraid of offending them, even if they do something terrible. These people wouldn't dare take action against them."[75]

China's *Liberation Army Daily* put it even more bluntly. "The counterattack in self-defense is a salutary remedy for those suffering from 'Sovietophobia,' " the paper said. "The victory has been a great encouragement to the people of Southeast Asia and the world as a whole in their struggle against hegemonism."[76]

Deng's outburst against the West's appeasement policy was, however, an indirect admission of China's failure to get applause for its tough action. Thanks to Brzezinski's support for the action, the United States was the only Western country that came close to endorsing China's war. In contrast with Washington's earlier condemnation of the Vietnamese invasion of Cambodia as "a threat to regional peace and stability [that] raises the danger of wider conflict," the United States implicitly justified the Chinese action. "In the last few weeks," Carter said, "we have seen a Vietnamese invasion of Cambodia and, as a result, a Chinese border penetration in Vietnam." The American spokesman called for immediate withdrawal of Vietnamese troops from Cambodia and Chinese troops from Vietnam, a formulation that was interpreted at the time as implying the United States would not object to the Chinese troops' staying in Vietnam as long as the Vietnamese were in Cambodia.[77]

Brzezinski successfully resisted a Vance demand that a planned trip to China by Treasury Secretary Michael Blumenthal be canceled to show American displeasure at the Chinese attack. "Thanks to Carter's steadfastness," and implicitly his own, Brzezinski wrote, "the new American-Chinese relationship had successfully weathered its baptism of fire."[78]

The Sino-Vietnamese war seems to have marked a new step in U.S. security cooperation with China after the beginning made during Brzezinski's May 1978 trip. Years later several American officials privately admitted to me that while heavy cloud cover over the Sino-Vietnamese border area in the first week of the conflict had prevented American spy satellites from monitoring Vietnamese deployment, Washington had quietly helped China by providing satellite intelligence about Soviet troop deployment along China's border and informing China when Soviet forces in Siberia were put on a state of alert after the Chinese invasion.[79]

A Lesson for All

The massiveness of the Chinese attack, the death and destruction it wrought on Vietnam, and the Soviets' inaction certainly added to China's credibility. The fact that the Soviets made only threatening maneuvers along China's border and stepped up their delivery of supplies to Vietnam was used by Peking propagandists as evidence that the Soviet Union was a "paper polar bear." However, the Chinese claim of success was somewhat clouded by reports that three Vietnamese regular divisions were advancing toward Lang Son when the Chinese announced their pullout, and by the fact that Moscow's stern warning to China to stop aggression "before it is too late," preceded the Chinese withdrawal. China's principal achievement in the end, as summed up by a pro-Peking analyst, was the destruction of Vietnam's military infrastructure and of its communication lines and basic social facilities in the north.[80]

By crippling Vietnam's weak economy even further and by saddling it with the costly responsibility of defending the northern border against future Chinese attack, Peking also raised the price that Hanoi would have to pay for opposing Chinese interests. But for all the sacrificing of soldiers and civilians—twenty thousand casualties by China's own estimate[81]—and squandering of resources, the invasion achieved very little else.

If Peking had any hope that the death and destruction would chasten the Vietnamese, it had a rude surprise when on the eve of Chinese withdrawal Vietnam passed a decree of general mobilization ordering the whole nation to be organized into combat units. "The war of resistance against the reactionary Chinese aggressors has begun," Hanoi declared defiantly.

Vietnam clearly had learned no lesson, nor did the operation have any effect on Cambodia Pham Van Dong carried on his visit in Phnom Penh as if nothing had happened. He signed a twenty-five-year treaty of friendship and cooperation with Heng Samrin that retroactively justified the presence of Vietnamese divisions in Cambodia. Far from diverting troops from Cambodia, a cocky Vietnamese leadership did not even send its regular divisions to the border, leaving the job instead to the militia and regional forces. The Vietnamese lost an enormous number of lives, perhaps ten thousand soldiers and civilians,[82] but by refusing to commit regular divisions to a set-piece battle against the Chinese, Hanoi deprived Peking of the chance to score a decisive victory.

The most important lesson from the operation was perhaps learned by the Chinese themselves. A confidential Chinese report concluded that the Chinese and Vietnamese losses had been "about equal" and that the PLA had "not been able to conduct a modern war." Heavy casualties suffered during the war, as well as failures of weapons and tactics, brought home to China the urgent need for modernizing its military.[83]

Whether the Chinese taught a lesson or the Vietnamese learned one, this was one war that nobody won. While visiting Cao Bang in July 1979, I saw a sullen, miserably poor populace trying to rebuild life in the ruins with undamaged bricks from the rubble. The market that had once thrived with an abundant supply of Chinese goods from across the border was now a skimpy collection of listless people selling recycled odds and ends. Traveling through China's Guangxi and Yunnan provinces the following month, I was struck by the incredible numbers of invalid PLA soldiers in green uniforms hobbling around with crutches and by the population's total apathy toward an exhibition in Kunming about China's victorious "counterattack in self-defense." The most telling evidence of how popular China's educational war had been came during a cultural show in Nanning. Accompanied by a Chinese official, I went to see a song and dance performed by various minorities in Guangxi Province. Every single piece of dance and music was lustily cheered by the audience in the jam-packed hall enjoying the lights and colors. Then came the performance "Heroic PLA punishes the Vietnamese bandits." Two men dressed in baggy green uniforms and Vietnamese pith helmets were on the stage scrounging for food, fighting between themselves over a morsel found on the street, blowing their noses, and wiping their fingers on their trousers—very similar to the way revolutionary opera of the Cultural Revolution days had depicted American imperialist GIs. Suddenly, onto the stage leaped a PLA hero in tight-fitting white clothes. In a mixture of acrobatics, ballet, and judo he quickly felled the Vietnamese bandits. As the curtain came down, there was an embarrassed silence in the hall. My Chinese companion kept looking at the ceiling. No one could know better than the people of Nanning how many thousands of coffins had returned from Vietnam.

11

Indochina: War Forever?

Iᴛ ᴀʟʟ sᴛᴀʀᴛᴇᴅ with a furtive clasp of hands with a U.S. Secret Service agent on the evening of Saturday, January 13, 1979. At the end of the last session of the UN Security Council meeting, Prince Norodom Sihanouk, accompanied by a number of dark-suited Khmer Rouge "associates" and Secret Service agents, was on his way back to his suite at New York's Waldorf-Astoria. Few had noticed that behind his fixed grin and his courteous bowing and waving Sihanouk was tense. In the crowded hotel elevator, he quietly grasped the hand of a Secret Service agent standing next to him. The agent was horrified, thinking that his charge was trying to push what felt like money in his palm. He half-groaned in protest, but, looking at Sihanouk's pleading eyes and discreet shaking of head, the agent hesitantly pocketed the "bill." Sihanouk's Khmer Rouge shadows concluded that the prince had tipped the American. They would find out later that it was a different kind of tip.

Sihanouk's four days in New York since his arrival on January 9 were packed with meetings, press conferences, interviews, and speeches, but very little sleep. The media, starved of firsthand news from inside Cambodia, hounded Sihanouk for details of the Cambodian "holocaust" and attacked him for representing the murderous regime. Exhausted, emotionally distraught Sihanouk lashed out at the Vietnamese for invading his country but reserved his harshest words for the regime he had come to defend. "Pol Pot may be a patriot," he told a newsman, "but he is a butcher. He treats the Cambodian people as cattle good for forced labor and pigs good for the slaughterhouse."[1]

Speaking at a specially convened UN Security Council meeting, Sihanouk made an emotional plea to the world body to expel the Vietnamese from Cambodia. His passionate speech and his personal popularity among many Third World countries drew sympathy and support, but an inevitable Soviet veto blocked unanimous censure of Vietnam. The question of his representation seemed overshadowed by his patriotism, honesty, and courage. At the United Nations Sihanouk met old friends and made new ones. He took a great liking to America's UN ambassador Andrew Young, a forceful advocate of human rights all over the world. The appreciation was mutual. Young thought Sihanouk was "an amazing guy." "The man," he said, "has maintained his integrity and courage in the face of real difficulties. Somehow he has survived without seeming to have compromised himself."[2]

Young perhaps did not realize how soon his admiration for the prince would be put to the test. The day the Security Council session ended with a Soviet veto, Sihanouk, unbeknownst to all but his wife, Monique, had already reached a serious decision about his career as a "high representative" of Democratic Kampuchea. It had become clear that his missing children and his sister-in-law and her husband had been liquidated by the Khmer Rouge. Talking to diplomats, journalists, and Khmer compatriots, he came to grasp the magnitude of what had happened in Cambodia. His personal agony and the condemnations he faced as representative of Pol Pot were added to grave personal loss at the hands of the Khmer Rouge. Despite the honor and attention showered on him by the Chinese representatives at the United Nations—"Please don't think anything about spending," the Chinese ambassador had entreated him after installing him in a luxury suite—and despite his access to the press, Sihanouk was still a prisoner. Three Khmer Rouge cadres, who had accompanied him from Phnom Penh, not only shadowed him in his every public appearance but even shared the suite with Sihanouk and his wife. If that was not demeaning enough for the "God King" and former head of state, he was informed that after Ieng Sary's arrival in a few weeks' time Sihanouk would be demoted to deputy leader of Democratic Kampuchea's UN delegation. That, as Sihanouk would later recall, was the last straw. He decided it was high time to make a dash for freedom.

That Saturday evening Andrew Young was stunned to read what Sihanouk had written in the note passed on to the Secret Service. On a scrap of paper the prince had scribbled with a pencil, "Dear inspector, I request the help of your team to free me from the control of the Khmer Rouge, who are now staying with me at Waldorf-Astoria. Tonight, exactly at two in the morning, I will surreptitiously leave my suite, alone with a suitcase. Please be kind to take me in a car directly to the office of Mr. Andrew Young, the permanent ambassador of the U.S. at the UN. Many thanks." The note carried Sihanouk's signature.

Young swiftly alerted Secretary Vance and Richard Holbrooke, who called an emergency meeting with intelligence and security officials. As Holbrooke recalled, "We decided to do a little cloak-and-dagger operation in the middle of the night." Secret Service agents would wait for him outside his suite at the hour chosen by the prince. Holbrooke went to the seventh floor operation room of the State Department to monitor the progress of the plan while Vance stood by the phone at home. "Everyone was very concerned," Holbrooke later explained, for "this was very dangerous. We were afraid that he might get killed. The Khmer Rouge after all imprisoned him."

In his suite Sihanouk waited nervously for the appointed hour. Normally his Khmer Rouge shadows went to bed at midnight, but that night they seemed not to be sleepy. Even at 12:30 A.M. he could hear the clacking of a typewriter in an adjacent room. But by 2:00 A.M. all was quiet. He said good-bye to a pale Monique and slipped out of the suite to be met by four hefty, grim-looking Americans. Before leaving he had instructed Monique to inform the Khmer Rouge and the Chinese of his decision to leave their company and return to the Khmer Rouge twenty thousand dollars in cash that they had given him prior to his departure from Phnom Penh. Surrounded by the agents, who towered over him, Sihanouk briskly walked to a service elevator and through a maze of corridors reached the road where a car waited to whisk him to Young's office. The whole experience, as Sihanouk would reminisce later, seemed like a scene out of a spy film.

This sudden development had upset Young's plan to be in Atlanta on January 14 for a ceremony to commemorate the anniversary of the late Martin Luther King's fiftieth birthday. President Carter had to explain away Young's absence to reporters by saying that he was called by the State Department at 2:30 A.M. that morning for a "special mission." When Young finally arrived in Atlanta later in the day he told reporters that he had been talking with Chinese representatives, "trying to settle some Cambodian difficulties."[3]

What Young could not say at the time was that he had spent the early hours of January 14 talking to a distraught Sihanouk and then discussing the prince's defection bid with the Chinese. The Chinese ambassador to the United Nations was called to Young's office to hear directly from Sihanouk his wish to seek provisional political asylum in the United States. "One day I will return to China to live there," the prince told the Chinese, "but for now I am exhausted and traumatized. I need to quickly go to a New York hospital for recuperation."

Sihanouk was a hot potato in the hands of the State Department. While there was great sympathy for the prince for the trials he had undergone in Cambodia, Vance and Holbrooke worried that his defection might leave the Cambodian political scene without an able leader and a unifying symbol. A matter of even more immediate concern was the chilling effect U.S. asylum for Sihanouk could have on the newly established Sino-American ties. It was essentially through Chinese initiative and entirely at China's expense that Sihanouk had been plucked out of Phnom Penh before the Vietnamese entered and sent to New York to represent the discredited Pol Pot regime. Peking clearly counted on using the prince's international stature to mobilize opinion against Vietnam. Vice-Premier Deng Xiaoping was to visit the United States within two weeks; for the

United States to grant asylum to Sihanouk on the eve of Deng's visit could be seen by Peking as an affront. Roger Sullivan, Holbrooke's deputy assistant secretary for China, was awakened in the middle of the night to come to the State Department to stand by in the Operations Room. It was his job to break the news to the Chinese. At 4:00 A.M. Sullivan called Han Xu, chief of the Chinese liaison office in Washington, to inform him that an exhausted Sihanouk was checking into a hospital. "Han Xu was surprised," Sullivan recalled, "but he quickly gained composure. 'Well, if that's what he wants, that's okay with us' was the thrust of his reply."[4]

The faint glimmer of dawn was breaking over the East River when the prince was driven to Lenox Hill Hospital on Park Avenue. The next morning his wife, Princess Monique, too, moved into the ninth floor suite of the hospital to be with the prince. This was to be a holding operation. The State Department had concluded that it was better to keep Sihanouk in a secluded place and give him time to think over his request rather than hastily grant him asylum. A bulletin was put out to announce that laboring under "extreme stress and exhaustion," Prince Sihanouk had checked into the hospital. French-speaking Foreign Service officer Frank Tatu, who had spent years in Cambodia, was dispatched to see the prince. Tatu assured him that he was not a prisoner. The security was to protect him and give him time to think over his decision. Later, Young went to see him. The American message essentially was "You can defect if you want to, but why don't you think it over for a while? Once a person defects and loses his identity, he loses his usefulness as a political leader." As Holbrooke recalled, "We also asked him, Who is going to support you? What are you defecting from? Are you defecting from the Khmer Rouge? Everyone knows you have broken with them. Are you defecting from a country you can't go back to anyway now?" On January 18, Vance himself visited the prince at the hospital and told him that he was a guest of the U.S. government and could stay in the United States as long as he wanted, but he avoided the question of political asylum.[5]

The prince was exhilarated to be out of the clutches of the Khmer Rouge and a free man again, but the hard reality was that unlike many Third World leaders this ex-king had no unnumbered account in foreign banks. Lenox Hill Hospital administrators were dumbfounded to learn from Tatu that this illustrious patient was not covered by medical insurance. Since neither of his sponsors— the Khmer Rouge and the Chinese—could be asked, the U.S. government paid the fifteen thousand dollar hospital bill. But after the Vance visit Sihanouk concluded that the United States was not ready to grant asylum. A demoralized Sihanouk hurriedly approached the French ambassador to the United Nations to convey to Paris his request for French passports for Monique and himself and permission to live in the little villa in Mougins owned by his mother. So certain was Sihanouk that he wrote to the State Department, assuring them that he was going to live in France. The French, however, agreed to grant the two asylum on the condition that Sihanouk would refrain from all political activity, including giving political interviews. Monique, who was born of a French father, could obtain a French passport but the prince could not. The choice for Sihanouk was stark—life as a penniless and stateless exile or as a pampered representative of a murderous regime. A third choice soon arrived, but was scarcely more attractive. Hanoi had sent him a message through a nonaligned ambassador that he would be welcome to return to Phnom Penh as head of the Vietnamese-installed regime.

The choice was finally made for him by China's Deng Xiaoping. Deng was deeply concerned by Sihanouk's public declarations against the Khmer Rouge and his plan to live in the West. With American cooperation, Deng's packed Washington schedule was altered to include a meeting with Sihanouk on January 31. Escorted by four State Department security officers, Sihanouk and his wife drove down from New York to Blair House—the U.S. guesthouse where Deng was staying—for an unpublicized dinner.

"Samdech Sihanouk, you are a great patriot. You should not abandon your homeland, Democratic Kampuchea," Deng urged him over a sumptuous Chinese meal. "My homeland," Sihanouk replied promptly, "is just Cambodia, not Democratic Kampuchea. I am not very democratic, I am a feudal prince." Deng vigorously protested, saying that indeed he was a democratic prince, and added, "We Chinese must confess that we do not appreciate some aspects of Pol Pot's policy. He is too tough." He said China had tried to soften him. "Really? You believe that you can change a tiger into a pussy-cat, really?" an incredulous prince asked with a nervous giggle. Deng acknowledged that China was not that powerful but mentioned the efforts the country had made to liberate him from the Khmer Rouge. Playing to the full on Sihanouk's gratitude to China, Deng told him that China had been an old friend and a second home to him since his overthrow in 1970. It would be a loss of face for China if the prince did not return to live in Peking. China, he assured Sihan-ouk, respected his wish not to work with the Khmer Rouge and would not pressure him to join in an alliance with them. Neither would China force him to go anywhere against his will. Deng also promised to use his good offices to urge the Khmer Rouge to search for Sihanouk's missing children, grandchildren, and relatives. In the warmth of Deng's invitation and his promises of total liberty, Sihanouk's two-week-old dilemma was resolved. Peking was to be his home again until political fortunes beckoned him to an indepen-dent Cambodia.[6]

Sihanouk's optimism for a quiet sojourn in China was, of course, mistaken. Very quickly the prince became an object of pressure, cajolement, and wooing by various parties to join in the new strug-gle for Cambodia that had begun in the wake of the Vietnamese occupation. Sihanouk's international stature and his immense pop-ularity in Cambodia had again made him into a key player in the Cambodian drama. Compared with 1970, when Sihanouk, the de-posed head of state, threw in his lot with the Khmer Rouge and their Vietnamese and Chinese backers, external stakes were now even higher. The Vietnamese occupation of Cambodia was not just a challenge to China: it was a worrisome development for ASEAN. More important, it removed the traditional buffer between Thailand and its age-old rival, Vietnam. What had begun as a conflict be-tween Vietnam and China and its protégé, Cambodia, now merged with another historic struggle—between Thailand and Vietnam for the control of trans-Mekong plains. While the new war opened up unprecedented opportunities for Soviet military advance in the Pa-cific, Thailand's regional allies and Western friends were also drawn into conflict, making Cambodia another hot spot for East-West con-frontation. As the resumed historic conflict burned on slowly and the friends and allies of the protagonists maneuvered to gain strategic advantage, the fate of the Khmer nation hung in the balance.

Three Countries, One Current

When the Vietnamese army overran Phnom Penh and fanned out toward the Thai border in pursuit of the Khmer Rouge, there was consternation in Bangkok. Where would the Vietnamese stop? Would the "Prussians of Asia" now pursue the remnants of Pol Pot's regime into Thai territory? Would they roll their tanks into Bangkok?

In hundreds of Cambodian villages, the Vietnamese invasion was greeted with joy and disbelief. The Khmer Rouge cadres and militia were gone. People were free again to live as families, to go to bed without fearing the next day. Some three hundred thousand people from the western provinces and from Phnom Penh were forced to join the retreating Khmer Rouge into the forest. But for the rest of Cambodia it was as if salvation had come. Villagers emptied the government granaries and slaughtered pigs and chickens to have their first hearty meals in four years. Hundreds of thousands took to the road to return to their hometowns. Men and women in black rags carried their meager belongings on improvised pushcarts and crisscrossed the country like lines of ants. Six months after the invasion, when I revisited Cambodia, the returnees were still on the road. Dog-tired and hungry after walking hundreds of miles, they trudged on to final destinations. One refrain that I heard constantly from the survivors was "If the Vietnamese hadn't come, we'd all be dead." That expression of gratitude was, however, often laced with apprehension that the traditional enemy—Vietnam—might now annex Cambodia. "I fear they [the Vietnamese] want to stay here to eat our rice," a former schoolteacher whispered to me on the road on his long march back home.

The Vietnamese certainly did not help to foster confidence. In the three months following the occupation of Phnom Penh they had systematically plundered the capital. Convoys of trucks carrying refrigerators, air conditioners, electrical gadgets, furniture, machinery, and precious sculptures headed toward Ho Chi Minh City. All these had been left behind by a population brutally evicted from the city in 1975 and had gone untouched by the Khmer Rouge rulers, who loathed these artifacts of bourgeois decadence. That booty from Phnom Penh might have brought some money to Hanoi's coffers, but it left a deep scar in the Khmer psyche; it reinforced prejudices about the detested *yuon*. It would also remain a large blot on the Vietnamese role as "savior" of Cambodia.

When I arrived in Phnom Penh in July 1979, it was a ghost town—barred to all but the most enterprising of returnees who waited in makeshift camps outside the city. Those who managed to enter prowled through the city, hunting for movable goods. Walking down Boulevard Monivong, I could hear the eerie echo of my footsteps. The once busy Chinese business section of Phnom Penh looked like a scene after a cataclysmic storm. Every house and shop had been ransacked, and remains of broken furniture and twisted pieces of household goods were strewn over the road. Damp nodules of cotton from ripped-open mattresses and pillows covered the ground. Clearly, marauders had gone through the households, searching for gold and jewelry.

If the Vietnamese had not expected the swift collapse of the Khmer Rouge resistance, they also were not fully prepared for what awaited them inside the country, nor for the serious international difficulties. It was not just a land without money, markets, postal system, or schools; it was a land littered with mass graves and charnel houses. A famine was facing the weak and dispirited survivors. Instead of a hearty round of applause for ousting the universally condemned regime, Vietnam found itself the butt of international criticism and censure.

Cambodia was to be nominally ruled by the People's Revolutionary Party of Kampuchea, which was hastily organized while the Vietnamese army was marching into Phnom Penh. The party's two hundred members and the inexperienced bunch of Khmer exiles and defectors that formed the Revolutionary Council were not up to the job of reviving a nation and restoring a modicum of normalcy to a population emerging from a nightmare. Most important, they could not hope to defend the new regime against armed opposition from the Khmer Rouge. The decimation of the Cambodian professional class and the reluctance of many of the survivors to serve another

Communist regime made the job of rebuilding the country even more difficult.

Thousands of Vietnamese officials and technicians were commandeered to Cambodia to restore the water supply and electricity in Phnom Penh, put the railway line back into service, and reopen rudimentary health clinics with Vietnamese doctors and paramedics and a handful of Cambodian doctors. Ministries were set up, with Vietnamese advisers running things behind the scenes. Hundreds of Khmers were sent to Vietnam to take crash courses in health care, education, banking, foreign trade, and security work.

After a period of a cashless economy, during which the revived market operated with bartered rice and gold, currency was reintroduced in Cambodia in 1980. Thanks to large-scale smuggling from the Thai border, markets flourished again. Massive international assistance averted the famine. Cambodian children went to school again. Some medicine returned to the empty shelves of hospitals. Cambodia's revival, as I was able to witness over a period of six years, was a true miracle. Like a phoenix, it emerged from its own ashes. Although the Vietnamese provided a valuable infrastructure, and international aid was generous, it was, above all, a triumph of Khmer resilience and tenacity.

Resuscitating Cambodia, however, was easier than resolving the question of its political future. As Cambodia's citizens went about their way, trying to rebuild life, Hanoi's major effort was focused on consolidating its hold over the country by creating a new Khmer state, a government, and party institutions.

"If Phnom Penh Falls, Saigon Falls"

In the spring of 1981, a new constitution was passed. It was followed by a national election that chose 117 members of the National Assembly from among 148 candidates. The candidates were a mixed bag of former Khmer Rouge, Khmer Issarak, and surviving intellectuals from the old regime united only in their opposition to Pol Pot. Elections were designed, Foreign Minister Hun Sen explained, "to select human beings and not the political line. We have chosen the political line through the sacrifice of blood."[7] Not sur-

prisingly, all the stalwarts of the new regime received over 99 percent of the votes cast.

After the elections the party congress officially unveiled a reor-
ganized party in Mimot in January of 1979. The new party, renamed the Kampuchean People's Revolutionary Party (KPRP), with
its eight hundred members was, in effect, the revived pro-Vietnamese wing of the Cambodian Communist Party that had almost been
destroyed by Pol Pot.[8] The new secretary of the party was Pen Sovan, a stern, hollow-cheeked Khmer Issarak exile from Hanoi.

The new party restored the Indochinese unity broken by Pol Pot.
Unlike Pol Pot, who had denied Vietnamese parentage of the party,
Pen Sovan acknowledged that the KPRP was carrying forward the
glorious tradition of the Ho Chi Minh–founded Indochinese Communist Party. One of Vietnam's principal efforts in Cambodia was
to educate the KPRP, especially its new members, about the dangers of what it termed "narrow nationalism" and of breaking away
from Indochinese solidarity. To ensure the purity of the new party,
Vietnamese advisers (at the provincial level) vetted applications of
would-be party members, and candidates were then sent to Vietnam
for political training.[9]

Militarily, Cambodia was brought under the responsibility of
Vietnam's Fourth Army Corps, which normally covered the Mekong
Delta provinces. While a Cambodian Ministry of Defense was established and, by 1983, three Khmer divisions had been raised[10] to
play a supporting role, the 180,000-strong Vietnamese army led by
Fourth Corps commander General Le Duc Anh provided the defensive shield for the fledgling regime.

Three shadowy Vietnamese organizations controlled the pulse of
the People's Republic of Kampuchea, as the new regime calls itself.
The highest of these organizations was a body called A-40 composed
of some experts from the Vietnamese party's Central Committee.
They maintained liaison between the Cambodian and Vietnamese
parties and offered advice on all key issues. Another group, called
B-68, was headed by Tran Xuan Bach, a member of Vietnamese
Party secretariat and consisted of midlevel Vietnamese experts at
tached to various Cambodian ministries and participating in day-to-
day decision making. A third group of advisers, A-50, consisted of
experts who worked with provincial administration.[11]

In rural areas, civilian advisers from Vietnamese "sister" provinces worked in Khmer provincial offices and services. Below the provincial level the advisory work was left to special teams from the Vietnamese army commanded by captains.[12]

In the years since its invasion and occupation of Cambodia the Vietnamese have refined their justifications for an Indochinese alliance and raised it to the level of some immutable natural law—a law dictated by geography and history. "For centuries," General Le Duc Anh wrote in a major article, "the three countries [Laos, Cambodia, Vietnam] shared the same fate as victims of aggression by the Chinese feudalistic forces, imperialism, and international reactionary forces." Dividing one country from another, using one as a springboard from which to annex another, and then annexing all three countries "became the law for all wars of aggression by outside forces against the Indochinese peninsula." Consequently, Anh argued, building a "strategic and combat alliance among the three Indochinese countries constitutes the law of survival and development for each individual country and the three countries as well."[13]

Vietnamese soldiers serving in Cambodia, dying of malaria and being maimed and killed in operations against Khmer Rouge ambushes, had been provided with the "law" in its most basic form. "If Phnom Penh falls, Saigon falls. If we have to fight and die, we do it here, not in Vietnam." This was the way Vietnamese officers explained the reason for their presence in Cambodia.[14]

Bloc Yes, Buffer No

The first public step toward formalizing the Indochinese alliance was taken in January 1980, when foreign ministers of the three countries met in Phnom Penh to announce a unified stand on Cambodian problems and other international issues. Thenceforward such gatherings became regular biannual affairs to present the latest Hanoi position as that of the whole Indochinese grouping. By associating Laos and Cambodia with its policy position, Hanoi not only formalized its leadership role vis-à-vis those countries but sought to boost the legitimacy of its client regime in Phnom Penh and to convey a sense of irreversibility to the newly formed alliance. Since

1980 Hanoi had developed the theme of two blocs in Southeast Asia—Indochina and ASEAN—and had flatly rejected the idea that Cambodia become a neutral buffer. "I don't insist on having an ASEAN country as a buffer state," Vietnamese foreign minister Nguyen Co Thach told his Thai counterpart, Sitthi Sawetsila, in May 1980. "Why do you then want a buffer country among the three Indochinese countries?"[15]

What Hanoi sought was not only the security of a political bloc, but the creation of an economically integrated unit in which to achieve "gradual implementation of labor distribution, ensuring an effective use of labor and land potentials of the three countries."[16] With its 6 million hectares of cultivated land and population of 60 million (1985), Vietnam clearly saw potential in sparsely populated Cambodia (7 million population) with its 1.5 million hectares of cultivable land and enormous fishing grounds.[17]

Pursuing a policy begun since the signing of the Lao-Vietnamese treaty in 1977, all the Lao and Cambodian provinces were coupled with sister provinces in Vietnam. Vietnamese advisers, technical experts, and doctors from the provinces were dispatched to sister provinces in Laos and Cambodia to help in small projects and to build a special Indochinese bond.

Following a summit conference of the Indochinese states in Vientiane in February 1983, a Vietnam-Laos-Cambodia Joint Economic Committee was established. Since then the body consisting of economic and planning ministers of the three countries has met twice a year "to accelerate the economic cooperation and the coordination of national plans of development."[18] Although the national committees for cultural and economic cooperation set up in each of the Indochinese countries were initially engaged only in consultations, Hanoi soon made it clear that its "long-term goal [was] to bring the three countries together and to achieve economic integration."[19]

The fact that prior to the 1970 coup d'état there were five hundred thousand Vietnamese residents in Cambodia, all of whom were either killed in the anti-Vietnamese pogroms of the Lon Nol and Pol Pot regimes or expelled to Vietnam, was presented as justification for a return. These returnees as well as new settlers could be an important element in long-term economic integration. A directive of the Cambodian council of ministers in May 1982 said that Vietnamese who had come into Cambodia since 1979 and were "engaged in occupations which contribute to the rehabilitation and development of the economy such as farming, fishing, salt-making, handicrafts" would be allowed to stay and work.[20]

Although the Vietnamese were concerned that an unrestricted flow of Vietnamese into Cambodia could fuel the traditional Khmer animosity toward the Vietnamese and cause tension, they could not possibly be oblivious to the benefits of some of its population's finding gainful employment in Cambodia or playing key economic roles. Whether it was Hanoi's deliberate policy to settle Vietnamese in Cambodia, as its opponents charged, or whether it was just the continuation of the historical pattern of spontaneous movement of the Vietnamese to less populated areas, the result could only be strengthening of the Vietnamese hold over the country. According to the estimate of a leading Western demographer, by 1985 more than one hundred and seventy-five thousand Vietnamese civilians— including former residents, new landless immigrants, traders, and discharged soldiers—had settled in Cambodia.[21] Other estimates were as high as six hundred thousand.[22]

While the Vietnamese army and civilian advisers were trying to consolidate the new Cambodian regime, the full weight of Hanoi's diplomacy was devoted to gaining international recognition for the People's Republic of Kampuchea. Worldwide criticism of Vietnamese intervention and the economic sanctions that followed made legitimization of the new Cambodian regime the highest-priority concern of Hanoi's foreign policy. It tried to achieve this by a steady effort to undermine the moral and legal standing of Pol Pot's Democratic Kampuchea rather than by promoting the virtue of the government it had installed.

Formal recognition of the PRK came from the Soviet bloc and eleven pro-Soviet countries and organizations among the eighty-eight-member Non-Aligned Movement (NAM). While Hanoi's friends in the NAM were unable to expel Democratic Kampuchea from the movement, Vietnamese diplomatic maneuvers at least succeeded in silencing the Khmer Rouge voice in the conference. A meeting of the NAM coordinating bureau in Colombo in June 1979 rejected the Vietnamese demand for seating Hun Sen, the young foreign minister of PRK, and allowed his DK counterpart, Ieng Sary, to occupy the Cambodian seat, but at a price. He could sit in the hall but could not address the floor. At the Non-Aligned Summit in Havana in September 1979, the new chairman of the movement, Cuban president Fidel Castro, delivered the coup de grace. Although Khieu Samphan, the president of the fallen regime, received a visa to enter Cuba, his delegation was housed in a hotel twenty miles away from the conference hall and was deprived of transportation and the identification tags needed to enter the hall. Despite strenuous opposition by the ASEAN delegates the Cambodian seat was announced as vacant, and it has since remained empty.

Similar tricks were not possible at the United Nations, nor was the power of a Soviet veto sufficient in matters of credentials. During the General Assembly session in September 1979, the Vietnamese attempt to unseat Democratic Kampuchea from the world body was defeated. By a vote of six (including the United States) to three, the UN Credential Committee allowed the DK to retain its seat. This was an ironic vote cast in favor of the regime Carter had earlier denounced as the "greatest violator of human rights" in the world. Vance agonized over the decision, since a U.S. vote for seating Pol Pot could be interpreted as support for his regime. But to vote against the DK would mean opposing China and ASEAN and legitimizing the Vietnamese invasion. "The choice for us," a senior U.S. official would later admit, "was between moral principles and international law. The scale weighed in favor of law because that also served our security interests." That fateful vote, however, linked U.S. support to a murderous group with whom U.S. officials were forbidden to shake hands.[23]

On September 21, 1979, the UN General Assembly accepted the Credential Committee's report by a vote of seventy-one in favor, thirty-five against, and thirty-four abstentions. Vietnam's military drive against Democratic Kampuchea, begun on Christmas of 1978, was finally checkmated on the green-and-gold floor of the United Nations. The Pol Pot regime might have been reduced to a band of guerrillas in the hills, but it was voted in as the only legitimate representative of the Cambodian people. Ever since that vote, for a few weeks every autumn the struggle for Cambodia has moved from the jungles of the Thai-Cambodian border to the high-domed UN General Assembly in Manhattan.

The battle waged at the United Nations to force Vietnam to withdraw from Cambodia and to allow self-determination for the Khmer people brought together a strange coalition of over a hundred nations in support of the very Khmer Rouge many of them had condemned and continued to denounce. The continued UN recognition of the DK meant the diplomatic isolation of Vietnam and gave China a favorable climate in which to wage its campaign to punish the Vietnamese and attempt to reverse Hanoi's military victory.

A Graduation Course for Vietnam

China's military "lesson" in February 1979 made no dent in the Vietnamese determination to stay in Cambodia, but Peking was convinced that a combination of military pressures (both at its own border and in Cambodia), diplomatic isolation, and economic sanctions by the international community would force Hanoi to seek peace. China's objective was to restore its Khmer Rouge allies, albeit chastened and reformed, to power in Phnom Penh. Even if that seemed a remote possibility, continuing the battle against Vietnam by proxy seemed a good enough medium-term objective for Chinese foreign-policy goals. The Soviet invasion of Afghanistan in December 1979 gave additional weight to China's anti-Soviet stance. China could claim to be the champion of independence and sovereignty for two small countries and a front-ranking fighter against Soviet hegemony and Vietnamese expansionism, a move that also promised to bring dividends in terms of Western support for China's modernization program.

But one of the most important, unspoken reasons why China was keen to leave the conflict in Cambodia unresolved was its fear that a quick settlement of the issue could only be favorable to Hanoi. If a pro-Vietnamese regime were legitimized in Cambodia and an Indochina bloc were consolidated under Hanoi, a severe blow would be dealt to China's regional power. Resolution of the Cambodian conflict and restoration of amity between Hanoi and ASEAN would also end the uneasy coalition between China and ASEAN. In the face of entrenched Vietnamese power in Indochina, Thailand might bend with the wind and become less cooperative. Other ASEAN countries, such as Indonesia and Malaysia, which viewed their own Chinese population with some suspicion and feared Peking's expansionism, would likely pay even less regard to China. On the other hand, a long, drawn-out conflict in Cambodia that pitted Vietnam and the Soviet Union against the rest of the world would drain Soviet resources and bleed Vietnam white. While China publicly demanded Vietnamese withdrawal from Cambodia, in a rare moment of candor, Deng Xiaoping admonished Japanese prime minister Masayoshi Ohira for Japan's and other Western countries' eagerness for a quick Vietnamese withdrawal. "It is wise for China," Deng told an astonished Ohira, "to force the Vietnamese to stay in Kampuchea because that way they will suffer more and more and will not be able to extend their hand to Thailand, Malaysia, and Singapore."[24]

In an April 1980 interview with me, China's vice–foreign minister, Han Nianlong, one of the principal architects of China's Indochina strategy, put the argument differently. To ask the Vietnamese to pull their troops out of Cambodia, he said, was impractical. "It is only when the Soviets can no longer support the Vietnamese that a political solution to the crisis will be possible." For the time being nothing should be done "to lighten their [the Soviets'] burden," he said. "We should exert efforts, and also use public opinion, to put pressure on them, to let them see that it won't do to continue their way. . . . We must ensure that the Soviet Union is very isolated."[25]

The Sino-Vietnamese conflict took on a new dimension in the summer of 1979, when China began to organize defectors and dissidents from Indochina into anti-Vietnamese resistance groups. While dozens of midlevel party cadres from Vietnam and Laos defected to Peking, and with Thai assistance refugee tribesmen from Laos were flown into China, Hoang Van Hoan, one of the comrades-in-arms of Ho Chi Minh's and a former Politburo member, made a dramatic escape to China. In July at a transit stop at Karachi on his way to

East Berlin for medical care, the seventy-six-year-old Hoan had complained of chest pain. He was rushed out of the transit lounge by Pakistani personnel for an emergency medical examination. As the flight was about to leave Hoan's bodyguard and companion discovered that the airport personnel knew nothing of his whereabouts. A month later he surfaced in Peking to denounce "Le Duan and company" for selling Vietnam to Moscow. While Hoan issued a call for a "second revolution" in Vietnam, the Chinese set up training schools for Vietnamese, Lao dissidents, and ethnic minorities, and began supporting anti-Communist guerrilla movements against Indochinese governments.[26]

"The Chinese," as one State Department China specialist noted with obvious relish, "are not giving Vietnam one or two lessons; they are administering an entire curriculum." They were applying unrelenting pressure on Laos and Cambodia, dissuading donors from helping Vietnam, and forcing the Vietnamese to militarize their economy. This course, he said, would continue for three to five years. "I don't know what graduation ceremony the Chinese envisage after the end of the curriculum."[27]

The development in Cambodia called for a new shift in regional alliance. Seen from Bangkok, the drama of the Vietnamese occupation of Cambodia, shorn of its modern props, was a replay of Nguyen dynasty expansionism in the early part of the nineteenth century. The arrival of the French in Indochina temporarily halted the Thai-Vietnamese rivalry for supremacy in mainland Southeast Asia. From the seventeenth century that rivalry was played out in an effort by both sides to control the buffers—the kingdoms of Laos and Cambodia—and to weaken each other. In the post-Geneva period Thailand had tried to contain Communist Vietnam by participating in the CIA-operated "secret war" in Laos, by supporting the anti-Communist Khmer Serei movement in Cambodia, and by sending troops to South Vietnam. Hanoi had responded by supporting the Thai Communist insurgency. Thai efforts, however, were in vain. The 1975 Communist victory in Laos, where some fifty thousand Vietnamese troops came to be stationed, and the subsequent Vietnamese invasion of Cambodia meant the loss of that vital space Thailand had fought for since the seventeenth century. Thailand was not ready to take it as the final verdict. In the old days Thailand would have responded to such a move by dispatching its army to fight the Vietnamese in Cambodia. That was no longer possible. At a heated strategy debate in early 1979 Kriangsak countered the argument for direct intervention by asking, "In whose name do we go in? The Khmer Rouge?" But thanks to the tenacious Khmer Rouge resistance and China's determination to curb Vietnamese power, Thailand found it still had powerful means to challenge Vietnamese supremacy. Not to do so, Thai strategists felt, would radically alter the power balance in mainland Southeast Asia. It would bring Vietnam to Thailand's doorstep and pave the way for subversion and an eventual Vietnamese attempt at subjugating Thailand. As one Thai military thinker put it, having lost Cambodia as buffer, the best that Thailand could do was to sustain the fighting that in itself constituted a buffer.[28]

Birth of a Deng Xiaoping Trail

At the government level, a de facto alliance between Peking and Bangkok opened a "Deng Xiaoping Trail" through Thailand and made the latter the linchpin of China's Cambodian strategy. Under secret arrangements, Chinese ships delivered arms and ammunition to Sattahip and Klong Yai ports, from which the Thai army transported the materiel to Khmer Rouge camps (and later to non-Communist resistance groups) along the Thai-Cambodian border. The Chinese embassy in Bangkok, working with Sino-Thai businessmen and the Thai army, has been responsible for supplying food, medicine, and other civilian supplies to the Khmer Rouge. Apart from paying the Thai army a transportation fee, China also allowed Thailand to retain a portion of the arms shipment. Under another arrangement China provided technology to coproduce antitank weapons in a Thai ordnance factory on the condition that part of the production would be given to the Khmer Rouge.

The transit arrangement not only helped to revive a Thai military-operated transport company, which had fallen on hard times since the closure of U.S. bases; it also opened opportunities for graft for some Thai officers, who demanded a "fee" for delivering the Chinese arms.[29]

Thanks to the generous Chinese supplies that started arriving in late 1979, Pol Pot's forces, which had been reduced to starving, malaria-ridden ragtag bands, were rejuvenated. At the time of the Vietnamese invasions a dozen Khmer Rouge divisions that survived were scattered and in disarray, out of touch with one another and even with their own commanders. While international relief aid revived the Khmer Rouge, Chinese supplies reequipped them to full strength. By the end of 1980 the Khmer Rouge fighting force was estimated to have grown from twenty thousand to forty thousand.[30]

While the Khmer Rouge headquarters remained only a few miles from the Thai border, guerrilla teams of ten to twelve men were sent to the interior of Cambodia to ambush Vietnamese forces, mine roads, and blow up bridges. By the end of 1981, the guerrilla war in Cambodia had increased sharply, rendering large parts of the country insecure.

Internationally, however, prospects did not look bright for the emerging anti-Hanoi coalition. Although the U.S.–ASEAN and Chinese joint effort at the United Nations had kept the Khmer Rouge in the Cambodian seat, there was growing anxiety about the erosion of international support. Since 1980, the Vietnamese had flung open Cambodia's door to Western media. Reporters and television crews were allowed to freely travel around the country, observe the mass graves, talk to countless survivors, and visit the notorious Tuol Sleng Prison in Phnom Penh, where thousands of pages of confessions were extracted under torture and where gruesome photographs of victims stood in silent testimony to the "efficiency" of Democratic Kampuchea's murder machine. The reports and television films that resulted from those visits caused worldwide revulsion and led Britain and Australia to withdraw their recognition of Democratic Kampuchea.[31]

In the fall of 1980 the new U.S. secretary of state, Edmund Muskie, was keen to follow departing secretary Vance's advice and abstain in the UN vote for Pol Pot's credentials. But eventually, under tremendous pressure from China, from American ambassadors in ASEAN capitals, and, of course, from Brzezinski, Muskie agreed to a U.S. vote in favor of Democratic Kampuchea. The Khmer Rouge retained their seat, and the lobbying by the U.S.–Chinese–ASEAN bloc won ninety-seven votes for its resolution calling for Vietnamese withdrawal. However, despite the success, there was an increasing awareness among ASEAN countries that in order to preserve the DK seat at the United Nations, it was essential not only to improve the Khmer Rouge image but also to broaden the base of the anti-Vietnamese resistance. In the autumn of 1980 Singapore premier Lee Kuan Yew publicly acknowledged that in order to "muster and maintain the support of the non-Communist world Democratic Kampuchea should be seen before the General Assembly of 1981 to have come under the leadership of Kampucheans of international standing." [32]

It was also necessary to think of an eventual solution without the Khmer Rouge, whom ASEAN could not support. As a senior Thai diplomat explained later, "There would be little sense in pushing for political settlement while ASEAN did not have an alternate political basket to offer." The idea of an anti-Vietnamese Khmer coalition was thus born, but its sponsors would have to log tens of thousands of miles in air travel and hold countless stormy meetings with various Khmer parties and the Chinese before the idea could take shape.

Peking was cool to the ASEAN effort at seeking a political solution by organizing an international conference under the UN auspices. China's prescription was maintenance of the DK as it was, but formation of a broad-based united front alongside it to carry on armed struggle. It was afraid that ASEAN's proposal of a coalition Khmer government with personalities like Prince Sihanouk and former premier Son Sann would dilute the Khmer Rouge power. Since Sihanouk's return to Peking in February 1979 his relationship with the Chinese had steadily deteriorated. The Chinese established him at an enormous palace, complete with an Olympic-size swimming pool and private movie theater, right in the heart of Peking. But contrary to the promise Deng made to Sihanouk in Washington, the Chinese had soon started pressuring him to accept the leadership of a united front. He not only repeatedly rejected the Chinese request but also called for expulsion of Democratic Kampuchea from the United Nations, keeping the seat empty until a representative government was formed. [33] The physical comfort and honor bestowed on the prince by China, however, had not prevented him from continuing shrill denunciation of the Khmer Rouge and criticizing China's policy of what he called "fighting Vietnam to the last Khmer." For Sihanouk the only way of solving the Cambodia problem was through a new Geneva conference that assured Vietnam's security and restored Cambodia's independence. He ridiculed the Chinese assertion that Vietnam would crack under pressure. Chinese leaders were so angry with the prince's pronouncements made right in Peking, especially his expressed desire in early 1980 to return to Cambodia as a private citizen, that they virtually quarantined Sihanouk. When in July 1980 the Thai foreign minister was barred from meeting the prince,[34] an angry, frustrated Sihanouk, who had flown from Pyongyang for that meeting, declared to the press that he was retiring from politics. After his experience in August 1979, when the Chinese had similarly blocked his planned meeting with the American vice-president, Walter Mondale, he had had enough.[35]

ASEAN, however, kept up the pressure on China. During successive visits to Peking in the fall of 1980 Thai premier Prem Tinsulanond and Singapore premier Lee Kuan Yew both urged the Chinese to drop the notorious Khmer Rouge trio—Pol Pot, Ieng Sary, and Khieu Samphan—from the DK leadership and accept Sihanouk and Son Sann. Deng Xiaoping bluntly told Prem that to drop the Khmer Rouge leaders would demoralize the very Khmer Rouge fighters who were acting as buffer between the Vietnamese forces and Thailand. Deng, however, agreed to the suggestion that Prince Sihanouk and Son Sann should be brought into a coalition with the Khmer Rouge—only on the condition that "they did not undermine the struggle against the Vietnamese."[36]

China had reasons to be wary not only about Sihanouk but also his old associate and premier, Son Sann. The frail, soft-spoken Son Sann, who commanded the loyalty of some six thousand men of the Khmer People's National Liberation Front (KPNLF) led by General Dien Del at the Thai-Cambodia border, had consistently refused cooperation with the Khmer Rouge until their notorious leaders were removed. He also demanded arms for his men before agreeing to get together with the Khmer Rouge. "Before I walk into the tiger's cage, I need a big stick," he had repeated tirelessly.

Deng, however, assured Lee that China did not insist on the Khmer

Rouge's regaining power in Cambodia. If in a free election held in Cambodia after the Vietnamese withdrawal they were defeated, China would accept that verdict. "Would you accept if the Khmer Rouge return to power in the election?" Deng had asked Lee in his new-found enthusiasm for bourgeois democracy. "Of course," Lee had replied, sure in the knowledge that it would never happen.[37] Lee returned satisfied from the visit as China had finally given its consent to holding an International Conference on Cambodia and to the idea of a political settlement through free elections.

The stage was now set for a new diplomatic initiative by ASEAN to develop a Cambodian coalition before holding an international conference. In February 1981, ASEAN's special envoy, Anwar Sany, an Indonesian diplomat, flew to Pyongyang to meet Sihanouk and urge him on behalf of the organization to head a coalition government. This was followed by visits from the ambassadors of China and Democratic Kampuchea in Pyongyang, both entreating the prince to join the coalition.

Renewed pressure on Sihanouk came at a time when he himself had begun to feel that his options were running out. In the autumn of 1979 he had assembled his supporters into a Confederation of Nationalist Khmers and offered to hold talks with the Vietnamese "to restore the independence and neutrality" of Cambodia. But the three letters he wrote to his old friend Vietnamese premier Pham Van Dong had gone unanswered. His public offer to return to Heng Samrin–ruled Cambodia as an "ordinary citizen" also had been spurned by Phnom Penh.[38] Further, the Vietnamese door appeared shut and his attempt to create an alternative focus to Democratic Kampuchea by creating a government-in-exile of his own was cold-shouldered by the West. Sihanouk had the unpleasant choice of withdrawing from political life altogether or rejoining his hated partners of a past struggle. Not only did Sihanouk chafe at the criticism of some of his émigré compatriots about what they called his selfishness in neglecting Cambodia's fight for independence, his own self-image as the father of modern Cambodia and his sense of history would not let him quit political life. He solved the dilemma by announcing his readiness to join the Khmer Rouge and then setting conditions that would make such an alliance impossible.

Shortly after the prince startled the world by announcing his readiness to work with the Khmer Rouge, he responded to my request for an interview. Since 1970, when he first took up exile in Peking, Sihanouk regularly spent several months a year in Pyongyang—at his enormous forty-room mansion just outside the capital, which North Korean president Kim II Sung, an old friend, had built for him. Armed with a visa that the prince had secured from President Kim, I flew to the frozen grandeur of the North Korean capital. In the middle of the interview at his palatial residence overlooking snow-covered hills and a frozen lake, the prince showed me a table. "This is where I will sit with Khieu Samphan for negotiation," he said with his habitual nervous giggle, "and there will be disagreement." Displaying a candor that had become his hallmark, he said, "I do not plan to say yes to the Khmer Rouge now or tomorrow or in November [his announced date for a second round of talks with Samphan]. I will just have a good time with the Chinese."

As Sihanouk had predicted, his meeting with Khieu Samphan in March broke down over his conditions for joining a united front with the Khmer Rouge. Of nine different conditions that Sihanouk had announced, the one dealing with the future proved to be the most intractable.[39]

Samphan refused to accept the condition that the Khmer Rouge disarm along with other resistance groups when, after a settlement, an international peacekeeping force replaced the withdrawing Vietnamese troops. Later events would prove that Sihanouk had touched upon a key issue that underlined the conflict of interest between China and its Khmer Rouge allies on the one hand and non-Communist Southeast Asia on the other.

Deng's American Nursemaids

ASEAN had not gauged how stubbornly the Khmer Rouge rejected the idea of disarmament and abdication of power as part of a settlement. ASEAN satisfaction at China's willingness to participate in an international conference on Cambodia was, however, short-lived, since Moscow and Hanoi made it clear they would have no part of it. Still, encouraged by China's claim that it did not seek restoration of its influence in Cambodia through the Khmer Rouge, ASEAN pressed on with organizing the conference. A reasonable peace plan that took care of Vietnam's security interests and was backed by major powers, including China and the United States, ASEAN calculated, would be attractive to Hanoi even if for the sake of face it stayed out of the conference. ASEAN, and Singapore in particular, were in for some unpleasant surprises.

In July 1981 the draft declaration for the International Conference on Kampuchea (ICK) proposed by ASEAN—drawn up principally at Lee Kuan Yew's initiative—was surprisingly conciliatory toward Vietnam. The draft reflected an ASEAN consensus that China's bleeding strategy for Vietnam did not serve the interests of the group. A weakened Vietnam and restoration of the pro-Chinese Khmer Rouge would seriously upset the regional balance. Establishing an independent and nonaligned government in Cambodia by eliminating the Khmer Rouge through the electoral process would allay both Vietnamese and Thai security concerns and deprive China of a pretext to intervene in mainland Southeast Asia.

The ASEAN draft acknowledged "the legitimate concerns of neighboring states of Kampuchea [i.e., Vietnam] that it should not in any way become a threat or be used by any state for subversion or armed aggression against them." This declaration implicitly laid part of the blame for Vietnamese intervention on the Khmer Rouge's adventurism and China's military presence in Cambodia. It also offered international aid to rebuild war-ravaged Vietnam after resolution of the Cambodian conflict. The ASEAN draft sought a Vietnamese withdrawal from Cambodia to be followed by the disarming of all the Khmers and institution of an interim administration to hold a free election.

Almost from the start of the conference at the United Nations on July 13, the ASEAN draft ran into heavy Chinese and Khmer Rouge opposition. The idea of inviting the pro-Vietnamese KPRP to participate in the conference was shelved. The wording about the legitimate concerns of neighboring states was watered down. But ASEAN put up a fight on the issue of disarming the Khmer factions and forming an interim government. Singapore diplomats discovered to their surprise that Deng's assurances to Lee about an electoral verdict did not mean what they seemed to mean. At a working group meeting on July 15 Singapore ambassador to the United Nations Tommy Koh, representing ASEAN, found himself in an acrimonious encounter with China's UN ambassador, Lin Qing, in the presence of forty observers, including American diplomats. Flustered by Lin's quoting international law to defend the Khmer Rouge, Koh, himself a former dean of the Faculty of Law in Singapore University, raised his voice: "I know at least as much of international law as you do, Mr. Ambassador, but law does not apply to this barbarous bunch." He then proceeded to detail their horrendous record of four years. Some of the Cambodians in the room began to sob.[40]

In another meeting with ASEAN foreign ministers, Chinese vice–foreign minister Han Nianlong thumped the table to state that he had had enough of this criticism of the Khmer Rouge. "If there were no persistent struggle of Democratic Kampuchea, what we would be discussing here today would not be the question of Cambodia but that of Thailand."[41] He reminded them that not only would disarming the Khmer Rouge demoralize the fighters, it would also deal a blow to the legitimacy of Democratic Kampuchea. "How can you ask a legitimate member of the United Nations to lay down its arms? How can you impose an interim government in the territory of a UN member that has been the victim of aggression?" Han agitatedly asked the ASEAN colleagues. In the Chinese view, after the Vietnamese withdrawal it would be the responsibility of only the rightful government of Democratic Kampuchea to organize elections.

If the Chinese stand at the ICK angered ASEAN the American role there came as a shock. In 1980 President Ronald Reagan had provoked the Chinese by his campaign promise of establishing official relations with Taiwan. Now his secretary of state, Alexander Haig, was bending over backward to please the Chinese. As he noted, in terms of U.S. strategic interests "China may be the most important country in the world."[42]

At the ICK Haig carried his Sinophilia to the extent of siding with Peking against America's non-Communist allies and friends. As one senior ASEAN diplomat recalled with bitterness, "Haig and [assistant secretary of state John] Holdridge walked out of the General Assembly as Ieng Sary rose to speak. That bit of theatrics made the front page of *The New York Times*, but behind the scenes they pressured us to accept the Chinese position."[43]

Holdridge and Deputy Assistant Secretary for Southeast Asia John Negroponte went around the ASEAN missions urging ASEAN foreign ministries not to push China for concessions since the pragmatic leader Deng Xiaoping was under pressure from the Left. An angry Indonesian foreign minister, Mochtar Kusumaatmadja, retorted, "If Deng is not in full control that's his problem. We are not his nursemaids."[44]

Failing to persuade Singapore foreign minister Suppiah Dhanabalan to drop the provisions objected to by China, Holdridge threatened to take up the matter with Prime Minister Lee. "Please go ahead," an enraged Dhanabalan challenged before storming out of the meeting. Lee never forgave Haig and Holdridge for the insult.[45]

On Haig's instruction American ambassadors in Manila and Bangkok raised the matter with President Marcos and Prime Minister Prem, urging them to rein in their foreign ministers in New York. Although angry at what many considered American "betrayal," ASEAN gave in to Sino-American pressure and accepted compromise language that amounted to giving away the two key points.

The deadlock was finally broken when ASEAN gave up its insistence on disarming the Khmers in favor of vague assurances of "appropriate arrangements to ensure that armed Kampuchean factions will not be able to prevent or disrupt" elections. The call for an interim administration was replaced by a reference to "appropriate measures for the maintenance of law and order." While the linguistic compromise saved the conference, the stormy encounter between ASEAN and China—which Singapore's Tommy Koh called the "bitterest in my thirteen years at the UN"—exposed the big gulf that had lain hidden under their common opposition to Vietnamese occupation of Cambodia and taught the group a lesson about big-power politics.[46]

A Fighting Coalition

Although Prince Sihanouk had refused to take part in the ICK, calling it a "tribunal" to try Vietnam rather than to find a settlement, by the summer of 1981 he moved closer to the idea of a coalition. In August he met Son Sann for the first time since 1970, when the former premier had left Phnom Penh for Paris. Son Sann, an economist by training, had been young King Sihanouk's private tutor and later his banker, minister of finance, and prime minister. Despite their long and close association the mutual chemistry had changed toward the end of Sihanouk's reign, and they were not on speaking terms until the August meeting. The pressure to patch up the old feud came from ASEAN. In an unpublicized meeting at the Royal Thai embassy in Paris, Thai foreign minister Sitthi Sawetsila—the first Thai official to meet Sihanouk in over fifteen years—urged the prince to forget the past and agree to lead a coalition.

For Thailand an alliance with Sihanouk signified a dramatic reversal of a bitter historic relation. In 1962 the prince had taken Thailand to the International Court of Justice and obtained the cession of a temple that Thailand claimed, and throughout the fifteen years of his rule he had warned his people against Thai expansionism and Thai military rulers. Now the interest of Thai security outweighed the historic ill feeling. An internal Thai debate on the wisdom of allying with Sihanouk was clinched when the Thai military got word from the royal palace that a reconciliation with Sihanouk now was in the Thai interest.[47]

After much coaxing and cajoling by ASEAN and the United States, both Sihanouk and Son Sann flew to Singapore in September 1981 to sign an accord agreeing to set up a coalition government.

While agreeing that a Democratic Kampuchean coalition was essential to sustain international support, ASEAN's five members had different ideas as to what else the coalition was supposed to do. The Malaysians and Indonesians viewed the coalition as a necessary framework within which a "third force" could be developed to represent the vast majority of Cambodians, who supported neither the Vietnamese nor the Khmer Rouge. For them, forming the coalition was a ploy by which the non-Communist leaders would usurp the legitimacy of Democratic Kampuchea and eventually reach a deal with Vietnam after pushing the Khmer Rouge overboard. Malaysian foreign minister Tan Sri Ghazali Shafie explained to me that "since the Chinese do not want to disarm the Khmer Rouge we'll have to build a countervailing non-Communist force." Creation of a coalition would pave the way for arming the non-Communists. The armed third force, he warned, "is not intended to fight the Vietnamese but aimed at creating parity among the coalition partners and lending credibility to the non-Communist force as a negotiating partner of the Vietnamese."[48]

The prevailing view in Thailand, however, attached greater importance to continuing military pressure on the Vietnamese through the Khmer Rouge and held that the coalition was useful only for bringing international support to this struggle. The Singapore view was close to the Thai, but Singapore was concerned that the Khmer Rouge should not gain any political advantage from the coalition. After reaching an agreement in principle in September the three parties, however, were bogged down in dispute over who could retain what portfolio, whether to have a centralized or decentralized command. Singapore intervened to resolve the dispute with its plan for a "loose coalition" that would allow the partners to retain their autonomy and deny the Khmer Rouge the chance to dominate. After eight months of hard negotiation, as well as threats from ASEAN to cut off supplies to the KPNLF and withdraw recognition from Democratic Kampuchea, an acceptable formula of a coalition was hammered out.

The final hurdle as to who would hold the top two posts in a coalition government was overcome in May 1982, when Sitthi flew to Peking to confer with Sihanouk (this time with full Chinese cooperation). Sihanouk was to be the president, Son Sann would be the prime minister, and Khieu Samphan would have the portfolio of foreign minister in addition to the title of vice-president. "After having tried to fly on our own wings we finally had to surrender," Sihanouk explained to me later. ASEAN and the United States had made it clear to him and to Son Sann that they could give assistance only to a legal government like the DK and not to a guerrilla movement. The three leaders finally assembled in Kuala Lumpur on June 22, 1982, for the ceremonial signing of the Coalition Government of Democratic Kampuchea—adding yet another set of initials, CGDK, to the expanding glossary of the Indochina conflict. On balance, the terms of the coalition seemed to favor the Khmer Rouge. The partners had not only accepted their four conditions—tripartite structure, nonpreponderance of any one side, consensus decision making, and acceptance of the Democratic Kampuchean flag and anthem— but granted the Khmer Rouge the right to withdraw from the coalition, taking the DK label with them. While few feared the Khmer Rouge's quitting the coalition on their own, the last condition nevertheless put an end to hopes that non-Communists could one day seize the mantle of DK legality from the Khmer Rouge. The Khmer Rouge also fought for and retained the right to conduct foreign policy and the right of all the Democratic Kampuchean diplomatic personnel abroad to remain in their posts.

Learning to Live with Resignations

Although Vietnam did not seem to be impressed with the CGDK, its formation did seem to strengthen ASEAN's international position and breathe new life into the resistance. From 1982 Vietnam stopped challenging the DK credential at the United Nations, and the number of countries voting for the ASEAN resolution against Vietnam increased from 91 in 1979 to a record 114 in 1985. ASEAN and the United States developed a program for economic and military aid and training for the non-Communist factions in the CGDK. China and North Korea had offered aid to the non-Communist factions in addition to Peking's massive assistance to the Khmer Rouge. Thanks to food and other humanitarian assistance supplied by international organizations to the Khmer population living in camps along the Thai border and military supplies given by China and ASEAN, the number of non-Communist fighters grew to a force of nearly thirty thousand.

While trying to build up the non-Communist factions as viable interlocutors for Vietnam, ASEAN also kept up diplomatic pressure on Hanoi with proposals for a negotiated settlement. In more than a dozen different proposals—which were variations of ASEAN's ICK declaration—the non-Communist nations urged Vietnam to withdraw its troops and allow self-determination of the Khmer people under international supervision. Behind the facade of this united ASEAN position, however, Indonesia and Malaysia, who were more concerned about the long-term Chinese threat to the region, tried to push for a more conciliatory approach. General Benny Murdani, then chief of Indonesian intelligence, made two unpublicized trips to Hanoi in 1980 and 1982 in a bid to work out a compromise formula. Apart from Jakarta's distrust of China for its alleged role in the abortive uprising by Indonesian Communists in 1965, it sympathized with Vietnam's national struggle and defiance of Peking. Benny, in particular, expressed understanding for the Vietnamese intervention in Cambodia as a legitimate act of self-defense. However, in the face of strong Thai and Singapore opposition his move to effect a settlement by accepting the fait accompli in Cambodia had to be abandoned. Malaysia's effort in early 1983 to bring about a dialogue between ASEAN and the two countries of Indochina— Vietnam and Laos—was shot down by Thailand and China on the ground that it would put a stamp of approval on the Indochina bloc concept. Another Malaysian proposal in 1985 to organize indirect talks between the Heng Samrin regime and the CGDK, too, was resisted by Thailand, China, and the Khmer Rouge because it would give legitimacy to the surrogate regime. An Indonesian proposal that U.S.–Vietnamese normalization be made a part of the package to induce Vietnamese withdrawal from Cambodia was also cold-shouldered by Thailand and Singapore.

After having achieved international recognition because of its Cambodia initiative, for ASEAN maintaining unity became as important a goal as finding a solution to the Cambodian problem. And unity of ASEAN was maintained by deferring to the wishes of the "frontline state" Thailand. Incidents of hardline Thai opposition created some bitter feeling in Indonesia, which felt that, despite its rank as the largest and most populous country in Southeast Asia, Bangkok was leading it "by the nose." In the Indonesian view a protracted conflict in Cambodia not only threatened to fragment the region but also opened the way for increasing big-power intervention. What Indonesians wanted was to bring Vietnam into a cooperative Southeast Asian community and to build a "protective moat" around it to keep out other powers, including China.[49]

Maintaining the cohesion of a patchwork coalition was in some ways an even more pressing task than maintaining ASEAN unity. Not only was there no coordination among the coalition partners, but they often publicly sniped at each other. The Khmer Rouge and non-Communists occasionally fought skirmishes. With some ASEAN partners' still trying to remove the unsavory Khmer Rouge characters from the coalition, mutual suspicion continued to haunt the coalition and its sponsors. In September 1983, during an ASEAN dinner in Sihanouk's honor at the Waldorf-Astoria Hotel in New York, Malaysian Foreign Minister Ghazali gingerly broached the subject to Khieu Samphan: "Would you please request Messrs. Pol Pot, Ieng Sary, and Ta Mok to retire for the sake of Cambodia?" Sihanouk jumped in with a generous offer. If "His Excellency Pol Pot" would give Samphan control of the army, Sihanouk would be delighted to put his own palace in Pyongyang and his little villa in Mougins at his disposal. Warming to the subject, the prince added that the palace in Pyongyang was equipped with a swimming pool, cinema hall, badminton and volleyball courts. "You will have all the cuisine you want—French, Khmer, Chinese. You'll pass your time very pleasantly," Sihanouk assured. A frowning Khieu Samphan firmly replied, "All that is not important. What is important is unity. We have always been united and we will always be. Nobody can separate us." After a moment of embarrassed silence, the ministers resumed their meal.[50]

Aware that at a ministerial meeting in July 1984 ASEAN again discussed retiring some of the notorious Khmer Rouge figures, Deng Xiaoping delivered a direct warning to the CGDK. Receiving Sihanouk, Son Sann, and Khieu Samphan together in Peking in October 1984, Deng threatened to cut off Chinese assistance altogether if one partner of the coalition were removed. As Sihanouk later recalled, Deng was in a rage. "I do not understand," he fumed, "why some people want to remove Pol Pot. It is true that he made some mistakes in the past but now he is leading the fight against the Vietnamese aggressors."[51]

The undercurrent of tension in the CGDK was not helped by Sihanouk's repeated threats to quit the coalition. "Before Cambodia's independence I had only one master—France—but after losing the independence again I have to deal with eight," a frustrated Sihanouk told an associate. The eight masters were the six countries of ASEAN, China, and the United States.

One of Sihanouk's more serious resignation threats came in November 1984 while he was visiting Paris amid strong rumors that he might meet Hun Sen, foreign minister of the Heng Samrin regime, then present in the city on a private visit. On November 22 Thai ambassador to France Arun Phanupong was at a UNESCO conference getting ready to deliver a speech, when he received a cable from his boss Sitthi Sawetsila, asking him to urgently seek for him an appointment with Sihanouk. Sitthi was already on a Thai International flight winging toward Paris in a bid to stop Sihanouk. Arun left in a hurry without making the speech.

He caught up with the prince and asked whether it was true he had tendered his resignation to Khieu Samphan. "He just exploded," Arun later recalled. "I am fed up," Sihanouk said. "I'll have nothing to do with the coalition." His outburst was provoked by pro–Son Sann demonstrators in Minneapolis who had hurled insults at the prince during a visit twelve days earlier. Later he calmed down and asked Sitthi to lunch at his hotel outside Paris. Through the Thai International communication channel Arun had radioed a message to Sitthi on the plane and had driven the red-eyed foreign minister directly from Charles de Gaulle Airport to lunch with Sihanouk. Over a twelve-course meal Sitthi condemned the actions of Son Sann's supporters and persuaded the prince to stay on as the head of the coalition. Speeding back to Paris in the evening, Sitthi had vomited. A soiled Mercedes was a small price to keep the CGDK alive.[52]

But four months later Sihanouk threatened again to resign, claiming poor health but obviously meaning to protest China's refusal to seek a dialogue with Hanoi. ASEAN foreign ministers meeting in Bandung went into an emergency huddle to draft a collective appeal to the prince not to quit. Sihanouk agreed, but in July 1985 he publicly denounced the Khmer Rouge coalition partners for killing thirty-eight of his partisans and warned that if one more were killed "my decision to leave the coalition would be irrevocable."

Although the coalition survived its internal crises, the biggest blow to the credibility of the CGDK came in the dry season of 1984–85. In five months of a sustained campaign in which the Vietnamese attacked civilian camps and military bases along the Thai-Cambodian border using artillery and tanks, they ended the fiction of a Democratic Kampuchean territory. The overrun encampments included several important Khmer Rouge logistical supply bases and their showpiece capital. The village named Phum Thmei, carved out amidst jungle close to the Thai border, served as the CGDK provisional capital where Prince Sihanouk received the credentials of foreign ambassadors while clinking glasses of champagne. When the campaign ended not a single resistance base was left on Cambodian soil. The Khmer Rouge were forced to break up in small units, disperse inside Cambodia, and send 46,000 civilians under their control to take refuge in Thailand. Supporters of Sihanouk and Son Sann and 250,000 civilian refugees who lived in resistance-controlled camps just inside Cambodia had to withdraw to Thai territory.

The military setback also brought to the surface the weaknesses of ideology, organization, and training of the non-Communist groups, especially the KPNLF. Unlike the fanatical Khmer Rouge, the non-Communist fighters were reluctant to leave their families behind and go deep inside the country to fight a guerrilla war. While Sihanoukist fighters made sporadic forays inside to generate political propaganda, some fourteen thousand KPNLF troops were virtually immobilized by the loss of their camps. The simmering discontent of some of the top military leaders of KPNLF against Son Sann's "dictatorial" ways, his interference in military matters, and his refusal to cooperate with Sihanouk finally erupted into an open revolt in December 1985. The revolt was subdued through ASEAN intervention but the effective command of the KPNLF was taken over by the Thai military.

Cam Ranh Bay: Bear in the South

While ASEAN maneuvered to keep alive the resistance war and the shaky coalition, one of its long-standing goals of a big-power-free Southeast Asia had taken a back seat. In the six years since the invasion of Cambodia the Soviet military presence had had a dramatic growth in the Pacific, which was followed by an increased American presence. Taking advantage of Vietnam's isolation and vulnerability vis-à-vis China and its dire economic position, Moscow emerged as principal patron of Hanoi. The price of that patronage was the military facilities that Hanoi had tenaciously denied to the Soviets for four years. In the two years following the Chinese invasion Moscow supplied Hanoi with weapons worth $2 billion—a more than tenfold increase over 1978. Although the arms deliveries slackened in subsequent years, aid was still estimated at an annual average of $750 million. Although most of what Hanoi received was second-generation equipment that the Warsaw Pact and other Soviet allies were phasing out, the Vietnamese had to be grateful to Moscow. Shifting its earlier posture Hanoi opened the door wide to Soviet personnel. The number of Soviet military advisers stationed in Vietnam in 1986 was estimated to be around two thousand compared with just twenty-five in early 1977. In addition there were three thousand Soviet experts working on aid projects, including offshore oil exploration. Since 1979 Soviet economic aid was estimated by U.S. intelligence to be worth $1 billion a year.[53] The Soviets simultaneously increased their economic and military aid to Laos and Cambodia and expanded their presence.

The price for Soviet aid was paid by the Vietnamese in small installments. Eleven days after the beginning of the Chinese invasion Pham Van Dong made an unpublicized trip to Moscow. Shortly after his return in early March 1979, support vessels from the Soviet intelligence-gathering task force assembled in the South China Sea anchored at Danang Harbor.[54] Agreement for that visit was presumably reached during the consultations he had held in Moscow. United States government analysts believe that Soviet military buildup in Vietnam began not on the basis of any open-ended commitment or "leasing" of Vietnamese facilities, but as a result of specific accords reached during periodic consultations held between Moscow and Hanoi officials. Article Six of the Soviet-Vietnamese treaty provided for consultation on security threats to the contracting parties and appropriate measures to counter them.

The more significant port call came on March 27, 1979. A small fleet—one cruiser, one frigate, and one minesweeper—became the first Russian ships to drop anchor at Cam Ranh Bay since April 12, 1905, when an armada of forty-two vessels led by czarist admiral

Zinovi Rozhdestvenski had steamed into the same port. The only difference was that in 1905 Cam Ranh Bay was an inhospitable coaling station maintained by the French—who ordered the fleet out of the bay in order to maintain neutrality in the Russo-Japanese War—and seventy-four years later it was a major air-naval base left behind by the United States. Since that small beginning Cam Ranh Bay had developed into Moscow's largest naval base and staging area outside the Soviet Union and a key outpost for greater Soviet power projection in the South China Sea and the Indian Ocean.

Although in line with their recent practice the Soviets did not undertake any major onshore construction that was not expendable (with the exception of an electronic intelligence-gathering station to monitor American and Chinese naval movements), in slow but steady steps they increased the number of ships and aircraft operating from Cam Ranh Bay. From the daily average of five to ten ships operating from Cam Ranh Bay in 1979 the number steadily rose from twenty-five to thirty-five by 1985. The daily average of aircraft deployed in Cam Ranh Bay increased from ten to fifteen a day to thirty-five to forty in the six years after 1979. By stationing sixteen naval Badger bombers and a squadron of all-weather MiG-23s in addition to the long-range reconnaissance and transport aircraft in Vietnam, Moscow acquired a strike capability in Southeast Asia that was beyond its wildest dreams before 1978. By early 1986, with some twenty to twenty-five ships, including submarines, deployed in the South China Sea and with refueling, dry-dock, and repair facilities at Cam Ranh Bay, doubling the Soviet naval deployment capacity in the Indian Ocean, the Soviet Union had emerged as a major naval power in Asia.[55] It is an ironic commentary on Brzezinski's effort to checkmate Soviet expansionism by backing China.

Thaw in Moscow, Chill in Hanoi

Soviet presence in Indochina and its military buildup continued to grow against the backdrop of a brushfire war in Cambodia. The strategic imperatives behind China's "American card," however, had begun to change within two years of Deng Xiaoping's historic trip to the United States. The Sino-American strategic alliance that

Brzezinski pushed so hard to achieve in 1978 and that had blossomed in 1980 (particularly in the wake of the Soviet invasion of Afghanistan) with a broad range of cooperative security measures ran into trouble with the election of Ronald Reagan.[56] His campaign pledge to improve relations with Taiwan had come at a time when for domestic political reasons China had begun to rethink its increasing strategic alignment with the United States. As a wrangle developed with Washington over the issue of arms sales to Taiwan—left unresolved by the two sides in December 1978 in their hurry to normalize relations—the Chinese foreign policy posture shifted from Deng's call for a united front against Moscow to a more Third World–oriented view seeking economic cooperation rather than confrontation. That cooperative approach was applied to every country—even the USSR and Eastern Europe—with the sole exception of Vietnam. In late 1981 Chinese vice-premier Li Xiannian announced that China was willing to resume the normalization talks with Moscow that were suspended after the Soviet invasion of Afghanistan.

Responding to China's new interest and in a clear attempt to exploit Sino-American tension, on March 24, 1982, Brezhnev issued a public call for improvement of relations with China. He not only gave China a self-serving reminder that Moscow had never supported a two-China policy but also moved away from past denunciations of China for its "betrayal of Marxism-Leninism." Brezhnev assured Peking, "We have not denied, and do not deny now the existence of a socialist system in China."[57]

Peking soon responded to the offering by calling upon Moscow to remove three obstacles to Sino-Soviet normalization. The obstacles viewed as threats to China's security were Soviet support for the Vietnamese occupation of Cambodia, Soviet occupation of Afghanistan, and massive deployment of Soviet forces along China's border. Within seven months normalization talks resumed.

Despite Brezhnev's public assurances that improvement of relations with China would not be "to the detriment of third countries," Hanoi was disconcerted by the opening of the talks. Vietnam had too often seen its interests sacrificed by its powerful friends for their own strategic gains. Seven rounds of talks held since the fall of

1982, however, did not produce any visible weakening of Soviet support. Moscow was obviously not ready to risk its military advantage in Vietnam in trying to satisfy China. Notwithstanding those "obstacles," however, economic, trade, and cultural ties between China and the Soviet Union improved significantly. In 1985 alone more than seventy visits were exchanged between the two countries. After the visit by the first senior Soviet leader—Vice-Premier Ivan Arkhipov—to China in December 1984 and that of Chinese Vice-Premier Yao Yilin to Moscow in July 1985, Moscow agreed to modernize seventeen industries in China and build seven new industrial enterprises. An agreement signed in 1985 stipulated that their trade was to register a twelvefold increase in five years. Despite Peking's assertion that political relations would not ameliorate without the Soviets' giving satisfaction on the "obstacles," especially Cambodia, a wide range of contacts involving trade unions and youth leagues took place, and the foreign ministers of the two countries were scheduled to visit each other's capital in 1986.

Of course, Peking still harbored deep distrust of Moscow and was concerned about the long-term threat that the Soviet Union posed to China. But it calculated that improvement of ties with Moscow not only would be economically beneficial but would also enable China to exert psychological pressure on Vietnam and make it more amenable to seeking a settlement with China. In an obvious bid to sow doubt between Moscow and Hanoi, Deng Xiaoping told an European leader in early 1985 than China had no objections to a Soviet base in Cam Ranh Bay if the Vietnamese withdrew from Cambodia.[58] Although the statement was in all probability a tactical ploy, it was an ironic reversal from the mid-1970s, when Peking incessantly warned the world against Soviet hegemonists' seeking a base in Cam Ranh Bay. Frustrated, however, by the lack of Soviet response on issues of concern to China, in early 1986 Peking stepped up its propaganda attacks on Moscow. In order to assure Thailand and the United States and signal to Moscow that China's resolve on Cambodia was not weakening, it simultaneously intensified shelling and infantry attacks on Vietnam.

While Moscow under Mikhail Gorbachev assured Vietnam continued economic and military assistance (albeit in exchange for increased Vietnamese agricultural exports and stricter management of aid) and publicly backed its position on Cambodia, there were signs of a cooling enthusiasm. In his first official presentation on Southeast Asian problems Soviet Deputy Foreign Minister Mikhail Kapitsa called the Cambodian situation "irreversible" and predicted that over time China's "three obstacles would become blurred." Privately, officials were less sanguine, however. They noted that the continuation of the conflict gave "the Americans a free ride in Southeast Asia," complicated Soviet relations with ASEAN, and limited its access to one of the world's most dynamic regions. They also pointed out that in view of emergent Khmer nationalism Vietnam would be better off withdrawing troops from Cambodia at an early date. In December 1985 a senior Soviet Asia specialist put it to me quite bluntly. He said, "Vietnam would have to seek an accommodation with China. They cannot afford to have a hostile China on their border in perpetuity."[59]

A Role for Uncle Sam

History turned full circle in January 1985 when, a decade after the last American helicopter left Saigon, the Indochinese foreign ministers issued an appeal to the United States to return to the region to play a constructive role. That turnaround had followed the budding Sino-Soviet détente and significant transformation in Sino-American relations. Hanoi was particularly encouraged by the Reagan administration's dispute with China over Taiwan.

After George Shultz took over responsibility for American foreign policy from Alexander Haig in 1982, the United States took a more hard-nosed view of China's value as a strategic partner. While Peking was viewed as an important regional player, a vast potential market for U.S. trade and investment, and a valuable counterpoint to the Soviet power in Asia, it no longer occupied the central place in American strategic thinking. Although Washington agreed with the Chinese line on pressuring Vietnam, there was clearer recognition that their objectives in Cambodia were not the same. To China's discomfort the Reagan administration repeatedly declared its opposition to a Khmer Rouge return to power in Cambodia. While the United States remained as hard-line in opposing the Vietnamese occupation as China, the stability and cohesion of ASEAN as an organization and, above all, the security interests of Thailand, rather than pleasing China, informed its policy. Washington refused to take any initiative of its own in Cambodia, but it worked behind the scenes with ASEAN to bring about the Cambodian coalition and ensure its success at the United Nations. In 1982 the United States began a program of covert assistance worth $15 million a year, channeled through ASEAN countries to the non-Communist partners of the coalition. Reflecting the new U.S. mood in support of anti-Communist "freedom fighters" all over the world in 1985, the Congress stepped in to authorize up to $5 million in overt economic or military aid to the Cambodian resistance.

One reminder of a change in Vietnam's perspective was the mild concern with which it reacted to that aid—the first direct American involvement in Indochina since 1975. Apart from its awareness of the symbolic nature of the move, Hanoi was sensitive to the changed strategic situation in East Asia. In some ways Vietnam's calculations about the United States in 1985 were similar to those of 1978. Prior to its treaty with Moscow and intervention in Cambodia, Vietnam made a desperate effort to normalize its relations with the United States. After seven years of consolidation of its influence in Cambodia, Vietnam was again seeking to establish ties with the United States and increase its margin of maneuver vis-à-vis Moscow. There was also a growing realization in Hanoi that though Soviet weapons might have helped it to eliminate the threat from Pol Pot, its long-term security interest in Indochina could only be ensured through an international settlement and guarantee. A key player in the diplomatic game would have to be the United States, which not only had shifted from its Brzezinski-style strategic alliance with China but had also come to acknowledge that despite a close alliance with Moscow, Vietnam was not a puppet. ("The Soviet-Vietnamese marriage is not made in heaven," Assistant Secretary of Defense Richard Armitage told me. He fully expected it to head for the rocks when the glue of mutual self-interest loosened.) The United States, however, was not ready to respond to the Indochinese appeal to return to the region as an active player. But the fact that the Reagan administration took keen interest in settling the issue of twenty-five-hundred Americans missing in Indochina ("a highest national priority" for Reagan) provided the Vietnamese with a useful lever to draw the United States into renewed dialogue. Encouraged by signals from Vietnam, Richard Armitage visited Hanoi in February 1982 to discuss the resolution of the MIA problem. Although very few concrete results were achieved, the Hanoi visit by the first senior American official since 1977 helped to relieve the Vietnamese feeling of isolation and created concern in Peking and some ASEAN capitals. Despite those worries a U.S. policy review in mid-1982 decided to push the MIA issue with Hanoi even if Hanoi did not budge on the question of Cambodia. Several high-level meetings and visits since that time resulted in the return of about one hundred remains of American servicemen. In 1985 Hanoi took a new step by allowing a U.S. military team to search a crash site in Vietnam. It promised that it would make unilateral efforts to resolve the MIA issue within two years. In early 1986 Armitage and Assistant Secretary of State for East Asian and Pacific Affairs Paul Wolfowitz led the highest-level U.S. delegation to Hanoi since Leonard Woodcock's mission nine years earlier and came back with assurance of full cooperation without any preconditions.

Hanoi also attempted to seduce the Americans by dangling the possibility of reduced Soviet use of Cam Ranh Bay. In late 1985 Hanoi began to hint to the Americans that Cam Ranh Bay was still under Vietnamese control and that in the event of a settlement on Cambodia the level of Soviet military presence could be reduced. Although the hints were tantalizing, Americans were too suspicious of the "tricky" Vietnamese even to peck at the suggestion. Washington did not want to be maneuvered into negotiations that could unravel the ASEAN, and particularly Thai strategy toward Cambodia.

While welcoming Vietnamese "humanitarian" cooperation as a positive move that would clear the deck for eventual normalization, the United States repeatedly said that it would not establish relations with Hanoi until its withdrawal from Cambodia. But the Vietnamese turned on their charm in the hope that cooperation on the emotionally charged MIA issue would earn them some goodwill. In an improved climate, Hanoi hoped, Washington would soften its stance on Cambodia, pressure China to be conciliatory, and also influence Thailand. Even without the hoped-for flexibility Hanoi calculated that stepped-up cooperation with the United States would help to defuse a growing anti-Hanoi campaign in the United States over allegations of prisoners of war still being held in Vietnam and would act as a brake on the Reagan administration's ideological impulse to support resistance in Cambodia.

Counting on Time

Ever since the Hanoi army had marched into Cambodia both the Vietnamese and their opponents believed time, like God, to be on their side. Hanoi thought that with every passing year the Heng Samrin regime would consolidate itself in a revived Cambodia, and, tired of backing a hopeless resistance war, the world would accept the fait accompli. Peking was convinced that as the Vietnamese became bogged down in an unwinnable guerrilla war in Cambodia and their economy and security deteriorated in the face of economic sanctions and military pressure, they would be forced to retreat. But as the Cambodian war entered its seventh year neither of these calculations seemed close to realization.

China's war of attrition against Vietnam drained Vietnamese resources. Denial of Western aid and loans deepened Vietnam's economic difficulties. Since the end of the war over a million Vietnamese had fled their homeland—a large number of them after 1979. Vietnam, once a hero of the Third World as a giant-killer, had become an international pariah—condemned by the same United Nations that once massively voted in favor of large-scale reconstruction aid to Hanoi. By the beginning of 1986 Vietnam's foreign debt had risen to $6.7 billion, and, because of their default in repayment, all Western lending institutions had closed their doors. Although liberal economic reforms, introduced since 1980, had pushed up food production and helped Vietnam through its worst economic crisis, the capital-starved country's future was still bleak. The prospect turned even gloomier as a result of gross mismanagement of the economy. Opposition to reform by some die-hard idealogues in the Party, especially an attempt to cut down consumption by replacing the old currency in September 1985, proved disastrous. Buffeted by a 500 percent inflation that followed the move, even the most loyal population in the north began clamoring for a change of leadership. In a bid to restore popular confidence in the summer of 1986, an ailing Party Secretary Le Duan was virtually stripped of power, and in a major reshuffle a number of reformers were brought into the cabinet. The Sixth Congress of the Communist Party of Vietnam, scheduled for the end of 1986, was expected to replace some of the old guard with younger and more modern-minded leaders. There was, however, no sign that the younger reformist leaders were any less committed on Cambodia than their elders.

Despite a certain demoralization among ASEAN partners there was no indication that Thailand and China—the two principal actors—were close to throwing in the towel. Vietnam had seriously erred in its assumption that the Khmer Rouge would be wiped out quickly or that the world would soon forget Cambodia. With every passing year the Vietnamese grip over Cambodia increased but so did the number of countries at the United Nations voting against Hanoi's occupation. Though still hated and feared by the population, aided by China and Thailand, the Khmer Rouge staged a comeback. Despite reverses suffered in the 1985 dry season they were increasingly active in mounting guerrilla attacks inside the country. With the Vietnamese occupation running into its seventh year, the old Khmer antagonism toward the Vietnamese began to surface. There were indications of disaffection within the Heng Samrin army and small signs of defiance against Hanoi within the PRK ranks.

By early 1986 there were few straws in the wind indicating the beginning of a realization by the Vietnamese that although Cambodia was in their hands, time might not be on their side. Vietnam could win the battle in Cambodia and still lose the bigger struggle for building a secure and prosperous country. As China was forging ahead with its modernizations and most of non-Communist Southeast Asia was flourishing, Indochina seemed to be disappearing into an economic sinkhole. While acknowledging that time was of the essence, Hanoi, however, did not change an iota its view of Cambodia as the key to its security. It continued its effort to snuff out the resistance but began looking more and more toward a diplomatic solution—a friendly coalition government headed by Sihanouk and international guarantee—to attain the same security objectives. If that search were blocked by its opponents, in the hope that a few more years would bring Hanoi to its knees, Vietnam—even under a new leadership—was determined to soldier on, regardless of cost.

Epilogue

Was the Third Indochina War inevitable? With the benefit of hindsight the answer is yes—and no. Given their scarred historical memory and the deep suspicion with which the Khmers and the Vietnamese, and the Vietnamese and the Chinese, viewed each other, a certain tension between them was inevitable. A re-emergence of irrendentism and a contest over resources, so long frozen by colonial rule and foreign intervention, too were natural to a degree. But these things in themselves did not insure war.

The Vietnamese view that Indochina was a unified theater for their security and vital space for their economic future was bound to produce friction between the ultranationalistic Khmer Rouge and Hanoi. But as the war ended Vietnam's primary concern was consolidation of the Communist party's control over the whole country and economic reconstruction, not the creation of an Indochinese empire. While the Vietnamese were concerned by the dissidence of the Khmer Rouge they were in no hurry to force them to change their line. But Pol Pot and his friends were pressed for time. Cambodian revolutionary power had to be built at a breakneck speed, and the nation had to be "purified" of all Vietnamese puppets and weaklings to prepare for the inevitable life-and-death struggle against the "expansionist" Vietnamese. Emboldened by Vietnam's prostrate economy and domestic troubles, the Khmer Rouge even thought it possible to preempt Vietnam's inevitable attack on Cambodia by taking the war into Vietnam itself. Khmer Rouge provocations forced Hanoi to alter its timetable and turn its full attention to its security in Indochina. While China had long suspected Vietnamese ambition and would have used its power and diplomacy to prevent a Hanoi hegemony in Indochina, its agenda too was modified by the Khmer Rouge initiative. After initial hesitation China had to throw in its weight behind Cambodia in the war that the Khmer Rouge had brought upon themselves.

An unfortunate conjunction of international events also exacerbated the situation in Indochina. For nearly three years—until late 1978—China was too involved in its internecine struggle to adopt a new, creative, or even pragmatic approach to Indochina. Instead of policy, it pursued an inertial course dictated by tradition and halfhearted implementation of Maoist dogma. In the United States a post-Vietnam indifference to Asia and strong congressional feeling ran counter to the Vietnamese hope of bringing back the United States as a new guarantor of regional power balance. Although Cyrus Vance and Richard Holbrooke understood the opportunity the Indochinese conflict offered to Washington, they lost the bureaucratic battle to the Manichaean anti-Sovietism of Zbigniew Brzezinski.

What does the future hold for Indochina? Judging by recent history the years ahead can bring more suffering and perhaps more bloodshed. China is determined to tame Vietnam and establish its own supremacy in Southeast Asia—a goal for which it has only partial support from ASEAN and the West. Vietnam is determined to maintain the dominance it has achieved by military might and deprivation of its own people. Unless there is a willingness in both Peking and Hanoi to lower their sights, Indochina will not know peace.

Although a giant in size and manpower, China finds itself incapable of bending Vietnam to its will. Vietnam, backed by Moscow, remains a redoubtable military power; however, its drive to achieve supremacy in Indochina is hamstrung by its economic and social problems, by the nationalism of the Khmers, and by stubborn opposition from the traditional rival Thailand.

If history has taught the protagonists to be wary of each other, it has also taught them that peace is possible. The bitterness of the Sino-Vietnamese conflict is matched by the intimate knowledge each has of the other. In the past, between bouts of war fought by China and Vietnam there have been long periods of peace, which were based on China's recognition of the difficulty of subordinating Vietnam and Vietnam's acknowledgment of the superiority of the Middle Kingdom. To achieve peace, China would need to acknowledge Vietnam's security concern in Cambodia in the same way it demands Hanoi be mindful of China's security interests. The proud masters of Vietnam today may not be ready to follow the example of their anti-Chinese hero Nguyen Hue—who followed up his military success against the Middle Kingdom with a tribute-bearing mission—but they cannot ignore the reality of China as a regional power. The failure of the nineteenth century Vietnamese attempt to control Cambodia and its own recent experience should also give Hanoi food for thought.

The history of Thai-Vietnamese relations also shows that the only period when Bangkok and Hue did not fight over Cambodia was in the early nineteenth century, when the Vietnamese exercised effective influence over Cambodia, but the court of Hue acknowledged equal Thai interest in Cambodian affairs. In the celebrated words of Vietnamese governor Le Van Duyet, "Cambodia was a child with Thailand as father and Vietnam as mother." Khmers would bristle at this suggestion of Cambodia's being a helpless child. But thanks to decades of warfare and the bloodletting by Pol Pot, Cambodia today is too weak to be a buffer. It may have to recommence its journey to full nationhood as a matter of course, not under a Vietnamese-Thai condominium but under international guarantee—an international guarantee against the return of the murderous policies of the Khmer Rouge and foreign intervention. Only a big power guarantee of that sort could reassure the Cambodian people, bridge the gulf of suspicion between Vietnam and Thailand, and ensure everybody's security interest in Cambodia.

409

An international guarantee, however, is possible only if Moscow accepts that it can gain more in political influence and trade in Southeast Asia if it abandons its single-minded search for supremacy through opportunistic use of military tools.

A heavy responsibility—and opportunity—however, lies with the United States. An ironic turn of the wheel has again placed Washington in the position of an arbiter in Asia. It is best placed to guarantee a new balance of power in Southeast Asia, guarantee Thai security against Vietnam, reassure Hanoi against Chinese hegemony while alleviating Chinese concerns about Moscow, and provide Hanoi with an alternative to total dependence on the Soviets. To achieve this, however, Washington would have to abandon its one-issue approach to Indochina—which consists of seeking accounting for MIAs—and play a more active and imaginative role than it has so far been willing to. The prestige and influence the U.S. once lost in its misguided military adventure in Indochina can still be regained through rightful use of its economic power and diplomacy, and above all in helping in the revival of Cambodia.

Chronology
of Events

1 9 7 5

April 17	Phnom Penh falls to the Khmer Rouge.
April 30	Saigon falls to the Vietnamese Communists.
May 4	Khmer Rouge attack Vietnamese islands.
May 12	Khmer Rouge capture U.S. freighter *Mayaguez*.
June 12	Vietnam occupies Cambodian island; Pol Pot is in Hanoi on an unpublicized visit.
June 21	Unpublicized meeting between Mao Zedong and Pol Pot in Peking.
August 18	China pledges massive economic aid to a visiting Cambodian delegation.
September 25	Le Duan ends discordant Peking visit.
October 30	Moscow pledges long-term economic aid to Vietnam during Le Duan visit.

November 21   Vietnam announces imminent reunification of North and South.

1 9 7 6

February 6   China signs secret military aid agreement with Cambodia.

April 2   Prince Norodom Sihanouk resigns as head of state of Cambodia.

April 14   A new government, Democratic Kampuchea, headed by Pol Pot, is announced.

July 20   Pol Pot receives a Vietnamese journalist delegation.

September 9   Chairman Mao Zedong dies.

October 6   Radical "Gang of Four" is arrested in China.

December 14   Vietnamese Communist party congress opens.

1 9 7 7

February 24   Peking tells Vietnam it is unable to give new aid.

March 16   Leonard Woodcock leads U.S. presidential delegation to Hanoi.

April 25   Pham Van Dong begins tour of Western Europe.

April 30   Khmer Rouge launch attack on Vietnamese villages.

May 3   U.S.–Vietnamese normalization talk opens in Paris.

June 7   Pham Van Dong meets Leonid Brezhnev in Moscow.

June 10   Pham Van Dong meets Li Xiannian in Peking.

July 17   Vietnam signs a twenty-five-year treaty of friendship with Laos.

September 24   Khmer Rouge attack Vietnamese village, killing hundreds of civilians.

September 28   Pol Pot begins triumphant tour of China.

October 10   High-level Soviet military delegation visits Vietnam.

November 21   Le Duan visits Peking in effort to disengage China from the Khmer Rouge.

December 3   Chinese vice-premier Chen Yonggui visits Cambodia.

December 25   Vietnam launches attack on Cambodia.

December 31   Cambodia severs diplomatic relations with Vietnam.

1 9 7 8

January 18   Madame Deng Yingchao visits Cambodia to urge moderation.

February 5   Hanoi proposes cease-fire and negotiation with Cambodia.

February 22   Vietnamese negotiator makes secret trip to Peking.

March 24   Vietnam begins clampdown on its ethnic Chinese.

April 22   First Khmer rebel brigade formed in Vietnam.

May 12   China cancels part of its aid to Vietnam.

May 20   Zbigniew Brzezinski arrives in Peking.

May 24   Pol Pot launches attack on his own party in the Eastern Zone; China denounces Vietnam for its treatment of ethnic Chinese.

June 28   Vietnam joins Soviet economic bloc COMECON.

July 5   Secret U.S.–Chinese negotiation for normalization begins in Peking.

July 11   Vietnam publicly renounces aid precondition for ties with the United States.

September 10   Pham Van Dong begins tour of non-Communist Southeast Asia.

September 27   Unpublicized U.S.–Vietnam talks in New York make breakthrough on normalization.

October 11 President Jimmy Carter decides to shelve normalization with Hanoi pending establishment of ties with Peking.

November 3 Vietnam signs twenty-five-year friendship treaty with Moscow.

November 5 Deng Xiaoping begins tour of non-Communist Southeast Asia; another Chinese delegation visits Cambodia.

November 11 Chinese party meeting begins, leading to Deng Xiaoping's ascendancy.

December 2 Anti–Pol Pot Cambodian national salvation front is announced by Hanoi.

December 15 U.S.–Chinese normalization is announced.

December 25 Vietnam launches invasion of Cambodia.

1 9 7 9

January 7 Phnom Penh falls to the Vietnamese.

January 14 Secret Thai-Chinese meeting to support guerrilla war against the Vietnamese in Cambodia.

January 28 Deng arrives in Washington; plans to teach a "lesson" to Vietnam.

February 17 China launches invasion against Vietnam.

March 27 Soviet naval contingent drops anchor at Cam Ranh Bay.

Notes

ABBREVIATIONS

BP	*Bangkok Post*
BR	*Beijing Review*
FEER	*Far Eastern Economic Review*
FBIS—PRC	*Foreign Broadcast Information Service—People's Republic of China*
FBIS—APA	*Foreign Broadcast Information Service—Asia Pacific*
ND	*Nhan Dan*
NYT	*The New York Times*
QDND	*Quan Doi Nhan Dan*
RR	*Renmin Ribao*
SWB	*Summary of World Broadcast (BBC)*
VNA	*Vietnam News Agency*
VC	*Vietnam Courier*
WP	*Washington Post*
Xinhua	*Xinhua News Agency*

415

Notes

Notes to Chapter 1

1. Roy Rowan, *The Four Days of Mayaguez* (New York: Norton, 1975), 38–48.

2. *The Vietnamese Air Force, 1951–1975: An Analysis of its Role in Combat and Fourteen Hours at Koh Tang*, Southeast Asia Monograph Series, Vol. 3 (Washington, D.C.: USAF, 1981), 106.

3. Rowan, *Four Days*, 223.

4. Personal communication from an Australian foreign service officer who had interviewed Tot in Malaysia on April 5, 1979.

5. Michael Chinoy, "A Close Look at the *Mayaguez*," *FEER*, May 30, 1975, 18.

6. R. M. Smith, *Cambodia's Foreign Policy* (Ithaca, N.Y.: Cornell University Press, 1965), 159.

7. Ben Kiernan, "Wild Chickens, Farm Chickens, and Cormorants: Kampuchea's Eastern Zone under Pol Pot," in *Revolution and its Aftermath in Kampuchea: Eight Essays*, David Chandler and Ben Kiernan, eds., Monograph Series no. 25 (New Haven, Conn.: Yale University Southeast Asia Studies, 1983), 178.

8. *Kampuchea Dossier*, Vol. 1, VC, Hanoi, 1979, 127.

9. Author's interview with Pham Van Ba, former Vietnamese ambassador to Democratic Kampuchea, Ho Chi Minh City, January 27, 1981.

10. *SWB*, August 5, 1975.

11. *Kampuchea Dossier*, 126.

12. Kenneth M. Quinn, "The Origin and Development of Radical Cambodian Communism" (Ph.D. diss., University of Maryland, 1982), 187.

13. Ibid.

14. Mimeographed transcript of Wang Shangrong–Son Sen meeting on February 6, 1976. (Translated from Khmer to French by People's Republic of Kampuchea, 1979.) This document was left behind by the Pol Pot regime in January 1979 and was later produced as evidence by the People's Republic of Kampuchea at the trial-in-absentia of Pol Pot and Ieng Sary. Although the original transcript was not available, the internal evidence in the translated version, especially the rather limited nature of the Chinese aid mentioned in the document, which contrasts with exaggerated Hanoi claims, suggests it to be authentic.

15. *FBIS—PRC*, April 16, 1976, A-7.

16. *The Straits Times*, November 13, 1974.

17. Henry Kissinger, *The White House Years* (Boston: Little, Brown, 1979), 1114.

18 *Kiessing's Contemporary Archives*, January 1974, 26488.

19. "Memorandum outlining Vice Premier Li Xiannian's talks with Premier Pham Van Dong on 10 June 1977," *Xinhua*, March 22, 1979.

20. *SWB*, May 1, 1975.

21. *SWB*, May 29, 1975.

22. *SWB*, May 22, 1975.

23. "Fighting a New Kind of War," *FEER*, September 26, 1975, 10.

24. *FBIS—PRC*, September 23, 1975, A-16.

25. Ibid., A-18–19.

26. A Chinese official in Hongkong told me on April 17, 1980, that Le Thanh Nghi was so insistent in demanding aid from China during his frequent trips that he was known by the nickname "the Beggar."

27. *BR*, June 16, 1978, 12–16. Although the article does not give the date of the meeting nor the name of the Vietnamese leader, the allusion to Zhou's "serious illness" when he met the visitor and reference to "during the war" make Nghi the most likely person to have heard this remark from Zhou. The Chinese media reported in August 1975 Nghi's meeting with Zhou, who was in his hospital bed.

28. Quoted by *Xinhua*, June 19, 1981.

29. *Vietnam's Sovereignty over Hoang Sa and Truong Sa Archipelagoes* (Hanoi: Ministry of Foreign Affairs, 1979), 60. This Vietnamese account was confirmed by Xinhua, August 14, 1979.

30. Author's interview with the deputy director of the Chinese Centre for Contemporary Affairs, Peking, March 8, 1982.

31. *SWB*, June 6, 1978.

32. *SWB*, May 2, 1975.

33. Carlyle A. Thayer and David G. Marr, *Vietnam Since 1975*, Centre for the Study of Australian-Asian Relations Research Paper no. 20 (Brisbane: Griffith University, 1980), 7.

34. *Ta Kung Pao*, Hongkong, November 27, 1975.

35. Gareth Porter, "Vietnamese Policy and the Indochina Crisis" in *The Third Indochina Conflict*, David W. P. Elliott, ed. (Boulder, Colo.: Westview Press, 1981), 80.

Notes

36. *SWB*, April 26, 1976.

37. Ieng Sary's interview with Patrice de Beer, Southeast Asia correspondent of *Le Monde* in Bangkok, October 1975. I am grateful to de Beer for sharing his notes with me.

38. Sarin Chhak, *Les Frontières du Cambodge* (Paris: Dalloz, 1966), 207–208; also see *Cambodia-Vietnam*, International Boundary Study no. 155, U.S. Department of State, Bureau of Intelligence and Research, Washington, D.C., 1976, 11–12.

39. Transcript of James Burnet's interview with Hoang Tung, Hanoi, January 12, 1986. Personal communication from James Burnet.

40. *SWB*, July 6, 1976.

41. *SWB*, August 18, 1976.

42. "Memorandum outlining Vice Premier Li Xiannian's talks with Premier Pham Van Dong on 10 June 1977," *Xinhua*, March 22, 1979.

43. Jurgen Domes, *China After the Cultural Revolution* (London: Hurst, 1976), 247–251.

44. Michel Oksenberg, "A Decade of Sino-American Relations," *Foreign Affairs*, Fall 1982, 180–181.

NOTES TO "PRINCE NORODOM SIHANOUK: THE VICTORY"

1. Henry Kissinger, *Years of Upheaval* (Boston: Little, Brown, 1982), 59.

2. Y Phandara, *Retour à Phnom Penh* (Paris: A. M. Métailié, 1982), 37.

NOTES TO CHAPTER 2

1. Paul Mus, *Vietnam: Sociologie d'une Guerre* (Paris: Editions du Seuil, 1952), 17.

2. Michael G. Cotter, "Towards a Social History of Vietnamese Southward Movement," *Journal of Southeast Asian History*, Vol. IX, No. 1, March 1968, 14.

3. Georges Maspero, *Le Royaume de Champa* (Paris: Van Houst, 1928), 26. The more recent figure is from the 1976 census of the Socialist Republic of Vietnam.

4. Alexander Barton Woodside, *Vietnam and the Chinese Model* (Cambridge: Harvard University Press, 1971), 247.

5. David Chandler, *Cambodia Before the French: Politics in a Tributary Kingdom, 1794–1848* (Ann Arbor, Mich.: University Microfilms, 1973), 108.

418

6. David Chandler, "An Anti-Vietnamese Rebellion in Early Nineteenth Century Cambodia: Pre-colonial Imperialism and a Pre-Nationalist Response," *Journal of Southeast Asian Studies*, Vol. VI, No. 1, March 1975, 16–24.

7. Personal communication from Dr. David Chandler, October 15, 1982; David Chandler, *Cambodia Before the French*, 154; David Chandler, "Kampuchea-Vietnam—the Roots of Strife" in *The Vietnam-Kampuchea-China Conflict*, Malcolm Salmon, ed., Working paper no. 1 (Canberra: Department of Political and Social Change, Research School of Pacific Studies, Australian National University, 1979), 4–5.

8. The "tea story" formed a regular part of the Khmer Rouge propaganda repertoire in the villages. See the account by a Cambodian survivor, Y Phandara, *Retour à Phnom Penh* (Paris: Métailié, 1982), 129; also A. Pannetier, *Notes Cambodgiennes: Au Coeur du Pays Khmer* (Paris: Payot, 1921; Paris: Cedoreck, 1983), 15–16.

9. Chandler, *Cambodia Before the French*, 153.

10. Press release, Democratic Kampuchea, Permanent Mission to UN, December 11, 1978, 2. Of course, that claim is false. Pol Pot or some of his friends might have secretly harbored and even sought such an objective, but it was not made the party's key mission until 1977.

11. Sarin Chhak, *Les Frontières du Cambodge* (Paris: Dalloz, 1966), Tome 1, 179.

12. Michael Leifer, *Cambodia: The Search for Security* (London: Pall Mall, 1967), 95; also Roger M. Smith, *Cambodia's Foreign Policy* (Ithaca, N.Y.: Cornell University Press, 1965), 158–159. In October 1964 negotiations between the South Vietnamese National Liberation Front (NLF) and Cambodia broke down because of the Cambodian insistence that NLF guarantee certain rights to the Khmer Krom population in South Vietnam. *Procès verbal de la Réunion de la délégation du FNL du Sud Vietnam au Palais d'hôtes à Pékin; le 1er Octobre 1964, à 16 heures*, typescript, private collection of Charles Meyer.

13. Alain Forest, *Le Cambodge et la Colonisation Française* (Paris: l'Harmattan, 1980), 452.

14. Quoted by Gareth Porter, "Vietnam and Cambodia," in *Third Indochina Conflict*, David Elliott, ed. (Boulder, Colo.: Westview, 1981), 124, note 101.

15. Declassified State Department cable no, 749-S.D.C.S. (October 1952) from Saigon provided the text of the document captured in Cambodia. The same directive said that the Chinese Communist party had authorized the VWP to "organise and direct the Chinese emigrant members of the Party residing in Vietnam, Laos and Cambodia."

16. The significance of the 1960 Congress is a debated issue among Cambodia scholars. Did it mark the founding of the Communist Party of Kampuchea

(CPK), as later claimed by Pol Pot? Or was it the second congress of the Kampuchean People's Revolutionary Party—which was a direct descendant of the ICP? The answer probably lies in the middle. As we have seen, although the ICP was broken into three national parties including the KPP it was, even in the Vietnamese eye, a proto-party, not a full-scale proletarian vanguard. The ambiguity in the status of the KPP in 1960 is indicated by the "Annotated History of the Party" prepared by the party's Eastern Zone Military Political Service in 1973. It called the 1960 meeting the second congress of the party, thus clearly denying it the glory of a founding congress. But at the same time it said that the meeting in September 1960 "decided to form the Marxist-Leninist Party in Cambodia, to continually wage the Cambodian revolution." *Summary of Annotated Party History*, typescript, translated by the U.S. Embassy in Phnom Penh, 1974.

17. Author's interview with Charles Meyer, Paris, June 18, 1977. According to Charles Meyer, former personal adviser of Sihanouk, under an arrangement worked out in 1964 with Peking and Hanoi 10 percent of the arms supplied by China was kept by Cambodia, and the remainder was transported by army trucks to the Cambodian border. Peking procured rice locally by directly paying the army chief, Lon Nol, who was in charge of the supply operation. Meyer recalled that once he conveyed to Sihanouk the Vietnamese complaint that Lon Nol cheated on the quantity of rice. "Sihanouk had a good laugh. 'Oh, Lon Nol is smart,' he said. But did not do anything about it."

18. Norodom Sihanouk, *La Calice Jusqu'à la Lie*, unpublished manuscript.

19. Harald Munthe-Kaas, "Interview with Prince Norodom Sihanouk," *FEER*, December 9, 1965.

20. Stephen Heder, "Kampuchea's Armed Struggle: The Origin of an Independent Revolution," *Bulletin of Concerned Asian Scholars*, Vol. 11, No. 1, 1979, 7.

21. Timothy Carney, "Cambodia: The Unexpected Victory," unpublished paper, February 1979, 10; Pol Pot later claimed that during the 1965 meeting in Hanoi the CPK agreed to give the Vietnamese refuge in the Khmer Rouge–controlled zones in Cambodia: *Interview of Comrade Pol Pot to the Democratic Kampuchean Press Agency* (Phnom Penh: Democratic Kampuchea, 1978), 4.

22. Heder, "Kampuchea's Armed Struggle," 14.

23. Author's interview with Charles Meyer, Paris, June 18, 1977.

24. Kissinger, *The White House Years*, 250; William Shawcross, *Sideshow: Kissinger, Nixon and the Destruction of Cambodia* (New York: Simon and Schuster, 1979), 70.

25. Quoted by Shawcross, *Sideshow*, 123. Shawcross also quotes William Colby, the former director of CIA, as saying "Lon Nol may well have been encouraged

by the fact that the United States was working with Son Ngoc Thanh (leader of anti-Sihanouk Khmer Serei movement). I don't know of any specific assurances he was given, but the obvious conclusion from him, given the political situation in South Vietnam and Laos, was that he would be given United States support," 122.

26. Sihanouk, *La Calice*, unpublished manuscript.

27. Heder, "Kampuchea's Armed Struggle, 14." In 1968 Sihanouk himself reportedly claimed to have put fifteen hundred Communists to death since 1956.

28. Ibid.

29. Shawcross, *Sideshow*, 250.

30. *Livre Noir, Faits et preuves des actes d'agression et d'annexion du Vietnam contre le Kampuchea* (Phnom Penh: Le Ministère des Affaires Étrangères du Kampuchea Démocratique, 1978), 86.

31. Kissinger, *The Years of Upheaval* (Boston: Little, Brown, 1981), 353.

32. Ibid., 341.

33. Ibid., 36.

34. Shawcross, *Sideshow*, 335–343.

35. Author's interview with Prince Norodom Sihanouk, Peking, April 5, 1980.

36. Donald Kirk, "Revolution and Political Violence in Cambodia, 1970–74" in *Communism in Indochina*, Joseph Zasloff and Paul Brown, eds. (Toronto: Lexington, 1975), 218.

37. The declassified Quinn cable is cited by Ben Kiernan, "Wild Chicken, Farm Chickens, and Cormorants: Kampuchea's Eastern Zone under Pol Pot," in *Revolution and its Aftermath in Kampuchea: Eight Essays*, David Chandler and Ben Kiernan, eds., Monograph Series no. 25 (New Haven, Conn.: Yale University Southeast Asia Studies, 1983), 176.

38. Ibid., 159.

39. *Kampuchea Dossier Chicago*, 9–10.

Notes to Chapter 3

1. The account of Sary's reaction to the radicals' arrest was provided to me by a close associate of Gaspari in Bangkok. In 1979–82 Gaspari served as the Yugoslav ambassador to Thailand.

2. J. B. Armstrong, *Revolutionary Diplomacy: Chinese Foreign Policy and the United Front Doctrine* (Berkeley: University of California Press, 1977), 180–181.

3. For the events of October 1976 in China, see Roger Garside, *Coming Alive: China after Mao* (New York: Mentor, 1981), 101–154; Andres D. Onate, "Hua Kuo-Feng and the Arrest of the Gang of Four," *China Quarterly*, September 1978, 540–565.

4. A Radio Phnom Penh broadcast reported that on October 31 ambassadors of Mali and Tanzania, who arrived from Peking to present credentials, were received by Defense Minister Son Sen as acting foreign minister, *SWB*, November 1, 1976. Most probably Sary returned to Phnom Penh by the same aircraft that the ambassadors took to go back to Peking on November 8.

5. Banquet speech by China's minister of foreign trade, Li Qiang, on October 28, 1976, *FBIS—APA*, October 29, 1976.

6. The account is based on interviews with Peking- and Hanoi-based diplomats conducted in mid-1977. By the end of 1976 Democratic Kampuchea bought only $1 million worth of goods in Hong Kong. See Nayan Chanda, "Phnom Penh's Undercover Men," *FEER*, December 10, 1976.

7. Ben Kiernan and Chanthou Boua, *Peasant and Politics in Cambodia* (London: Zed, 1982), 291.

8. David P. Chandler, "A Revolution in Full Spate: Communist Party Policy in Democratic Kampuchea, December 1976," unpublished paper, 7.

9. Kenneth M. Quinn, "The Origins," 136–37.

10. David P. Chandler, "Revising the Past in Democratic Kampuchea: When Was the Birthday of the Party?" *Pacific Affairs*, Summer 1983, 297–99; Ben Kiernan and Chanthou Boua, *Peasant and Politics in Cambodia* (London: Zed, 1982), 291.

11. Chandler, "Revising the Past," Ibid., 297.

12. Chanthou Boua and Ben Kiernan, "Bureaucracy of Death," *New Statesman*, May 2, 1980; David Hawk, "Tuol Sleng Extermination Centre," *Index on Censorship*, January 1986, 25–31.

13. Chandler, "Revising the Past," Ibid., 298.

14. Translation of the *Revolutionary Flag* article done by Timothy Carney and Kem Sos will appear in a volume edited by Karl Jackson.

15. This paragraph is based on information provided by Timothy Carney, Cambodia expert of the U.S. embassy in Bangkok. Also see Barry Kramer, "Cambodia's Communist regime begins to purge its own ranks while continuing a crack-down," *Wall Street Journal*, October 19, 1977.

16. *SWB*, November 1, 1976.

17. VNA, December 21, 1976.

18. Author's interview with Dr. Pramoj Nakhonthap, former lecturer in political science at Bangkok's Thammasat University, on February 4, 1982, Vientiane. Pramoj made a secret visit to Hanoi after going into voluntary exile in the wake of the October 6, 1976, coup d'état in Thailand.

19. Information about Loi's secret visit was provided to me in May 1977 by a well-connected Asian diplomat based in Hanoi.

20. Author's interview with Kham Kon, official of the People's Committee of Svay Rieng Province, January 14, 1981, Svay Rieng.

21. Parti Communist du Vietnam: IVème Congrès National Documents (Hanoi: Éditions des Langues Étrangères, 1977), 161–162.

22. Author's interview with Ros Saroeun, January 14, 1981, Phnom Penh.

23. Personal communication from Michael Strulovici, Hanoi correspondent of l'Humanité, November 1977.

24. Interview with a Peking-based Indian diplomat, October 27, 1977, Hongkong.

25. "Memorandum outlining Vice Premier Li Xiannian's talks with Premier Pham Van Dong on 10 June 1977," Xinhua, March 22, 1979.

26. Author's interview with Singapore foreign minister Sinnathamby Rajaratnam, February 19, 1982, Singapore.

27. Xinhua, March 14, 1977.

28. SWB, April 19, 1977.

29. SWB, January 9, 1978.

30. Kampuchea Dossier, 133.

31. SWB, June 28, 1977.

32. According to Sankei Shimbun, quoted in Issues and Studies, March 1978. In November 1977 Vietnamese sources also claimed to me that during a counterattack inside Cambodia Hanoi forces captured a number of Chinese technical advisers. However, Peking reportedly refused to recognize them as PRC nationals. No independent confirmation of this private claim has been available.

33. "Memorandum outlining Vice Premier Li Xiannian's talks with Premier Pham Van Dong on 10 June 1977," Xinhua, March 22, 1979.

34. SWB, July 19, 1977.

35. SWB, July 20, 1977. Three other documents were also signed—a treaty delineating Lao-Vietnamese borders, an agreement for three-year nonrepayable aid

and an interest-free loan from Vietnam, and an accord providing exemption from entrance and exit visas to diplomats and officials of both countries. Most Vietnamese economic aid was, as Vietnamese ambassador to Laos, Nguyen Xuan, told me in 1979, to pay the salary and upkeep of Vietnamese soldiers stationed in Laos.

36. *Interview of Comrade Pol Pot to the Delegation of Yugoslav journalists in visit to Democratic Kampuchea* (Phnom Penh: Democratic Kampuchea, March 1978).

37. Pol Pot's speech before the Permanent Committee of the Party on August 2, 1978, cited in Document no. 2.5.11 submitted before the People's Revolutionary Tribunal in Phnom Penh in August 1979, 2.

38. Quoted in Nayan Chanda, "Laos, Vietnam: Best of Friends," *FEER*, July 29, 1977.

39. Quoted in Gareth Porter, "Vietnamese Policy and the Indochina Crisis," 97, and also mimeographed translation of page 84 of the resolution obtained from Hanoi. Cambodia experts who examined the Khmer original provided by Hanoi concluded the document to be authentic.

40. Kiernan and Boua, *Peasants*, 170.

41. Document no. 2.5.11 cited in note 37.

42. *SWB*, May 14, 1977.

43. *SWB*, October 22, 1977.

44. *BR*, October 7, 1977, 20–30.

45. Transcript of Pol Pot's meeting with the Chinese leaders on September 29, 1977, captured in Phnom Penh, was submitted as Document no. 2.5.28 at the People's Revolutionary Tribunal in August 1979. The ideas expressed by Pol Pot tally with other captured Khmer Rouge documents that outline their revolutionary plans. The Khmer Rouge were in close touch with the Communist Party of Thailand (CPT) and in fact ran a dozen training camps for the CPT in western Cambodia. The Khmer Rouge also maintained contact with the pro-Chinese Partai Kommunis Indonesia (PKI) and the Communist Party of Malay (CPM) and Communist Party of Burma (CPB), all of whom had representations in Peking. A party and guerrilla warfare training school for the Southeast Asian revolutionaries was run in Kunming in south China.

46. Huang Hua's report smuggled out of China by Taiwanese intelligence was published in *Issues and Studies*, December 1977, 77–79. In view of the fact that it was published a month before the Cambodia-Vietnam conflict broke into the open, the report seems authentic.

47. *BR*, October 7, 1977, 20–30.

NOTE TO "PRINCE NORODOM SIHANOUK: THE RETREAT"

1. Author's interview with Phạm Văn Ba, former Vietnamese ambassador to Democratic Kampuchea, Ho Chi Minh City, January 27, 1981.

NOTES TO CHAPTER 4

1. Wang Gungwu, *Community and Nation: Essays on Southeast Asia and the Chinese* (Singapore: Heinemann, 1981), 53.

2. Georges Maspero, *Le Royaume de Champa* (Paris: Van Houst, 1928), 224.

3. *Realités Cambodgiennes*, June 24, 1965.

4. Huynh Sanh Thong, ed. and trans., *The Heritage of Vietnamese Poetry* (New Haven, Conn.: Yale University Press, 1979), 3.

5. Henri Maspero, quoted by M. Coughlin, "Vietnam in China's Shadow," *Journal of Southeast Asian History*, September 1967, 242.

6. Quoted by Keith W. Taylor, "The rise of Dai Viet and the establishment of Thang Long," in Kenneth R. Hall and John K. Whitmore, eds. *Explorations in Early Southeast Asian History: The Origins of Southeast Asian Statecraft*, Michigan Papers on South and Southeast Asia, no. 11 (Ann Arbor, 1976), 165–166; Taylor has translated the letter from a Vietnamese annal, but the original Chinese text is not available. Historian Wang Gungwu considers the letter to be plausible but perhaps with some embellishment by Vietnamese chroniclers to heighten nationalist feeling.

7. Gungwu, *Community and Nation*, 64.

8. Thomas Hodgkin, *Vietnam: the Revolutionary Path* (New York: St. Martin's Press), 56.

9. Hodgkin, *Vietnam*, 89.

10. Professor George Mct. Kahin, personal communication, July 19, 1984.

11. Trung Buu Lam, "Intervention versus Tribute in Sino-Vietnamese Relations, 1788–1790," in *The Chinese World Order*, John K. Fairbank, ed. (Cambridge: Harvard University Press, 1968), 178.

12. Le Thanh Khoi, *Histoire du Vietnam des origines à 1858* (Paris: Sudestasie, 1981), 214.

13. Lloyd Eastman, *Throne and Mandarins: China's Search for a Policy during the Sino-French Controversy 1880–1885* (Cambridge: Harvard University Press, 1967), 13.

14. Lam, "Intervention," 174–175.

15. John K. Whitmore, "The Development of Le Government in Fifteenth Century Vietnam," Ph.D. diss., Cornell University, 1968, 208; also Maspero, *Le Royaume de Champa*, 231.

16. Chandler, *Cambodia Before the French*, 63.

17. Woodside's argument is nicely put in his *Vietnam and the Chinese Model* (Cambridge: Harvard University Press, 1971), 253–254.

18. Dao Vang Vy, *Nguyen Tri Phuong* (Saigon, Nha Van Hoa, Ba Van Hoa Giao Duc Va Than Nien, 1974), 53. I am grateful to Michael Eiland for pointing out the passage and translating it.

19. John T. McAlister, Jr., "The possibilities for diplomacy in Southeast Asia," *World Politics*, Vol. XIX, No. 2, January 1976, 273.

20. Quoted by Huynh Kim Khanh, *Vietnamese Communism* (Ithaca, N.Y.: Cornell University Press, 1982), 129.

21. *Kampuchea Dossier*, 95.

22. Ibid.

23. William Turley, "Vietnam's View of Regional Order," paper presented at the 26th Annual Convention of the International Studies Association, Washington, D.C., March 8, 1985, 6.

24. Ibid.

25. Che Viet Tan's article "Redistribute the work force in order to build and defend the fatherland," *Tap Chi Cong San*, August 1979, is translated by Joint Publications Research Service, *Vietnam Report*, No. 2148 (Washington, D.C.: National Technical Information Service, 1979), 21.

26. *FBIS—APA*, January 4, 1985, K6.

27. Quoted by Suebsaeng Promboon, *Sino-Siamese Tributary Relations, 1282–1853*, Ph.D. diss., University of Wisconsin, 1971, 173.

28. Quoted by Gungwu, *Community and Nation*, 46–47.

29. Cited by Eastman, *Throne and Mandarins*, 39.

30. Ben Kiernan, *How Pol Pot Came to Power* (London: Verso, 1985), 140.

31. The following account of China's role in the Geneva Conference draws mainly on François Joyaux, *La Chine et le règlement du premier conflit d'Indochine, Genève 1954* (Paris: Publications de la Sorbonne, 1979), 231–323.

32. For a detailed analysis of China's attitude toward reunification of South and North Vietnam, see Eugene K. Lawson, *The Sino-Vietnamese Conflict* (New York: Praeger, 1984), 52–69.

33. Roxane Witke, *Comrade Chiang Ching* (Boston: Little, Brown, 1977), 271.

34. Mohamed Heikal, *Nasser: the Cairo Documents* (London: New English Library, 1973), 269.

35. Madame Wang Guangmei to Dr. David G. Marr, Peking, September 7, 1980. I am grateful to Dr. Marr for sharing his notes with me.

36. Kissinger, *The Years of Upheaval,* 58–59.

37. "A pro-Peking Lao, General Phomma, was killed in action in 1971, but there were 'rumours' that he was eliminated by the Vietnamese," a Vietnamese official in Vientiane told the author in an interview, May 26, 1978. The way he put it implied that the rumors might not be baseless.

38. Pierre Mendès-France, *Face to Face with Asia*, Susan Dannon, trans. (New York: Liveright, 1974), 107–108.

39. Mendès-France, *Face to Face,* 189.

40. Etienne M. Manac'h, *Une terre Traversée de Puissance Invisibles: Chine-Indochine 1972–73* (Paris: Fayard, 1982), 575.

41. Porter, "Vietnamese Policy and the Indochina Crisis," 74–75.

42. *FEER*, June 15, 1979, 39.

43. Lawson, *Sino-Vietnamese Conflict,* 193–194.

44. Tang's observations were later indirectly confirmed by a Hanoi official who said that four months before Nixon's trip to China (February 1972) China had advised Vietnam to defer the question of Thieu's status, and concede instead to a quick agreement aimed at getting the last American troops out of Vietnam. Quoted by Stanley Karnow, *Vietnam: A History* (New York: Viking, 1983), 638.

45. François Missoffe, *Duel Rouge* (Paris: Ramsey, 1977), 128.

46. Thanh Nam, "Pekin au secours de Saigon" in *Courrier du Vietnam*, June 1979; Philippe Richer, *Jeu de Quatre en Asie du Sudest* (Paris: Presse Universitaire de France, 1982), 49.

47. Joyaux, *La Chine,* 355.

48. Lawson, *Sino-Vietnamese Conflict,* 242.

49. Author's interview with a Vietnamese diplomat, February 14, 1983, Bangkok.

NOTES TO CHAPTER 5

1. Seymour Hersh, *The Price of Power: Kissinger in the Nixon White House* (New York: Summit Books, 1983), 623–625.

2. The Paris Agreement signed by the United States and Vietnam committed Vietnam "to facilitate the exhumation and repatriation of (MIA) remains" and the United States to "contribute to healing the wounds of war."

3. Author's interview with Leonard Woodcock, August 17, 1984, Washington.

4. Office of the White House Press Secretary, *Presidential Commission on Americans Missing and Unaccounted for in Southeast Asia: A Report on Trip to Vietnam and Laos March 16–20, 1977,* Washington, D.C., March 23, 1977, 11.

5. *WP,* March 18, 1977.

6. From 1977 Col. Paul Mather, an official of the Joint Casualty Resolution Center in Hawaii, was attached to the U.S. Embassy in Bangkok to monitor the MIA issue.

7. Although the overwhelming feeling in the U.S. administration in 1975 was of bitterness toward Vietnam, some were interested in making a new beginning with Hanoi. Major Michael Eiland, who had been involved in the U.S. war effort in Indochina, wrote a memorandum for the assistant secretary of defense on June 5, 1975, calling for normalization with Hanoi even at the price of giving some aid. Calling the trade embargo "an act of sullenness, even petulance, which has no place in the world politics of mature nations," Eiland suggested bold, sophisticated moves to deal with the fact of a new Vietnam.

8. *NYT,* November 19, 1975.

9. Quoted by Murray Hiebert, "Playing Politics with the MIAs," *Southeast Asia Chronicle,* No. 85, August 1982, 16.

10. *NYT,* April 25, 1976.

11. Author's interview with Richard Holbrooke, June 5, 1983, Peking.

12. According to the Department of Defense, of the 2,546 men missing in Indochina, 753 were missing in action, 33 were prisoners of war, 647 had a presumptive finding of death, and 1,113 were among those killed in action whose bodies were not recovered; Bill Herod, "The Unfinished Business of America's MIAs," *Indochina Issues,* No. 17, June 1981; also his "America's Missing: A Look behind the Numbers," *Indochina Issues,* No. 54, February 1985.

13. *WP,* December 17, 1976.

14. Cyrus Vance, *Hard Choices: Critical Years in American Foreign Policy* (New York: Simon and Schuster, 1983), 450.

15. President Carter's press conference on March 24, 1977, in Washington, Transcript, U.S. Information Service, Washington, D.C.

16. *SWB,* March 29, 1977.

17. For instance, Michel Oksenberg, Asia specialist in the National Security Council under Carter, said: "The Woodcock mission was badly handled. Some people tried to use the trip, which was purely for the MIA question, to take steps toward normalization with Vietnam. Vietnam was given a more central role in U.S. foreign policy than it really had. This gave a false impression to the Vietnamese. During the talks with Woodcock they were flexible on the question of reparation. But soon thereafter they retreated from that position and hung grimly to the demand for aid." Interview with author, Hongkong, March 3, 1983.

18. Author's interview with Nguyen Lam, chairman of Vietnam's State Planning Commission, January 31, 1981, Hanoi; FEER, February 28, 1981. One observer argues that in addition to these planners, another group in the Vietnamese leadership pushed hard for American money because they hoped that "a cornucopia of U.S.-financed commodities would ease the pressure for economic liberalization." Gareth Porter, "Linkage between Domestic and Foreign Policy Debates in Vietnam: 1975–1983," paper presented at the Association for Asian Studies Annual Meeting in Washington, D.C., March 23, 1984.

19. Author's interview with Richard Holbrooke, June 5, 1983, Peking.

20. Vance, Hard Choices, 122; Carter also said that he was inclined to "aggressively challenge" the Soviets for influence in crucial areas around the world, including Vietnam. NYT, June 12, 1977.

21. Arkady N. Shevchenko, Breaking with Moscow (New York: Knopf, 1985), 265.

22. Zbigniew Brzezinski, Power and Principle: Memoirs of the National Security Adviser (1977–1981), (New York: Farrar, Straus, Giroux, 1983), 197.

23. Socialist Republic of Vietnam: An Introductory Economic Report, World Bank, Washington, D.C., August 1977, 66.

24. Declassified U.S. Embassy cable from Ambassador Charles Whitehouse in Bangkok, no. 09191-271744z, on April 27, 1977.

25. Asian Wall Street Journal, May 5, 1977.

26. The details of the U.S.–Vietnam talks in May and June are based on the author's interview with Vice–Foreign Minister Phan Hien, June 21, 1977, Paris, and with former assistant secretary Richard Holbrooke, July 24, 1981, Washington, D.C.

27. FBIS—APA, June 7, 1977, k-5.

28. Marc Menguy, "Hanoi versus Peking," Center for International Affairs, Harvard University, 1979, 36.

29. Ibid., 40.

30. Ibid., 41.

31. *Information-Documents*, No. 3, April 1, 1982, edited by VC, Hanoi, 11.

NOTES TO CHAPTER 6

1. The account of the incident at Thang Loi is based on interviews with a number of diplomats present at the reception. A French diplomat then posted in Hanoi, Marc Menguy, also mentions the incident in his monograph "Hanoi versus Peking," Center for International Affairs, Harvard University, 1979, 33.

2. Ho Chi Minh, "The Path Which Led Me to Leninism," in *Selected Works,* Vol. IV (Hanoi: Foreign Language Publishing House, 1977), 448–450.

3. For an account of Ho Chi Minh's career, see Jean Lacouture, *Ho Chi Minh* (London: Penguin Books, 1969); for one of the best accounts of the Vietnamese Communist movement, see Huynh Kim Khanh, *Vietnamese Communism 1925– 45,* (Ithaca, N.Y.: Cornell University Press, 1982).

4. Gareth Porter, "Vietnam and the Socialist Camp: Center or Periphery," in *Vietnamese Communism in Comparative Perspective*, William Turley, ed. (Boulder, Colo.: Westview Press, 1980), 228–231.

5. Bernard Fall, *Le Vietminh: La République Démocratique du Vietnam 1945–60* (Paris: Presse de la Fondation Nationale des Sciences Politiques, 1960), 116– 119.

6. Jean Lacouture and Philippe Devillers, *End of a War: Indochina 1954* (New York: Praeger, 1969), 291–293.

7. Porter, "Vietnam and the Socialist Camp," 247.

8. Quoted by Douglas Pike, "The Impact of the Sino-Soviet Dispute on Southeast Asia," in *The Sino-Soviet Conflict*, Herbert Ellison, ed. (Seattle: University of Washington Press, 1982), 196.

9. Donald S. Zagoria, *Vietnam Triangle: Moscow, Peking, Hanoi* (New York: Pegasus, 1967), 127.

10. For an incisive analysis of Vietnamese policy toward the Soviet Union and China, see W. R. Smyser, *The Independent Vietnamese: Vietnamese Communism between Russia and China, 1956–69*, Papers on International Studies, Southeast Asia series, no. 55 (Athens, Ohio: Ohio University Center for International Studies, 1980).

11. David Butler, *The Fall of Saigon* (New York: Simon and Schuster, 1985), 299.

12. Daniel S. Papp, *Vietnam: The View from Moscow, Peking, Washington* (Jefferson, N.C.: McFarland, 1981), 195.

13. Shevchenko, *Breaking with Moscow*, 262–263.

14 Author's interview with a Vietnamese Foreign Ministry official, January 24, 1981, Hanoi.

15. Joseph Alsop, "Showdown Over Southeast Asia," *Reader's Digest*, December 1975, 128.

16. Author's interview with Hoang Tung, July 25, 1975, Hanoi; author's interview with a Vietnamese Foreign Ministry official, July 26, 1975, Hanoi.

17. *Quan Doi Nhan Dan*, October 7, 1974, quoted in *Asian Analyst*, November 1975, 4.

18. Personal communication from Peter Limqueco, February 11, 1976.

19. Editorial in *Giaiphong*, November 28, 1975, quoted by Le Thi Tuyet, *Vietnam: Socialism in Search of Capital* (Washington, D.C.: Center for Strategic and International Studies, 1976), 9.

20. Nayan Chanda, "Hanoi Opts For a Broad Approach," *FEER*, February 25, 1977.

21. Testimony of Evelyn Colbert, former deputy assistant secretary of state for East Asian and Pacific affairs, before the House Subcommittee on Asian and Pacific Affairs, July 26, 1983, in *The Soviet Role in Asia* (Washington, D.C.: U.S. Government Printing Office, 1983), 193.

22. Shevchenko, *Breaking with Moscow*, 263.

23. Author's interview with a European diplomat, November 25, 1977, Hanoi; author's interview with a senior Soviet diplomat, June 6, 1983, Peking.

24. A correspondent, "Le Duan backs the loners," *FEER*, March 19, 1976.

25. Personal communication from Massimo Loche, correspondent of *l'Unità* in Hanoi, December 1976.

26. "IMF, IBRD Tools of Imperialist Exploitation," *Tass*, April 6, 1983, FBIS, USSR, April 8, 1983, CC2.

27. Author's interview with an Indian diplomat based in Hanoi, January 2, 1977, Hongkong.

28. Author's interview with a Vietnamese diplomat in Vientiane, March 9, 1977.

29. Author's interview with a Hanoi-based Asian diplomat, November 4, 1976, Hongkong; author's interview with an Australian trade official in April 1977, Hongkong; author's interview with an American banker in Hongkong, May 4, 1977; also Nayan Chanda, "Hanoi Opts For Broad Approach," *FEER*, February 25, 1977.

30. Robert Ross, "China's Vietnam Policy, 1975–1979; The Politics of Alliance Termination," Ph.D diss., Columbia University, 1984, 140.

31. Nayan Chanda, "Vietnam's Economy: New Priorities," *FEER*, November 19, 1976.

32. Author's interview with a Hanoi-based Asian diplomat on May 5, 1977, Hongkong.

33. *SWB*, December 17, 1976.

34. Author's interview with an Indian diplomat based in Hanoi, August 19, 1977, Hongkong.

35. Author's interview with Philippe Richer, the former French ambassador to Hanoi, June 13, 1982, Paris.

36. The account of Soviet-Vietnamese negotiations is based on the author's interviews with non-Communist and Eastern bloc diplomats and East European journalists in Hanoi in November 1977 and the author's interview with a senior Soviet diplomat, June 6, 1983, Peking.

37. Ross, "China's Vietnam Policy," 211.

38. The account of the unpublicized Soviet visit and military cooperation is based on interviews with a number of Asian and East European diplomats in Hanoi in November 1977, and with an Indian diplomat with good access to Soviet sources, September 17, 1978, New Delhi; author's interview with a U.S. intelligence analyst, January 17, 1986, Washington, D.C.

Notes to Chapter 7

1. Personal communication from Sandor Gyori, October 12, 1985.

2. Author's interview with Stephen Heder, June 30, 1983, Bangkok.

3. The account of the Vietnamese operation is based on private conversation with three Vietnamese officials, including a colonel, and also on non-Communist diplomats in Hanoi in March 1978.

4. *Livre Noir: Faits et Preuves des actes d'aggression et annexion du Vietnam contre le Kampuchea* (Phnom Penh: Ministère des Affaires Étrangères, 1978), 99.

5. *Kampuchea Dossier*, Vol. 2, VC, Hanoi, 1979, 63–65.

6. Stephen Heder's interview with Hun Sen, conducted in Phnom Penh in July 1981. (Transcript.)

7. Author's interview with Stephen Heder, Bangkok, June 30, 1983.

8. Author's interview with a Hanoi-based Indian diplomat, Hongkong, August 1978.

9. Both Hun Sen and Hem Samin told this separately to Stephen Heder in interviews in July 1981. (Transcript.)

10. According to Hem Samin, who in 1979 became an important functionary of the Kampuchean National United Front for National Salvation and the chairman of Kandal Province People's Revolutionary Committee, the core group consisted of eight persons. Besides himself, they were Hun Sen, Nuch Than, Nhek Huon, Meas Kroch, Meas Huon, Ung Phan, and Peng Path (Heder interview, July 8, 1981, Phnom Penh). Clearly this group was not in touch with other defectors who had entered Vietnam earlier—for example, Tapuon minority leader from Ratanakiri Bou Thang fled to Vietnam in 1974. Later he was to become the defense minister of the Vietnamese-backed government. Almost all of the core group, in fact, rose to prominence in the government later installed in Phnom Penh with Vietnamese help. Timothy Carney, "Heng Samrin armed forces and a military balance in Cambodia," paper presented at the Princeton Conference on Cambodia, November 12–14, 1982, 8–9.

11. This account is based on interviews with Vietnamese and Asian diplomats in Hanoi in March 1978.

12. The border disputes between Vietnam and China were more a symptom than a cause of conflict. They arose in the early 1970s as their perceived national interest and hence strategies began to differ. Although the Sino-Vietnamese land border was delineated by conventions signed between the Tsing court and France, it was not properly marked, leading to dispute over small pockets of land. China also disputed the Vietnamese claim that those conventions provided the demarcation line in the Gulf of Tonkin (*Bac Bo* gulf in Vietnamese, and *Beibu* gulf in Chinese), which was becoming important as a possible source for offshore oil. In October 1977 the Vietnamese proposed a draft agreement on the land border leaving aside the question of the gulf, but China rejected that. China has not published any details of these negotiations; for a Vietnamese account, see *Memorandum of the Ministry of Foreign Affairs of the Socialist Republic of Vietnam concerning the Chinese authorities' provocations and territorial encroachments in the border region of Vietnam* (Hanoi: Ministry of Foreign Affairs, 1979), 17–22. For details concerning the land border, see *China-Vietnam Boundary*, International Boundary Study, no. 38, Bureau of Intelligence and Research, U.S. Department of State, Washington, D.C., October 29, 1964. The study noted, "no territorial disputes are known to exist."

13. *VNA*, October 10, 1977.

14. Hoang Van Hoan defected to China in July 1979. His close association with China was, however, well known. It is curious that in 1977 alone Hoang Van Hoan was allowed to make three private trips to Peking—in June, September, and December. Hanoi perhaps sought to use his access to Chinese leaders to win Chinese support, without fearing that he would betray the party. Peking

could have received valuable intelligence from Hoan about Vietnamese thinking on major issues. Although Hoang Van Hoan was stripped of his Politburo post in 1976 and held only the ceremonial position of vice-chairman of the National Assembly, his son was in an important position in the party, and he had many friends and followers to enable him to follow the trends.

15. Text of the agreement was captured by the Vietnamese forces in Phnom Penh in January 1979. A French translation from the original Khmer was presented as Document no. 2.5.25 at the People's Revolutionary Tribunal in Phnom Penh in August 1979. The tribunal condemned Pol Pot and Ieng Sary to death in absentia.

16. *SWB*, November 14, 1977.

17. This purported statement by Le Duan was reported by *Xinhua*, November 23, 1979, only after the beginning of open hostility between China and Vietnam in 1978 to underline the Vietnamese volte-face. But the remark seems to have been made to contrast Vietnam's fidelity to China with Peking's lack of fidelity.

18. *SWB*, November 22, 1977.

19. *SWB*, November 22, 1977.

20. *FBIS—PRC*, September 23, 1975, A-18–19.

21. "Keng Piao's Report on the Situation of the Indochina Peninsula," in *Issues and Studies*, Taipei, January 1981, 85. A well-placed Peking official privately confirmed to me the authenticity of the document smuggled out by Taiwanese agents.

22. Several Chinese officials interviewed in Peking and Hongkong in 1979 indicated continued difference within the leadership over Cambodia until late 1978, when the Deng Xiaoping line emerged triumphant. But by then Cambodia-Vietnam conflict had reached a critical point, threatening China's strategic position in Southeast Asia. A reluctant Deng Xiaoping leadership was drawn into deeper involvement in Cambodia. Deng Yingchao's critical approach to Cambodia almost caused a diplomatic incident during her trip to Phnom Penh in January 1978.

23. *NYT*, December 23, 1977, 5.

24. Hanoi media later quoted this statement, commenting, "One easily understands whom this hint was directed against." *The Vietnam-Kampuchea Conflict: A Historical Record* (Hanoi: Foreign Language Publishing House, 1979), 23.

25. *FBIS—APA*, December 16, 1977, H-3.

26. Author's interview with Chanpheng Sihaphom, senior Lao Foreign Ministry official, July 28, 1983, Vientiane.

27. Author's interview with Hoang Tung, March 22, 1978, Hanoi. Hem Samin, a former Khmer Rouge cadre who rallied to the Vietnamese and who was involved in the December operations, later explained, "The aim was to do something to force Pol Pot to negotiate, to demonstrate that Vietnam's forces' condition was such that they could hold off Pol Pot, and to do something to get Pol Pot to negotiate to stop the bloodshed and to cease making the same provocations." Stephen Heder's interview with Hem Samin, July 1981.

28. The mood in Phnom Penh is described by a rare foreign resident. Laurence Picq, married to a high-ranking Khmer Rouge cadre, lived in Cambodia from 1975 to 1979 before leaving her husband and country of adoption. See her *Au delà du Ciel: Cinq ans chez les Khmer Rouges* (Paris: Barrault, 1984), 116.

29. Ibid., 115.

30. *FBIS—APA*, January 1, 1978.

31. Author's interview with Kieu Ming, January 16, 1981, Phnom Penh. Kheang's name appears on the list of executed "traitors" in Phnom Penh's Tuol Sleng interrogation center. Laurence Picq recalls how shortly after his return to Phnom Penh a distraught So Kheang and his wife disappeared from the camp. Picq, *Au delà*, 117.

32. Addressing a press conference in Peking on the morning of December 31, the Democratic Kampuchean ambassador, Pich Cheang, said, "Our only alternative is to fight for the attention of our friends, near and far, on the five continents. It is a fight for world opinion." Quoted by Douglas Pike, *Vietnam-Cambodia Conflict*, report prepared for the Subcommittee on Asian and Pacific Affairs, Committee on International Relations, Washington, D.C.: U.S. Congress, October 4, 1978, 11.

33. *Agence France-Presse*, October 21, 1977.

34. At the third plenary session of the Chinese Communist party in July 1977 Deng Xiaoping gave a speech strongly criticizing the direction of Chinese foreign policy for being narrowly based on class struggle (*Issues and Studies*, Taipei, May 1979, 55). A month later during the eleventh congress of the party nearly half of the new Central Committee members were rehabilitated friends of Deng, formerly purged for being rightist. By late 1977 a general purge of the leftists in the party had begun. See Philip Short, *The Dragon and the Bear* (London: Pall Mall, 1982), 226–229. It is fair to assume that the Cambodian embassy in Peking closely watched this ebbing influence of the Left in China.

35. *FBIS*, "Trend in Communist Media," January 11, 1978, 10–11, quoted by Ross, "China's Vietnam Policy," 286.

36. On January 11 Vietnamese negotiator Phan Hien left for Peking, where he met a Cambodian representative. The meeting failed to produce any result as

the Cambodians demanded a Vietnamese admission of its aggression before holding any substantive talk on the border dispute. Author's interview with a Third World diplomat, March 4, 1978, Hanoi.

37. Picq, 52.

38. On the occasion of the second death anniversary of Zhou Enlai (January 8, 1978) Princess Bopha Devi had sent a letter to Madame Deng Yingchao requesting her help in getting Sihanouk out of Cambodia. Later Madame Deng communicated to the princess her regrets about failing to meet Sihanouk. Author's interview with Sihanouk's close associate Khek Vandy, January 30, 1985, Paris.

39. *SWB*, January 21, 1978.

40. *SWB*, January 20, 1978.

41. *FBIS—APA*, January 20, 1978, H-2.

42. *SWB*, February 23, 1978.

43. According to Western intelligence, Chinese-supplied long-range artillery and antitank weapons started arriving in Cambodia in late January and early February. See Evelyn Colbert, "Issues of Power, Balance and Security in Indochina," paper presented at the Security Conference on Asia and the Pacific held in Palm Springs, January 8–10, 1982, 14, and Douglas Pike, op.cit., 11.

44. Hua's speech at the Fifth National People's Congress quoted by Ross, op.cit., 290.

45. Visiting Yugoslav journalists were told by the Khmer Rouge cadres in Cambodia's Takeo Province that twenty-four Vietnamese tanks were destroyed by the combatants. Asked where the remains were, the cadres replied, "The peasants have taken them away to melt them and forge tools and utensils." One of the reporters noted that during their approximately 744-mile journey through Cambodia they had seen many destroyed tanks of the Lon Nol era and nobody had bothered to transform them into utensils and tools. Dragoslav Rancic, "At the Vietnamese Border," *Politika*, Belgrade, March 24, 1978.

46. Ben Kiernan, " 'Khmer Bodies with Vietnamese Minds': Kampuchea's Eastern Zone, 1975–1978," 31.

47. *SWB*, January 7, 1978.

48. The account of the happenings in the Eastern Zone is based on interviews I conducted with several dozen people in Kompong Cham and Prey Veng provinces in March 1980 and January 1981. In Takeo I asked an old man whether he knew Ta Mok. He spat on the ground and asked, "You mean A Mok?" (*Ta* is a prefix meaning "venerable," "elderly," and the prefix A means "contempt-

ible.") "A Mok is evil. He killed people as if they were ants," he said, recalling the dark days in 1978. Also the author's interview with Stephen Heder, June 30, 1983, Bangkok.

49. Author's interview (January 1981) with a well-placed Vietnamese official, who, "for the sake of history," provided me with many of the details about Vietnamese preparation for military intervention in Cambodia. For obvious reasons, he wants to remain unnamed.

50. The only known armed resistance to Pol Pot—led by veteran leader Say Puthang and continued in the southwestern corner of Cambodia (1974–79)—without any Vietnamese support. Say Puthang later joined the movement launched from Vietnam and became a senior leader in the newly formed Cambodian Communist Party. See Timothy Carney, "Heng Samrin Armed Forces and A Military Balance in Cambodia," paper presented at Princeton Conference on Cambodia, November 12–14, 1982, 7.

51. Information about the training camps was provided by more than a dozen officials of the Heng Samrin regime interviewed in Phnom Penh and in Kompong Cham, Svay Rieng, and Kompong Thom in March 1980.

52. In April 1981, the founding date of the first brigade came to light as the unit celebrated its third anniversary. *FBIS—APA*, April 29, 1981, H-4.

53. Kissinger, *The White House Years*, 1414.

54. Richard Dudman, "Cambodia Versus the 'Crocodile,' " *Asian Wall Street Journal*, December 27, 1978.

55. *FBIS—APA*, March 20, 1978, H-2.

NOTES TO CHAPTER 8

1. *SWB*, May 3, 1978.

2. Roland-Pierre Parringaux, *Le Monde*, April 20, 1978.

3. Tsai Maw-Kuey, *Les Chinois au Sud Vietnam* (Paris: Bibliothèque Nationale, 1968), 23–29. Also see Michael Eiland's forthcoming Ph.D. dissertation, Cornell University, on Thai-Vietnamese relations in the eighteenth century. It is a great historic irony that while a group of Chinese helped the Vietnamese to occupy Ha Tien, two hundred years later with Peking's military aid Cambodians would attempt to recover that territory (see Chapter 7, "Calm Before the Storm").

4. Minh Mang said, "Nowadays within Siam, the Malay and Chinese [minorities] reside confusedly and are not restrained and controlled. If there are foreign instabilities, how can the Siamese be certain that people who are not of their

race will remain unalienated?" Quoted in Alexander Woodside, *Vietnam and the Chinese Model* (Cambridge: Harvard University Press, 1971), 244. Ironically, 145 years later, very similar arguments were employed by Vietnam's Communist rulers in warning Thailand against China: ". . . The great influence of Chinese over the economic life of this country [Thailand] should be taken into account. Sixty-five great capitalist families, mostly of Chinese origin, now control 75 percent of the gross social production value and strongly manipulate the Thai economy. They have exercised control over banking operations and the export of rice, tin, rubber and have influenced all kinds of service sectors. They have placed their men in the parliament and in various state organs. They have also owned the so-called Maoist Communist Party of Thailand which, when necessary, will be used as directed by Beijing's baton of command to conduct harassment and sabotage activities and exercise pressure on the Thai government" (commentary broadcast by Radio Hanoi domestic service, April 9, 1985).

5. Fujiwara Riichiro, "Vietnamese Dynasties' Policies Toward Chinese Immigrants," *Acta Asiatica*, No. 18, March 1970, 68–69.

6. *Hoa in Vietnam Dossier* (Hanoi: Foreign Language Publishing House, 1978), 24. An official of the Overseas Chinese Affairs Commission in Peking told me that Vietnamese rendering of that verbal agreement dropped a key word— *voluntarily*. Asked about it, Nguyen Trong Vinh, Vietnamese ambassador to Peking, told me that it was China who distorted the agreement. See Nayan Chanda, "Southeast Asia Comes into Focus," *FEER*, July 7, 1978.

7. Pao-min Chang, *Beijing, Hanoi and the Overseas Chinese* (Berkeley: Institute of East Asian Studies, University of California, 1982), 11. Interestingly, as the relations between Hanoi and Peking deteriorated in the mid-1970s the Chinese embassy in Hanoi discreetly started issuing passports to Chinese residents. Vietnamese security would be surprised to find such passports in 1978. See Nayan Chanda, "Cholon's Merchants Feel the Border Backlash," *FEER*, May 5, 1978.

8. Quoted by Charles Benoit, "Vietnam's 'Boat People,' " in *The Third Indochina Conflict*, David W. P. Elliott, ed. (Boulder, Colo.: Westview Press, 1981), 144.

9. Gareth Porter, "Vietnamese Policy and the Indochina Crisis," in *The Third Indochina Conflict*, David W. P. Elliott, ed. (Boulder, Colo.: Westview Press, 1981), 74.

10. To Huu's speech at the Nguyen Ai Quoc Cadre school, *Giao Duc Ly Luan* (translated) in *JPRS—Southeast Asia*, March 1, 1985.

11. Author's interview with Nguyen Trong Vinh, Vietnamese ambassador to China, Peking, June 1978.

12. "Memorandum outlining Vice Premier Li Xiannian's talk with Premier Pham Van Dong on 10 June 1977," *Xinhua*, March 22, 1979.

13. *BR*, August 18, 1978, 28. Ibid., June 16, 1978, 15.

14. For an account of the economic problem facing Vietnam at the beginning of 1978, see Nayan Chanda, "Hanoi Takes the Campaign behind the Lines," *FEER*, March 3, 1978; "Hanoi Takes a Grip on the South," *FEER*, May 26, 1978.

15. *FBIS*, January 5, 1978, E-11–21.

16. Author's interview with a Vietnamese official, Ho Chi Minh City, July 1979.

17. Author's interview with a Vietnamese diplomat, March 2, 1978, Vientiane.

18. *SWB*, March 28, 1978.

19. Nayan Chanda, "Peking Says It Out Loud to Hanoi," *FEER*, May 12, 1978.

20. *On Vietnam's Expulsion of Chinese Residents* (Peking: Foreign Languages Publishing House, 1978), 2–6.

21. Benoit, *Third Indochina Conflict*, 151.

22. For details about Chinese aid cut, see the June 17 communiqué of the Vietnamese Foreign Ministry, *SWB*, June 18, 1978. An indication of how rushed and emotional Peking's decision to terminate aid was the total surprise with which it took Chinese officials abroad. Barely two weeks earlier a Chinese official in Hong Kong, who was extremely well informed, firmly excluded the possibility of aid cut. "We would never do to anybody what the Russians did to us," he had said, referring to the abrupt Soviet withdrawal of technical and economic aid in July 1960 that left Chinese industry crippled and the Chinese bitter.

23. Author's interview with a Vietnamese diplomat, March 2, 1978, Vientiane.

24. *FBIS—APA*, June 6, 1978, K1–7. Vietnam's eleventh-century hero, Ly Thuong Kiet, encouraged his men to fight the Chinese invaders by a chant, "The southern emperor rules the southern land. . . ."

25. *SWB*, June 27, 1978. A CIA study would later estimate that some two hundred thousand Chinese lost their lives in Cambodia under Pol Pot. *Kampuchea: A Demographic Catastrophe* (Washington, D.C.: CIA, 1980), 14.

26. *SWB*, July 7, 1978.

27. Michael Godley, "A Summer Cruise to Nowhere: China and the Vietnamese Chinese in Perspective," *The Australian Journal of Chinese Affairs*, No. 4, July 1980, 41.

28. Pao-Min Chang, *Beijing, Hanoi and the Overseas Chinese*, 40.

29. Benoit, *Third Indochina Conflict*, 153.

30. The best account of Hanoi's refugee operation is provided by Barry Wain, *The Refused: The Agony of Indochina Refugees* (Hongkong: Dow Jones, 1981), 85–106.

31. *The Boat People: An "Age" Investigation*, introduction by Bruce Grants (Victoria, Australia: Penguin, 1979), 80–81.

32. Stephen Heder, *From Pol Pot to Pean Sovan* (Bangkok: Chulalongkorn University, 1980), 16.

33. According to a witness cited by Michael Vickery, So Phim reportedly said that the purpose of the revolution was to improve the standard of living, not to regress from rich to poor or to force people into misery just to learn how it was to be poor (Pol Pot's policy). Michael Vickery, *Cambodia, 1975–1982* (Boston: South End Press, 1984), 137. It is also interesting to note that unlike Pol Pot's 1977 version of the history of the CPK, which denied any Vietnamese role, a history published by the Eastern Zone in 1973 acknowledged "firm support" of the Vietnamese Communists in the party's 1951 founding and expressed views about socialism that were strikingly similar to those of the Vietnamese. Ben Kiernan, "Wild Chickens, Farm Chickens and Cormorants: Kampuchea's Eastern Zone under Pol Pot," in *Revolution and Its Aftermath in Kampuchea: Eight Essays* (New Haven, Conn.: Yale University Southeast Asia Studies, 1983), 161.

34. For an interesting analysis of the regional differences in Cambodia see Vickery, *Cambodia*, 65–188, especially 131–138; for an account of Eastern Zone life, also see Kiernan, "Wild Chickens," 136–198.

35. One of the earliest attempts on Pol Pot's life is believed to have been made by Chan Chakrey, a popular Eastern Zone leader. After the abortive attempt, he was arrested and executed on May 19, 1976. Other senior leaders from the Eastern Zone executed on a charge of treason included So (March 1977), Suos Neou alias Chhouk (August 28, 1976), and Seat Chhe alias Tum (April 29, 1977). A list of eliminated leaders is to be found in the "Last Joint Plan," a report by Democratic Kampuchean counterintelligence found at Tuol Sleng interrogation center. I am grateful to Murray Hiebert for providing me with an English translation of the report.

36. Kiernan, "Wild Chickens," 187.

37. *SWB*, May 15, 1978.

38. Author's interview with Stephen Heder, New York, September 20, 1984. Heder's conclusion is based on a reading of confessions made by some of So Phim's associates such as Phuong and on interviews with leaders who knew So Phim.

Hem Samin, one of the early defectors from Pol Pot, told Heder, "The affair of the Cham foreign [sic] nationals . . . was a matter of orders from So Phim. He was a real savage. Therefore, if I had met him, I wouldn't have let him live. I would have disposed of him, shoved him into his grave. Because if this guy had taken the correct position, when there was trouble, he absolutely could have gotten in touch with Vietnam, but he was precisely the one who gave the orders to attack Vietnam. The trouble between Ta [elderly] Phim and Vietnam was not something recent. It had been this way ever since 1970 between him and Vietnam. On the outside he seemed to talk nice, inside that was not the way it was, he was not satisfied with Vietnam. . . . If Ta Phim had been good, then under the condition of the time fighting broke out, Ta Phim absolutely had to search for our base [in Vietnam] to fall back on. But why didn't Phim come? Because Phim was aware that if he had gone, there was no way he would have stayed alive, because he had already created the conditions for attacking Vietnam. He was afraid the Vietnamese would kill him." I am grateful to Heder for providing me with the transcript of his July 8, 1981, interview.

Interestingly in their public statements the Vietnamese have tended to present Phim as one with "correct" policy and as leading the resistance against Pol Pot. Other Khmer leaders, such as Heng Samrin and Hun Sen, had said that Phim was a good revolutionary. On the basis of information provided by Hanoi to a Third World diplomat I had reported in the *FEER* (August 11, 1978) that So Phim was leading anti–Pol Pot resistance in Cambodia. As I would learn later, by the time the report appeared Phim was dead. Didn't the Vietnamese know he was dead? Or was it a Machiavellian trick, "a little disinformation to spark the anger of the Khmer Rouge center"? as suggested by Timothy Carney. "Heng Samrin's Armed Forces and a Military Balance in Cambodia," paper presented at the Princeton Conference on Cambodia, November 12–14, 1982), 8. A Phnom Penh–based Vietnamese diplomat told me in January 1981, "So Phim had the intention of revolting against Pol Pot but was pre-empted."

39. *Livre Noir*, 101–104. Documents later found in Tuol Sleng Prison, where hundreds of Eastern Zone cadres were tortured for information prior to the May 24 attack, show that the Pol Pot leadership believed in a bizarre series of plots involving not only the Vietnamese but Soviet, Taiwanese, American, and East German intelligence services. However incredible it may seem, Pol Pot and his associates genuinely believed that all these different intelligence agencies were in cahoots in their effort to snuff out Cambodia's unique revolution. See, for example, "Last Joint Plan."

According to Timothy Carney, "the isolation of the regions, the existence of dissent over the harsh line after 1975 and consequent anti-Party activity, and the real activity of various foreign powers, particularly the Vietnamese, doubtless fueled this counterespionage paranoia: "The Organisation of Power in Democratic Kampuchea" in a forthcoming book on Cambodia, Karl Jackson, ed. (Berkeley: University of California Press).

40. The account of So Phim's end is based on Kiernan, op.cit., 188–191; Heder's research; and my own interviews with several cadres from the Eastern Zone conducted in Kompong Cham and Svay Rieng in March 1980 and January 1981. While most testimonies about the last days of So Phim are in accord on the fact that he headed in the direction of Phnom Penh, there are divergences on the exact location and manner in which he met his end. Some said he was killed by Pol Pot troops, but most believe that he committed suicide. A Chinese official in Hongkong told me in October 1978 that the Vietnamese claim about So Phim's leading a resistance force was false because, according to confidential information received from Phnom Penh, So Phim had committed suicide after being surrounded by Democratic Kampuchean troops. As the world outside then knew nothing at all about the So Phim affair, later independent accounts made the same point, rendering suicide the most plausible case. Besides, given the fact that Phim had no troops with him, it would have been more likely for Pol Pot to try to capture and interrogate him than to order him killed.

41. Battalion commander Run Dun's account in VNA, June 21, 1978.

42. This terminology has been in use since 1971, when the Pol Pot group began their discreet purge of cadres returned from Vietnam; Heder interview with Hem Samin, July 8, 1981.

43. When a new Cambodian Communist Party Central Committee would be formed in January 1979, sixteen of the twenty members would be from provinces bordering Cambodia, particularly the Eastern Zone.

44. Author's interview with Heng Samkai, January 15, 1981, Svay Rieng. A well-placed Vietnamese official also provided the detail concerning this key meeting.

45. Quoted by Banning Garrett, "The 'China Card' and Its Origins: U.S. Bureaucratic Politics and the Strategic Triangle," Ph.D. diss., Brandeis University, 1983, 132.

46. During an interview in January 1981, a well-placed Vietnamese official provided me with the details about Soviet-Vietnamese secret meetings in early 1978. Although revealing this information might not help Vietnam's cause nor his career, he said he felt that this should be told "for the sake of history."

47. Commentator, "Who is the Instigator?" RR, reproduced in On Vietnam's Expulsion of Chinese Residents, Peking, 1978, 131.

48. SWB, July 12, 1978.

49. Michael Pillsbury, "Strategic Acupuncture," *Foreign Policy*, No. 41, Winter 1980–81, 56. Pillsbury was the first U.S. defense specialist to call publicly for the arming of China in 1975. See his "U.S.-Chinese Military Ties?" *Foreign Policy*, Fall 1975.

50. Michel Oksenberg, "A Decade of Sino-American Relations," *Foreign Affairs*, Fall 1982, 185.

51. *Jiji Press*, quoting a Hongkong source, July 26, 1978. The *Jiji Press* report was cited by Masashi Nishihara, "The Sino-Vietnamese War of 1979: Only the First Round?" unpublished paper.

52. Author's interview with a Chinese official, Hongkong, May 12, 1980. For a perceptive analysis of Chinese policy toward Vietnam in this period, see Robert G. Sutter, "China's Strategy Towards Vietnam and Its Implications for the United States," David W. P. Elliott, ed. *The Third Indochina Conflict* (Boulder, Colo.: Westview Press, 1981), 175–190.

53. Author's interview with a Chinese official in Hongkong, April 10, 1979. In his secret speech on January 16, 1979, Chinese Politburo member Geng Biao mentioned the Chinese effort "to reestablish the Sihanouk regime." See "Keng Piao's Report on the Situation of the Indochinese Peninsula," *Issues and Studies*, Taipei, January 1981, 83.

NOTES TO CHAPTER 9

1. Author's interview with Robert Oakley, currently assistant secretary of state for counter-terrorism, December 19, 1984, Washington, D.C.

2. Author's interview with an Indian official, March 22, 1978, Hanoi.

3. Transcript of Phan Hien's July 10 press conference in the unclassified State Department cable from Tokyo, July 14, 1978.

4. Author's interview with Andrew Peacock, November 26, 1982, Canberra.

5. Transcript of John D. Murtha–Phan Hien conversation in Hanoi, on August 21, 1978, was provided to me by one of the U.S. participants present during the meeting.

6. *Congressional Record*, August 22, 1978.

7. *Los Angeles Times*, August 23, 1978.

8. Daniel Southerland, "US Wary over Vietnam's Overtures," *Christian Science Monitor*, August 29, 1978.

9. Zbigniew Brzezinski, *Power and Principle*, 224.

10. Ibid., p. 562.

11. "Teng Hsiao-ping's speech on Foreign Policy at the Third Plenum, July 20, 1977," *Issues and Studies*, Taipei, May 1979, 55.

12. Jimmy Carter, *Keeping Faith, Memoirs of a President* (London: Collins, 1982), 189.

13. Cyrus Vance, *Hard Choices: Critical Years in American Foreign Policy* (New York: Simon and Schuster, 1983), 81.

14. Author's interview with Cyrus Vance, August 15, 1980, New York.

15. William Gleysteen, who does not have any softness for Brzezinski, believes that the leak from the NSC was more out of "misplaced enthusiasm rather than a Machiavellian plot to derail" Vance's talks. Author's interview with William Gleysteen, May 27, 1985, Washington, D.C.

16. Brzezinski, *Power and Principle*, 197.

17. Ibid., 560.

18. Oksenberg, "A Decade of Sino-American Relations," 183.

19. Vance, *Hard Choices*, 116.

20. Jonathan D. Pollack, *The Lessons of Coalition Politics: Sino-American Security Relations* (Santa Monica: Rand, 1984), 29.

21. Brzezinski, *Power and Principle*, Annex 1, 1–3.

22. Garrett, "The 'China Card' and Its Origins," 46.

23. In an interview with the author (May 1985) a member of the Brzezinski delegation refused to talk about intelligence, but he said, "Your observations do not clash with what I know." *Electronic Warfare/Defense Electronics* (August 1978, 23–24) reported that Brzezinski had offered the Chinese "eyes and ears of the West." The same magazine, in its January 1979 issue, reported what proved to be surprisingly accurate: that under an "accommodation" agreement with China, the United States had arranged to set up, install, man, equip, and service a series of SIGINT (signal intelligence) stations along China's border with the Soviet Union. The fact that the United States was operating such stations in China was confirmed in 1981 after *The New York Times* and major networks reported it. See Murray Marder's analysis of the way the story was broken, "Monitoring: Not-So-Secret Secret," *WP*, June 19, 1981.

24. Brzezinski, *Power and Principle*, 212. In a secret report on the Cambodian situation presented to the Chinese Central Committee on January 16, 1979, Geng Biao, a Politburo member in charge of international liaison, said of a mid-1978 plan to bolster Cambodia with U.S. help: "As long as our plan can maintain peace in Southeast Asia and contain the expansion of social-imperialism, the Americans will exert themselves more than we do. Because of this

we are sure that the Americans will lend a helping hand. But now the plan is of no use." *Issues and Studies*, Taipei, January 1981, 83. The authenticity of this report obtained by Taiwanese intelligence has been confirmed to me by a well-placed Peking source.

25. Author's interview with Cyrus Vance, August 15, 1980, New York.

26. Vance, *Hard Choices*, 117.

27. Author's interview with a former NSC staffer, Hongkong, November 19, 1981.

28. Author's interview with Michel Oksenberg, March 3, 1983, Hongkong.

29. Author's interview with Michel Oksenberg, March 3, 1983, Hongkong.

30. Author's interview with Raphael Iungerich, December 22, 1984, Washington, D.C.

31. Author's interview with Raphael Iungerich, December 22, 1984, Washington, D.C.

32. Author's interview with Andrew Peacock, November 26, 1982, Canberra.

33. Author's interview with Richard Holbrooke, July 11, 1985, Washington, D.C.

34. Brzezinski, *Power and Principle*, 228.

35. Author's interview with Zbigniew Brzezinski, July 27, 1981.

36. Author's interview with Leonard Woodcock, October 4, 1984, Washington, D.C.

37. Author's interview with Richard Holbrooke, July 11, 1985, Washington, D.C. The view that normalization with China would be derailed by normalization with Vietnam was strongly challenged by State Department officials in Peking and in Washington. One official who served in the State Department's East Asia Bureau in 1978 said that Brzezinski was a globalist and not very involved in domestic issues. It was people like Oksenberg and Roger Sullivan who were overconcerned about Chinese reaction to Vietnam normalization. They would weigh every word the Chinese said and interpret it in a way to suggest that establishing relations with Vietnam would hurt those with China. "As far as I could see from my vantage point," he said, "the Chinese were concerned but not opposed." Another senior American diplomat and a China specialist posted in Asia told me, "People like Brzezinski and Oksenberg would bend over backward and do triple somersaults to please the Chinese. It upset me no end that this single-minded passion for things Chinese would put the brakes on normalization with Vietnam. I even wrote a memo to Dick Holbrooke that we should not allow the Chinese angle to get into the way of normalization with Vietnam."

38. Carter, *Keeping Faith*, 195. Seven years later, after visiting a Khmer refugee camp on the Thai-Cambodian border, Carter told the press, "The U.S. should, as a matter of principle, have relations with Vietnam, since, even when countries have differences, it is better to maintain contacts." *Philadelphia Inquirer*, June 5, 1985.

39. This information was provided by a State Department official closely involved in the issue at the time. That less-than-full explanation from the White House remains a sore point. Talking six years after the event, the official still insisted that I not use his name while mentioning the White House guidance.

40. Author's interview with Pham Binh, director of the International Research Division of the Vietnamese Foreign Ministry, January 28, 1981, Hanoi.

41. Author's interview with an Indian diplomat July 17, 1979, Hanoi. Since the beginning of 1978 the Vietnamese had made increasing use of the Indian air corridor to fly to Moscow. The Vietnamese request for overflight rights gave the Indians a useful clue to developments in Soviet-Vietnamese relations.

42. Aside from the fact that a bilateral treaty with a third country should not influence U.S. recognition, the simple fact is that the Soviet-Vietnamese treaty of friendship and cooperation was signed on November 3, 1978. The Vietnamese invasion of Cambodia began on December 25, 1978.

43. Author's interview with Richard Holbrooke, July 11, 1985, Washington, D.C.

44. Author's interview with Robert Oakley, December 19, 1984, Washington, D.C.

45. Author's interview with Richard Holbrooke, July 11, 1985, Washington, D.C.

46. Rowland Evans and Robert Novak, "A Case of Soviet 'Disinformation,'" *WP*, November 13, 1978.

NOTE TO "PRINCE NORODOM SIHANOUK: THE SURVIVOR"

1. *SWB*, May 15, 1978.

NOTES TO CHAPTER 10

1. This account is based on the following interviews conducted by the author: Ambassador Khamphan Vilachit, February 9, 1983, Vientiane; another Lao diplomat who served in Phnom Penh, February 7, 1983, Vientiane; a Yugoslav official, Bangkok, January 22, 1979; Colonel Bui Tin, January 28, 1981, Hanoi; workers of Phnom Penh distillery, January 23, 1981; Prince Norodom Sihanouk, April 5, 1980, Peking. Also Y Phandara, *Retour à Phnom Penh* (Paris: Métailié, 1982), 183–186.

2. *ND*, December 1, 1971.

3. Author's interview with a Malaysian diplomat, October 12, 1978, Hongkong.

4. "Vietnam—Economic Situation," Washington, D.C.. World Bank, 1979, 3.

5. In the last two weeks of October the Foreign Ministry in Hanoi had requested permission from the Indian Embassy for Vietnamese aircraft to fly through Indian airspace on its way to Taskhent and Moscow. Such requests for over-flights had become routine since the deterioration of relations with China. But what struck the Indian diplomats was that two flight plans submitted by the Vietnamese were canceled on short notice. The overflight request was revived again toward the end of October. Author's interview with an Indian diplomat, July 12, 1979, Hanoi.

6. *Visite en Union Soviétique de la délégation du Parti et du Gouvernement de la République Socialiste du Vietnam* (Moscow: Novosti, 1978), 17.

7. Ibid.

8. Gareth Porter, "Vietnam's Soviet Alliance: A Challenge to U.S. Policy," *Indochina Issues*, No. 6, May 1980, 4.

9. Author's interview with a U.S. analyst in an Asian capital, July 13, 1983; Don Oberdorfer, "Reds vs. Reds in Indochina: A New, Confusing Kind of War," *WP*, April 1, 1979.

10. A summary of the debriefing report dated April 30, 1982, was made available to me by a Western analyst who wishes to remain anonymous. Wei's role in Vietnam was underlined to me by a Chinese official in Nanning, interview, August 25, 1979.

11. *FEER*, November 17, 1978.

12. Michael Chinoy's interview with a well-placed Thai official, November 11, 1978, Bangkok. I am grateful to Chinoy for providing me his notes of the interview. In a public statement Deng also evoked the possibility of the fall of Phnom Penh in a way that seemed as if he almost wished it. Prior to his visit to Thailand he told a group of Thai journalists: "If my expectation is correct Cambodia then will be completely overrun, and it will prove to the world what kind of regime the Vietnamese have. Then will be the time for ASEAN to play an important role in solving the problem." Nayan Chanda, "Cambodia: Waiting for the Inevitable," *FEER*, November 24, 1978.

13. Author's interview with a Thai Foreign Ministry official closely involved in the Kriangsak–Deng talks, December 21, 1981, Hongkong.

14. Chanda, "Cambodia: Waiting for the Inevitable."

15. According to a confidential Chinese document the Cambodian government put forward such a demand. See "Keng Piao's Report on the Situation of the In-

dochinese Peninsula," *Issues and Studies*, Taipei, January 1981, 85. Confirmation is given in Picq, *Au delà du Ciel,* 141.

16. Jurgen Domes, *The Government and Politics of the PRC: A Time of Transition,* (Boulder, Colo.: Westview Press, 1985), 163.

17. Parris Chang, *Elite Conflict in the Post Mao China* (Baltimore: University of Maryland, Occasional Papers/Reprint Series in Contemporary Asian Studies, No. 2, 1983), 10–11.

18. King C. Chen, *Politics and Process of Peiping's Decision to Attack Vietnam* (Taipei: Institute of International Relations, 1983), 81. See also "Keng Piao's Report on the Situation of the Indochinese Peninsula," 85–86.

19. "Keng Piao's Report," op.cit., 88–89.

20. Chen, *Politics and Process,* 86–87.

21. Oksenberg, "A Decade of Sino-American Relations," 187.

22. Ibid.

23. Author's interview with Ambassador Leonard Woodcock, October 8, 1980, Hongkong.

24. Carter, *Keeping Faith,* 198–199.

25. Ibid., 197.

26. Vance, *Hard Choices,* 118–119.

27. Author's interview with Ambassador Leonard Woodcock, October 8, 1980, Hongkong; October 4, 1984, Washington, D.C.

28. Whether as a result of faulty intelligence or paranoia, the Vietnamese estimate of Chinese presence appears to have been inflated. Most knowledgeable analysts believe that the figure did not exceed five thousand. Later, a Vietnamese army colonel told me that on the basis of indications observed after the capture of Phnom Penh Chinese advisers totaled eight thousand. Author's interview with Colonel Bui Tin, January 28, 1981, Hanoi.

29. Daniel Burstein, "On Cambodia: But, Yet," *NYT*, November 21, 1978.

30. *BP*, December 9, 1978.

31. Author's interview with Chatchai Choonhavan, December 14, 1981, Bangkok. As part of Cambodia's image-building effort in November 1978 Ieng Sary ordered preparations for Radio Phnom Penh broadcasting in English and French to begin from December 1. "The battle of the air waves has begun! It's your battle!" an excited Sary had exhorted the broadcasters. Picq, *Au delà du Ciel,* 143.

32. *SWB*, October 2, 1978.

33. Author's interview with Prince Norodom Ranaridh, October 26, 1982, Canberra.

34. Dinh Can's account of the KNUFNS founding meeting was obtained by a Vietnamese-speaking Australian official in November 1979 after Can arrived in Malaysia as a refugee. I am grateful to the official, who wishes to remain anonymous, for providing me with his notes. Most of the information provided by Can was confirmed to me by several Khmer cadres who participated in the December 2 meeting.

35. *Front d'Union Nationale Pour le Salut du Kampuchea*, Service d'Information du FUNSK, 1979, 31 ff (place of publication not given).

36. The United Issarak Front was set up after the First National Congress of the Khmer Resistance on April 17, 1950. A Khmer document published in 1952 ascribed the success of resistance to the leadership of Khmer patriots and "to the influence of the Vietnamese resistance and the assistance of the Vietnamese people": *Khmer Armed Resistance* (The Khmer Peace Committee, October 1952), 22.

37. Timothy Carney, "Heng Samrin's Armed Forces and a Military Balance in Cambodia," paper presented at the Princeton Conference on Kampuchea, November 12–14, 1982, 4.

38. The fourteen members of KNUFNS were Heng Samrin (former Khmer Rouge, or KR), Chea Sim (KR), Ros Samay (Khmer Issarak, or KI), Mat Ly (KR), Bun Mi (KR), Hun Sen (KR), Mrs. Mean Saman (KR), Meas Samnang (KR), Neou Samon (KI), Monk Long Sim, Hem Samin (KI), Mrs. Chey Kanha, Chan Ven, and Prach Sun.

39. Author's interview with a Vietnamese official, January 29, 1981, Hanoi.

40. Author's interview with Col Bui Tin, January 28, 1981, Hanoi.

41. Author's interview with Prince Norodom Sihanouk, April 5, 1980, Peking. Sihanouk did not know that one of the commandos survived and later fled to Thailand.

42. Phandara, *Retour à Phnom Penh*, 180.

43. Personal comunication from Ben Kiernan, September 30, 1982, Melbourne.

44. Van Tien Dung, *Our Great Spring Victory* (New York: Monthly Review Press, 1977); Tran Van Tra, *Vietnam: History of the Bulwark B-2 Theatre*, Vol 5. *Concluding the 30 Years War* (Washington, D.C.: Joint Publication Research Service, 1983).

45. Dung, op.cit., 25.

46. Stephen Heder's interview with Chea Soth, July 6, 1981, Phnom Penh (transcript).

47. Stephen Heder's interview with Hem Samin, July 8, 1981, Phnom Penh (transcript).

48. Stephen Heder, unpublished paper. According to Heder the congress elected a seven-member standing committee headed by Pen Sovan. Other members were Hun Sen, Bou Thang, Chan Kiri, Vann Sonn, Heng Samrin, and Chea Soth. Only two of them—Hun Sen and Heng Samrin—were ex–Khmer Rouge, and the rest were Khmer Issarak.

49. Author's interview with a U.S. Embassy Indochina analyst, February 11, 1983, Bangkok.

50. Excerpts from the transcript are in "Record of a conversation between Deng Xiaoping and Ieng Sary on 13 January," VC, October 1979. Certain passages not included in this version were later published in *The Chinese Rulers' Crimes Against Kampuchea*, Phnom Penh: Ministry of Foreign Affairs, People's Republic of Kampuchea, 1984. Considerable other evidence corroborates the thrust of the conversation. Besides, the authenticity of the transcript has never been denied by Peking.

51. *The Chinese Rulers' Crimes Against Kampuchea*, 111. In an interview on March 25, 1983 (before these documents were published), a high Thai Foreign Ministry official in Bangkok had told me about the secret visit. A senior U.S. official then serving in Bangkok also confirmed the secret meeting. Author's interview with the U.S. official, October 4, 1984, Washington, D.C.

52. Excerpts from Geng Biao's conversation are quoted in *The Chinese Rulers' Crimes Against Kampuchea*, 112.

53. Ibid.

54. Don Oberdorfer, "Reds vs. Reds," WP, April 1, 1979.

55. *Newsweek*, February 5, 1979.

56. Brzezinski, *Power and Principle*, 409.

57. *U.S. State Department Bulletin*, February 1979, 7–11.

58. Brzezinski, op.cit., 409.

59. Zbigniew Brzezinski, "East Asia and Global Security: Implications for Japan," *The Journal of International Affairs*, Vol. 37, No. 1, Summer 1983, 8.

60. Carter said Deng's visit was "one of the delightful experiences of my presidency. To me everything went right, and the Chinese leader seemed equally pleased." He also noted in his diary on January 29, 1979: "I was favorably impressed with Deng. He's small, tough, intelligent, frank, courageous, per-

sonable, self-assured, friendly, and it's a pleasure to negotiate with him." *Keeping Faith*, 202.

61. Brzezinski, *Power and Principle*, 25.

62. Vance, *Hard Choices*, 122.

63. Brzezinski, *Power and Principle*, 408. On February 2 Vance submitted to Carter a proposed statement to be issued on Deng's visit. The statement would state the importance of Sino-American relations for a stable structure of peace and would attach equal importance to improvement of relations with the Soviet Union. Before even reading the statement, Carter muttered, "Is it another apology?" A statement like this, Brzezinski convinced Carter, would give the impression of a weak and zigzagging United States. In the end no statement was issued.

64. Carter, *Keeping Faith*, 209.

65. Brzezinski, *Power and Principle*, 412. Just prior to the Chinese attack, U.S. Ambassador to Moscow Malcolm Toon conveyed to Gromyko the hope that the Soviets would show restraint if an attack came. *Christian Science Monitor*, February 26, 1979.

66. Author's interview with Leonard Woodcock, October 8, 1980, Hongkong.

67. *BR*, February 9, 1979, 13–14.

68. Author's interview with a senior Japanese Foreign Ministry official, May 31, 1983, Tokyo.

69. In a separate meeting with Foreign Minister Huang Hua the Japanese foreign minister Sunao Sonoda said, "China should not use force to settle its border dispute with Vietnam. . . . Japan wanted to see China act with prudence." *Mainichi Daily News*, February 8, 1979.

70. Author's interview with a Chinese official, March 7, 1979, Hongkong.

71. Brzezinski, *Power and Principle*, 410. Author's interview with a senior Japanese Foreign Ministry official, May 31, 1983, Tokyo.

72. Author's interview with a French diplomat, February 3, 1985, Paris.

73. When the news of the attack broke Vajpayee cut short his visit and returned to India. Pham Van Dong, however, continued his.

74. *NYT*, February 25, 1979.

75. *Time*, March 12, 1979.

76. Daniel Tretiak, "China's Vietnam War and Its Consequences," paper presented at a seminar on China at the Chinese University of Hong Kong, December 5–7, 1979, 7.

77. Garrett, "The 'China Card' and Its Origins," 156.

78. Brzezinski, *Power and Principle*, 414.

79. Only published reference to the secret help is in a paper entitled "Major Power Interests in the Asia Pacific Region," presented to Indonesia-Australia Symposium in Bali, December 5–8, 1982. T. B. Miller mentioned "practical aid apparently provided by the U.S. through its satellite photography." Dr. Miller, who as head of the Australian Strategic and Defence Studies Centre had access to confidential information, told me in an interview (Canberra, December 17, 1982) that "irreproachable sources" informed him that the United States passed on to the Chinese intelligence about Soviet troop movements. Since Australian facilities at Pine Gap play a key role in U.S. electronic surveillance Miller certainly was well placed to know about that particular collaboration. Since 1973 U.S. Rhyolite satellite *Bird I* was directed at snooping intelligence from Vietnam and China and transmitting it to Pine Gap station. See Desmond Ball, *The Ryolite Programme* (Canberra: Strategic and Defence Studies Centre, 1981), 5. The Vietnamese are convinced that the PLA began their withdrawal from Lang Son only after U.S. intelligence alerted them about movement of Vietnamese regular divisions toward the town. Author's interview with Vietnamese diplomat in Vientiane, March 25, 1979.

80. Li Man Kin, *Sino-Vietnamese War* (Hongkong: Kingsway International Publications, 1981), 61.

81. Ibid., 60.

82. This is a Chinese estimate. Vietnam did not release any figure. *FBIS–PA*, March 22, 1979, L1.

83. For an analysis of the domestic cost borne by China, see Daniel Tretiak, op.cit. A high-level PLA defector later told a Western intelligence official that all in all it was a "disastrous operation." Of the three hundred men in his battalion forty-five were killed and ninety-five injured—nearly 50 percent casualty. With poor maps (some were of the Qing dynasty period) and poorer map-reading ability, the soldiers wandered about in the hills looking for targets and falling into traps. For the lack of basic skill the few radio sets they had often were unusable after the operator was hit. Similar cases involved infantrymen in his battalion who were asked to use a machine gun after the original gunner had been killed. Porters and mules took days of trudging through the hills to bring supplies while forward units waited for fuel and ammunition.

Notes to Chapter 11

1. *Le Matin*, January 19, 1979.

2. Elizabeth Becker, "Sihanouk Center Stage," *WP*, January 15, 1979.

3. *NYT*, January 15, 1979.

4. Author's interview with Roger Sullivan, July 17, 1985, Washington, D.C.

5. In his memoir *La Calice Jusqu'à la Lie* (manuscript), Sihanouk wrote: "In the face of this silence [of Vance], my wife suggested that I immediately approach France to seek asylum which the U.S. seems to be refusing us."

6. The account of Sihanouk's dinner meeting with Deng Xiaoping is based on the author's interview with the prince, April 5, 1979, Peking, and in August 1979 on the telephone from Pyongyang.

7. Nayan Chanda, "The Ballot-box Response," *FEER*, May 8, 1981.

8. Eighty percent of the KPRP Central Committee members are former anti-French fighters (Khmer Issarak) allied with the Vietnamese and 20 percent are former Khmer Rouge: Stephen Heder, in a paper entitled "The Elite of the People's Republic of Kampuchea," presented at a Cornell University seminar, November 12, 1981 (transcript). Heder points out that 80 percent of the KPRP Central Committee members are from provinces bordering Vietnam, and 60 percent of the CC members have spent twenty or more years in Vietnam.

9. Timothy Carney, "Kampuchea in 1982: Political and Military Escalation," *Asian Survey*, January 1983, 82.

10. Ibid., 79.

11. Author's interview with a diplomat from a socialist country, March 2, 1980, Phnom Penh; also see John McBeth, "Bureaucrats from B68," *FEER*, October 15, 1982. Thai intelligence sources, however, told McBeth that A-40 dealt with the whole country and A-50 handled affairs in the Phnom Penh area. I would trust my informant as to their respective roles.

12. Ibid., 82.

13. *FBIS—APA*, January 4, 1985, K-6.

14. Paul Quinn-Judge, "View From the Front," *FEER*, April 9, 1982.

15. Nayan Chanda, "Making of a Bloc," *FEER*, May 30, 1980.

16. Vo Van Kiet, speaking at the First Indochinese Planning Conference in February 1984, quoted in an unsigned article, "The Vietnamisation of Kampuchea: A New Model of Colonialism," *Indochina Report*, October 1984, Singapore.

17. Compared to 0.09 hectare of cultivated land per capita in Vietnam in 1985, it could reach 0.13 hectare in 2000 if Vietnam succeeds in increasing the cultivated area by 85 percent to 10 million hectares. By then, according to conservative estimates, Vietnamese population is expected to reach 75 million.

Stewart E. Fraser, "Vietnam Struggles with Exploding Population," *Indochina Issues*, No. 57, May 1985, 5.

18. *FBIS—APA*, February 25, 1983, I-6.

19. A senior Vietnamese official said this to William S. Turley during an interview in Hanoi on March 31, 1983 (personal communication from Turley).

20. *Policy of the People's Republic of Kampuchea with Regard to Vietnamese Residents*, Phnom Penh, September 1983, 12. In June 1983 Vietnamese Foreign Minister Nguyen Co Thach told his Australian counterpart, Bill Hayden, that Vietnamese settlement in Cambodia would not exceed five hundred thousand but indicated that because many of the original residents have since died, some of their friends and relatives could now take their place. Author's interview with Bill Hayden, June 27, 1983, Hongkong.

21. Fraser, op.cit., 6.

22. Marie-Alexandrine Martin, "Le Processus de Vietnamisation au Cambodge" *Politique Internationale*, Summer 1984, 184.

23. As Robert Rosenstock, the U.S. representative to the UN Credentials Committee, rose from his seat after voting to seat the DK, someone grabbed his hand and congratulated him. "I looked up and saw it was Ieng Sary," Rosenstock told a writer. "I felt like washing my hand." Gareth Porter, "Kampuchea's UN Seat: Cutting the Pol Pot Connection," *Indochina Issues*, No. 8, July 1980, 1. In 1981 the State Department had issued a circular forbidding U.S. officials from shaking hands with the Khmer Rouge. During a reception at the UN in July 1981 Secretary of State Alexander Haig had pumped the hand of an eager diplomat without apparently realizing that the man in the dark suit was Ieng Sary.

24. A Japanese Foreign Ministry official in Tokyo showed me the transcript of Ohira's December 9, 1979, conversation with Deng in Peking (Tokyo, December 10, 1979). See Nayan Chanda, "Japan's Kampuchean Diplomacy," *FEER*, December 21, 1979.

25. "Last Chance for the Khmer Rouge," *FEER*, April 18, 1980.

26. In an interview with the author, a Lao defector confirmed the existence of a training camp for anti-Vietnamese Lao resistance in south China. Author's interview with Dr. Khamsengkeo Sengsathit, February 1982, Peking. A group of American academics, too, ran into a group of Thais in a small town in Yunnan. They were engaged in training Lao dissidents. Personal communication from an American academic, July 2, 1985. For details of Peking's support for anti-Communist guerrillas, see Nayan Chanda, "Fancy meeting you here," *FEER*, July 24, 1981, 14–15.

27. Author's interview with a State Department official, August 20, 1980, Washington, D.C.

28. Thai Supreme Commander General Saiyud Kerdphol quoted in *The Nation Review*, July 19, 1982.

29. I heard about the "fees" from Khmer Rouge porters as well as from non-Communist Khmer resistance leaders. When at a Peking dinner in 1982 I mentioned the business of a fee, my official Chinese hosts had a good laugh. "We are used to that," one of them had said without any bitterness. "We had to grease many palms in Phnom Penh when we used to supply arms to the Vietcong through Cambodia."

30. Steve Heder, "Democratic Kampuchea: The regime's postmortem," *Indochina Issues*, No. 13, January 1981, 5.

31. Australian derecognition was announced on October 14, 1980, when Foreign Minister Andrew Peacock told the parliament, "Australia cannot prolong its recognition of such a loathsome regime as that of Pol Pot." See Frank Frost, "The Conflict over Cambodia: Implications of the Khmer Coalition Agreement," Canberra, Department of the Parliamentary Library, 1982, Basic Paper No. 14.

32. Lee Kuan Yew, quoted in *FEER*, September 26, 1980.

33. Responding to a letter from Khieu Samphan on August 21, 1979, offering to him the presidency of the front, Sihanouk wrote: "The new front and the new political programme presented by the Khmer Rouges are incontestably a new deception. Only idiots and imbeciles will fall into the trap of your new delusions."

34. Author's interview with a senior Thai diplomat, January 14, 1986, Washington, D.C.

35. Author's interview with a senior U.S. diplomat who accompanied Mondale to Peking, July 23, 1985, Washington, D.C.

36. The account of the Prem visit to China is based on interviews with a Chinese official in Hongkong, November 15, 1980, and with a Thai Foreign Ministry official, November 29, 1980, Bangkok.

37. The account of the Lee visit to Peking is based on an interview with a Chinese official in Hongkong, December 3, 1980, and with a Singapore Foreign Ministry official, December 5, 1980. In an interview in Bangkok, February 1983, the Singapore foreign minister Suppiah Dhanabalan also confirmed Chinese assurance about accepting the electoral verdict on the Khmer Rouge.

38. Sihanouk told me in an interview on April 5, 1980, in Peking: "I am a Cambodian and a patriot. I cannot imagine Sihanouk dying in a foreign soil. I want

to die in the land of my ancestors, my people. I love China, I love North Korea but they are not my homeland. My homeland is Cambodia and only Cambodia. . . . Before dying my dream is this, I confess very sincerely, I want to have a good name as the rebuilder of Cambodia, mainly in the social and cultural field. The little people, the common people in Cambodia have always been for me. Before dying if I could serve them. . . . But the Vietnamese and Heng Samrin should know that if I go there (Cambodia) they will gain a lot. That will be the end, battle against the Khmer Rouge would be won."

39. The nine conditions were as follows: (a) His willingness to join the Khmer Rouge in a united front and government of national union is conditional. If any one of the conditions is not accepted by the Khmer Rouge or China, he will not be able to cooperate. (b) The name of the country should be changed from *Democratic Kampuchea* to *Cambodia* and the pre-1970 flag and national anthem should be used. (c) The pro-Sihanoukist resistance force should be armed by China as substantially as the Khmer Rouge. While cooperating with the Khmer Rouge, they must remain totally independent. (d) Sihanouk could be head of the united front without taking responsibility for its administration. (e) He will have the right to work and travel with the main functionaries of the government. (f) Sihanouk should have the right to express his views as a journalist and writer. (g) Light should be shed on the fate of his relatives and associates who disappeared during the Khmer Rouge rule. (h) Neutralization of Cambodia after the Vietnamese withdrawal, disarmament of all the forces, and introduction of international peacekeeping army before Vietnamese withdrawal. (i) General elections and the replacement of international peacekeeping force with an international control commission.

40. Author's interview with an ASEAN diplomat who was present at the meeting, July 15, 1981, New York.

41. Han Nianlong himself recalled this remark to me in an interview several months later: "Han Fires a Warning Volley," *FEER*, March 12, 1982.

42. Alexander M. Haig, *Caveat: Realism, Reagan, and Foreign Policy* (New York: Macmillan, 1984), 194.

43. Author's interview with a senior ASEAN official, May 20, 1985, Washington, D.C.

44. Author's interview with Mochtar Kusumaatmadja, July 17, 1981, New York.

45. Ibid.

46. Recalling the episode with the Americans one ASEAN diplomat later told me, "ICK had taught us [a] good lesson. When the chips are down small countries cannot count on any friend." Most of the Western countries refused to get involved in a clash with China on ASEAN's side. The Japanese ambassador to

the UN even wrote a letter to ASEAN expressing inability to oppose China although his heart was with them. Privately some State Department officials called U.S. performance at the ICK a "shameful episode," but others justified American pressure for a compromise as necessary.

47. Author's interview with a senior Thai diplomat, November 11, 1985, Washington, D.C.

48. Author's interview with Tan Sri Ghazali Shaffie, December 25, 1981, Hongkong.

49. Sabam Siagian, "Potentials of Conflict and Potentials of Peace in Southeast Asia," paper presented at the Third Indonesia-Germany Conference, Hamburg, April 15–17, 1985.

50. Author's interview with Prince Norodom Sihanouk, October 14, 1984, New York.

51. Nayan Chanda, "Sihanouk Stonewalled," FEER, November 1, 1984.

52. Author's interview with Arun Phanupong, January 31, 1985, Paris.

53. Author's interview with a U.S. intelligence analyst, January 17, 1986, Washington, D.C.; The USSR in Indochina, Report no. 334, Bureau of Intelligence and Research, Department of State, Washington, D.C., March 1982.

54. WP, March 10, 1979.

55. Author's interview with Richard Armitage, assistant secretary of defense for international security affairs, December 28, 1985, Washington, D.C.

56. For an excellent summary of Sino-American security cooperation in 1979–80, see Jonathan D. Pollack, The Lessons of Coalition Politics: Sino-American Security Relations (Santa Monica: Rand Corporation, 1984), 39–72.

57. Banning N. Garrett and Bonnie S. Glaser, War and Peace: The Views from Moscow and Beijing, Policy Papers in International Affairs no. 20, Institute of International Studies (Berkeley: University of California Press, 1984), 48–49.

58. Richard Nations, "Great Leap Sideways," FEER, May 30, 1985.

59. Author's interview with a senior Soviet academic specialist on Southeast Asia, December 7, 1985, Bellagio.

Index

aftermath of, 370–72

anti-Vietnamese resistance groups and, 379, 380, 396; ASEAN and, *see* Association of Southeast Asian Nations (ASEAN), anti-Vietnamese Khmer coalition; Chinese lessons in, 378–81, 408–409; Deng Xiaoping Trail in, 381–82; Hoan's defection, 379–80; Khmer Rouge in, *see* Khmer Rouge, in post-Cambodia-Vietnam War years; new government, 346, 356, 371–72; offer to Sihanouk, 368; old prejudices and, 370, 371, 401, 405, 407, 409; Phnom Penh, 370–71; reaction of Cambodians, 370; revival, 372; severity of problems, 371–72, 409; Thai fears and, 369–70, 379, 380–81, 409, 410; time aspect of, 404–405; U.S. role in, 410; Vietnamese booty during, 370–71; Vietnamese help in, 372; *see also* People's Republic of Kampuchea (PRK)

ASEAN and, 318–20; *Black Book* and, 196; break in diplomatic relations, 207–208, 214, 215–16, 218, 297; Cambodian purges and, 213–14, 218, 248–55; China-Vietnam War and, 258–62, 325, 359, 361; Chinese support for Cambodia and, 195, 198–204, 209–16, 261–62, 281, 325–29, 342, 347, 348; Chinese volunteers for, 260, 326–27, 328, 334; Cholon district and, 232, 234–35; defectors from the Khmer Rouge, 196–98, 248, 254–55, 339–41; Eastern Zone rebellion, 213–14, 247–55

defections resulting from, 254–55; insane policies and, 251; savage repression of, 253–55; So Phim and, 248, 250–53; toll of, 250, 251, 253–54; Vietnamese influence and, 249–50

epilogue to, 407–10; fall of Phnom Penh, 343–47

aftermath of, 370–71; Deng on, 325; Laotian embassy and, 313–17; new government and, 346, 356; Sihanouk and, 300–304, 343;

strategic opportunism and, 345–47; suddenness of, 343–45; Thai border and, 347; withdrawal of diplomats, 315–16, 347

first Vietnamese operation, 196; foreign journalists and, 219–25; inevitability of, 407–408; Khmer "Liberation Army," 214–19, 301, 336–41

call for rebellion against Pol Pot, 215–16, 298, 340; Cambodian civilians and, 340; Eastern Zone massacres and, 254–55; flag of, 340; headquarters of, 341; Khmer Krom and, 338; nucleus of, 196–98, 217–18, 255, 330, 339, 340–41, 371; predecessors to, 340; refugees for, 214–15, 217, 248, 336–41; secret camps for recruitment and training, 218–19, 320

Khmer Rouge atrocities and, 193–95, 220–25, 227; Laos and, 204–206, 326, 342

embassy in Phnom Penh, 313–17

lifting the veil on, 207–10, 214

China and, 209–10; Radio Phnom Penh, 207–208, 211; Vietnamese propaganda, 209

mediation attempts by Vietnam, 199–206

China and, 209–12; Souphanouvong and, 204–206

outbreak of, 206–207; Pol Pot's final solution and, 86, 251, 298; prewar Khmer Rouge attacks, 72–73, 86–87, 91–92, 96–97, 101–102, 186, 188

brutality of, 79–80, 86–87, 193–95, 286; refugees from, 16, 67–68, 71–72, 73, 79–80, 85, 195; suppression of news of, 92, 194–95; Tay Ninh massacres and, 194–95, 197–98, 220–21

prewar strained relations, 66–73; propaganda war and, 219, 224–25, 334–35, 336; refugees from, 214–15, 220, 227, 248, 301, 334–35; as a secret war, 193–99, Sihanouk and, 229–30, 297–304, 316, 335–36, 343